Management and Organizational Behavior Classics

Management and Organizational Behavior Classics

Fifth Edition

Edited by

Michael T. Matteson
Professor of Organizational Behavior and Management
University of Houston

John M. Ivancevich
Cullen Chair
and
Professor of Organizational Behavior and Management
University of Houston

IRWIN

Homewood, IL 60430
Boston, MA 02116

The first edition of this book was published under the title Management Classics.

© RICHARD D. IRWIN, INC., 1986, 1989, and 1993

Sponsoring editor: *Kurt L. Strand*
Project editor: *Karen J. Nelson*
Production manager: *Bette K. Ittersagen*
Cover designer: *Nina Lisowski*
Art coordinator: *Mark Malloy*
Compositor: *Carlisle Communications, Inc.*
Typeface: *10/12 Century Schoolbook*
Printer: R. R. Donnelley & Sons Company

Library of Congress Cataloging-in-Publication Data
Management and organizational behavior classics / edited by Michael T.
    Matteson, John M. Ivancevich.—5th ed.
        p.   cm.
    Includes index.
    ISBN 0-256-08750-4
    1. Industrial management.   2. Organizational behavior.
I. Matteson, Michael T.   II. Ivancevich, John M.
HD31.M2917   1993
658—dc20   91–47499

Printed in the United States of America
2 3 4 5 6 7 8 9 0 DOC 9 8 7 6 5 4 3

Preface

The practice of management is as old as humankind. Throughout time, people have joined with others to accomplish goals, first in families, later in tribes, and still later in more sophisticated political and organizational units. Ancient peoples transported entire nations across great distances; pyramids, temples, shrines, ships, and cities were constructed; sophisticated systems of government, farming, and commerce were created; wars were waged against other tribes and nation-states. These elaborate social endeavors were undertaken through the use of management techniques and processes. Despite the use of management procedures by our forebears, virtually no attempts were made to accumulate and synthesize knowledge of management practice. What knowledge that did exist was passed along between tribal leaders or parents and offspring or was learned through experience.

The principal objective of the first three previous editions of this book of readings was to provide the reader with what the editors believed were classics in the field of management—writings that have had a demonstrated and continuing impact on the development of management thought, practice and education. In the fourth edition, we expanded that focus beyond the classical management processes, which provided the framework for the earlier editions, and included organizational behavior topics as well. This new fifth edition continues that orientation. It is becoming increasingly difficult (if not impossible) to separate the topics of *management* and *organizational behavior,* whether one is a practitioner, student, or teacher.

Thus, the primary objective of this fifth edition is to make available to the reader outstanding contributions to the management *and* organizational behavior literature. Attainment of this objective is facilitated by three major subgoals of the book. First, an anthology of management and organizational behavior must *include the works of recognized, respected, and pioneer scholars in the field.* Perusal of the list of contributors on page ix will confirm that a veritable Who's Who of management and organizational behavior is represented. Second, the readings should *broaden the understanding of management and organizational behavior* that the reader receives from studying textbooks in the field. A major assist in using these readings as a supplement in both management and organizational behavior courses is presented in the Cross-Reference Guide beginning on page xv.

Indexed by topic, this guide presents reading selections for over two dozen major topic areas typically covered in either management or organizational behavior courses. Finally, the readings, many written years ago, need to *have relevance for contemporary managers and students* who spend much of their time working in, learning about, coping with, and shaping organizations. We have attempted to ensure that the selections included are directly applicable to present—and future—management challenges.

The importance and diversity of management and organizational behavior as fields of inquiry necessitates a book of readings such as this. The complexity and dynamic nature of these fields stems in part from the variety of disciplines from which they borrow principles, procedures, and models; economics, sociology, statistics, mathematics, engineering, and psychology are several of the contributing disciplines. Not surprisingly, this diversity of background produces different interpretations of organizations and employee dimensions with which managers must deal daily. The practicing manager, consequently, is faced with sorting out these differences and, hopefully, reaching some point where enlightened and successful practice can be initiated.

Some, understandably, might ask why a book composed of "classics" needs to undergo periodic revision. There are a number of reasons. In every edition, we have been forced to make choices among many excellent articles. Not every article meeting the criteria of being a classic could be included in previous editions. In this edition we have included several articles which, were it not for space limitations, would have appeared in earlier editions.

Second, it has been over 15 years since the first edition of *Management and Organizational Behavior Classics*. In the intervening time, the range of selections that could be considered "classic" has increased. Indeed, this fifth edition includes four selections that had not yet appeared when the first edition was published.

Finally, and perhaps most importantly, feedback from users of previous editions has played a significant role in shaping this edition. It was this kind of feedback that validated our decision to include organizational behavior topics in the most recent previous edition. The ultimate test of any book, of course, is how useful it is. Using your feedback, we have revised this edition to make it an even more effective and useful tool.

This edition is organized into five sections with editorial comments for each section. We have so prepared these comments that the section is clearly introduced and the reader understands the management process or organizational behavior topic that will be covered. Additional comments introduce each reading selection and provide an introduction to that selection. Part One includes six articles, which discuss traditional behavioral, and systems approaches to understanding management and organizational behavior. Part Two contains nine articles that address three classical management processes: planning, organizing, and controlling. In Part Three, four articles focus on individual behavior, while in Part Four the same number of readings emphasize group behavior topics. Finally, Part Five is comprised of 12 articles on managing organizational behavior and is evenly divided between the topics of influence and leadership, motivation, decision making, and organizational change and development.

This edition of *Management and Organizational Behavior Classics* could not have been compiled without the contribution of the writers of the articles to the fields of management and organizational behavior. To each of these writers, and to their publishers, we extend sincere thanks for permission to publish the articles in this anthology. And most importantly, we wish to thank all the users of the four previous editions who gave us the benefit of their experiences. We hope you find this edition continues and improves upon the usefulness of the earlier volumes.

Michael T. Matteson
John M. Ivancevich

Contributors

Robert C. Albrook

Warren Bennis

C. West Churchman

Lester Coch

L. L. Cummings

Peter F. Drucker

Amitai Etzioni

Henri Fayol

Daniel C. Feldman

Fred E. Fiedler

Mary Parker Follett

John R. P. French, Jr.

John W. Gardner

Luther Gulik

Frederick Herzberg

George C. Homans

Arthur G. Jago

David B. Jemison

Robert L. Kahn

Fremont E. Kast

Steven Kerr

Harold Koontz

Rensis Likert

David C. McClelland

Douglas M. McGregor

Abraham H. Maslow

Fred Massarik

C. Northcote Parkinson

Jeffrey Pfeffer

Bertram Raven

James E. Rosenzweig

William G. Scott

Stanley E. Seashore

Herbert A. Simon

Adam Smith

George A. Steiner

Max Weber

Contents

Cross-Reference Guide

The purpose of this cross-reference guide is to match a variety of topical areas in management and organizational behavior with the articles in this text. Since the content of the articles makes them suitable for use in principles of management courses, as well as in organizational behavior courses, articles have been cross-referenced with topics typically found in both courses. Reference to this guide should greatly facilitate the course and the reading assignment planning.

PART ONE

Foundations for Understanding Management and Organizational Behavior

There is continued debate about whether management and organizational behavior theories are or are not useful. First, it is difficult to isolate any particular set of principles or models in "pure" form from various modifications and efforts to translate those principles into practice. Second, particular principles of management and organizational behavior are interpreted differently by various individuals, and the result is often confusion and misunderstanding. Third, the major schools of thought in management and organizational behavior house people with differing backgrounds, values, and experiences. These differences create some conflict among the disciples of management and organizational behavior theory, which is manifested by their turning a deaf ear on ideas, propositions, and principles proposed by individuals outside their particular orientation. The classicist ignores the behavioralist, the field researcher ignores the laboratory researcher, and the academic ignores the practitioner. All of which delays our efforts to understand what is going on in organizations and what we can do to improve organizational efficiency and effectiveness.

Each of the major schools of management thought, along with the contributions made by organizational behavior research, has provided the following positive contributions:

- Knowledge that can be used by practicing managers.
- The translation of knowledge so it can be used by managers.
- Propositions and hypotheses that can be used scientifically to research managerial and organizational behavior processes, functions, and theories.
- Adding to the already existing theories, models, and techniques that serve as the foundation for theorists, researchers, and managers.
- Terminology that has been used to understand what managers do.

1

These positive contributions should suggest that a variety of approaches need to be thoroughly examined when attempting to comprehend the workings of living human organizations.

The pioneers of management thought and organizational behavior, such as Fayol, Smith, Follett, Gulik, Homans, and Likert, intended their ideas about the processes of management to be a cumulative body of knowledge. For example, Fayol argued that, because of their widespread value and applicability, management concepts should be taught in universities. The long-range goal of a cumulative body of knowledge in management and organizational behavior has not yet been achieved. Instead, what we find are different approaches, principles, models, and theories. In this first section of *Management and Organizational Behavior Classics* we have purposely included articles of such pioneers as Luther Gulik and Mary Parker Follett, as well as more contemporary contributors. In this and later sections we will include articles that are associated with a variety of orientations to management and organizational behavior. As you will see, these different orientations are seldom mutually exclusive; rather, in many ways they draw from and build upon one another, with each contributing to the goal of a meaningful cumulative body of knowledge.

1

Management as a Profession

Mary Parker Follett

*In this article, Mary Follett, whose philosophy was that any productive or-
ganization must give recognition to the human element, argues for the pro-
fessionalism of management and for the need for managers to prepare themselves as seriously for the profession of management as for any other. Written
over 65 years ago, its contents are as timely today as if they were written
yesterday.—Eds.*

The word "profession" connotes for most people a foundation of *science* and
a motive of *service*. That is, a profession is said to rest on the basis of a
proved body of knowledge, and such knowledge is supposed to be used in the
service of others, rather than merely for one's own purposes. Let us tonight
ask ourselves two questions: (1) How far does business management rest on
scientific foundations? (2) What are the next steps to be taken in order that
business management shall become more scientific?

PRESENT SIGNS OF A SCIENTIFIC BASIS FOR
BUSINESS MANAGEMENT

We have many indications that scientific method is being more and
more applied to business management. First, of course, is the development
of so-called scientific management, which, after its early stages, began to
concern itself with the technique of management as well as with the technique of operating.

Second, there is the increasing tendency toward specialized, or what is
being called "functionalized," management. Functionalized management
has, indeed, not yet been carried far. In some cases the only sign we see of
it, beyond the recognition that different departments require different kinds

SOURCE: Reprinted from Chapter IV of *Business Management as a Profession*, edited by Henry
C. Metcalf (Chicago: A. W. Shaw Company, 1927), pp. 73–87, by permission of McGraw-Hill
Book Company.

of knowledge, different kinds of ability, is the employing of experts for special problems. In other cases a further step is taken and a planning department is created; but the powers given to planning departments vary greatly from plant to plant—some take up only occasional problems as they are asked, some are only advisory bodies. Yet in most plants the functionalization of management is a process which in one way or another has gained a good deal of ground recently. That is, the fact is very generally accepted that different types of problems require different bodies of knowledge.

In the third place, arbitrary authority is diminishing, surely an indication that more value is being put on scientific method. The tendency today is to vest authority in the person who has most knowledge of the matter in question and most skill in applying that knowledge. Hiring, for instance, is now based on certain principles and special knowledge. The job of hiring is given to those who have that knowledge. It is not assumed by someone by virtue of a certain position.

Perhaps nowhere do we see more clearly the advance of business management toward becoming a profession than in our conception of the requirements of the administrative head. It would be interesting to take some firm and note how one duty after another has in recent years passed from the president to various experts, down to that most recent addition to many businesses, the economic adviser. One president, of whom I inquired what he thought exactly his job to be, said to me: "I can't define my job in terms of specific duties because I can't tell what special duty which I have today may be given at any moment to someone better able than I to handle it." One of the interesting things about that remark (there are several) is that he recognized that someone might handle some of his duties better than he could; and yet he is an exceedingly able man. He saw that some particular task might develop a special technique and that men might be trained as experts in that technique.

The stereotype of the successful businessman is indeed changing. The image of the masterful man carrying all before him by the sheer force of his personality has largely disappeared. One good result of this is that we now consider that executive leadership can in part (remember, I say only "in part") be learned. Sheldon calls executive leadership "an intangible capacity." I do not wholly agree. Someone else says it is "beyond human calculation." There are many things, we hope, which have not yet been calculated which are not beyond calculation. I think that one of the hopes for business management lies in the fact that executive leadership is capable of analysis and that men can be trained to occupy such positions. I do not, of course, mean every man; but not every man can become a doctor or an architect. I mean that for business management, exactly as for other professions, training is gaining in importance over mere personality. I know a man who told me 10 or 15 years ago that he relied on his personality in business dealings. He has not made a success of his business. It was once thought that the executive's work rested largely on "hunch," and his subordinates' on obeying—no science in either case. The administrative head who relies first on the magic shortcut of "hunch," and secondly on his adroitness or masterfulness in getting others to accept his "hunch," is, I believe, about to be superseded by a man of different type.

Can you not remember the picture we used to have of the man in the swivel chair? A trembling subordinate enters, states his problem; snap goes the decision from the chair. This man disappears only for another to enter. And so it goes. The massive brain in the swivel chair all day communicates to his followers his special knowledge. An excellent plan if—there seem to be too many if's in the way! And so we resort to the humbler method of scientific research, the method of all the professions.

But with this agreed to, there is another misconception in regard to the administrative head. Many writers speak as if he were only the glue to hold together all these departments and functions of our big modern plants. As the need of coordination is daily and hourly felt in these vast, complex organizations, it is said that the president must do the coordinating. True; but I think that coordination is very different from matching up the pieces of a picture puzzle, to change our metaphor. Later, I am going to say just what I think it is; but let me say now that those of us who think of the administrative head as more than a mere coordinator and those of us who think that administrative decisions should rest on more than "hunch" (although "hunch," too, is important) are thinking of scientific foundations for business management.

A significant indication of the different type of management required today is the fact that managers are somewhat less inclined to justify their behavior by a claim of abstract "rights." An employer used to say, "I have a right to treat my men so and so." Or, "My behavior in this matter is perfectly reasonable." Today there are many who are more inclined to say: "If I treat my men so and so, how will they behave? *Why* will they behave in that way?" It takes far more science to understand human beings—and their "rights"—than to proclaim loudly our own rights and reasonableness.

We have a very interesting indication of the new demand made upon management in the fact that the idea, which is everywhere gaining ground, that we may have greater conscious control of our lives is seen in the business world most significantly. For example, those fatalistic rhythms, business cycles, are now considered susceptible to study, not as mysteries wholly beyond the comprehension of man. Again, take unemployment. Consider the steel industry. There you have an imperishable commodity. Moreover, you can calculate pretty well the demand. And you have rather permanently located firms and mills. There seems no reason, therefore, why the steel industry should not eventually be stabilized. Every time we take a problem out of the unsolvable class and put it into the solvable, and work at it as such, we are helping to put business management on a scientific basis. Mr. John Maynard Keynes, in an address last summer, spoke of the three great epochs of history described by Dr. John R. Commons,[1] and stated his belief that we are on the threshold of the third of those epochs. The first of these was the era of scarcity, which came to an end in about the 15th century. Next came the era of abundance, the dominating idea of which was the doctrine of laissez faire. Finally, there has come the era of stabilization, upon which we are now entering and in which the doctrine of laissez faire must be abandoned in favor of deliberate, conscious control of economic forces for the sake of the general social good.

Many people today think of business not as a game of chance, not as a speculative enterprise depending on rising and falling markets, but as largely controllable. The mysteriousness of business is in fact disappearing as knowledge in regard to business methods steadily increases.

This is seen in the increased sense of responsibility for failure. You know the old excuses if a business failed or was not getting on well: the hard terms of bankers, the unscrupulousness of competitors, the abominable behavior of trade unions. I think that today there is less inclination to take refuge in such excuses; that there is a tendency to seek the difficulty in the running of the business. There is greater frankness in facing difficulties and a keener zest in overcoming them. You know, perhaps, the story of little Mary who was naughty and was told by her mother to go into the next room and ask God to forgive her. When she came back her mother said, "Did you do what I told you to?" And received the reply, "Yes, I did; and God said, 'Mercy me, little Mary, I know heaps worse'n you.' " Many an employer takes this attitude, but their numbers are diminishing.

Moreover, many of the points disputed with trade unions, many points which both sides have thought to be legitimate fighting issues, are now considered problems which we should try to solve. To increase wages without increasing price is sometimes a solvable problem. Wherever thinking takes the place of fighting, we have a striking indication that management is coming to rest on scientific foundations. In international relations—but I have only to mention that term for you to see the analogy, for you to see the barbarous stage we are yet in, in international relations. Businessmen have the chance to lead the world in substituting thinking for fighting. And businessmen are thinking. One of the things I have been most struck with in the last four or five years has been the vitality of the thinking of businessmen. I said last winter to a professor of philosophy, "Do you realize that you philosophers have got to look to your laurels, that businessmen are doing some very valuable thinking and may get ahead of you?" And he acknowledged this fully and generously, which I thought was a significant concession.

Finally, management, not bankers nor stockholders, is now seen to be the fundamental element in industry. It is good management that draws credit, that draws workers, that draws customers. Moreover, whatever changes come, whether industry is owned by individual capitalists or by the state or by the workers, it will always have to be managed. Management is a permanent function of business.

There are many circumstances, let us note in concluding the first part of this talk, which are impelling us toward a truly scientific management: (1) efficient management has to take the place of that exploitation of our natural resources whose day is now nearly over; (2) keener competition; (3) scarcity of labor; (4) a broader conception of the ethics of human relations; (5) the growing idea of business as a public service, which carries with it a sense of responsibility for its efficient conduct.

WHAT ARE THE NEXT STEPS TOWARD MAKING BUSINESS MANAGEMENT MORE SCIENTIFIC?

Recognizing that business management is every day coming more and more to rest on scientific foundations, what has it yet to do? First, the scientific standard must be applied to the whole of business management; it is now often applied to only one part. Business management includes: (1) on the technical side, as it is usually called, a knowledge of production and distribution, and (2) on the personnel side, a knowledge of how to deal fairly and fruitfully with one's fellows. While the first has been recognized as a matter capable of being taught, the latter has been often thought to be a gift which some men possess and some do not. That is, one part of business management rested on science; the other part, it was thought, never could. Oliver Sheldon says: "Broadly, management is concerned with two primary elements—things and men. The former element is susceptible to scientific treatment, the latter is not."[2] And again: "Where human beings are concerned, scientific principles may be so much waste paper."[3] If we believed that, we should not be here tonight in a Bureau of Personnel Administration. Let us take that statement—that human relations are not susceptible of scientific treatment—and ask what scientific treatment is. Science has been defined as "knowledge gained by systematic observation, experiment, and reasoning; knowledge coordinated, arranged, and systematized." Can we not accumulate in regard to human relations knowledge gained by systematic observation, experiment, and reasoning? Can we not coordinate, arrange, and systematize that knowledge? I think we can.

Sheldon says further: "There may be a science of costing, of transportation, of operation, but there can be no science of cooperation."[4] The reason we are here studying human relations in industry is that we believe there can be a science of cooperation. By this I mean that cooperation is not, and this I insist on, merely a matter of good intentions, of kindly feeling. It must be based on these, but you cannot have successful cooperation until you have worked out the methods of cooperation—by experiment after experiment, by a comparing of experiments, by a pooling of results. . . . It is my plea above everything else that we learn *how* to cooperate. Of course, one may have a special aptitude for dealing with men as others may have for dealing with machines, but there is as much to learn in the one case as in the other.

In all our study of personnel work, however, we should remember that we can never wholly separate the human and the mechanical problem. This would seem too obvious to mention if we did not so often see that separation made. Go back to that sentence of Sheldon's: "There may be a science of costing, of transportation, of operation, but there can be no science of coöperation." But take Sheldon's own illustration, that of transportation. The engineering part of transportation is not the larger part. Please note that I do not say it is a small part. It is a large part, and it is the dramatic part, and it is the part we have done well, and yet the chief part of transportation is the personal thing. Everyone knows that the main difficulty about transportation is that there have not always been sensible working arrangements between the men concerned. But you all see every day that the study of human relations in business and the study of technique of operating are bound up together. You know that the way the worker is treated affects output. You know that the routing of materials and the maintenance of machines is a matter partly of human relations. You know, I hope, that there is danger in "putting in" personnel work if it is superadded instead of being woven through the plant. You remember the man who wanted to know something about Chinese metaphysics and so looked up China in the encyclopedia and then metaphysics, and put them together. We shall not have much better success if we try merely to add personnel work. Even although there is, as I certainly believe there should be, a special personnel department run by a trained expert, yet it seems to me that every executive should make some study of personnel work a part of that broad foundation which is today increasingly felt to be necessary for the businessman.

If, then, one of the first things to be done to make business management more scientific is to apply scientific methods to those problems of management which involve human relations, another requirement is that we should make an analysis of managers' jobs somewhat corresponding to the analysis of workers' jobs in the Taylor system. We need to get away from tradition, prejudice, stereotypes, guesswork, and find the factual basis for managerial jobs. We know, for instance, what has been accomplished in elimination of waste by scientific methods of research and experiment applied to operating, to probable demand for commodities, and so on. I believe that this has to be carried further, and that managerial waste, administrative waste, should be given the same research and experiment. How this can be done, I shall take up later.

The next step business management should take is to organize the body of knowledge on which it should rest. We have defined science as an organized body of exact knowledge. That is, scientific method consists of two parts: (1) research and (2) the organization of the knowledge obtained by research. The importance of research, of continued research, receives every year fuller and fuller appreciation from businessmen; but methods of organizing the results of such research have not kept pace with this appreciation. While business management is collecting more and more exact knowledge, while it is observing more keenly, experimenting more widely, it has not yet gone far in organizing this knowledge. We have drawn a good many conclusions, have thought out certain principles, but have not always seen the relation between these conclusions or these principles.

I have not time to speak here of more than one way of organizing in industrial plants our accumulating knowledge in regard to executive technique. There should be, I think, in every plant, an official, one of whose duties should be to classify and interpret managerial experience with the aid of the carefully kept records which should be required of every executive. From such classification and interpretation of experience—this experience which in essentials repeats itself so often from time to time, from department to department, from plant to plant—it would be possible to draw useful conclusions. The importance of this procedure becomes more obvious when we remember that having experience and profiting by experience are two different matters. Experience may leave us with mistaken notions, with prejudice or suspicion.

A serious drawback to a fuller understanding of and utilization of executive experience is that we have at present (1) no systematic follow-up of decisions, of new methods, of experiments in managing; and (2) no carefully worked out system of recording. Poorly kept records, or the absence of any systematic recording, are partly responsible for what seems in some plants like a stagnant management, and in all plants for certain leaks in management. For instance, the fact that we have no follow-up for executive decisions with a comparing of results—a procedure necessary before business management can be considered fully on a scientific basis—is partly a deficiency in recording. The fact that an executive, if he wishes to introduce a certain method (not in operating but in management itself), cannot find in any records whether that method has been tried before or anything like it, and what the results have been, is a serious deficiency in recording. If an executive is facing a certain problem, he should be able to find out: (1) whether other executives have had to meet similar problems, (2) how they met them, (3) what the results were. It seems to me very unfortunate that it is possible for one man to say to another, as I heard someone say at the suggestion of a new method, "I believe our department tried that a few years ago, but I've forgotten what we thought of it."

I have heard it said that the Harvard football team was put on its feet when Percy Haughton introduced the system of recording football experience. After that, if someone thought he had a brilliant idea that such and such a play could be tried on Yale, the first thing done was to examine the records; and it might be found that that play had been tried two years before and failed. It might even be discovered why it had failed. This system of recording—I believe it already existed at Yale—was Mr. Haughton's great contribution to Harvard football. Because of it, the team could not, at any rate, go on making the *same* mistakes.

The recording of executive experiences, which will probably need a technique somewhat different from that used for the rest of business recording, should have, I think, our immediate attention. The system of both recording and reporting should be such that records and reports can be quickly mastered, and thus be practically useful to all, instead of buried underneath their own verbiage, length, and lack of systematization. And there should be required, from every executive, training in the technique of keeping records and making reports.

But we need more than records. We need a new journal, or a new department in some present journal; we need sifted bibliographies of reports; ways of getting information from other parts of the country, from other countries; above all, we need executive conferences with carefully worked out methods for comparing experience which has been scientifically recorded, analyzed, and organized. When many different plants are willing to share with one another the results of their experience, then we shall have business policies based on wider data than those of the present.

The Graduate School of Business Administration and the Bureau of Business Research of Harvard University are now collecting cases of business policy, thus opening the way for classifying and cross-indexing. Harvard has, of course, been able to get hold of a very small number of cases, but this seems to be a valuable and significant undertaking.

I have been interested also in what a certain recent committee, with representatives from various firms, deliberately stated as its object: "the comparison of experience." I should like to know how frank and full their exchange of experience was; but any attempt of this kind is interesting, indicating, as it does, the attitude on the part of those participating that they expect to gain more by working together than they will lose (the old idea) by allowing other firms to gain any intimate knowledge of their affairs.

Moreover, not only should we analyze and compare our experience but we should deliberately experiment. We should make experiments, observe experiments, compare and discuss these with each other, and see what consensus we can come to in our conclusions. For this we should be wholly frank with one another. If we have the scientific attitude toward our work, we shall be willing to tell our failures. I heard of a man who made an ice machine which did not work, and the following conversation took place between him and a friend he met:

Friend:

I was sorry to hear your experiment was a failure!

Man:

Who told you it was a failure?

Friend:

Why, I heard your ice machine wouldn't work.

Man:

Oh, that was true enough, but it was a great success as an experiment. You can learn as much from your failures as from your successes.

From such experimenting and from the comparison of experience, I think certain standards would emerge. But we should remember that, as no Taylorite thinks there is anything final in "standardization," so we should not aim at a static standardization of managerial method, executive technique. We should make use of all available present experience, knowing that experience and our learning from it should be equally continuous matters.

If science gives us research and experimentation as its two chief methods, it at the same time shows us that nothing is too small to claim our attention. There is nothing unimportant in business procedure. For instance, I spoke above of record keeping. I know a firm where they tell me that they are not getting nearly so much advantage as they should from their records because they have not yet worked out a system of cross-indexing. Yet to some, cross-indexing may not seem to be of great importance. I know a man who says frequently about this detail or that, "Oh, that doesn't matter." Everything matters to the scientist. The following incident seems to me to have some significance. I told a man that I was working at the technique of the business interview, at which he seemed rather amused and said, "I guess most businessmen know how to conduct interviews." It was evident that he thought he did—but he is a man who has never risen above a small position. Later, I said the same thing to a clever man in a good position, a New York man, by the way. I said it a little hesitatingly, for I thought he, too, might consider it beneath his notice, but he was much interested and asked if he might see my paper when finished.

I have spoken of the classification of experience, the organizing of knowledge, as one of the necessary preliminaries to putting business management on a scientific basis. This organized body of knowledge tends at first to remain in the hands of a few. Measures should be taken to make it accessible to the whole managerial force. There should be opportunities for the training of executives through talks, suggested readings (including journals on management), through wisely led discussion groups and conferences, through managers' associations, foremen's associations, and the like. The organized knowledge of managerial methods which many of the higher officials possess should spread to the lower executives. In some cases, the higher official does not even think of this as part of his responsibility. He will say to a subordinate, "Here is what I want done; I don't care how you do it, that's up to you." Indeed, many an official has prided himself on this way of dealing with subordinates. But this is changing. It is part of the Taylor system that standards and methods for each worker's job are made accessible to the worker; also knowledge of the quality of work expected, which is shown him by specifications or drawings. Some such system should be developed for management. To develop it might be made part of that analysis of managerial jobs which I spoke of a few moments ago. Indeed, more and more of the higher executives are seeing now that managers' jobs as well as workers' jobs are capable of carrying with them accepted standards and methods.

Of course, it is recognized that many of these standards and methods need the sanction of custom, rather than of authority, that they should be indicated, rather than prescribed, also that much more elasticity should be allowed than in the detailed instructions of the Taylor system—but this is all part of that large subject, the method of training executives. Possibly, in time, as business organization develops, we shall have an official for executives corresponding to the functional foreman who is sometimes known as the "methods instructor," an official whose duty it will be to see that certain managerial methods are understood and followed, as it is the duty of the functional foreman to see that certain operating methods are understood and followed. But I should not advocate this unless the executives were allowed fullest opportunity for contributing to such prescribed methods. The development of managerial technique has been thought by some to involve the risk of crushing originality, the danger of taking away initiative. I think that, rightly managed, it should give executives increased opportunity for the fruitful exercise of initiative and originality, for it is they themselves who must develop this technique even if helped by experts. The choice here presented is not that between originality and a mechanical system, but between a haphazard, hit-or-miss way of performing executive duties and a scientifically determined procedure.

Yet when business management has gained something of an accepted technique, there still remains, as part of the training of executives, the acquiring of skill in its application. Managerial skill cannot be painted on the outside of executives; it has to go deeper than that. Like manual workers, managerial workers have to acquire certain habits and attitudes. And just as in the case of manual workers, for the acquisition of these habits and attitudes three conditions must be given: (1) detailed information in regard to a new method; (2) the stimulus to adopt this method; and (3) the opportunity to practice it so that it may become a habit.

A businessman tells me that I should emphasize the last point particularly. He says that his firm has been weak just here; that they have done more preaching than giving opportunity for practice. He says: "We've given them a lecture on piano playing and then put them on the concert stage. This winter we are going to try to invent ways of giving real practice to foremen so that a set of habits can be formed." No subject is more important than the training of executives; but as it is a subject which would require an evening for the most superficial consideration, we cannot speak further of it tonight. Let me just say, however, as a hint of what I shall elaborate later, that, if you wish to train yourself for higher executive positions, the first thing for you to decide is what you are training for. Ability to dominate or manipulate others? That ought to be easy enough, since most of the magazines advertise sure ways of developing something they call "personality." But I am convinced that the first essential of business success is the capacity for organized thinking.

In conclusion: What does all this imply in regard to the profession of business management? It means that men must prepare themselves as seriously for this profession as for any other. They must realize that they, as all professional men, are assuming grave responsibilities, that they are to take a creative part in one of the large functions of society, a part which, I believe, only trained and disciplined men can in the future hope to take with success.

NOTES AND REFERENCES

1. John Rogers Commons, 1862–1945. American economist, educator, and author. Also had considerable influence in labor legislation.—Editor
2. Oliver Sheldon, *Bulletin of Taylor Society* 8, no. 6 (December 1913), p. 211.
3. Oliver Sheldon, *The Philosophy of Management* (London: Sir Isaac Pitman & Sons, Ltd., 1923), p. 36.
4. Ibid., p. 35.

2
Notes on the Theory of Organization

Luther Gulick

This selection represents one of the first statements of the "principles" approach to management. It reflects the application of scientific management ideals to the operation of the human organizational element. This selection includes Gulick's famous mnemonic device, POSDCORB.—Eds.

Every large-scale or complicated enterprise requires many men to carry it forward. Wherever many men are thus working together the best results are secured when there is a division of work among these men. The theory of organization, therefore, has to do with the structure of coordination imposed upon the work-division units of an enterprise. Hence, it is not possible to determine how an activity is to be organized without, at the same time, considering how the work in question is to be divided. Work division is the foundation of organization; indeed, the reason for organization.

1. THE DIVISION OF WORK

It is appropriate at the outset of this discussion to consider the reasons for and the effect of the division of work. It is sufficient for our purpose to note the following factors.

Why Divide Work?

Because men differ in nature, capacity, and skill, and gain greatly in dexterity by specialization; Because the same man cannot be at two places at the same time; Because the range of knowledge and skill is so great that a man cannot within his life-span know more than a small fraction of it. In other words, it is a question of human nature, time, and space.

SOURCE: Luther Gulick and Lyndall Urwick, eds., *Papers on the Science of Administration* (New York: Institute of Public Administration, 1937), pp. 3–13.

In a shoe factory it would be possible to have 1,000 men each assigned to making complete pairs of shoes. Each man would cut his leather, stamp in the eyelets, sew up the tops, sew on the bottoms, nail on the heels, put in the laces, and pack each pair in a box. It might take two days to do the job. One thousand men would make 500 pairs of shoes a day. It would also be possible to divide the work among these same men, using the identical hand methods, in an entirely different way. One group of men would be assigned to cut the leather, another to putting in the eyelets, another to stiching up the tops, another to sewing on the soles, another to nailing on the heels, another to inserting the laces and packing the pairs of shoes. We know from common sense and experience that there are two great gains in this latter process: first, it makes possible the better utilization of the varying skills and aptitudes of the different workmen, and encourages the development of specialization; and second, it eliminates the time that is lost when a workman turns from a knife, to a punch, to a needle and awl, to a hammer, and moves from table to bench, to anvil, to stool. Without any pressure on the workers, they could probably turn out twice as many shoes in a single day. There would be additional economies, because inserting laces and packing could be assigned to unskilled and low-paid workers. Moreover, in the cutting of the leather there would be less spoilage because the less-skillful pattern cutters would all be eliminated and assigned to other work. It would also be possible to cut a dozen shoe tops at the same time from the same pattern with little additional effort. All of these advances would follow, without the introduction of new labor-saving machinery.

The introduction of machinery accentuates the division of work. Even such a simple thing as a saw, typewriter, or a transit requires increased specialization, and serves to divide workers into those who can and those who cannot use the particular instrument effectively. Division of work on the basis of the tools and machines used in work rests no doubt in part on aptitude, but primarily upon the development and maintenance of skill through continued manipulation.

Specialized skills are developed not alone in connection with machines and tools. They evolve naturally from the materials handled, like wood, or cattle, or paint, or cement. They arise similarly in activities which center in a complicated series of interrelated concepts, principles, and techniques. These are most clearly recognized in the professions, particularly those based on the application of scientific knowledge, as in engineering, medicine, and chemistry. They are none the less equally present in law, ministry, teaching, accountancy, navigation, aviation, and other fields.

The nature of these subdivisions is essentially pragmatic, in spite of the fact that there is an element of logic underlying them. They are therefore subject to a gradual evolution with the advance of science, the invention of new machines, the progress of technology, and the change of the social system. In the last analysis, however, they appear to be based upon differences in individual human beings. But it is not to be concluded that the apparent stability of "human nature," whatever that may be, limits the probable development of specialization. The situation is quite the reverse. As each field of knowledge and work is advanced, constituting a continually larger and more complicated nexus of related principles, practices, and skills, any individual will be less and less able to encompass it and maintain intimate knowledge and facility over the entire area, and there will thus arise a more minute specialization because knowledge and skill advance while man stands still. Division of work and integrated organization are the bootstraps by which mankind lifts itself in the process of civilization.

The Limits of Division

There are three clear limitations beyond which the division of work cannot to advantage go. The first is practical and arises from the volume of work involved in man-hours. Nothing is gained by subdividing work if that further subdivision results in setting up a task which requires less than the full time of one man. This is too obvious to need demonstration. The only exception arises where space interferes, and in such cases the part-time expert must fill in his spare time at other tasks, so that as a matter of fact a new combination is introduced.

The second limitation arises from technology and custom at a given time and place. In some areas nothing would be gained by separating undertaking from the custody and cleaning of churches, because by custom the sexton is the undertaker; in building construction it is extraordinarily difficult to redivide certain aspects of electrical and plumbing work and to combine them in a more effective way, because of the jurisdictional conflicts of craft unions; and it is clearly impracticable to establish a division of cost accounting in a field in which no technique of costing has yet been developed.

This second limitation is obviously elastic. It may be changed by invention and by education. If this were not the fact, we should face a static division of labor. It should be noted, however, that a marked change has two dangers. It greatly restricts the labor market from which workers may be drawn and greatly lessens the opportunities open to those who are trained for the particular specialization.

The third limitation is that the subdivision of work must not pass beyond physical division into organic division. It might seem far more efficient to have the front half of the cow in the pasture grazing and the rear half in the barn being milked all of the time, but this organic division would fail. Similarly there is no gain from splitting a single movement or gesture like licking an envelope, or tearing apart a series of intimately and intricately related activities.

It may be said that there is in this an element of reasoning in a circle; that the test here applied as to whether an activity is organic or not is whether it is divisible or not—which is what we set out to define. This charge is true. It must be a pragmatic test. Does the division work out? Is something vital destroyed and lost? Does it bleed?

The Whole and the Parts

It is axiomatic that the whole is equal to the sum of its parts. But in dividing up any "whole," one must be certain that every part, including unseen elements and relationships, is accounted for. The marble sand to which the Venus de Milo may be reduced by a vandal does not equal the statue, though every last grain be preserved; nor is a thrush just so much feathers, bones, flesh, and blood; nor a typewriter merely so much steel, glass, paint, and rubber. Similarly a piece of work to be done cannot be subdivided into the obvious component parts without great danger that the central design, the operating relationships, the imprisoned idea, will be lost.

A simple illustration will make this clear. One man can build a house. He can lay the foundation, cut the beams and boards, make the window frames and doors, lay the floors, raise the roof, plaster the walls, fit in the heating and water systems, install the electric wiring, hang the paper, and paint the structure. But if he did, most of the work would be done by hands unskilled in the work, much material would be spoiled, and the work would require many months of his time. On the other hand, the whole job of building the house might be divided among a group of men. One man could do the foundation, build the chimney, and plaster the walls; another could erect the frame, cut the timbers and the boards, raise the roof, and do all the carpentry; another all the plumbing; another all the paper hanging and painting; another all the electric wiring. But this would not make a house unless someone—an architect—made a plan for the house, so that each skilled worker could know what to do and when to do it.

When one man builds a house alone he plans as he works; he decides what to do first and what next, that is, he "coordinates the work." When many men work together to build a house this part of the work, the coordinating, must not be lost sight of.

In the "division of the work" among the various skilled specialists, a specialist in planning and coordination must be sought as well. Otherwise, a great deal of time may be lost, workers may get in each other's way, material may not be on hand when needed, things may be done in the wrong order, and there may even be a difference of opinion as to where the various doors and windows are to go. It is self-evident that, the more the work is subdivided, the greater is the danger of confusion, and the greater is the need of overall supervision and coordination. Coordination is not something that develops by accident. It must be won by intelligent, vigorous, persistent, and organized effort.

2. THE COORDINATION OF WORK

If subdivision of work is inescapable, coordination becomes mandatory. There is, however, no one way to coordination. Experience shows that it may be achieved in two primary ways. These are:

1. By organization; that is, by interrelating the subdivisions of work by allotting them to men who are placed in a structure of authority, so that the work may be coordinated by orders of superiors to subordinates, reaching from the top to the bottom of the entire enterprise.

2. By the dominance of an idea; that is, the development of intelligent singleness of purpose in the minds and wills of those who are working together as a group, so that each worker will of his own accord fit his task into the whole with skill and enthusiasm.

These two principles of coordination are not mutually exclusive; in fact, no enterprise is really effective without the extensive utilization of both.

Size and time are the great limiting factors in the development of coordination. In a small project, the problem is not difficult; the structure of authority is simple, and the central purpose is real to every worker. In a large complicated enterprise, the organization becomes involved, the lines of authority tangled, and there is danger that the workers will forget that there is any central purpose, and so devote their best energies only to their own individual advancement and advantage.

The interrelated elements of time and habit are extraordinarily important in coordination. Man is a creature of habit. When an enterprise is built up gradually from small beginnings the staff can be "broken in" step by step. And when difficulties develop, they can be ironed out, and the new method followed from that point on as a matter of habit, with the knowledge that that particular difficulty will not develop again. Routines may even be mastered by drill as they are in the army. When, however, a large new enterprise must be set up or altered overnight, then the real difficulties of coordination make their appearance. The factor of habit, which is thus an important foundation of coordination when time is available, becomes a serious handicap when time is not available; that is, when change rules. The question of coordination therefore must be approached with different emphasis in small and in large enterprises; in simple and in complex situations; in stable and in new or changing organizations.

Coordination through Organization

Organization as a way of coordination requires the establishment of a system of authority whereby the central purpose or objective of an enterprise is translated into reality through the combined efforts of many specialists, each working in his own field at a particular time and place.

It is clear from long experience in human affairs that such a structure of authority requires not only many men at work in many places at selected times but also a single directing executive authority.[1] The problem of organization thus becomes the problem of building up between the executive at the center and the subdivisions of work on the periphery an effective network of communication and control.

The following outline may serve further to define the problem:

I. First Step: define the job to be done, such as the furnishing of pure water to all of the people and industries within a given area at the lowest possible cost.

II. Second Step: provide a director to see that the objective is realized.

III. Third Step: determine the nature and number of individualized and specialized work units into which the job will have to be divided. As has been seen above, this subdivision depends partly upon the size of the job (no ultimate subdivision can generally be so small as to require less than the full time of one worker) and upon the status of technological and social development at a given time.

IV. Fourth Step: establish and perfect the structure of authority between the director and the ultimate work subdivisions.

It is this fourth step which is the central concern of the theory of organization. It is the function of this organization (IV) to enable the director (II) to coordinate and energize all of the subdivisions of work (III) so that the major objective (I) may be achieved efficiently.

The Span of Control

In this undertaking we are confronted at the start by the inexorable limits of human nature. Just as the hand of man can span only a limited number of notes on the piano, so the mind and will of man can span but a limited number of immediate managerial contacts. The problem has been discussed brilliantly by Graicunas in his paper included in this collection. The limit of control is partly a matter of the limits of knowledge, but even more is it a matter of the limits of time and of energy. As a result the executive of any enterprise can personally direct only a few persons. He must depend upon these to direct others, and upon them in turn to direct still others, until the last man in the organization is reached.

This condition placed upon all human organization by the limits of the span of control obviously differs in different kinds of work and in organizations of different sizes. Where the work is of a routine, repetitive, measurable and homogeneous character, one man can perhaps direct several score workers. This is particularly true when the workers are all in a single room. Where the work is diversified, qualitative, and particularly when the workers are scattered, one man can supervise only a few. This diversification, dispersion, and nonmeasurability is of course most evident at the very top of any organization. It follows that the limitations imposed by the span of control are most evident at the top of an organization, directly under the executive himself.

But when we seek to determine how many immediate subordinates the director of an enterprise can effectively supervise, we enter a realm of experience which has not been brought under sufficient scientific study to furnish a final answer. Sir Ian Hamilton says, "The nearer we approach the supreme head of the whole organization, the more we ought to work towards groups of three; the closer we get to the foot of the whole organization (the Infantry of the Line), the more we work towards groups of six."[2]

The British Machinery of Government Committee of 1918 arrived at the conclusion that "The Cabinet should be small in number—preferably ten or, at most, twelve."[3]

Henri Fayol said "[In France] a minister has twenty assistants, where the Administrative Theory says that a manager at the head of a big undertaking should not have more than five or six."[4]

Graham Wallas expressed the opinion that the Cabinet should not be increased "beyond the number of ten or twelve at which organized oral discussion is most efficient."[5]

Léon Blum recommended for France a Prime Minister with a technical cabinet modelled after the British War Cabinet, which was composed of five members.[6]

It is not difficult to understand why there is this divergence of statement among authorities who are agreed on the fundamentals. It arises in part from the differences in the capacities and work habits of individual executives observed, and in part from the non-comparable character of the work covered. It would seem that insufficient attention has been devoted to three factors: first, the element of diversification of function; second, the element of time; and third, the element of space. A chief of public works can deal effectively with more direct subordinates than can the general of the army, because all of his immediate subordinates in the department of public works will be in the general field of engineering, while in the army there will be many different elements, such as communications, chemistry, aviation, ordnance, motorized service, engineering, supply, transportation, etc., each with its own technology. The element of time is also of great significance as has been indicated above. In a stable organization the chief executive can deal with more immediate subordinates than in a new or changing organization. Similarly, space influences the span of control. An organization located in one building can be supervised through more immediate subordinates than can the same organization if scattered in several cities. When scattered there is not only need for more supervision, and therefore more supervisory personnel, but also for a fewer number of contacts with the chief executive because of the increased difficulty faced by the chief executive in learning sufficient details about a far-flung organization to do an intelligent job. The failure to attach sufficient importance to these variables has served to limit the scientific validity of the statements which have been made that one man can supervise but three, or five, or eight, or twelve immediate subordinates.

These considerations do not, however, dispose of the problem. They indicate rather the need for further research. But without further research we may conclude that the chief executive of an organization can deal with only a few immediate subordinates; that this number is determined not only by the nature of the work but also by the nature of the executive; and that the number of immediate subordinates in a large, diversified, and dispersed organization must be even less than in a homogeneous and unified organization to achieve the same measure of coordination.

One Master

From the earliest times it has been recognized that nothing but confusion arises under multiple command. "A man cannot serve two masters" was adduced as a theological argument because it was already accepted as a principle of human relation in everyday life. In administration this is known as the principle of "unity of command."[7] The principle may be stated as follows: A workman subject to orders from several superiors will be confused, inefficient, and irresponsible; a workman subject to orders from but one superior may be methodical, efficient, and responsible. Unity of command thus refers to those who are commanded, not to those who issue the commands.[8]

The significance of this principle in the process of coordination and organization must not be lost sight of. In building a structure of coordination, it is often tempting to set up more than one boss for a man who is doing work which has more than one relationship. Even as great a philosopher of management as Taylor fell into this error in setting up separate foremen to deal with machinery, with materials, with speed, etc., each with the power of giving orders directly to the individual workman.[9] The rigid adherence to the principle of unity of command may have its absurdities; these are, however, unimportant in comparison with the certainty of confusion, inefficiency and irresponsibility which arise from the violation of the principle.

Technical Efficiency

There are many aspects of the problem of securing technical efficiency. Most of these do not concern us here directly. They have been treated extensively by such authorities as Taylor, Dennison, and Kimball, and their implications for general organization by Fayol, Urwick, Mooney, and Reiley. There is, however, one efficiency concept which concerns us deeply in approaching the theory of organization. It is the principle of homogeneity.

It has been observed by authorities in many fields that the efficiency of a group working together is directly related to the homogeneity of the work they are performing, of the processes they are utilizing, and of the purposes which actuate them. From top to bottom, the group must be unified. It must work together.

It follows from this (1) that any organizational structure which brings together in a single unit work divisions which are nonhomogeneous in work, in technology, or in purpose will encounter the danger of friction and inefficiency; and (2) that a unit based on a given specialization cannot be given technical direction by a layman.

In the realm of government it is not difficult to find many illustrations of the unsatisfactory results of nonhomogeneous administrative combinations. It is generally agreed that agricultural development and education cannot be administered by the same men who enforce pest and disease control, because the success of the former rests upon friendly cooperation and trust of the farmers, while the latter engenders resentment and suspicion. Similarly, activities like drug control established in protection of the consumer do not find appropriate homes in departments dominated by the interests of the producer. In the larger cities and in states it has been found that hospitals cannot be so well administered by the health department directly as they can be when set up independently in a separate department, or at least in a bureau with extensive autonomy; and it is generally agreed that public welfare administration and police administration require separation, as do public health administration and welfare administration, though both of these combinations may be found in successful operation under special conditions. No one would think of combining water supply and public education, or tax administration and public recreation. In every one of these cases, it will be seen that there is some element either of work to be done, or of the technology used, or of the end sought which is non-homogeneous.

Another phase of the combination of incompatible functions in the same office may be found in the common American practice of appointing unqualified laymen and politicians to technical positions or to give technical direction to highly specialized services. As Dr. Frank J. Goodnow pointed out a generation ago, we are faced here by two heterogeneous functions, "politics" and "administration," the combination of which cannot be undertaken within the structure of the administration without producing inefficiency.

Caveamus Expertum

At this point a word of caution is necessary. The application of the principle of homogeneity has its pitfalls. Every highly trained technician, particularly in the learned professions, has a profound sense of omniscience and a great desire for complete independence in the service of society. When employed by government he knows exactly what the people need better than they do themselves, and he knows how to render this service. He tends to be utterly oblivious of all other needs, because, after all, is not his particular technology the road to salvation? Any restraint applied to him is "limitation of freedom," and any criticism "springs from ignorance and jealousy." Every budget increase he secures is "in the public interest," while every increase secured elsewhere is "a sheer waste." His efforts and maneuvers to expand are "public education" and "civic organization," while similar efforts by others are "propaganda" and "politics."

Another trait of the expert is his tendency to assume knowledge and authority in fields in which he has no competence. In this particular, educators, lawyers, priests, admirals, doctors, scientists, engineers, accountants, merchants, and bankers are all the same—having achieved technical competence or "success" in one field, they come to think this competence is a general quality detachable from the field and inherent in themselves. They step without embarrassment into other areas. They do not remember that the robes of authority of one kingdom confer no sovereignty in another; but that there they are merely a masquerade.

The expert knows his "stuff." Society needs him, and must have him more and more as man's technical knowledge becomes more and more extensive. But history shows us that the common man is a better judge of his own needs in the long run than any cult of experts. Kings and ruling classes, priests and prophets, soldiers and lawyers, when permitted to rule rather than serve mankind, have in the end done more to check the advance of human welfare than they have to advance it. The true place of the expert is, as A. E. said so well, "on tap, not on top." The essential validity of democracy rests upon this philosophy, for democracy is a way of government in which the common man is the final judge of what is good for him.

Efficiency is one of the things that is good for him, because it makes life richer and safer. That efficiency is to be secured more and more through the use of technical specialists. These specialists have no right to ask for, and must not be given freedom from supervisory control, but in establishing that control, a government which ignores the conditions of efficiency cannot expect to achieve efficiency.

3. ORGANIZATIONAL PATTERNS

Organization Up or Down?

One of the great sources of confusion in the discussion of the theory of organization is that some authorities work and think primarily from the top down, while others work and think from the bottom up. This is perfectly natural, because some authorities are interested primarily in the executive and in the problems of central management, while others are interested primarily in individual services and activities. Those who work from the top down regard the organization as a system of subdividing the enterprise under the chief executive, while those who work from the bottom up look upon organization as a system of combining the individual units of work into aggregates which are in turn subordinated to the chief executive. It may be argued that either approach leads to a consideration of the entire problem, so that it is of no great significance which way the organization is viewed. Certainly it makes this very important practical difference: Those who work from the top down must guard themselves from the danger of sacrificing the effectiveness of the individual services in their zeal to achieve a model structure at the top, while those who start from the bottom, must guard themselves from the danger of thwarting coordination in their eagerness to develop effective individual services.

In any practical situation the problem of organization must be approached from both top and bottom. This is particularly true in the reorganization of a going concern. May it not be that this practical necessity is likewise the sound process theoretically? In that case one would develop the plan of an organization or reorganization both from the top downward and from the bottom upward, and would reconcile the two at the center. In planning the first subdivisions under the chief executive, the principle of the limitation of the span of control must apply; in building up the first aggregates of specialized functions, the principle of homogeneity must apply. If any enterprise has such an array of functions that the first subdivisions from the top down do not readily meet the first aggregations from the bottom up, then additional divisions and additional aggregates must be introduced, but at each further step there must be a less and less rigorous adherence to the two conflicting principles until their juncture is effected.

An interesting illustration of this problem was encountered in the plans for the reorganization of the City of New York. The Charter Commission of 1934 approached the problem with the determination to cut down the number of departments and separate activities from some 60 to a manageable number. It was equally convinced after conferences with officials from the various city departments that the number could not be brought below 25 without bringing together as "departments" activities which had nothing in common or were in actual conflict. This was still too many for effective supervision by the chief executive. As a solution it was suggested by the author that the charter provide for the subdividing of the executive by the appointment of three or four assistant mayors to whom the mayor might assign parts of his task of broad supervision and coordination. Under the plan the assistant mayors would bring all novel and important matters to the mayor for decision, and through continual intimate relationship know the temper of his mind on all matters and, thus, be able to relieve him of great masses of detail without in any way injecting themselves into the determination of policy. Under such a plan one assistant mayor might be assigned to give general direction to agencies as diverse as police, parks, hospitals, and docks without violating the principle of homogeneity any more than is the case by bringing these activities under the mayor himself, which is after all a paramount necessity under a democratically controlled government. This is not a violation of the principle of homogeneity, *provided* the assistant mayors keep out of the technology of the services and devote themselves to the broad aspects of administration and coordination, as would the mayor himself. The assistants were conceived of as parts of the mayoralty, not as parts of the service departments. That is, they represented not the apex of a structure built from the bottom up but, rather, the base of a structure extended from the top down, the object of which was to multiply by four the points of effective contact between the executive and the service departments.[10]

Organizing the Executive

The effect of the suggestion presented above is to organize and institutionalize the executive function as such so that it may be more adequate in a complicated situation. This is in reality not a new idea. We do not, for example, expect the chief executive to write his own letters. We give him a private secretary, who is part of his office and assists him to do this part of his job. This secretary is not a part of any department, he is a subdivision of the executive himself. In just this way, though on a different plane, other phases of the job of the chief executive may be organized.

Before doing this, however, it is necessary to have a clear picture of the job itself. This brings us directly to the question, "What is the work of the chief executive? What does he do?"

The answer is POSDCORB.

POSDCORB is, of course, a made-up word designed to call attention to the various functional elements of the work of a chief executive because "administration" and "management" have lost all specific content.[11] POSDCORB is made up of the initials and stands for the following activities:

Planning, that is working out in broad outline the things that need to be done and the methods for doing them to accomplish the purpose set for the enterprise.

Organizing, that is the establishment of the formal structure of authority through which work subdivisions are arranged, defined and coordinated for the defined objective.

Staffing, that is the whole personnel function of bringing in and training the staff and maintaining favorable conditions of work.

Directing, that is the continuous task of making decisions and embodying them in specific and general orders and instructions and serving as the leader of the enterprise.

Coordinating, that is the all important duty of interrelating the various parts of the work.

Reporting, that is keeping those to whom the executive is responsible informed as to what is going on, which thus includes keeping himself and his subordinates informed through records, research and inspection.

Budgeting, with all that goes with budgeting in the form of fiscal planning, accounting, and control.

This statement of the work of a chief executive is adapted from the functional analysis elaborated by Henri Fayol in his "Industrial and General Administration." It is believed that those who know administration intimately will find in this analysis a valid and helpful pattern, into which can be fitted each of the major activities and duties of any chief executive.

If these seven elements may be accepted as the major duties of the chief executive, it follows that they *may* be separately organized as subdivisions of the executive. The need for such subdivision depends entirely on the size and complexity of the enterprise. In the largest enterprises, particularly where the chief executive is as a matter of fact unable to do the work that is thrown upon him, it may be presumed that one or more parts of POSDCORB should be suborganized.

NOTES

1. That is, when *organization is the basis of coordination.* Wherever the central executive authority is composed of several who exercise their functions jointly by majority vote, as on a board, this is from the standpoint of organization still a "single authority"; where the central executive is in reality composed of several men acting freely and independently, then organization cannot be said to be the basis of coordination; it is rather the dominance of an idea and falls under the second principle stated above.
2. Sir Ian Hamilton, "The Soul and Body of an Army." Arnold, London, 1921, p. 230.
3. Great Britain. Ministry of Reconstruction. Report of the Machinery of Government Committee. H. M. Stationery Office, London, 1918, p. 5.
4. Henri Fayol, "The Administrative Theory in the State." Address before the Second International Congress of Administrative Science at Brussels, September 13, 1923. Paper IV in this collection.
5. Graham Wallas, "The Great Society." Macmillan, London and New York, 1919, p. 264.
6. Léon Blum, "La Réforme Gouvernementale." Grasset, Paris, 1918. Reprinted in 1936, p. 59.
7. Henri Fayol, "Industrial and General Administration." English translation by J. A. Coubrough. International Management Association, Geneva, 1930.
8. Fayol terms the latter "unity of direction."
9. Frederick Winslow Taylor, "Shop Management." Harper and Brothers, New York and London, 1911, p. 99.
10. This recommendation was also presented to the Thatcher Charter Commission of 1935, to which the author was a consultant. A first step in this direction was taken in Sec. 9, Chap. 1 of the new charter which provides for a deputy mayor, and for such other assistance as may be provided by ordinance.
11. See Minutes of the Princeton Conference on Training for the Public Service, 1935, p. 35. See also criticism of this analysis in Lewis Meriam, "Public Service and Special Training," University of Chicago Press, 1936, pp. 1, 2, 10 and 15, where this functional analysis is misinterpreted as a statement of qualifications for appointment.

3

The Management Theory Jungle

Harold Koontz

A true modern-day classic, this selection is perhaps the most frequently re-printed article in the management literature. In it, Koontz classifies the major schools of management theory into six main groups which, he argues, have resulted in a "semantics jungle." The article describes the need to disentangle the resulting confusion and integrate management and other disciplines.— Eds.

Although students of management would readily agree that there have been problems of management since the dawn of organized life, most would also agree that systematic examination of management, with few exceptions, is the product of the present century and more especially of the past two decades. Moreover, until recent years almost all of those who have attempted to analyze the management process and look for some theoretical underpinnings to help improve research, teaching, and practice were alert and perceptive practitioners of the art who reflected on many years of experience. Thus, at least in looking at *general* management as an intellectually based art, the earliest meaningful writing came from such experienced practitioners as Fayol, Mooney, Alvin Brown, Sheldon, Barnard, and Urwick. Certainly not even the most academic worshipper of empirical research can overlook the empiricism involved in distilling fundamentals from decades of experience by such discerning practitioners as these. Admittedly done without questionnaires, controlled interviews, or mathematics, observations by such men can hardly be accurately regarded as a priori or "armchair."

The noteworthy absence of academic writing and research in the formative years of modern management theory is now more than atoned for by a deluge of research and writing from the academic halls. What is interest-

SOURCE: Reprinted by permission of the author and publisher from "The Management Theory Jungle," *The Academy of Management Journal*, December 1961, pp. 174-88.

ing and perhaps nothing more than a sign of the unsophisticated adolescence of management theory is how the current flood has brought with it a wave of great differences and apparent confusion. From the orderly analysis of management at the shop-room level by Frederick Taylor and the reflective distillation of experience from the general management point of view by Henri Fayol, we now see these and other early beginnings overgrown and entangled by a jungle of approaches and approachers to management theory.

There are the behavioralists, born of the Hawthorne experiments and the awakened interest in human relations during the 1930s and 1940s, who see management as a complex of interpersonal relationships and the basis of management theory the tentative tenets of the new and undeveloped science of psychology. There are also those who see management theory as simply a manifestation of the institutional and cultural aspects of sociology. Still others, observing that the central core of management is decision making, branch in all directions from this core to encompass everything in organization life. Then, there are mathematicians who think of management primarily as an exercise in logical relationships expressed in symbols and the omnipresent and ever revered model. But the entanglement of growth reaches its ultimate when the study of management is regarded as a study of one of a number of systems and subsystems, with an understandable tendency for the researcher to be dissatisfied until he has encompassed the entire physical and cultural universe as a management system.

With the recent discovery of an ages old problem area by social, physical, and biological scientists, and with the supersonic increase in interest by all types of enterprise managers, the apparent impenetrability of the present thicket which we call management theory is not difficult to comprehend. One can hardly be surprised that psychologists, sociologists, anthropologists, sociometricists, economists, mathematicians, physicists, biologists, political scientists, business administration scholars, and even practicing managers should hop on this interesting, challenging, and profitable band wagon.

This welling of interest from every academic and practicing corner should not upset anyone concerned with seeing the frontiers of knowledge pushed back and the intellectual base of practice broadened. But what is rather upsetting to the practitioner and the observer, who sees great social potential from improved management, is that the variety of approaches to management theory has led to a kind of confused and destructive jungle warfare. Particularly among academic disciplines and their disciples, the primary interests of many would-be cult leaders seem to be to carve out a distinct (and hence "original") approach to management. And to defend this originality, and thereby gain a place in posterity (or at least to gain a publication which will justify academic status or promotion), it seems to have become too much the current style to downgrade, and sometimes misrepresent, what anyone else has said, or thought, or done.

In order to cut through this jungle and bring to light some of the issues and problems involved in the present management theory area so that the tremendous interest, intelligence, and research results may become more meaningful, it is my purpose here to classify the various "schools" of management theory, to identify briefly what I believe to be the major source of differences, and to offer some suggestions for disentangling the jungle. It is hoped that a movement for clarification can be started so at least we in the field will not be a group of blind men identifying the same elephant with our widely varying and sometimes viciously argumentative theses.

THE MAJOR "SCHOOLS" OF MANAGEMENT THEORY

In attempting to classify the major schools of management theory into six main groups, I am aware that I may overlook certain approaches and cannot deal with all the nuances of each approach. But it does seem that most of the approaches to management theory can be classified in one of these so-called schools.

The Management Process School

This approach to management theory perceives management as a process of getting things done through and with people operating in organized groups. It aims to analyze the process, to establish a conceptual framework for it, to identify principles underlying it, and to build up a theory of management from them. It regards management as a universal process, regardless of the type of enterprise, or the level in a given enterprise, although recognizing, obviously, that the environment of management differs widely between enterprises and levels. It looks upon management theory as a way of organizing experience so that practice can be improved through research, empirical testing of principles, and teaching of fundamentals involved in the management process.[1]

Often referred to, especially by its critics, as the "traditional" or "universalist" school, this school can be said to have been fathered by Henri Fayol, although many of his offspring did not know of their parent, since Fayol's work was eclipsed by the bright light of his contemporary, Frederick Taylor, and clouded by the lack of a widely available English translation until 1949. Other than Fayol, most of the early contributors to this school dealt only with the organization portion of the management process, largely because of their greater experience with this facet of management and the simple fact that planning and control, as well as the function of staffing, were given little attention by managers before 1940.

This school bases its approach to management theory on several fundamental beliefs:

(1) that managing is a process and can best be dissected intellectually by analyzing the functions of the manager;

(2) that long experience with management in a variety of enterprise situations can be grounds for distillation of certain fundamental truths or generalizations—usually referred to as principles—which have a clarifying and predictive value in the understanding and improvement of managing;

(3) that these fundamental truths can become focal points for useful research both to ascertain their validity and to improve their meaning and applicability in practice;

(4) that such truths can furnish elements, at least until disproved, and certainly until sharpened, of a useful theory of management;

(5) that managing is an art, but one like medicine or engineering, which can be improved by reliance on the light and understanding of principles;

(6) that principles in management, like principles in the biological and physical sciences, are nonetheless true even if a prescribed treatment or design by a practitioner in a given case situation chooses to ignore a principle and the costs involved, or attempts to do something else to offset the costs incurred (this is, of course, not new in medicine, engineering, or any other art, for art is the creative task of compromising fundamentals to attain a desired result); and

(7) that, while the totality of culture and of the physical and biological universe have varying effects on the manager's environment and subjects, as indeed they do in every other field of science and art, the theory of management does not need to encompass the field of all knowledge in order for it to serve as a scientific or theoretical foundation.

The basic approach of this school, then, is to look, first, to the functions of managers. As a second step in this approach, many of us have taken the functions of managers and further dissected them by distilling what we see as fundamental truths in the understandably complicated practice of management. I have found it useful to classify my analysis of these functions around the essentials involved in the following questions:

(1) What is the nature of the function?

(2) What is the purpose of the function?

(3) What explains the structure of the function?

(4) What explains the process of the function?

Perhaps there are other more useful approaches, but I have found that I can place everything pertaining to management (even some of the rather remote research and concepts) in this framework.

Also, purely to make the area of management theory intellectually manageable, those who subscribe to this school do not usually attempt to include in the theory the entire areas of sociology, economics, biology, psychology, physics, chemistry, or others. This is done not because these other areas of knowledge are unimportant and have no bearing on management, but merely because no real progress has ever been made in science or art without significant partitioning of knowledge. Yet, anyone would be foolish not to realize that a function which deals with people in their various activities of producing and marketing anything from money to religion and education is not completely independent of the physical, biological, and cultural universe in which we live. And, are there not such relationships in other "compartments" of knowledge and theory?

The Empirical School

A second approach to management I refer to as the "empirical" school. In this, I include those scholars who identify management as a study of experience, sometimes with intent to draw generalizations but usually merely as a means of teaching experience and transferring it to the practitioner or student. Typical of this school are those who see management or "policy" as the study and analysis of cases and those with such approaches as Ernest Dale's "comparative approach."[2]

This approach seems to be based upon the premise that, if we study the experience of successful managers, or the mistakes made in management, or if we attempt to solve management problems, we will somehow understand and learn to apply the most effective kinds of management techniques. This approach, as often applied, assumes that, by finding out what worked or did not work in individual circumstances, the student or the practitioner will be able to do the same in comparable situations.

No one can deny the importance of studying experience through such study, or of analyzing the "how-it-was-done" of management. But management, unlike law, is not a science based on precedent, and situations in the future exactly comparable to the past are exceedingly unlikely to occur. Indeed, there is a positive danger of relying too much on past experience and on undistilled history of managerial problem solving for the simple reason that a technique or approach found "right" in the past may not fit a situation of the future.

Those advocating the empirical approach are likely to say that what they really do in analyzing cases or history is to draw from certain generalizations which can be applied as useful guides to thought or action in future case situations. As a matter of fact, Ernest Dale, after claiming to find "so little practical value" from the principles enunciated by the "universalists," curiously drew certain "generalizations" or "criteria" from his valuable study of a number of great practitioners of management.[3] There is some question as to whether Dale's "comparative" approach is not really the same as the "universalist" approach he decries, except with a different distiller of basic truths.

By the emphasis of the empirical school on study of experience, it does appear that the research and thought so engendered may assist in hastening the day for verification of principles. It is also possible that the proponents of this school may come up with a more useful framework of principles than that of the management process school. But, to the extent that the empirical school draws generalizations from its research, and it would seem to be a necessity to do so unless its members are satisfied to exchange meaningless and structureless experience, this approach tends to be and do the same as the management process school.

The Human Behavior School

This approach to the analysis of management is based on the central thesis that, since managing involves getting things done with and through people, the study of management must be centered on interpersonal relations. Variously called the "human relations," "leadership," or "behavioral sciences" approach, this school brings to bear "existing and newly developed theories, methods, and techniques of the relevant social sciences upon the study of inter- and intrapersonal phenomena, ranging fully from the personality dynamics of individuals at one extreme to the relations of cultures at the other."[4] In other words, this school concentrates on the "people" part of management and rests on the principle that, where people work together as groups in order to accomplish objectives, "people should understand people."

The scholars in this school have a heavy orientation to psychology and social psychology. Their primary focus is the individual as a sociopsychological being and what motivates him. The members of this school vary from those who see it as a portion of the manager's job, a tool to help him understand and get the best from people by meeting their needs and responding to their motivations, to those who see the psychological behavior of individuals and groups as the total of management.

In this school are those who emphasize human relations as an art that the manager should advantageously understand and practice. There are those who focus attention on the manager as a leader and sometimes equate management to leadership, thus, in effect, tending to treat all group activities as "managed" situations. There are those who see the study of group dynamics and interpersonal relationships as simply a study of sociopsychological relationships and seem, therefore, merely to be attaching the term *management* to the field of social psychology.

That management must deal with human behavior can hardly be denied. That the study of human interactions, whether in the environment of management or in unmanaged situations, is important and useful one could not dispute. And it would be a serious mistake to regard good leadership as unimportant to good managership. But whether the field of human behavior is the equivalent of the field of management is quite another thing. Perhaps it is like calling the study of the human body the field of cardiology.

The Social System School

Closely related to the human behavior school and often confused or intertwined with it is one which might be labeled the social system school. This includes those researchers who look upon management as a social system, that is, a system of cultural interrelationships. Sometimes, as in the case of March and Simon,[5] the system is limited to formal organizations, using the term *organization* as equivalent to enterprise, rather than the authority-activity concept used most often in management. In other cases, the approach is not to distinguish the formal organization, but rather to encompass any kind of system of human relationships.

Heavily sociological in flavor, this approach to management does essentially what any study of sociology does. It identifies the nature of the cultural relationships of various social groups and attempts to show these as a related, and usually an integrated, system.

Perhaps the spiritual father of this ardent and vocal school of management theorists is Chester Barnard.[6] In searching for an answer to fundamental explanations underlying the managing process, this thoughtful business executive developed a theory of cooperation grounded in the needs of the individual to solve, through cooperation, the biological, physical, and social limitations of himself and his environment. Barnard then carved from the total of cooperative systems so engendered one set of interrelationships which he defines as "formal organization." His formal organization concept, quite unlike that usually held by management practitioners, is any cooperative system in which there are persons able to communicate with each other and who are willing to contribute action toward a conscious common purpose.

The Barnard concept of cooperative system pervades the work of many contributors to the social system school of management. For example, Herbert Simon at one time defined the subject of organization theory and the nature of human organizations as "systems of interdependent activity, encompassing at least several primary groups and usually characterized, at the level of consciousness of participants, by a high degree of rational direction of behavior toward ends that are objects of common knowledge."[7] Simon and others have subsequently seemed to have expanded this concept of social systems to include any cooperative and purposeful group interrelationship or behavior.

This school has made many noteworthy contributions to management. The recognition of organized enterprise as a social organism, subject to all the pressures and conflicts of the cultural environment, has been helpful to the management theorist and the practitioner alike. Among some of the more helpful aspects are the awareness of the institutional foundations of organization authority, the influence of informal organization, and such social factors as those Wight Bakke has called the "bonds of organization."[8] Likewise, many of Barnard's helpful insights, such as his economy of incentives and his theory of opportunism, have brought the power of sociological understanding into the realm of management practice.

Basic sociology, analysis of concepts of social behavior, and the study of group behavior in the framework of social systems do have great value in the field of management. But one may well ask the question whether this *is* management. Is the field of management coterminous with the field of sociology? Or is sociology an important underpinning like language, psychology, physiology, mathematics, and other fields of knowledge? Must management be defined in terms of the universe of knowledge?

The Decision Theory School

Another approach to management theory, undertaken by a growing and scholarly group, might be referred to as the decision theory school. This group concentrates on rational approach to decision—the selection from among possible alternatives of a course of action or of an idea. The approach of this school may be to deal with the decision itself, or with the persons or organizational group making the decision, or with an analysis of the decision process. Some limit themselves fairly much to the economic rationale of the decision, while others regard anything which happens in an enterprise the subject of their analysis, and still others expand decision theory to cover the psychological and sociological aspect and environment of decisions and decision makers.

The decision-making school is apparently an outgrowth of the theory of consumer's choice with which economists have been concerned since the days of Jeremy Bentham early in the 19th century. It has arisen out of such economic problems and analyses as utility maximization, indifference curves, marginal utility, and economic behavior under risks and uncertainties. It is, therefore, no surprise that one finds most of the members of this school to be economic theorists. It is likewise no surprise to find the content of this school to be heavily oriented to model construction and mathematics.

The decision theory school has tended to expand its horizon considerably beyond the process of evaluating alternatives. That point has become for many only a springboard for examination of the entire sphere of human activity, including the nature of the organization structure, psychological and social reactions of individuals and groups, the development of basic information for decisions, an analysis of values and particularly value considerations with respect to goals, communications networks, and incentives. As one would expect, when the decision theorists study the small, but central, area of decision *making*, they are led by this keyhole look at management to consider the entire field of enterprise operation and its environment. The result is that decision theory becomes no longer a neat and narrow concentration on decision but, rather, a broad view of the enterprise as a social system.

There are those who believe that, since management is characterized by its concentration on decisions, the future development of management theory will tend to use the decision as its central focus and the rest of management theory will be hung on this structural center. This may occur, and certainly the study of the decision, the decision process, and the decision maker can be extended to cover the entire field of management as anyone might conceive it. Nevertheless, one wonders whether this focus cannot also be used to build around it the entire area of human knowledge. For, as most decision theorists recognize, the problem of choice is individual, as well as organizational, and most of what has been said that is pure decision theory can be applied to the existence and thinking of a Robinson Crusoe.

The Mathematical School

Although mathematical methods can be used by any school of management theory, and have been, I have chosen to group under a school those theorists who see management as a system of mathematical models and processes. Perhaps the most widely known group I arbitrarily so lump are the operations researchers or operations analysts, who have sometimes anointed themselves with the rather pretentious name of "management scientists." The abiding belief of this group is that, if management, or organization, or planning, or decision making is a logical process, it can be expressed in terms of mathematical symbols and relationships. The central approach of this school is the model, for it is through these devices that the problem is expressed in its basic relationships and in terms of selected goals or objectives.

There can be no doubt of the great usefulness of mathematical approaches to any field of inquiry. It forces upon the researcher the definition of a problem or problem area, it conveniently allows the insertion of symbols for unknown data, and its logical methodology, developed by years of scientific application and abstraction, furnishes a powerful tool for solving or simplifying complex phenomena.

But it is hard to see mathematics as a truly separate school of management theory, any more than it is a separate "school" in physics, chemistry, engineering, or medicine. I only deal with it here as such because there has appeared to have developed a kind of cult around mathematical analysts who have subsumed to themselves the area of management.

In pointing out that mathematics is a tool, rather than a school, it is not my intention to underestimate the impact of mathematics on the science and practice of management. By bringing to this immensely important and complex field the tools and techniques of the physical sciences, the mathematicians have already made an immense contribution to orderly thinking. They have forced on people in management the means and desirability of seeing many problems more clearly, they have pressed on scholars and practitioners the need for establishing goals and measures of effectiveness, they have been extremely helpful in getting the management area seen as a logical system of relationships, and they have caused people in management to review and occasionally reorganize information sources and systems so that mathematics can be given sensible quantitative meaning. But with all this meaningful contribution and the greater sharpness and sophistication of planning which is resulting, I cannot see that mathematics is management theory any more than it is astronomy.

THE MAJOR SOURCES OF MENTAL ENTANGLEMENT IN THE JUNGLE

In outlining the various schools, or approaches, of management theory, it becomes clear that these intellectual cults are not drawing greatly different inferences from the physical and cultural environment surrounding us. Why, then, have there been so many differences between them and why such a struggle, particularly among our academic brethren, to obtain a place in the sun by denying the approaches of others? Like the widely differing and often contentious denominations of the Christian religion, all have essentially the same goals and deal with essentially the same world.

While there are many sources of the mental entanglement in the management theory jungle, the major ones are the following.

The Semantics Jungle

As is so often true when intelligent men argue about basic problems, some of the trouble lies in the meaning of key words. The semantics problem is particularly severe in the field of management. There is even a difference in the meaning of the word "management." Most people would agree that it means getting things done through and with people, but is it people in formal organizations, or in all group activities? Is it governing, leading, or teaching?

Perhaps the greatest single semantics confusion lies in the word "organization." Most members of the management process school use it to define the activity-authority structure of an enterprise and certainly most practitioners believe that they are "organizing" when they establish a framework of activity groupings and authority relationships. In this case, organization represents the formal framework within an enterprise that furnishes the environment in which people perform. Yet a large number of "organization" theorists conceive of organization as the sum total of human relationships in any group activity; they thus seem to make it equivalent to *social* structure. And some use "organization" to mean "enterprise."

If the meaning of organization cannot be clarified and a standard use of the term adopted by management theorists, understanding and criticism should not be based on this difference. It hardly seems to me to be accurate for March and Simon, for example, to criticize the organization theories of the management process, or "universalist," school for not considering the management planning function as part of organizing, when they have chosen to treat it separately. Nor should those who choose to treat the training, selecting, guiding, or leading of people under staffing and direction be criticized for a tendency to "view the employee as an inert instrument" or a "given rather than a variable."[9] Such accusations, proceeding from false premises, are clearly erroneous.

Other semantic entanglements might be mentioned. By some, decision making is regarded as a process of choosing from among alternatives; by others, the total managerial task and environment. Leadership is often made synonymous with managership and is analytically separated by others. Communications may mean everything from a written or oral report to a vast network of formal and informal relationships. Human relations to some implies a psychiatric manipulation of people, but to others the study and art of understanding people and interpersonal relationships.

Differences in Definition of Management as a Body of Knowledge

As was indicated in the discussion of semantics, "management" has far from a standard meaning, although most agree that it at least involves getting things done through and with people. But, does it mean the dealing with all human relationships? Is a street peddler a manager? Is a parent a manager? Is a leader of a disorganized mob a manager? Does the field of management equal the fields of sociology and social psychology combined? Is it the equivalent of the entire system of social relationships?

While I recognize that sharp lines cannot be drawn in management any more than they are in medicine or engineering, there surely can be a sharper distinction drawn than at present. With the plethora of management writing and experts, calling almost everything under the sun management, can one expect management theory to be regarded as very useful or scientific to the practitioner?

The a Priori Assumption

Confusion in management theory has also been heightened by the tendency for many newcomers in the field to cast aside significant observations and analyses of the past on the grounds that they are a priori in nature. This is an often-met accusation made by those who wish to cast aside the work of Fayol, Mooney, Brown, Urwick, Gulick, and others who are branded as "universalists." To make the assumption that the distilled experiences of men such as these represent a priori reasoning is to forget that experience in and with managing *is* empirical. While the conclusions that perceptive and experienced practitioners of the art of management draw are not infallible, they represent an experience which is certainly real and not "armchair." No one could deny, I feel sure, that the ultimate test of accuracy of management theory must be practice and management theory and science must be developed from reality.

The Misunderstanding of Principles

Those who feel that they gain caste or a clean slate for advancing a particular notion or approach often delight in casting away anything which smacks of management principles. Some have referred to them as platitudes, forgetting that a platitude is still a truism and a truth does not become worthless because it is familiar. (As Robert Frost has written, "Most of the changes we think we see in life are merely truths going in or out of favor.") Others cast away principles of Fayol and other practitioners, only to draw apparently different generalizations from their study of management; but many of the generalizations so discovered are often the same fundamental truths in different words that certain criticized "universalists" have discovered.

One of the favorite tricks of the managerial theory trade is to disprove a whole framework of principles by reference to one principle which the observer sees disregarded in practice. Thus, many critics of the universalists point to the well-known cases of dual subordination in organized enterprise, coming to the erroneous conclusion that there is not substance to the principle of unity of command. But this does not prove that there is no cost to the enterprise by designing around, or disregarding, the principle of unity of command; nor does it prove that there were not other advantages which offset the costs, as there often are in cases of establishing functional authorities in organization.

Perhaps the almost hackneyed standby for those who would disprove the validity of all principles by referring to a single one is the misunderstanding around the principle of span of management (or span of control). The usual source of authority quoted by those who criticize is Sir Ian Hamilton, who never intended to state a universal principle, but, rather, to make a personal observation in a book of reflections on his Army experience, and who did say, offhand, that he found it wise to limit his span to three to six subordinates. No modern universalist relies on this single observation, and, indeed, few can or will state an absolute or universal numerical ceiling. Since Sir Ian was not a management theorist and did not intend to be, let us hope that the ghost of his innocent remark may be laid to deserved rest!

What concerns those who feel that a recognition of fundamental truths, or generalizations, may help in the diagnosis and study of management, and who know from managerial experience that such truths or principles do serve an extremely valuable use, is the tendency for some researchers to prove the wrong things through either misstatement or misapplication of principles. A classic case of such misunderstanding and misapplication is in Chris Argyris's interesting book on *Personality and Organization*.[10] This author, who in this book and his other works has made many noteworthy contributions to management, concludes that "formal organization principles make demands on relatively healthy individuals that are incongruent with their needs," and that "frustration, conflict, failure, and short-time perspective are predicted as results of this basic incongruency."[11] This startling conclusion—the exact opposite of what "good" formal organization based on "sound" organization principles should cause, is explained when one notes that, of four "principles" Argyris quotes, one is not an organization principle at all but the economic principle of specialization and three other "principles" are quoted incorrectly.[12] With such a postulate, and with no attempt to recognize, correctly or incorrectly, any other organization and management principles, Argyris has simply proved that wrong principles badly applied will lead to frustration; and every management practitioner knows this to be true!

The Inability or Unwillingness of Management Theorists to Understand Each Other

What has been said above leads one to the conclusion that much of the management theory jungle is caused by the unwillingness or inability of the management theorists to understand each other. Doubting that it is inability, because one must assume that a person interested in management theory is able to comprehend, at least in concept and framework, the approaches of the various "schools," I can only come to the conclusion that the roadblock to understanding is unwillingness.

Perhaps this unwillingness comes from the professional "walls" developed by learned disciplines. Perhaps the unwillingness stems from a fear that someone or some new discovery will encroach on professional and academic status. Perhaps it is fear of professional or intellectual obsolescence. But whatever the cause, it seems that these walls will not be torn down until it is realized that they exist, until all cultists are willing to look at the approach and content of other schools, and until, through exchange and understanding of ideas some order may be brought from the present chaos.

DISENTANGLING THE MANAGEMENT THEORY JUNGLE

It is important that steps be taken to disentangle the management theory jungle. Perhaps, it is too soon and we must expect more years of wandering through a thicket of approaches, semantics, thrusts, and counter thrusts. But in any field as important to society where the many blunders of an unscientifically based managerial art can be so costly, I hope that this will not be long.

There do appear to be some things that can be done. Clearly, meeting what I see to be the major sources of the entanglement should remove much of it. The following considerations are important:

1. The Need for Definition of a Body of Knowledge. Certainly, if a field of knowledge is not to get bogged down in a quagmire of misunderstandings, the first need is for definition of the field. Not that it need be defined in sharp, detailed, and inflexible lines, but, rather, along lines which will give it fairly specific content. Because management is reality, life, practice, my suggestion would be that it be defined in the light of the able and discerning practitioner's frame of reference. A science unrelated to the art for which it is to serve is not likely to be a very productive one.

Although the study of managements in various enterprises, in various countries, and at various levels made by many persons, including myself, may neither be representative nor adequate, I have come to the conclusion that management is the art of getting things done through and with people in *formally organized groups,* the art of creating an environment in such an organized group where people can perform as individuals and yet cooperate toward attainment of group goals, the art of removing blocks to such performance, the art of optimizing efficiency in effectively reaching goals. If this kind of definition of the field is unsatisfactory, I suggest at least an agreement that the area should be defined to reflect the field of the practitioner and that further research and study of practice be done to this end.

In defining the field, too, it seems to me imperative to draw some limits for purposes of analysis and research. If we are to call the entire cultural, biological, and physical universe the field of management, we can no more make progress than could have been done if chemistry or geology had not carved out a fairly specific area and had, instead, studied all knowledge.

In defining the body of knowledge, too, care must be taken to distinguish between tools and content. Thus, mathematics, operations research, accounting, economic theory, sociometry, and psychology, to mention a few, are significant *tools* of management but are not, in themselves, a part of the *content* of the field. This is not to mean that they are unimportant or that the practicing manager should not have them available to him, nor does it mean that they may not be the means of pushing back the frontiers of knowledge of management. But they should not be confused with the basic content of the field.

This is not to say that fruitful study should not continue on the underlying disciplines affecting management. Certainly knowledge of sociology, social systems, psychology, economics, political science, mathematics, and other areas, pointed toward contributing to the field of management, should be continued and encouraged. And significant findings in these and other fields of knowledge might well cast important light on, or change concepts in, the field of management. This has certainly happened in other sciences and in every other art based upon significant science.

2. Integration of Management and Other Disciplines.   If recognition of the proper content of the field were made, I believe that the present crossfire of misunderstanding might tend to disappear. Management would be regarded as a specific discipline and other disciplines would be looked upon as important bases of the field. Under these circumstances, the allied and underlying disciplines would be welcomed by the business and public administration schools, as well as by practitioners, as loyal and helpful associates. Integration of management and other disciplines would then not be difficult.

3. The Clarification of Management Semantics.   While I would expect the need for clarification and uniformity of management semantics would largely be satisfied by definition of the field as a body of knowledge, semantics problems might require more special attention. There are not too many places where semantics are important enough to cause difficulty. Here again, I would suggest the adoption of the semantics of the intelligent practitioners, unless words are used by them so inexactly as to require special clarification. At least, we should not complicate an already complex field by developing a scientific or academic jargon which would build a language barrier between the theorist and the practitioner.

Perhaps the most expeditious way out of this problem is to establish a commission representing academic societies immediately concerned and associations of practicing managers. This would not seem to be difficult to do. And even if it were, the results would be worth the efforts.

4. Willingness to Distill and Test Fundamentals.   Certainly, the test of maturity and usefulness of a science is the sharpness and validity of the principles underlying it. No science, now regarded as mature, started out with a complete statement of incontrovertibly valid principles. Even the oldest sciences, such as physics, keep revising their underlying laws and discovering new principles. Yet any science has proceeded, and more than that has been useful, for centuries on the basis of generalizations, some laws, some principles, and some hypotheses.

One of the understandable sources of inferiority of the social sciences is the recognition that they are inexact sciences. On the other hand, even the so-called exact sciences are subject to a great deal of inexactness, have principles which are not completely proved, and use art in the design of practical systems and components. The often-encountered defeatist attitude of the social sciences, of which management is one, overlooks the fact that management may be explained, practice may be improved, and the goals of research may be more meaningful if we encourage attempts at perceptive distillation of experience by stating principles (or generalizations) and placing them in a logical framework. As two scientists recently said on this subject:

> The reason for this defeatist point of view regarding the social sciences may be traceable to a basic misunderstanding of the nature of scientific endeavor. What matters is not whether or to what extent inexactitudes in procedures and predictive capability can eventually be removed . . . : rather it is *objectivity,* i.e., the intersubjectivity of findings independent of any one person's intuitive judgment, which distinguishes science from intuitive guesswork however brilliant. . . . But once a new fact or a new idea has been conjectured, no matter how intuitive a foundation, it must be capable of objective test and confirmation by anyone. And it is this crucial standard of scientific objectivity rather than any purported criterion of exactitude to which the social sciences must conform.[13]

In approaching the clarification of management theory, then, we should not forget a few criteria:

1. The theory should deal with an area of knowledge and inquiry that is "manageable"; no great advances in knowledge were made so long as man contemplated the whole universe.
2. The theory should be *useful* in improving practice and the task and person of the practitioner should not be overlooked.
3. The theory should not be lost in semantics, especially useless jargon not understandable to the practitioner.
4. The theory should give direction and efficiency to research and teaching.
5. The theory must recognize that it is a part of a larger universe of knowledge and theory.

NOTES AND REFERENCES

1. It is interesting that one of the scholars strongly oriented to human relations and behavioral approaches to management has recently noted that "theory can be viewed as a way of organizing experience" and that "once initial sense is made out of experienced environment, the way is cleared for an even more adequate organization of this experience." See Robert Dubin in "Psyche, Sensitivity, and Social Structure," critical comment in Robert Tannenbaum, I. R. Weschler, and Fred Massarik, *Leadership and Organization: A Behavioral Science Approach* (New York: McGraw-Hill, 1961), p. 401.
2. *The Great Organizers* (New York: McGraw-Hill, 1960), pp. 11–28.
3. Ibid., pp. 11, 26–28, 62–68.
4. R. Tannenbaum; I. R. Weschler; and F. Massarik, *Leadership and Organization* (New York: McGraw-Hill, 1961), p. 9.
5. *Organizations* (New York: John Wiley & Sons, 1958).
6. *The Functions of the Executive* (Cambridge, Mass.: Harvard University Press, 1938).

7. "Comments of the Theory of Organizations," *American Political Science Review* 46, no. 4 (December 1952), p. 1130.

8. *Bonds of Organization* (New York: Harper & Row, 1950). These "bonds" or "devices" of organization are identified by Bakke as (1) the functional specifications system (a system of teamwork arising from job specifications and arrangements for association); (2) the status system (a vertical hierarchy of authority); (3) the communications system; (4) the reward and penalty system; and (5) the organization charter (ideas and means which give character and individuality to the organization, or enterprise).

9. J. G. March and H. A. Simon. *Organizations* (New York: John Wiley & Sons, 1958), pp. 29–33.

10. New York: Harper & Row, 1957.

11. Ibid., p. 74.

12. Ibid., pp. 58–66.

13. O. Helmer and N. Rescher, "On the Epistemology of the Inexact Sciences" (Santa Monica, Cal.: The Rand Corporation, P-1513, 1958), pp. 4–5.

4

Toward Organizational Behavior

L. L. Cummings

This article presents three bases for conceptualizing organizational behavior as a field of inquiry different from other related fields. OB is characterized by three dimensions and three themes that impact the articulation of these dimensions in teaching, research, and application. Cummings then draws implications for the evolution of OB as a discipline.—Eds.

Attempting to describe a field as dynamic and as multifaceted, or even as confusing, as organizational behavior (OB) is not a task for the timid. It may be a task that only the foolish, yet concerned, would even tackle.

What motivates one toward accepting such an undertaking? Two forces are operating. First, there is a clear need to parcel out knowledge into more understandable and convenient packages. Students, managers, and colleagues in other departments request that we respond to straightforward, honest questions like: What is OB? How is OB different from management? How is it different from human relations? It is difficult for students to understand the philosophy or the systematic nature of a program or curriculum if they cannot define the parts. Our credibility with the managerial world is damaged when OB comes out in executive programs as "a little of everything," as "a combination of behavioral jargon and common sense," or as "touchy-feely" without content. The field's lack of confidence in articulating its structure is occasionally reflected in ambiguous and fuzzy suggestions for improvement in the world that managers face.

Second, identification or assertion of the themes and constructs underlying OB, or any other discipline, represents an important platform for expanding knowledge. Without assumptions about what is included, excluded, and on the boundary, duplication among disciplines results. The efficiency of knowledge generation and transmission is hampered. Until a

---

SOURCE: Reprinted by permission of the publisher from "Toward Organizational Behavior," *Academy of Management Review*, January 1978, pp. 90–98.

field is defined in relation to its intellectual cousins, it may develop in redundant directions. This leads to the usual awakening that parallel, and perhaps even superior, developments already have occurred in adjacent fields about which we are ignorant. Repetition of such occurrences in a field lessens its intellectual credibility among scholars. All of this is not to deny the benefits to be gained from cross-fertilization and exchange across sub-fields once these are delineated and common concerns and interests are discovered.

These are the forces underlying the concern. What is said here represents an unfinished product—a thought in process—not a finished, static, intellectually frozen definition. In fact, the argument is made that stimulating, dynamic fields are defined *in process* and that the processes of emergence and evolution should never end.

PERSPECTIVES ON ORGANIZATIONAL BEHAVIOR

Several partitions have been used in attempting to distinguish OB from related disciplines. Tracing some of these provides perspective on our task and builds a critical platform for appraising where the field is today.

Probably the most common segmentation of subfields relating behavior and organization is based on *units of analysis* where the units are differentiated by level of aggregation. Typically, using this framework, OB is defined as the study of individuals and groups within organizations. The units of analysis are individual and micro (e.g., dyadic) interactions among individuals. Organizational characteristics (e.g., structure, process, climate) are seen either as "givens" which assume a constant state or as independent variables whose variations are assumed to covary with or cause variations in the relevant dependent variables. These relevant dependent variables are measures of individual or micro unit affective and/or behavioral reactions.

Organizational theory (OT) is typically defined by its focus upon the *organization as the unit of analysis*. Organizational structure, process, goals, technology, and, more recently, climate are the relevant dependent variables, assumed to vary systematically with variations in environmental characteristics but not with characteristics embedded within systematically clustered individuals. A comparative, cross-organizational framework is essential for development of knowledge in OT. Studies of single organizations add little to understanding of organizations when the unit of analysis and variation is assumed to be the organization itself. This realization is increasingly reflected in the empirical literature of OT.[1]

Some have distinguished the field of inquiry based upon an attribution of *typical* or *modal methodologies* to the respective subfields. OB is defined as studies utilizing laboratory and, occasionally, field experimentation. OT is identified with the predominant use of survey and, occasionally, case designs. While the simplicity of this methodological distinction is attractive, it does not reflect the current diversity of designs underlying current research on people in organizations and on organizations per se.

The adjective pairs "normative-descriptive" and "empirical-theoretical" are attractive labels for describing *epistemological differences*. Certainly, the two predominant versions of classical OT have been characterized, and criticized, as excessively normative and not descriptive of behavioral and organizational realities. Both Taylor and Fayol on the one hand, and Weber on the other, have provided much of the focus for the normative critics. Some OB scholars view their field's mission as adding descriptive, empirically based facts to what they see as the essentially normative and theoretical biases of classical OT. With the advent of data among OT scholars and the infusion of organizational development (OD) into the OB tent, these distinctions are no longer descriptive of our domain. Descriptive, empirical, theoretical, and normative can each be used to characterize some work in both OB and OT. Complexity now overshadows the simple straw man of yesterday.

As OD began to emerge a few years ago, the theme of several corridor conversations was that OB *was becoming the applied cousin of OT*. After all, some claimed, OT deals with the theory of organizations by definition. For a moment the distinctions between OB and OD became blurred, and that opaqueness was attractive for some. Reading between the lines, OT was to become the reservoir of accepted and evolving constructs, and OB would emerge as the behavioral engineering function. For managers and consultants we would have OB; for scholars, OT. The largest obstacle to enacting such a distinction is that scholars and appliers do not generally read or listen to one another. The OB people must have their own constructs and theories. The OT people need their own applications, their own means of establishing credibility within the world of action. From this insulation, two OD camps have emerged with their own strategies for change. One focuses on change via the individual and micro unit within the organization and the other on change through structural and environmental manipulation. Alas, another simple, definitional distinction melts!

My preference among these alternative taxonomic bases is the first. The unit of analysis perspective seems cleanest. The most severe problem with this view is finding intellectual bridges to link the subfields. This linkage is crucial for understanding the way organizations function, the impacts they exert, and the opportunities they provide. Some bridges begin to emerge which are at least suggestive. For example, an organization's structure (i.e., number of levels, average span of supervision, degree of horizontal differentiation) can be viewed as a construct linking OT and OB. In OT, structure is typically positioned in a nomological network as a dependent variable. In OB, structure is typically positioned as an independent variable. This differential positioning of the same construct suggests a possible general role that several constructs might take in linking OT and OB. Structure, climate, task design, reward systems, and leader behavior can each be conceived of as intervening between causal forces in the environment of organizations and the behavior and attitudes of persons within organizations. Each is beginning to be modeled as a dependent variable in one context and an independent variable in another.

This differentiation of subfields by unit of analysis and their integration by intervening constructs is subject to limitations. The boundaries of aggregation between levels of analysis are arbitrary, with no fundamental laws underlying the distinctions. That is a limitation shared with the biological and physical sciences, where subfields have arisen as linking mechanisms (e.g., biophysics, biochemistry, psychopharmacology). The conception also lacks feedback loops with reversible intervening constructs. It is likely that such reciprocal causation reflects reality and that models that omit these loops will not provide a full understanding.

If we were to assume this posture of differentiation, what would be the result? Remembering that the distinctions are based primarily on levels of analysis with a slight nod toward the other distinctions, we can propose the definitions in Figure 1.

A DIMENSIONAL CHARACTERIZATION OF ORGANIZATIONAL BEHAVIOR

I believe that OB is evolving toward the model presented in Figure 2. The field is being enacted, not defined in some a priori sense, by scholars and teachers in ways that imply the dimensional, thematic conception suggested in that figure.

Three dimensions define the conceptual domain of OB. Most disciplines and emerging fields of inquiry that stand at the interface between science and professional practice are describable in terms of these dimensions. The specific articulation of the dimensions depends significantly upon the underlying epistemological themes adopted by the discipline.

A Way of Thinking

OB is a *way of thinking,* a manner of conceiving problems and articulating research and action solutions which can be characterized by five postures.

First, problems and questions are typically formulated within an independent variable(s)-dependent variable(s) framework. Recently, OB has begun to incorporate personal and situational moderators into this framework. OB's assertion that behavior within organizations is subject as systematic study is based on conceptualization of the object of study as nonrandom, systematic, and generally purposive. This way of thinking is significantly influencing our methodologies. The field is engaged in a sometimes painful search for cause and effect within our models.

FIGURE 1   Distinctions among Organizational Behavior, Organizational
Psychology, Organizational Theory, and Personnel and Human
Resources

Organizational Behavior- Organizational Psychology (OP)	Both fields focus upon explaining human behavior within organizations. Their difference centers on the fact that OP restricts its explanatory constructs to those at the psychological level. OB draws constructs from multiple disciplines. As the domain of OP continues to expand, the difference between OB and OP is diminishing, perhaps to the point of identity between the fields.
Organizational Behavior- Organizational Theory (OT)	The distinction is based on two differences: unit of analysis and focus of dependent variables. OB is defined as the study of individual and group behavior within organizations and the application of such knowledge. OT is the study of structure, processes, and outcomes of the organization per se. The distinction is neither that OB is atheoretical and concerned only with behavior nor that OT is unique or exclusive in its attention to theory. Alternatively, the distinction can be conceived as between micro and macro perspectives on OB. This removes the awkward differentiation of behavior and theory.
Organizational Behavior- Personnel and Human Resources (P&HR)	This distinction usually depicts OB as the more basic of the two and P&HR as more applied in emphasis. OB is seen as more concept oriented while P&HR is viewed as emphasizing techniques or technologies. The dependent variables—behavior and affective reactions within organizations—are frequently presented as similar. P&HR can be seen as standing at the interface between the organization and the individual, focusing on developing and implementing the system for attracting, maintaining, and motivating the individual within the organization.

FIGURE 2 Dimensions and Themes of Organizational Behavior

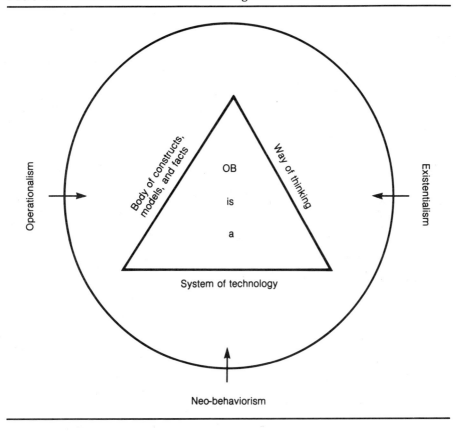

A second component of OB as a way of thinking is its orientation toward change as a desirable outcome for organizations and persons within organizations. Static phenomena possess diminishing prestige as topics of study. Conditions for stimulating change and models for evaluating change are an increasingly important part of the field.

Third, there is a distinctly humanistic tone within OB, reflected in concern for self-development, personal growth, and self-actualization. Although its influence on research and teaching seems to ebb and flow, and its reflection in scholarship and pedagogy varies by school, it is there, and its presence is causing both strain (given its positioning adjacent to scientism) and excitement, even relevance, within OB. The striving is toward humanism without softness. OB shares this dilemma with most of the person-oriented disciplines that attempt to combine basic, good science with a change orientation. Yet this tone of humanism is only one side of the current, slightly schizophrenic posture of OB. The other side is reflected in a heavy emphasis on operant learning models and behavioral modification techniques, an orientation toward environmental determinism rather than self actualization.

Fourth, OB is becoming increasingly performance oriented, with more studies including a performance-oriented dependent variable. The field is beginning to capture an important distinction between two types of dependent variables. One perspective focuses on description of a behavior, activity, or outcome, that is, the proper focus for scientific analysis and thinking. The other aims at application of a preference function to these behaviors, activities, or outcomes, resulting in a scaling of effectiveness or success. This is the proper focus for an engineering analysis—a managerial mind set.[2] We are beginning to hear the demands for relevance in our research and teaching. Unless OB can increase its performance payoffs, the field may be in danger of losing some of its hard battles for a niche in the curriculum or a moment in the board room.

Finally, OB uses the discipline imposed by the scientific method. The field is substantially influenced by norms of skepticism, caution, replication, and public exposure of knowledge based on facts. In many ways, this posture of "scientism" confuses some students and clients. It can be seen as the antithesis of several other postures that characterize OB thinking. Yet it is generally accepted as a crucial posture. It helps to keep the field straight, and it is the key ingredient in whatever longevity the field may possess. Scientific method, applied to OB, provides the mechanism for feedback and self-renewal.

A Body of Constructs, Models, and Facts

Even though OB is characterized by some definitional confusion, an implicit agreement is emerging about some of its components. Differences exist concerning the relative weighting of components and the emphasis given to basic science versus application in transmitting the field to others. But most treatments of the field now include coverage of constructs, models, and facts on: motivation, learning or socialization, group structure and process, leader behavior, task design, interpersonal communication, organizational structure, interpersonal change and conflict, and material on relevant dependent variables (e.g., satisfaction, other attitudes, participation measures, performance dimensions, and other behaviors).

This emergence of an identity for the field is evidenced by the second generation of OB textbooks, which are more similar in topical coverage than their ancestors. Some models sell and are thus influential in structuring the introductory level curricula underlying our field. Others stretch the field at its boundaries but do not become a part of the core. That core is gradually developing toward an identifiable body of components.

A System of Technology

OB is also a system or a collection of technologies. These have evolved out of the primary areas of study identified as the independent variables of OB. Techniques now exist for: training leaders, designing tasks, designing organizations, evaluating performances, rewarding behaviors, and modeling behaviors.

The uncritical eye might be pleased with OB's tool kit. Superficially, it appears that the field is ready to move into the world of action with vigor and confidence. But our posture of scientism keeps the field honest. These technologies are largely exploratory, unvalidated, and, in a few cases, under evaluation. The field has even spawned an occasional technology that has been adopted and later found damaging to an organization and its participants. In most cases, even when the technologies work, the field's theoretical models are not sufficiently developed to explain why they were effective. So, a system or collection of technologies? Yes. A behavioral engineering discipline? No.

THEMES INFLUENCING ORGANIZATIONAL BEHAVIOR

As depicted in Figure 2, three themes span the dimensions defining OB and influence the way each dimension is articulated. The relative emphasis given to each theme over time, by the various schools of thought within OB, determines our ways of thinking, constructs and facts, and development of technologies.

Existentialism

The emphasis here is upon the uncertain, contingent environment of people within organizations (and organizations). Existentialism emphasizes that, in the face of this type of environment, persons must exercise self-control in pursuit of their own objectives. The ultimate responsibility for designing productive and satisfying organizational environments rests with human beings. It is their responsibility to fashion themselves—to implement self-control. This philosophical posture leaves a legacy of concepts within OB—goal, purpose, expectation, expectancy, instrumental, path, and contingency.

This theme is forcing OB to become a more complex discipline. It asserts that no meaning exists in absolutes. All meaning derives from comparison; meaning is always relative. Activities and outcomes within organizations are meaningful only within a context including implicit or explicit statements of purpose. This is at the core of one important, current development in conceptualizing the influence of most of the independent variables treated in OB—the concept of contingency.

With the realization that an independent variable's effects depend, the next logical question becomes: Depends upon what? When? etc. *Why did who do what* with *whom* with what *outcomes?* This seemingly simple question can be applied to most independent-dependent variable linkages currently of concern in OB. The *why* focuses on the causes, the reasons, the antecedents of variance in the dependent variable. The *who* focuses on the initiating party (individual, group, or organization). The *what* requires description of the behavior in question. The *whom* provides the interaction component, adding dimensionality to the search for meaningfulness. It provides a vertical, horizontal, or diagonal vector to the reality that OB attempts to understand. The *outcomes* provide the ultimate meaning to the field. Existentialism implies that the meaning in any act exists in its consequences, and OB seems to be moving toward this realization.

Operationalism

Operationalism is reflected in three ways. First, the field is searching for theories of the middle range in most of its subareas. The grand, general, abstract models of motivation, leadership, environment-structure interaction, and change are not yielding satisfying, systematic, cumulative data. Some models posit relations between environmental and organizational characteristics and individual attitudes and behaviors. Models are needed to describe the processes through which environment impacts structure and structure impacts attitudes and behavior.

Second, emphasis is being given to the operations or behaviors through which people within organizations function. Whether describing what managers do or analyzing the impact of leaders, the importance of formulating the issue in operational terms is being realized. The literature is beginning to be characterized by questions like:

1. Through what operations is structure actually designed?
2. Through what operations does a leader impact a subordinate?
3. Through what operations do rewards and punishments effect change?
4. Through what operations do groups actually make decisions?

In each case, the field is beginning to examine the physiology of behavior within organizations. The anatomy of OB is important, but its study has not led to understanding the processes through which persons and organizations interact.

Third, measurement issues are impacting the field. Questions of reliability and validity must be faced, and questions of scaling and measurement confronted. We are increasingly anxious about our inability to explain large amounts of variance in dependent variables. Three rather lengthy streams of research have reached the point where lack of early attention to how we operationalized constructs and validated measures has caused major problems for continued, meaningful work. Cases in point are research on: the two-factor model of motivation (with faulty measurement procedures); expectancy formulations of motivation (with testing of inappropriate models); and the impact of organizational design on attitudes and behaviors (with designs that confound independent variables). While not completely pessimistic, I believe that the field has been extremely inefficient and myopic in the research strategies applied in some areas.

Neo-behavioralism

Finally, many causal assumptions and models in OB are moving toward a behavioristic orientation with a cognitive overtone. Motivation theory, under the influence of expectancy models, has moved in this direction. Leadership studies reflect the notion of instrumental, goal-oriented behavior with a significant emphasis on leader behavior being partially a function of the consequences which it produces. The concept of contingency plays a major role in several fields within OB, its general intellectual structure deriving directly from the behavioristic notion of structure and process evolving toward forms that are reinforcing to the organism. The behavioristic perspective also has surfaced in literature dealing with organizational design and organizational control and power. Distributions of influence and power are partially explained by environmental consequences of attempts at influence. The exercise of power generates consequences which, in turn, affect structural configurations of the organization.

Radical behaviorism is not the dominant theme, but, rather, a combination of general behavioral constructs *and* cognitions. It is not clear what functions are provided by the incorporation of cognitions within OB models. Little research has been addressed to the question of the variance explained in most OB models by cognitions beyond that explained by environmental determinants. Perhaps cognitive concepts do explain added variance, or perhaps they constitute a residual reservoir of unexplained variance to which we inappropriately attribute meaning.

CONCLUSIONS AND IMPLICATIONS

What are the implications of this perspective on the field? First, ultimately the definitions of the domains of OB, OT, OP, and OD are arbitrary. Definitions should be tested by their usefulness in specifying constructs and functional relations. Definitions are needed to guide the field toward middle range and operational theory. Movement toward definition by induction is needed. It may prove fruitful to aim toward definition through describing what is happening in the main streams of research within OB. Definitions established by assertion lead to debate without fruitful results.

Second, realities in organizations change so rapidly that our descriptions (ways of thinking, constructs, and technologies) do not keep pace with the rate of change in the objects of our study.[3] I see two implications of this for OB. First, incredibly long periods of time are needed to assess organizations and to identify the fundamental, underlying nature of the field. Second, increasing energy will be devoted to collapsing the time intervals needed to develop relevant constructs and models and to testing these models. This implies that management, as a general field, will accelerate adoption of both simulation and experimental designs. These designs permit the modeling of time lags. Contrary to the usual evaluation of such designs, they will allow us to become more realistic in our modeling and measurement of OB.

Third, what might this line of reasoning mean for the Academy of Management and its members? The academy is presently the only camp which attempts to house OB, OT, OD, and P&HR. For the moment, these fields have separate tents within the camp, but I believe that the traditional distinctions are beginning to melt. Several examples illustrate this permeability. The 1976 doctoral consortium conducted at the National Academy Convention included topics from both OT and OB. I suspect it is impossible to talk at an advanced level about one domain without the other. The P&HR division's program at the 1976 National Academy Convention consists of about 40 percent OB material. This reflects a healthy trend for both P&HR and OB. It is naive to deal with many of the important issues in P&HR without incorporating OB models and research. The *Academy of Management Journal,* the *Academy of Management Review, Organizational Behavior and Human Performance,* and *Administrative Science Quarterly* exhibit trends in submissions that reflect an increasing emphasis on *multiple* levels of analysis in both the independent and dependent variable domains.

I believe we are moving toward an enacted field, perhaps best labeled organizational analysis or organizational science (if we wish to emphasize the scientific lineage of our interests and our aspirations). Basically, we now have five divisions within the Academy, composing organizational analysis or science. These are Organizational Behavior, Organization and Management Theory, Personnel and Human Resources, Organization Development, and Organizational Communication. Such segmentation continues to provide important functions for the academy and its members, but it remains an open question whether segmentation is the most efficient strategy to advance our common interest in behavior *in* and *of* organizations.

As Thurstone said:

> It is the faith of all science that an unlimited number of phenomena can be comprehended in terms of a limited number of concepts or ideal constructs. Without this faith no science could ever have any motivation. To deny this faith

is to affirm the primary chaos of nature and the consequent futility of scientific effort. The constructs in terms of which natural phenomena are comprehended are man-made inventions. To discover a scientific law is merely to discover that a man-made scheme serves to unify, and thereby to simplify, comprehension of a certain class of natural phenomena. A scientific law is not to be thought of as having an independent existence which some scientist is fortunate to stumble upon. A scientific law is not a part of nature. It is only a way of comprehending nature.

NOTES

1. Hannan and Freeman (1) have argued quite convincingly that comparative analyses of organizational effectiveness are inappropriate for scientific purposes.
2. My thinking here has been significantly influenced by Robert Kahn of the University of Michigan. His comments at the 1976 Carnegie-Mellon Workshop on Organizational Effectiveness have been particularly helpful.
3. I am indebted to Professor Lou Pondy for stimulating this notion.

REFERENCES

1. Hannan, M. T., and J. Freeman. "Obstacles for Comparative Studies." *New Perspectives in Organizational Effectiveness*, ed. P. S. Goodman and J. M. Pennings. San Francisco: Jossey-Bass, 1977, pp. 106–31.
2. Thurstone, L. S. *Multiple-Factor Analysis*. Chicago: University of Chicago Press, 1947.

5

The Contributions of Administrative Behavior to Strategic Management

David B. Jemison

In this article the author examines the role that the behavioralists have played in increasing our understanding of general management, including such contributions as systems thinking, studies of managerial activity, and examination of the relationships between strategy, structure, and performance.— Eds.

The contributions of researchers in the field of administrative behavior (AB) are difficult to distill and synthesize because of problems of definition, level of analysis, and the variety of theoretical reference points. Accordingly, definitions of both strategic management and administrative behavior are in order at the outset to inform the reader of my biases.

Strategic management is the process by which general managers of complex organizations develop and use a strategy to coalign their organization's competences and the opportunities and constraints in the environment. A *strategist* is a person whose primary responsibilities are to the enterprise as a whole, rather than to a specific subunit. *Administrative behavior* refers to the collection of disciplines that focus their efforts on understanding either the management of organizations (administration) or the actions of the members of those organizations (behavior). Thus, scholars from sociology, organization theory, psychology, social psychology, organizational behavior, and political science are among those contributing to the field.

The contributions to strategic management by AB scholars can be grouped into three primary categories: (1) the study of organizations in the context of their environment, (2) the study of managerial action in the

SOURCE: Reprinted by permission of the author and publisher from "The Contributions of Administrative Behavior to Strategic Management," *The Academy of Management Review*, October 1981, pp. 663-642.

context of an organization, and (3) the study and development of methods to improve the strategic alignment between an organization's capabilities and its environment.

These three categories are summarized in Table 1, and exemplary authors are listed according to their subcategory of contribution. It should be noted that Table 1 is not intended to exhaustively recognize all AB scholars who have contributed to our understanding of strategic management issues. Instead, it is intended to outline the generic contributions from AB on which the field of strategic management depends and is being built today.

The three categories are of course entirely arbitrary. In fact, there is a great deal of interchange among the work of researchers in each of the three categories. But the artificial distinction does serve two important purposes. First, it helps in understanding the focus and perspective of different research approaches. Second, it allows me to highlight the important role of the strategist or general manager in the integration of the external and internal perspectives.

Before discussing the contributions of each of these three categories, some general observations and a statement of implicit assumptions are in order. Contributions from the AB field focus on the *processes* used to develop and rationalize a strategy, whereas contributions from industrial organization and marketing deal with the *content* of a strategy. Although AB researchers are becoming somewhat more prescriptive, most of their writing related to strategic management has been descriptive.

ORGANIZATIONS IN THE CONTEXT OF THEIR ENVIRONMENT

A focus on environmental context has enabled AB scholars to make three important contributions to our understanding of strategic management issues. The first is the recognition that organizations should be viewed and studied as open systems. This includes an application of systems theory to organizations, an elaboration of the concept of environment, and an exploration of the relationship of the environment to strategic decisions. The second is the recognition that organizations must have a favorable balance in their exchange relationships with their environments to gain legitimacy and to survive. The third is the definition of strategy as the means by which an organization's relationship with its environment is defined and articulated.

Organizations Seen as Open Systems

The open systems view of organizations posits that all organizations must have support and feedback from their environment in order to survive [von Bertalanffy, 1950; Weiner, 1954]. Thus, all organizations are seen as

TABLE 1   Contributions of Administrative Behavior to Strategic Management
Research

Categorical Contribution	Exemplary Authors
Organizations in the context of their environment	
Organizations seen as open systems	
Systems theory as applied to organizations	Barnard, 1938
	Beer, 1959
	Katz & Kahn, 1966
	Selznick, 1957
	Von Bertalanffy, 1950
	Weiner, 1954
Articulation of concept of environment	Dill, 1958
	Duncan, 1972
	Emery & Trist, 1965
	Kast & Rosenzweig, 1974
	Levine & White, 1961
	Terreberry, 1968
	Thompson, 1967
Relations of environment to strategic decisions	Anderson & Paine, 1975
	Bourgeois, 1980
	Hambrick, in press
	Jemison, 1981
	Lenz, 1980a
Necessity for favorable balance of exchange between organization and environment	Aldrich, 1979
	Barnard, 1938
	Blau, 1964
	Emerson, 1962
	Simon, 1946
	Thompson, 1967
Strategy defines environmental interactions	Barnard, 1938
	·Bourgeois, 1980
	Child, 1972
	Lenz, 1980b
	Newman, 1967
	Pfeffer & Salancik, 1978
	Selznick, 1957
	Summer, 1980
Managerial actions in the context of their organizations	
What managers do	Barnard, 1938
	Chandler, 1962
	Fayol, 1949
	Koontz, & O'Donnell, 1976
	Miles & Snow, 1978
	Mintzberg, 1973

TABLE 1 *(concluded)*

Categorical Contribution	*Exemplary Authors*
How managers act	
Rationality in decision making	Andrews, 1971
	Ansoff, 1965
	Dewey, 1933
	Learned et al., 1965
	Steiner, 1980
	Uyterhoeven et al., 1977
Limits to rationality	Cyert & March, 1963
	Lindblom, 1959
	Quinn, 1977, 1980
	Simon, 1946
	Wrapp, 1967
Political analyses of managerial actions	Allison, 1971
	Cyert & March, 1963
	Hah & Lindquist, 1975
	MacMillan, 1978
	March & Simon, 1958
	Mazzolini, 1979
	Murray, 1978
Improving strategic alignment	—
Improving decision-making processes	Ackoff, 1970
	Cosier et al., 1978
	Delbecq et al., 1975
	Lorange & Vancil, 1977
	MacMillan, 1978
	Mason, 1969
	Mitroff et al., 1977
	Roman, 1970
	Schelling, 1960
	Steiner, 1980
Improving organization design	Burns & Stalker, 1961
	Chandler, 1962
	Channon, 1971
	Dalton et al., 1980
	Fouraker & Stopford, 1968
	Galbraith, 1973
	Galbraith & Nathanson, 1978
	Grinyer et al., 1980
	Lawrence & Lorsch, 1967
	Rumelt, 1974
	Scott, 1971
	Woodward, 1965
	Wrigley, 1970

systems interacting with larger systems (their environment) and engaging in the life-sustaining processes of exchange.

Barnard [1938] was perhaps the first management-oriented writer to conceptualize the organization as a system. However, little application was made of his concept until after a more general theoretical exposition of the nature and properties of systems [Katz & Kahn, 1966; von Bertalanffy, 1950; Weiner, 1954]. The organization soon became the focus of analysis as scholars in the AB area began to translate systems thinking into organizational terms [Beer, 1959; Kast & Rosenzweig, 1974; Selznick, 1957].

This translation focused researchers' efforts on the concept of the environment as it applies to organizations (and thus to strategic management) and encouraged an identification of the characteristics by which an environment can be viewed. It also led to the beginning of a debate on whether an organization's environment is real or a figment of strategists' imaginations.

A definition of the environment as "everything out there" is not very useful for action-oriented executives. Dill's [1958] pioneering effort in defining the task environment provided guidance for most of the subsequent work on operationalizing the concept with respect to organizations. Thompson [1967], building on the work of Levine and White [1961], further extended our understanding of the relevant environment with his concept of domain—that part of the task environment for which specific products or services are provided.

The specification of the task environment and domain were important initial contributions by AB scholars. However, the elements of the environment still needed to be dealt with descriptively. Here, the valuable insights of Emery and Trist [1965], Terreberry [1968], and Duncan [1972] improved our ability to conceptualize the effect of an environmental segment on certain aspects of an organization's operations.

All definitions of the concept of environment suffer from a primary flaw—the lack of a solid grounding in theory that would allow measurement of the environment and its characteristics. In fact, the characteristics of the environment with which researchers deal (e.g., uncertainty, munificence) are often totally unrelated to the ways in which executives view the environment (e.g., a series of trends or events that have significance for their firm). This difference has led to a debate on whether a manager responds to the real external environment or merely to a set of perceptions about that environment. The question is an important contribution in itself because of the research attention it has focused on how the environment is related to strategists [Anderson & Paine, 1975; Bourgeois, 1980; Hambrick, in press; Jemison, 1981; Lenz, 1980a]. Researchers focusing on the strategic level asked "What must this organization do to survive in its environment?" Exploration of this question led naturally to the next contribution of AB scholars to strategic thinking—exchange theory.

Environmental Exchange

Exchange theory (first elaborated by Emerson [1962] and Blau [1964] recognizes that any organization depends on a network of other organizations for support and that these organizations in turn depend on the organization for some output. The key contribution of exchange theorists to the study of strategic issues is the implicit acknowledgement that the strategist is responsible for deciding what product or service output to produce, what internal rationalization or throughput procedures to use, and what resource inputs to acquire, so the outputs pay off the values received from external constituencies.

All organizations must provide some inducement to each group that contributes to its vitality [Barnard, 1938; Simon, 1946]. But these inducements do not take place in the metaphysical world of social scientists. In fact, they are developed through a process by which one organization gains sufficient power over another to make the other dependent on it for some aspect of its output. Two perspectives have emerged regarding the extent to which an organization is dependent on others in its environment. One, generally following exchange theory traditions, emphasizes having enough power to ensure that the exchange balance is in your organization's favor [Thompson, 1967]. The other perspective is the population-ecology model of organizations, which holds that organizations adapt to their environments in ways similar to those proposed by Darwin [1859]. In this view, organizations have very little control over their destiny because generally most organizations are not powerful enough to influence their environment [Aldrich, 1979].

The differences between these two viewpoints should not be understated. The exchange theory view implies that strategists can gain power for their organizations by improving alignment with the environment. The population-ecology view is that the organization is not controlled by strategists but, rather, is subject to the vagaries of the task environment. This important and substantive dispute raises an important question that strikes at the heart of the field of strategic management: "Are strategists really necessary or can organizations survive and prosper with minimal strategic direction?" This question leads us to the next point—organizational purpose.

Organizational Purpose

The conception and definition of organizational purpose is not a unique contribution of the AB school to strategy research. However, AB writers have acted as a stimulus and counterpoint for writers in the strategy area in a way that has reinforced the importance of organizational purpose.

An organization's purpose defines the ways in which it relates to its environment. If this purpose is not aligned with its constituencies' demands, the organization will atrophy and die. Conversely, if the purpose is fulfilled, the organization will survive and prosper [Barnard, 1938; Pfeffer & Salancik, 1978; Summer, 1980].

It is in the development, articulation, and operationalization of an organization's purpose that the strategist becomes a critical resource. The organization's strategy defines the ways in which its purpose will be fulfilled. The development of strategy involves the building of organizational competences that will allow the organization to survive in the niche chosen by the strategists [Newman, 1967]. The more distinctive the strategist can make these competences, the greater the organization's chances for survival [Selznick, 1957]. Lenz [1980b] speaks of an organization's strategic capability as its capacity to undertake action that will affect its long-term growth and development. Thus, the more that strategists can build and sustain distinctive competences and translate them into strategic capabilities, the better are their organizations' chances for survival.

MANAGERIAL ACTIONS IN THE CONTEXT OF THEIR ORGANIZATIONS

Strategic capabilities and competences are initiated and developed by specific managerial actions in the context of the organization. The actions with which we are concerned here are those encompassed by the general management or strategic managerial functions within an organization. I have defined a strategist as a person whose primary responsibilities are to the enterprise *as a whole.* Thus, the managers with whom we are concerned have a total organizational perspective. Our focus here will be on the institutional and to some extent managerial levels of Parsons [1960] or the strategic and middle management groups of Summer [1980].

The authors and subcategories listed in this category in Table 1 represent a broad spectrum. The primary criterion for inclusion is that an author has in some way advanced our knowledge in two primary areas of managerial action in the context of organizations: (1) an understanding of *what* managers actually do and (2) an understanding of *how* managers do their jobs and the *constraints* under which they operate.

What Managers Do

AB writers have described the process of strategic management both in terms of specific executive actions and the types of decisions with which strategies are concerned. Early descriptions of executive duties were based on the writers' judgment of what managers *should* be doing. Barnard [1938] provided the first real codification of managerial activity. He argued that the key executive functions directly paralleled the organization's needs of having a common goal toward which the members could work, having members who were willing to contribute, and having members who were able to communicate with one another. Thus, while Barnard directed our attention to what an executive should do for the organization to survive, he also couched his recommendations in light of the *organization's needs*. In the same prescriptive vein, Koontz and O'Donnell [1976] listed five primary functions in which managers engage: planning, organizing, staffing, directing, and controlling. This categorization has proven conceptually useful in separating the functions of management.

Another way to describe managerial activities is to focus on the types of decisions facing a manager. Chandler [1962] speaks of entrepreneurial decisions, involving allocating resources for the entire enterprise, and operating decisions, involving utilizing resources already allocated. Miles and Snow [1978], through their field research, expanded our understanding of these types of decisions by describing the key decisions made by managers as entrepreneurial, engineering, or administrative. Entrepreneurial decisions involve a choice of domain or product-market segments, engineering decisions operationalize the organization's approach to its domain, and administrative decisions develop and implement the internal processes and structures necessary for the organization to continue to evolve.

These descriptions of managerial activities were generally based on the writers' perception of the manager as a decision maker. Mintzberg's [1973] field study of managerial work attempted to identify what managers actually do. His three sets of managerial roles—figurehead, informational, and decisional—provided for the first time a description of managerial activity based on detailed clinical observation, rather than on theoretical generalizations. The essential contribution of his work was to inform academicians of something every general manager already knew: the job is much more than just making decisions. To the scholars studying executive action, this must have been like a blast of cold, fresh air—stinging at first, but ultimately exhilarating.

How Managers Act

The second important contribution of AB to research on managerial action in an organizational context is an understanding of how managers act as they go about doing the things that scholars say that they do. Any description of how managers act must logically be coupled with reasons for those actions. AB has contributed to research on rationality in decision making and to descriptions of decision processes.

Rationality in Decision Making. Early writers described strategy formulation as a rational process in which all the alternatives available were considered in light of the organization's history, external environment, and internal competences. A decision that provided the maximum benefit for the organization, given the situation constraints, was presumed to be the outcome of this process. Most early writers in this rational-comprehensive school of strategy formulation [e.g., Andrews, 1971; Ansoff, 1965; Learned, Christensen, Andrews, & Guth, 1969; Uyterhoeven, Ackerman, & Rosenblum, 1977] based their logical processes on John Dewey's [1933] model of the way humans think.

This emphasis on a rational, comprehensive perspective of strategy formulation was important and useful. It provided a general model through which other scholars could conceptualize strategic decision making—a straw man for purposes of study. These rational models were also useful for managers who had never before dealt with strategic thinking and who needed templates to guide their actions. These earlier normative models served that purpose by enabling the manager to temporarily suspend rationality and, among other things, presume that there was a clean slate on which to work in developing a strategy.

The rational-comprehensive view of strategy formulation is now all but obsolete as an accurate representation of reality. One of the first AB writers to call rationality into question was Lindblom [1959]. His arguments about the limits of rationality due to human considerations were similar to those proposed earlier by Simon [1946] Lindblom's real contribution to the debate in strategic decision making was his argument that "nonrational" incrementalism itself is logical because of the inherently iterative nature of strategic decisions and the resultant need to make and remake them.

Lindblom's arguments have in general been supported by other writers [e.g., Cyert & March, 1963; Quinn, 1980; Wrapp, 1967] as the appropriate way in which executives should (and do) act. Wrapp argues that successful strategists are able to work at a strategic and an operating level simultaneously and with ease The strategist keeps in mind the ultimate goals of the organization while making incremental adjustments to the firm's direction as opportunities from the environment present themselves and because political factors in the organization inhibit change on a grand scale.

Quinn [1980] describes as logical incrementalism the process by which strategists maintain a balance among products, markets, and internal structures and processes. His in-depth study of nine large corporations that faced major changes concluded that the successful firms were ones in which the strategist was able to incrementally adjust to changes in customers' needs or in which the internal structures and processes were appropriate.

Descriptions of Decision Processes.   Scholars in AB are progressing to a more detailed understanding of the underlying processes involved in strategic decision making. Increasing attention is being paid to strategy development and implementation as a political process [e.g., MacMillan, 1978]. Allison [1971] provided an important bridge to more recent writers by contrasting and comparing multiple paradigms as explanations of strategic behavior. This work and others that followed [e.g., Mazzolini, 1979] was instrumental in focusing scholars' attention on the variables that lead to organizational action.

Power has been identified as one of the key independent variables in the study of organizational political processes. Power often has perjorative connotations, but such connotations are not intended here. I agree with Russell's [1938] view of power as "the fundamental concept in social science in the same sense in which energy is the fundamental concept in physics." Thus, power is one of the tools the strategist uses both outside and within the organization. The strategist is not solely concerned with power relationships in the external environment. In fact, some of the most important contributions of AB scholars in this area have been to explore the concept of power as it applies to getting things done within an organization.

There seems to be general agreement among AB writers that intra-organizational power is derived from an individual's or a subunit's ability to cope with uncertainties that the organization faces [Perrow, 1970; Thompson, 1967]. March and Simon [1958] speak of reducing uncertainty as a way to gain and maintain power. This ability to deal with uncertainty may be due to the individual's or subunit's formal position in the organization [Weber, 1964], control over information [Pettigrew, 1972], or the performance of a critical function [Crozier, 1964; Hickson, Hinings, Lee, Schneck, & Pennings, 1971]. The strategist must balance the internal power available in a way that will simultaneously accomplish the organization's purposes and induce the organization's members to participate.

IMPROVING STRATEGIC ALIGNMENT

The strategist's primary task is to ensure a good strategic alignment between the organization and its environment. This alignment process involves two functions: (1) matching the organizations competences with the demands of the environment and (2) arranging internal structures and processes so other people can come up with creative strategic alternatives and develop new competences to meet the challenges of the future.

Both of these functions have been studied by AB researchers, whose contributions include aids for improving the strategic decision-making process and a better understanding of the options available in designing the organization.

Descriptions of the Decision-Making Process

A precondition of improving strategic decision making is a good description of the process. The normative approaches to how strategy should be formulated have provided this description [Ackoff, 1970; Lorange & Vancil, 1977; Steiner, 1980].

The contributions of AB scholars to our understanding of strategic decision making go beyond normative description. For example, Allison [1971] argued that, because of the complex nature of strategic decisions, multiple paradigms are necessary for adequately explaining the factors involved in difficult, unstructured decisions. Mintzberg, Raisinghani, & Théorêt [1976] pointed out the inherently structured nature of these seemingly unstructured decisions. Other writers such as Lindblom [1959] and Quinn [1980] have discussed the methodically incremental nature of the process as it occurs within organizations. Summer [1980] supports this view in pointing out that strategic decisions are made through a process of heuristic logic. That is, the strategist approaches decisions by connecting the entire strategic situation into a single comprehensive and logical framework of ends, means, goals, and resources by attacking a series of related decisions over a long period of time.

A problem with normative templates is the lack of guidance about how to understand and manage the interpersonal processes inherent in strategy formulation and implementation. These interpersonal processes have been theoretically explained in terms of intra-organizational bargaining behavior as well as inherent human cognitive limits [e.g., Cyert & March, 1963; Katz & Kahn, 1966; MacMillan, 1978; Schelling, 1960].

Improvements in the Process

Research from AB on ways in which the actual process of strategic decision making can be improved can be separated into two classes—improving the ability to forecast trends in the environment, and specific methods of formulating strategies. Techniques for improving environmental forecasting (e.g., the Delphi [Roman, 1970] and nominal group [Delbecq, Van de Ven, & Rustafson, 1975]) are useful in providing a general outline of future conditions. However, they are not helpful to the strategist who is interested in actually *managing* the process of strategy development more effectively.

Research directed toward improving the effectiveness of strategic planning includes explorations of dialectical inquiry and the devil's advocate approach. Dialectical inquiry is a Hegelian approach among the group of decision makers to create a synthesis that is supposed to be more effective than a decision taken by other methods [Mason, 1969; Mitroff, Barabba, & Kilmann, 1977]. Another group of researchers has argued that dialectical inquiry is not a superior method of improving strategic decision making [Cosier, Ruble, & Aplin, 1978]. They claim that a devil's advocate approach appears to be as effective as dialectical inquiry [Cosier, 1978]. It is much too early to bless either approach to strategy formulation, but such intensive, applied work as that of Mitroff et al. and Cosier et al. is precisely the kind of contribution that can be expected from AB scholars with respect to improving the effectiveness of the strategic decision process.

Organization Design

A fundamental set of decisions facing any strategist is how to design the organization in a way that maximizes the likelihood of successfully implementing strategy. Organization design is a set of conscious decisions, according to which the strategist divides the organization into smaller subunits for task effectiveness and develops a set of linkages among the subunits to ensure coordination and control. AB's contribution to our understanding of organization design has been to highlight how structure and process design decisions can enhance or inhibit a strategy.

The primary relationships that have been studied by AB scholars are those of strategy with structure, structure with performance, and the congruence of strategy and structure with performance. The general conclusions from researchers are that the organization must have a fit between structure and process(es) if the strategy is to bear fruit [Chandler, 1962; Channon, 1971; Scott, 1970; Wrigley, 1970]. In addition, existing structure and processes have been shown to constrain a firm's strategic options [Fouraker & Stopford, 1968; Miles & Snow, 1978].

The relationship between structure and performance is less definite. Beginning with Woodward [1965], the direct relationship between a "correct" structure and organizational performance has been debated. Although this argument has face validity, the extensive review of this subject by Dalton, Tudor, Spendolini, Fielding, and Porter [1980] indicates that the relationship between structure and performance is tenuous at best.

The next step has been to examine whether the fit between strategy and structure will lead to improved performance. Rumelt [1974] addressed this question but found no conclusive relationship. However, his study raised more questions than it answered, because it did not address the relative contribution of strategy, structure, or congruence between the two to performance, or the link between congruence and performance. Grinyer, Al-Bazzaz, and Yasai-Ardekani [1980] replicated Rumelt's work in UK firms and found the same tenuous relationship between congruence of structure and strategy and financial performance.

CONCLUDING REMARKS

AB scholars have improved our understanding of strategic management, but their work can be seen only as a beginning, owing to their focus on processes, the complex nature of the variables, and the essentially descriptive nature of the findings.

It probably is unreasonable to expect AB scholars to study anything other than processes. The variables in which they are interested do not allow them to comment knowledgeably on strategic content, and their training and expertise naturally lead them to explore the many concepts surrounding strategy formulation and implementation. Their more precise articulation and definition of these concepts has benefitted strategists and other scholars. Ultimately, an understanding of the processes of strategy formulation and implementation will be accompanied by a better understanding of the relationships among the complex set of variables with which the strategist must work.

It is precisely this complexity that prevents AB researchers from being more prescriptive. In fact, the problems of being more prescriptive are a classic example of the impediments to discovering causal relationships in social science research. Organizations and their managers won't hold still for researchers. The application of rigorous research techniques in field settings in which the real-time action of the managerial world exists is very difficult if not impossible. The difficulty of controlling for certain variables, the lack of comparability across organizations, different units of analysis, and the changing nature of the organizations and their environments restrict researchers' abilities to make causal attributions among these sets of variables.

AB scholars have made some tentative prescriptions, but these have usually concerned managerial action within the context of an organization (e.g., improving strategic planning processes), or organizational actions in the context of their environment (e.g., the structure must fit the strategy). However, these prescriptions have been drawn more from descriptive case studies than from rigorously controlled research.

There are several reasons to expect still more contributions from AB-based research in the future. First, the field of strategic management is becoming more accepted and is receiving more attention in schools of business, which means more young scholars may be attracted to the field. It is from their efforts that most of the contributions will come.

Second, a redirection of research methods is currently taking place, as seen in the gradual return to in-depth studies of a few organizations and the attempt to apply more controlled research procedures to a few variables. Recently, many authors have been applying highly sophisticated statistical techniques to AB-related strategic management research questions—probably owing in equal measure to the requirements of journals for "rigorous" research and to their own methodological training. Although quantitative studies can be useful and informative, they can also be futilely applied in a managerial environment that is inherently more complex than the degrees of freedom available to the researcher.

Third, there is an increasing trend to linking variables from AB with variables from other disciplines (e.g., economics and marketing). Studies of this type have real promise for the field of strategic management. The direction of research in the field should be to discover and explore the relationships between the processes of strategy formulation and implementation and strategy content. In this way, researchers will be catching up (in a sense) with strategists, who have always needed to balance these elements.

REFERENCES

Ackoff, R. L. *A concept of corporate planning.* New York: Wiley-Interscience, 1970.

Aldrich, H. *Organizations and environments.* Englewood Cliffs, N.J.: Prentice-Hall, 1979.

Allison, G. T. *Essence of decision: Explaining the Cuban missile crisis.* Boston: Little, Brown, 1971.

Anderson, C.; & Paine, F. Managerial perceptions and strategic behavior. *Academy of Management Journal* 1975, *18*, 811–823.

Andrews, K. R. *The concept of corporate strategy.* Homewood, Ill.: Dow Jones-Irwin, 1971.

Ansoff, H. I. *Corporate strategy.* New York: McGraw-Hill, 1965.

Barnard, C. I. *The functions of the executive.* Cambridge: Harvard University Press, 1938.

Beer, S. *Cybernetics and management.* New York: Wiley, 1959.

Blau, P. *Exchange and power in social life.* New York: Wiley, 1964.

Bourgeois, L. J. Strategy and environment: A conceptual integration. *Academy of Management Review,* 1980, *5*, 25–40.

Burns, T.; & Stalker, G. *The management of innovation.* London: Tavistock Institute, 1961.

Chandler, A. D. *Strategy and structure.* Cambridge: MIT Press, 1962.

Channon, D. *Strategy and structure of British enterprise.* Unpublished doctoral dissertation, Harvard University, 1971.

Child, J. Organization structure, environment, and performance: The role of strategic choice. *Sociology,* 1972, *6*, 1–22.

Cosier, R. A. The effects of three potential aids for making strategic decisions on prediction accuracy. *Organizational Behavior & Human Performance,* 1978, *22*, 295–306.

Cosier, R. A.; Ruble, T. L.; & Aplin, J. An evaluation of the effectiveness of the dialectical inquiry system. *Management Science,* 1978, *24*, 1483–1490.

Crozier, M. *The bureaucratic phenomenon.* Chicago: University of Chicago Press, 1964.

Cyert, R. M.; & March, J. G. *A behavioral theory of the firm.* Englewood Cliffs, N.J.: Prentice-Hall, 1963.

Dalton, D. R.; Tudor, W. D.; Spendolini, M. J.; Fielding, G. J.; & Porter, L. W. Organization structure and performance: A critical review. *Academy of Management Review,* 1980, *5*, 49–64.

Darwin, C. *On the origin of the species by means of natural selection, or the preservation of favoured races in the struggle for life.* London: John Murray, 1859.

Delbecq, A.; Van deVen, A.; & Rustafson, D. *Group techniques for program planning.* Glenview, Ill.: Scott-Foresman, 1975.

Dewey, J. *How we think.* Lexington, Mass.: D.C. Heath, 1933.

Dill, W. R. Environment as an influence on managerial autonomy. *Administrative Science Quarterly,* 1958, *2*, 409–443.

Duncan, R. B. Characteristics of organizational environments and perceived environmental uncertainty. *Administrative Science Quarterly,* 1972, *17*, 313–327.

Emerson, R. M. Power dependence relations. *American Sociological Review,* 1962, *27*, 31–41.

Emery, F.; & Trist, E. The causal texture of organizational environments. *Human Relations,* 1965, *18*, 21–31.

Fayol, H. *General and industrial administration.* London: Pitman & Sons, 1949.

Fouraker, L.; & Stopford, J. Organization structure and multinational strategy. *Administrative Science Quarterly,* 1968, *13*, 57–70.

Galbraith, J. *Designing Complex Organizations.* Reading, Mass.: Addison-Wesley, 1973.

Galbraith, J.; & Nathanson, D. *Strategy implementation: The role of structure and process.* St. Paul: West Publishing, 1978.

Grinyer, P.; Al-Bazzaz, S.; & Yasai-Ardekani, M. Strategy, structure, the environment, and financial performance. *Academy of Management Journal,* 1980, *23,* 193–220.

Hah, C.; & Lindquist, R. M. The 1952 steel seizure revisited: A systematic study in presidential decision making. *Administrative Science Quarterly,* 1975, *20,* 587–605.

Hambrick, D. L. Environment, strategy, and power within top management teams. *Administrative Science Quarterly,* in press.

Hickson, D. N.; Hinings, C. R.; Lee, C. A.; Schneck, R. E.; & Pennings, J. M. A strategic contingencies theory of intraorganizational power. *Administrative Science Quarterly,* 1971, *16,* 216–229.

Jemison, D. B. Organizational vs. environmental sources of influence in strategic decision making. *Strategic Management Journal,* 1981, *2,* 77–89.

Kast, F. E.; & Rosenzweig, J. E. *Organization and management.* 2nd ed. New York: McGraw-Hill, 1974.

Katz, D.; & Kahn, R. L. *The social psychology of organizations.* New York: Wiley, 1966.

Koontz, H.; & O'Donnell, C. *Management.* 6th ed. New York: McGraw-Hill, 1976.

Lawrence, P. R.; & Lorsch, J. W. *Organization and environment: Managing differentiation and integration.* Homewood, Ill.: Richard D. Irwin, 1967.

Learned, E. P.; Christensen, C. R.; Andrews, K. R.; & Guth, W. *Business policy.* Homewood, Ill.: Richard D. Irwin, 1965.

Lenz, R. T. Environment, strategy, organization structure, and performance: Patterns in one industry. *Strategic Management Journal,* 1980, *1,* 209–226. (a)

Lenz, R. T. Strategic capability: A concept and framework for analysis. *Academy of Management Review,* 1980, *5,* 225–234. (b)

Levine, S.; & White, P. Exchange and interorganizational relationships. *Administrative Science Quarterly,* 1961, *5,* 583–601.

Lindblom, C. E. The science of muddling through. *Public Administration Review,* 1959, *19*(2), 79–88.

Lorange, P.; & Vancil, R. *Strategic planning systems.* Englewood Cliffs, N.J.: Prentice-Hall, 1977.

MacMillan, I. *Strategy formulation: Political concepts.* St. Paul: West Publishing, 1978.

March, J.; & Simon, H. *Organizations.* New York: Wiley, 1958.

Mason, R. O. A dialectical approach to strategic planning. *Management Science,* 1969, *15,* B403–B414.

Mazzolini, R. *Government-controlled enterprises: International strategic and policy decisions.* New York: Wiley, 1979.

Miles, R. E.; & Snow, C. C. *Organizational strategy, structure, and process.* New York: McGraw-Hill, 1978.

Mintzberg, H. *The nature of managerial work.* New York: Harper & Row, 1973.

Mintzberg, H.; Raisinghani, D.; & Théorêt, A. The structure of unstructured decision processes. *Administrative Science Quarterly,* 1976, *21,* 246–275.

Mitroff, I. I.; Barabba, V. P.; & Kilmann, R. H. The application of behavioral and philosophical technologies to strategic planning: A case study of a large federal agency. *Management Science,* 1977, *24,* 44–58.

Murray, E. A. Strategic choice as a negotiated outcome. *Management Science,* 1978, *24,* 960–971.

Newman, W. H. Shaping the master strategy of your firm. *California Management Review,* 1967, *9,* 77–88.

Parsons, T. *Structure and process in modern societies.* New York: Free Press, 1960.

Pfeffer, J.; & Salancik, G. R. *The external control of organizations.* New York: Harper & Row, 1978.

Pettigrew, A. M. Information control as a power resource. *Sociology,* 1972, *6,* 187–204.

Perrow, C. *Organizational analysis: A sociological view.* Belmont, Calif.: Wadsworth, 1970.

Quinn, J. B. Strategic goals: Process and politics. *Sloan Management Review,* Fall 1977, *19,* 21–37.

Quinn, J. B. *Strategies for change: Logical incrementalism.* Homewood, Ill.: Richard D. Irwin, 1980.

Roman, D. D. Technological forecasting in the decision process. *Academy of Management Journal,* 1970, *13,* 127–138.

Rumelt, R. *Strategy, structure, and economic performance.* Cambridge: Harvard University Press, 1974.

Russell, B. *Power.* New York: Norton, 1938.

Schelling, T. *The strategy of conflict.* London: Oxford University Press, 1960.

Scott, B. *Stages of corporate development: A descriptive model.* ICCH No. 9-371-294. Boston: International Case Clearing House, 1971.

Selznick, P. *Leadership in administration.* New York: Harper & Row, 1957.

Simon, H. A. *Administrative behavior.* New York: Free Press, 1946.

Steiner, G. *Strategic planning.* New York: Free Press, 1980.

Summer, C. E. *Strategic behavior in business and government.* Boston: Little, Brown, 1980.

Terreberry, S. The evolution of organizational environments. *Administrative Science Quarterly,* 1968, *12,* 590–613.

Thompson, J. D. *Organizations in action.* New York: McGraw-Hill, 1967.

Uyterhoeven, H.; Ackerman, R.; & Rosenblum, J. *Strategy and organization* (2nd ed.). Homewood, Ill. Richard D. Irwin, 1977.

Von Bertalanffy, L. The theory of open systems in physics and biology. *Science,* January 13, 1950, pp. 23–29.

Weber, M. *The theory of social and economic organization* (A. M. Henderson & T. Parsons, trans.). New York: Free Press, 1964.

Weiner, N. *The human use of human beings.* New York: Doubleday, 1954.

Woodward, J. *Industrial organization: Theory and practice.* Fair Lawn, N.J.: Oxford University Press, 1965.

Wrapp, E. Good managers don't make policy decisions. *Harvard Business Review,* 1967, *45,* 91–99.

Wrigley, L. *Divisional autonomy and diversification.* Unpublished doctoral dissertation, Harvard University, 1970.

6

General Systems Theory: Applications for Organizations and Management

Fremont E. Kast
and
James E. Rosenzweig

World War II marked the beginning of the Systems Age, although it was not until many years after the war that systems science found its way into the management literature. This article discusses applying systems theory to the real world of organizations and concludes by looking at what steps need to be taken to make general systems theory a more useful model for both organizational analysis and application by practicing managers who must function on a day-to-day basis.—Eds.

Biological and social scientists generally have embraced systems concepts. Many organization and management theorists seem anxious to identify with this movement and to contribute to the development of an approach which purports to offer the ultimate—the unification of all science into one grand conceptual model. Who possibly could resist? General systems theory seems to provide a relief from the limitations of more mechanistic approaches and a rationale for rejecting "principles" based on relatively "closed-system" thinking. This theory provides the paradigm for organization and management theorists to "crank into their systems model" all of the diverse knowledge from relevant underlying disciplines. It has become almost mandatory to have the word "system" in the title of recent articles and books (many of us have compromised and placed it only in the subtitle).[1]

But where did it all start? This question takes us back into history and brings to mind the long-standing philosophical arguments between mechanistic and organismic models of the 19th and early 20th centuries. As Deutsch says:

SOURCE: From *Academy of Management Journal*, December 1972, pp. 447–65. Reprinted by permission.

Both mechanistic and organismic models were based substantially on experiences and operations known before 1850. Since then, the experience of almost a century of scientific and technological progress has so far not been utilized for any significant new model for the study of organization and in particular of human thought [12, p. 389].

General systems theory even revives the specter of the "vitalists" and their views on "life force" and most certainly brings forth renewed questions of teleological or purposeful behavior of both living and nonliving systems. Phillips and others have suggested that the philosophical roots of general systems theory go back even further, at least to the German philosopher Hegel (1770–1831) [29, p. 56]. Thus, we should recognize that in the adoption of the systems approach for the study of organizations we are not dealing with newly discovered ideas—they have a rich genealogy.

Even in the field of organization and management theory, systems views are not new. Chester Barnard used a basic systems framework.

> A cooperative system is a complex of physical, biological, personal, and social components which are in a specific systematic relationship by reason of the cooperation of two or more persons for at least one definite end. Such a system is evidently a subordinate unit of larger systems from one point of view; and itself embraces subsidiary systems—physical, biological, etc.—from another point of view. One of the systems comprised within a cooperative system, the one which is implicit in the phrase "cooperation of two or more persons," is called an "organization" [3, p. 65].

And Barnard was influenced by the "systems views" of Vilfredo Pareto and Talcott Parsons. Certainly this quote (dressed up a bit to give the term "system" more emphasis) could be the introduction to a 1972 book on organizations.

Miller points out that Alexander Bogdanov, the Russian philosopher, developed a theory of tektology or universal organization science in 1912, which foreshadowed general systems theory and used many of the same concepts as modern systems theorists [26, pp. 249–250].

However, in spite of a long history of organismic and holistic thinking, the utilization of the systems approach did not become the accepted model for organization and management writers until relatively recently. It is difficult to specify the turning point exactly. The momentum of systems thinking was identified by Scott in 1961, when he described the relationship between general systems theory and organization theory:

> The distinctive qualities of modern organization theory are its conceptual-analytical base, its reliance on empirical research data, and above all, its integrating nature. These qualities are framed in a philosophy which accepts the premise that the only meaningful way to study organization is to study it as a system. . . . Modern organization theory and general system theory are similar in that they look at organization as an integrated whole [33, pp. 15–21].

Scott said explicitly what many in our field had been thinking and/or imply-ing—he helped us put into perspective the important writings of Herbert Simon, James March, Talcott Parsons, George Homans, E. Wight Bakke, Kenneth Boulding, and many others.

But how far have we really advanced over the past decade in applying general systems theory to organizations and their management? Is it still a "skeleton"; or have we been able to "put some meat on the bones"? The systems approach has been touted because of its potential usefulness in understanding the complexities of "live" organizations. Has this approach really helped us in this endeavor or has it compounded confusion with chaos? Herbert Simon describes the challenge for the systems approach:

> In both science and engineering, the study of "systems" is an increasingly popular activity. Its popularity is more a response to a pressing need for syn-thesizing and analyzing complexity than it is to any large development of a body of knowledge and technique for dealing with complexity. If this popularity is to be more than a fad, necessity will have to mother invention and provide substance to go with the name [35, p. 114].

In this article we will explore the issue of whether we are providing substance for the term *systems approach* as it relates to the study of orga-nizations and their management. There are many interesting historical and philosophical questions concerning the relationship between the mechanis-tic and organismic approaches and their applicability to the various fields of science, as well as other interesting digressions into the evolution of sys-tems approaches. However, we will resist those temptations and plunge directly into a discussion of the key concepts of general systems theory, the way in which these ideas have been used by organization theorists, the limitations in their application, and some suggestions for the future.

KEY CONCEPTS OF GENERAL SYSTEMS THEORY

The key concepts of general systems theory have been set forth by many writers [6, 7, 13, 17, 25, 28, 39] and have been used by many organization and management theorists [10, 14, 18, 19, 21, 22, 24, 32]. It is not our purpose here to elaborate on them in great detail, because we anticipate that most readers will have been exposed to them in some depth. Figure 1 provides a very brief review of those characteristics of systems which seem to have wide acceptance. The review is far from complete. It is difficult to identify a "complete" list of characteristics derived from general systems theory; moreover, it is merely a first-order classification. There are many derived second- and third-order characteristics which could be considered. For example, James G. Miller sets forth *165* hypotheses, stemming from open systems theory, which might be applicable to two or more levels of systems [25]. He suggests that they are *general* systems theoretical hypoth-

FIGURE 1   Key Concepts of General Systems Theory

Subsystems or Components: A system by definition is composed of interrelated parts or elements. This is true for all systems—mechanical, biological, and social. Every system has at least two elements, and these elements are interconnected.

Holism, Synergism, Organicism, and Gestalt: The whole is not just the sum of the parts; the system itself can be explained only as a totality. Holism is the opposite of elementarism, which views the total as the sum of its individual parts.

Open Systems View: Systems can be considered in two ways: (1) closed or (2) open. Open systems exchange information, energy, or material with their environments. Biological and social systems are inherently open systems; mechanical systems may be open or closed. The concepts of open and closed systems are difficult to defend in the absolute. We prefer to think of open-closed as a dimension; that is, systems are relatively open or relatively closed.

Input-Transformation-Output Model: The open system can be viewed as a transformation model. In a dynamic relationship with its environment, it receives various inputs, transforms these inputs in some way, and exports outputs.

System Boundaries: It follows that systems have boundaries which separate them from their environments. The concept of boundaries helps us understand the distinction between open and closed systems. The relatively closed system has rigid, impenetrable boundaries; whereas the open system has permeable boundaries between itself and a broader suprasystem. Boundaries are relatively easily defined in physical and biological systems, but are very difficult to delineate in social systems, such as organizations.

Negative Entropy: Closed, physical systems are subject to the force of entropy, which increases until eventually the entire system fails. The tendency toward maximum entropy is a movement to disorder, complete lack of resource transformation, and death. In a closed system, the change in entropy must always be positive; however, in open biological or social systems, entropy can be arrested and may even be transformed into negative entropy—a process of more complete organization and ability to transform resources—because the system imports resources from its environment.

Steady State, Dynamic Equilibrium, and Homeostasis: The concept of steady state is closely related to that of negative entropy. A closed system eventually must attain an equilibrium state with maximum entropy—death or disorganization. However, an open system may attain a state where the system remains in dynamic equilibrium through the continuous inflow of materials, energy, and information.

Feedback: The concept of feedback is important in understanding how a system maintains a steady state. Information concerning the outputs or the process of the system is fed back as an input into the system, perhaps leading to changes in the transformation process and/or future outputs. Feedback can be both positive and negative, although the field of cybernetics is based on negative feedback. Negative feedback is informational input, which indicates that the system is deviating from a prescribed course and should readjust to a new steady state.

Hierarchy: A basic concept in systems thinking is that of hierarchical relationships between systems. A system is composed of subsystems of a lower order and is also part of a suprasystem. Thus, there is a hierarchy of the components of the system.

FIGURE 1 *(concluded)*

Internal Elaboration: Closed systems move toward entropy and disorganization. In contrast, open systems appear to move in the direction of greater differentiation, elaboration, and a higher level of organization.

Multiple Goal Seeking: Biological and social systems appear to have multiple goals or purposes. Social organizations seek multiple goals, if for no other reason than that they are composed of individuals and subunits with different values and objectives.

Equifinality of Open Systems: In mechanistic systems there is a direct cause and effect relationship between the initial conditions and the final state. Biological and social systems operate differently. Equifinality suggests that certain results may be achieved with different initial conditions and in different ways. This view suggests that social organizations can accomplish their objectives with diverse inputs and with varying internal activities (conversion processes).

eses and qualifies them by suggesting that they are propositions applicable to general systems *behavior* theory and, thus, would exclude nonliving systems. He does not limit these propositions to individual organisms, but considers them appropriate for social systems as well. His hypotheses are related to such issues as structure, process, subsystems, information, growth, and integration. It is obviously impossible to discuss all of these hypotheses; we want only to indicate the extent to which many interesting propositions are being posed which might have relevance to many different types of systems. It will be a very long time (if ever) before most of these hypotheses are validated; however, we are surprised at how many of them can be agreed with intuitively, and we can see their possible verification in studies of social organizations.

We turn now to a closer look at how successful or unsuccessful we have been in utilizing these concepts in the development of "modern organization theory."

A BEGINNING: ENTHUSIASTIC BUT INCOMPLETE

We have embraced general systems theory but, really, how completely? We could review a vast literature in modern organization theory which has explicitly or implicitly adopted systems theory as a frame of reference, and we have investigated in detail a few representative examples of the literature in assessing the "state of the art" [18, 19, 21, 22, 31, 38]. It was found that most of these books professed to utilize general systems theory. Indeed, in the first few chapters, many of them did an excellent job of presenting basic systems concepts and showing their relationship to organizations; however, when they moved further into the discussion of more specific subject matter, they departed substantially from systems theory. The studies appear to use a "partial systems approach" and leave for the reader the problem of integrating the various ideas into a systemic whole. It also appears that many of the authors are unable, because of limitations of knowledge about subsystem relationships, to carry out the task of using general systems theory as a conceptual basis for organization theory.

Furthermore, it is evident that each author had many "good ideas" stemming from the existing body of knowledge or current research on organizations which did not fit neatly into a "systems model." For example, they might discuss leadership from a relatively closed-system point of view and not consider it in relation to organizational technology, structure, or other variables. Our review of the literature suggests that much remains to be done in applying general systems theory to organization theory and management practice.

SOME DILEMMAS IN APPLYING GST TO ORGANIZATIONS

Why have writers embracing general systems theory as a basis for studying organizations had so much difficulty in following through? Part of this difficulty may stem from the newness of the paradigm and our inability to operationalize "all we think we know" about this approach. Or it may be because we know too little about the systems under investigation. Both of these possibilities will be covered later, but first we need to look at some of the more specific conceptual problems.

Organizations as Organisms

One of the basic contributions of general systems theory was the rejection of the traditional closed-system or mechanistic view of social organizations. But, did general systems theory free us from this constraint only to impose another, less obvious one? General systems theory grew out of the organismic views of von Bertalanffy and other biologists; thus, many of the characteristics are relevant to the living organism. It is conceptually easy to draw the analogy between living organisms and social organizations. "There is, after all, an intuitive similarity between the organization of the human body, and the kinds of organizations men create. And so, undaunted by the failures of the human-social analogy through time, new theorists try afresh in each epoch" [2, p. 660]. General systems theory would have us accept this analogy between organism and social organization. Yet, we have a hard time swallowing it whole. Katz and Kahn warn us of the danger:

> There has been no more pervasive, persistent, and futile fallacy handicapping the social sciences than the use of the physical model for the understanding of social structures. The biological metaphor, with its crude comparisons of the

physical parts of the body to the parts of the social system, has been replaced by more subtle but equally misleading analogies between biological and social functioning. This figurative type of thinking ignores the essential difference between the socially contrived nature of social systems and the physical structure of the machine or the human organism. So long as writers are committed to a theoretical framework based upon the physical model, they will miss the essential social-psychological facts of the highly variable, loosely articulated character of social systems [19, p. 31].

In spite of this warning, Katz and Kahn do embrace much of the general systems theory concepts which are based on the biological metaphor. We must be very cautious about trying to make this analogy too literal. We agree with Silverman who says, "It may, therefore, be necessary to drop the analogy between an organization and an organism: organizations may be systems but not necessarily natural systems" [34, p. 31].

Distinction between Organization and an Organization

General systems theory emphasizes that systems are organized—they are composed of interdependent components in some relationship. The social organization would then follow logically as just another system. But, we are perhaps being caught in circular thinking. It is true that all systems (physical, biological, and social) are by definition organized, but are all systems organizations? Rapoport and Horvath distinguish "organization theory" and "the theory of organizations" as follows:

> We see organization theory as dealing with general and abstract organizational principles; it applies to any system exhibiting organized complexity. As such, organization theory is seen as an extension of mathematical physics or, even more generally, of mathematics designed to deal with organized systems. The theory of organizations, on the other hand, purports to be a social science. It puts real human organizations at the center of interest. It may study the social structure of organizations and so can be viewed as a branch of sociology; it can study the behavior of individuals or groups as members of organizations and can be viewed as a part of social psychology; it can study power relations and principles of control in organizations and so fits into political science [30, pp. 74–75].

Why make an issue of this distinction? It seems to us that there is a vital matter involved. All systems may be considered to be organized, and more advanced systems may display differentiation in the activities of component parts—such as the specialization of human organs. However, all systems *do not* have purposeful entities. Can the heart or lungs be considered as purposeful entities in themselves or are they only components of the larger purposeful system, the human body? By contrast, the social organization is composed of two or more purposeful elements. "An organization consists of elements that have and can exercise their own wills" [1, p. 669].

Organisms, the foundation stone of general systems theory, do not contain purposeful elements which exercise their own will. This distinction between the organism and the social organization is of importance. In much of general systems theory, the concern is primarily with the way in which the organism responds to environmentally generated inputs. Feedback concepts and the maintenance of a steady state are based on internal adaptations to environmental forces. (This is particularly true of cybernetic models.) But, what about those changes and adaptations which occur from *within* social organizations? Purposeful elements within the social organization may initiate activities and adaptations which are difficult to subsume under feedback and steady state concepts.

Opened and Closed Systems

Another dilemma stemming from general systems theory is the tendency to dichotomize all systems as opened or closed. We have been led to think of physical systems as closed, subject to the laws of entropy, and to think of biological systems as open to their environment and, possibly, becoming negentropic. But applying this strict polarization to social organizations creates many difficulties. In fact, most social organizations and their subsystems are "partially open" and "partially closed." Open and closed are a matter of degree. Unfortunately, there seems to be a widely held view (often more implicit than explicit) that *open-system thinking is good and closed-system thinking is bad.* We have not become sufficiently sophisticated to recognize that both are appropriate under certain conditions. For example, one of the most useful conceptualizations set forth by Thompson is that the social organization *must seek* to use closed-system concepts (particularly at the technical core) to reduce uncertainty and to create more effective performance at this level.

Still Subsystems Thinking

Even though we preach a general systems approach, we often practice subsystems thinking. Each of the academic disciplines and each of us personally have limited perspective of the system we are studying. While proclaiming a broad systems viewpoint, we often dismiss variables outside our interest or competence as being irrelevant, and we only open our system to those inputs which we can handle with our disciplinary bag of tools. We are hampered because each of the academic disciplines has taken a narrow "partial systems view" and find comfort in the relative certainty which this creates. Of course, this is not a problem unique to modern organization theory. Under the more traditional process approach to the study of management, we were able to do an admirable job of delineating and discussing planning, organizing, and controlling as separate activities. We were much less successful in discussing them as integrated and interrelated activities.

How Does Our Knowledge Fit?

One of the major problems in utilizing general systems theory is that we know (or think we know) more about certain relationships than we can fit into a general systems model. For example, we are beginning to understand the two-variable relationship between technology and structure. But, when we introduce another variable, say psychosocial relationships, our models become too complex. Consequently, in order to discuss all the things we know about organizations, we depart from a systems approach. Perhaps it is because we know a great deal more about the elements or subsystems of an organization than we do about the interrelationships and interactions between these subsystems. And, general systems theory forces us to consider those relationships about which we know the least—a true dilemma. So we continue to elaborate on those aspects of the organization which we know best—a partial systems view.

Failure to Delineate a Specific System

When the social sciences embraced general systems theory, the total system became the focus of attention and terminology tended toward vagueness. In the utilization of systems theory, we should be more precise in delineating the specific system under consideration. Failure to do this leads to much confusion. As Murray suggests:

> I am wary of the word "system" because social scientists use it very frequently without specifying which of several possible different denotations they have in mind; but more particularly because, today, "system" is a highly cathected term, loaded with prestige; hence, we are all strongly tempted to employ it even when we have nothing definite in mind and its only service is to indicate that we subscribe to the general premise respecting the interdependence of things—basic to organismic theory, holism, field theory, interactionism, transactionism, etc. . . . When definitions of the units of a system are lacking, the term stands for no more than an article of faith, and is misleading to boot, insofar as it suggests a condition of affairs that may not actually exist [27, pp. 50–51].

We need to be much more precise in delineating both the boundaries of the system under consideration and the level of our analysis. There is a tendency for current writers in organization theory to accept general systems theory and then to move indiscriminately across systems boundaries and between levels of systems without being very precise (and letting their readers in on what is occurring). James Miller suggests the need for clear delineation of levels in applying systems theory, "It is important to follow one procedural rule in systems theory in order to avoid confusion. Every discussion should begin with an identification of the level of reference, and the discourse should not change to another level without a specific statement that this is occurring" [25, p. 216]. Our field is replete with these confusions about systems levels. For example, when we use the term *orga-*

nizational behavior are we talking about the way the organization behaves as a system or are we talking about the behavior of the individual participants? By goals, do we mean the goals of the organization or the goals of the individuals within the organization? In using systems theory we must become more precise in our delineation of systems boundaries and systems levels if we are to prevent confusing conceptual ambiguity.

Recognition That Organizations Are "Contrived Systems"

We have a vague uneasiness that general systems theory truly does not recognize the "contrived" nature of social organizations. With its predominate emphasis on natural organisms, it may understate some characteristics which are vital for the social organization. Social organizations do not occur naturally in nature; they are contrived by man. They have structure; but it is the structure of events, rather than of physical components, and it cannot be separated from the processes of the system. The fact that social organizations are contrived by human beings suggests that they can be established for an infinite variety of purposes and do not follow the same life-cycle patterns of birth, growth, maturity, and death as biological systems. As Katz and Kahn say:

> Social structures are essentially contrived systems. They are made of men and are imperfect systems. They can come apart at the seams overnight, but they can also outlast by centuries the biological organisms which originally created them. The cement which holds them together is essentially psychological, rather than biological. Social systems are anchored in the attitudes, perceptions, beliefs, motivations, habits, and expectations of human beings [19, p. 33].

Recognizing that the social organization is contrived again cautions us against making an exact analogy between it and physical or biological systems.

Questions of Systems Effectiveness

General systems theory with its biological orientation would appear to have an evolutionary view of system effectiveness. That living system which best adapts to its environment prospers and survives. The primary measure of effectiveness is perpetuation of the organism's species. Teleological behavior is therefore directed toward survival. But, is survival the only criterion of effectiveness of the social system? It is probably an essential but not all-inclusive measure of effectiveness.

General systems theory emphasizes the organism's survival goal and does not fully relate to the question of the effectiveness of the system in its supra-system—the environment. Parsonian functional-structural views provide a contrast. "The *raison d'etre* of complex organizations, according to this analysis, is mainly to benefit the society in which they belong, and that society is, therefore, the appropriate frame of reference for the evaluation of organizational effectiveness" [41, p. 896].

But, this view seems to go to the opposite extreme from the survival view of general systems theory—the organization exists to serve the society. It seems to us that the truth lies somewhere between these two viewpoints. And it is likely that a systems viewpoint (modified from the species survival view of general systems theory) will be most appropriate. Yuchtman and Seashore suggest:

> The organization's success over a period of time in this competition for resources—i.e., its bargaining position in a given environment—is regarded as an expression of its overall effectiveness. Since the resources are of various kinds, and the competitive relationships are multiple, and since there is interchangeability among classes of resources, the assessment of organizational effectiveness must be in terms not of any single criterion but of an open-ended multidimensional set of criteria [41, p. 891].

This viewpoint suggests that questions of organizational effectiveness must be concerned with at least three levels of analysis: the level of the environment, the level of the social organization as a system, and the level of the subsystems (human participants) within the organization. Perhaps much of our confusion and ambiguity concerning organizational effectiveness stems from our failure to clearly delineate the level of our analysis and, even more important, our failure really to understand the relationships among these levels.

Our discussion of some of the problems associated with the application of general systems theory to the study of social organizations might suggest that we completely reject the appropriateness of this model. On the contrary, we see the systems approach as the new paradigm for the study of organizations; but, like all new concepts in the sciences, one which has to be applied, modified, and elaborated to make it as useful as possible.

SYSTEMS THEORY PROVIDES THE NEW PARADIGM

We hope the discussion of GST and organizations provides a realistic appraisal. We do not want to promote the value of the systems approach as a matter of faith; however, we do see systems theory as vital to the study of social organizations and as providing the major new paradigm for our field of study.

Thomas Kuhn provides an interesting interpretation of the nature of scientific revolution [20]. He suggests that major changes in all fields of science occur with the development of new conceptual schemes or "paradigms." These new paradigms do not just represent a step-by-step advancement in "normal" science (the science generally accepted and practiced) but, rather, a revolutionary change in the way the scientific field is perceived by the practitioners. Kuhn says:

> The historian of science may be tempted to exclaim that when paradigms change, the world itself changes with them. Led by a new paradigm, scientists adopt new instruments and look in new places. Even more important, during revolutions scientists see new and different things when looking with familiar instruments in places they have looked before. It is rather as if the professional community has been suddenly transported to another planet where familiar objects are seen in a different light and are joined by unfamiliar ones as well. . . . Paradigm changes do cause scientists to see the world of their research-engagement differently. Insofar as their only recourse to that world is through what they see and do, we may want to say that after a revolution scientists are responding to a different world [20, p. 110].

New paradigms frequently are rejected by the scientific community. (At first they may seem crude and limited—offering very little more than older paradigms.) They frequently lack the apparent sophistication of the older paradigms which they ultimately replace. They do not display the clarity and certainty of older paradigms which have been refined through years of research and writing. But, a new paradigm does provide for a "new start" and opens up new directions which were not possible under the old. "We must recognize how very limited in both scope and precision a paradigm can be at the time of its first appearance. Paradigms gain their status because they are more successful than their competitors in solving a few problems that the group of practitioners has come to recognize as acute. To be more successful is not, however, to be either completely successful with a single problem or notably successful with any large number" [20, p. 23].

Systems theory does provide a new paradigm for the study of social organizations and their management. At this stage it is obviously crude and lacking in precision. In some ways it may not be much better than older paradigms which have been accepted and used for a long time (such as the management process approach). As in other fields of scientific endeavor, the new paradigm must be applied, clarified, elaborated, and made more precise. But, it does provide a fundamentally different view of the reality of social organizations and can serve as the basis for major advancements in our field.

We see many exciting examples of the utilization of the new systems paradigm in the field of organization and management. Several of these have been referred to earlier [7, 13, 19, 21, 22, 24, 31, 38], and there have been many others. Burns and Stalker made substantial use of systems views in setting forth their concepts of mechanistic and organic managerial systems [8]. Their studies of the characteristics of these two organization types lack precise definition of the variables and relationships, but their colleagues have used the systems approach to look at the relationship of organizations to their environment and also among the technical, structural, and behavioral characteristics within the organization [24]. Chamberlain used a system view in studying enterprises and their environment, which is substantially different from traditional microeconomics [9]. The emerging field of "environmental sciences" and "environmental administration" has found the systems paradigm vital.

Thus, the systems theory paradigm is being used extensively in the investigation of relationships between subsystems within organizations and in studying the environmental interfaces. But, it still has not advanced sufficiently to meet the needs. One of the major problems is that the practical need to deal with comprehensive systems of relationships is overrunning our ability to fully understand and predict these relationships. *We vitally need the systems paradigm, but we are not sufficiently sophisticated to use it appropriately.* This is the dilemma. Do our current failures to fully utilize the systems paradigm suggest that we reject it and return to the older, more traditional, and time-tested paradigms? Or do we work with systems theory to make it more precise, to understand the relationships among subsystems, and to gather the informational inputs which are necessary to make the systems approach really work? We think the latter course offers the best opportunity.

Thus, we prefer to accept current limitations of systems theory, while working to reduce them and to develop more complete and sophisticated approaches for its application. We agree with Rapoport who says:

> The system approach to the study of man can be appreciated as an effort to restore meaning (in terms of intuitively grasped understanding of wholes) while adhering to the principles of *disciplined* generalizations and rigorous deduction. It is, in short, an attempt to make the study of man both scientific and meaningful [7, p. xxii].

We are sympathetic with the second part of Rapoport's comment, the need to apply the systems approach but to make disciplined generalizations and rigorous deductions. This is a vital necessity and yet a major current limitation. We do have some indication that progress (although very slow) is being made.

WHAT DO WE NEED NOW?

Everything is related to everything else—but how? General systems theory provides us with the macro paradigm for the study of social organizations. As Scott and others have pointed out, most sciences go through a macro-micro-macro cycle or sequence of emphasis [33]. Traditional bureaucratic theory provided the first major macro view of organizations. Administrative management theorists concentrated on the development of macro "principles of management" which were applicable to all organizations. When these macro views seemed incomplete (unable to explain important phenomena), attention turned to the micro level—more detailed analysis of components or parts of the organization, thus the interest in human relations, technology, or structural dimensions.

The systems approach returns us to the macro level with a new paradigm. General systems theory emphasizes a very high level of abstraction. Phillips classifies it as a third-order study [29] that attempts to develop macro concepts appropriate for all types of biological, physical, and social systems.

In our view, we are now ready to move down a level of abstraction to consider second-order systems studies or midrange concepts. These will be based on general systems theory but will be more concrete and will emphasize more specific characteristics and relationships in social organizations. They will operate within the broad paradigm of systems theory but at a less abstract level.

What should we call this new midrange level of analysis? Various authors have referred to it as a "contingency view," a study of "patterns of relationships," or a search for "configurations among subsystems." Lorsch and Lawrence reflect this view:

> During the past few years there has been evident a new trend in the study of organizational phenomena. Underlying this new approach is the idea that the internal functioning of organizations must be consistent with the demands of the organization task, technology, or external environment, and the needs of its members if the organization is to be effective. Rather than searching for the panacea of the one best way to organize under all conditions, investigators have more and more tended to examine the functioning of organizations in relation to the needs of their particular members and the external pressures facing them. Basically, this approach seems to be leading to the development of a "contingency" theory of organization with the appropriate internal states and processes of the organization contingent upon external requirements and member needs [21, p. 1].

Numerous others have stressed a similar viewpoint. Thompson suggests that the essence of administration lies in understanding basic configurations which exist between the various subsystems and with the environment. "The basic function of administration appears to be co-alignment, not merely of people (in coalitions) but of institutionalized action—of technology and task environment into a viable domain, and of organizational design and structure appropriate to it [38, p. 157].

Bringing these ideas together we can provide a more precise definition of the contingency view:

> The contingency view of organizations and their management suggests that an organization is a system composed of subsystems and delineated by identifiable boundaries from its environmental suprasystem. The contingency view seeks to understand the interrelationships within and among subsystems as well as between the organization and its environment and to define patterns of relationships or configurations of variables. It emphasizes the multivariate nature of organizations and attempts to understand how organizations operate under varying conditions and in specific circumstances. Contingency views are ultimately directed toward suggesting organizational designs and managerial systems most appropriate for specific situations.

But, it is not enough to suggest that a "contingency view" based on systems concepts of organizations and their management is more appropriate than the simplistic "principles approach." If organization theory is to advance and make contributions to managerial practice, it must define more explicitly certain patterns of relationships between organizational variables. This is the major challenge facing our field.

Just how do we go about using systems theory to develop these midrange or contingency views? We see no alternative but to engage in intensive comparative investigation of many organizations following the advice of Blau:

> A theory of organization, whatever its specific nature, and regardless of how subtle the organizational processes it takes into account, has as its central aim to establish the constellations of characteristics that develop in organizations of various kinds. Comparative studies of many organizations are necessary, not alone to test the hypotheses implied by such a theory, but also to provide a basis for initial exploration and refinement of the theory by indicating the conditions on which relationships, originally assumed to hold universally are contingent. . . . Systematic research on many organizations that provides the data needed to determine the interrelationships between several organizational features is, however, extremely rare [5, p. 332].

Various conceptual designs for the comparative study of organizations and their subsystems are emerging to help in the development of a contingency view. We do not want to impose our model as to what should be considered in looking for these patterns of relationships. However, the tentative matrix shown in Figure 2 suggests this approach. We have used as a starting point the two polar organization types which have been emphasized in the literature—closed/stable/mechanistic and open/adaptive/organic.

We will consider the environment suprasystem and organizational subsystems (goals and values, technical, structural, psychosocial, and managerial) plus various dimensions or characteristics of each of these systems. By way of illustration we have indicated several specific subcategories under the Environmental Suprasystem as well as the Goals and Values subsystem. This process would have to be completed and extended to all of the subsystems. The next step would be the development of appropriate descriptive language (based on research and conceptualization) for each relevant characteristic across the continuum of organization types. For example, on the "stability" dimension for Goals and Values we would have High, Medium, and Low at appropriate places on the continuum. If the entire matrix were filled in, it is likely that we would begin to see discernible patterns of relationships among subsystems.

We do not expect this matrix to provide *the* midrange model for everyone. It is highly doubtful that we will be able to follow through with the field work investigations necessary to fill in all the squares. Nevertheless, it does illustrate a possible approach for the translation of more abstract general

FIGURE 2   Matrix of Patterns of Relationships between Organization Types and Systems Variables

Organizational Supra- and Subsystems	Continuum of Organization Types	
	Closed/Stable/Mechanistic	Open/Adaptive/Organic
Environmental relationships		
General nature	Placid.	Turbulent.
Predictability	Certain, determinate.	Uncertain, indeterminate.
Boundary relationships	Relatively closed; limited to few participants (sales, purchasing, etc.); fixed and well-defined.	Relatively open; many participants have external relationships; varied and not clearly defined.
Goals and values		
Organizational goals in general	Efficient performance, stability, maintenance.	Effective problem-solving innovation, growth.
Goal set	Single, clear-cut.	Multiple, determined by necessity to satisfy a set of constraints.
Stability	Stable.	Unstable.
Technical		
Structural		
Psychosocial		
Managerial		

systems theory into an appropriate midrange model which is relevant for organization theory and management practice. Frankly, we see this as a major long-term effort on the part of many researchers, investigating a wide variety of organizations. In spite of the difficulties involved in such research, the endeavor has practical significance. Sophistication in the study of organizations will come when we have a more complete understanding of organizations as total systems (configurations of subsystems) so that we can prescribe more appropriate organizational designs and managerial systems. Ultimately, organization theory should serve as the foundation for more effective management practice.

APPLICATION OF SYSTEMS CONCEPTS TO MANAGEMENT PRACTICE

The study of organizations is an applied science, because the resulting knowledge is relevant to problem solving in on-going institutions. Contributions to organization theory come from many sources. Deductive and inductive research in a variety of disciplines provide a theoretical base of propositions, which are useful for understanding organizations and for managing them. Experience gained in management practice is also an important input to organization theory. In short, management is based on the body of knowledge generated by practical experience *and* eclectic scientific research concerning organizations. The body of knowledge developed through theory and research should be translatable into more effective organizational design and managerial practices.

Do systems concepts and contingency views provide a panacea for solving problems in organizations? The answer is an emphatic *no;* this approach does not provide "ten easy steps" to success in management. Such cookbook approaches, while seemingly applicable and easy to grasp, are usually shortsighted, narrow in perspective, and superficial—in short, unrealistic. Fundamental ideas, such as systems concepts and contingency views, are more difficult to comprehend. However, they facilitate more thorough understanding of complex situations and increase the likelihood of appropriate action.

It is important to recognize that many managers have used and will continue to use a systems approach and contingency views intuitively and implicitly. Without much knowledge of the underlying body of organization theory, they have an intuitive "sense of the situation," are flexible diagnosticians, and adjust their actions and decisions accordingly. Thus, systems concepts and contingency views are not new. However, if this approach to organization theory and management practice can be made more explicit, we can facilitate better management and more effective organizations.

Practicing managers in business firms, hospitals, and government agencies continue to function on a day-to-day basis. Therefore, they must use whatever theory is available; they cannot wait for the *ultimate* body of knowledge (there is none!). Practitioners should be included in the search for new knowledge, because they control access to an essential ingredient— organizational data—and they are the ones who ultimately put the theory to the test. Mutual understanding among managers, teachers, and researchers will facilitate the development of a relevant body of knowledge.

Simultaneously with the refinement of the body of knowledge, a concerted effort should be directed toward applying what we do know. We need ways of making systems and contingency views more usable. Without oversimplification, we need some relevant guidelines for practicing managers.

The general tenor of the contingency view is somewhere between simplistic, specific principles and complex, vague notions. It is a midrange concept, which recognizes the complexity involved in managing modern organizations but uses patterns of relationships and/or configurations of subsystems in order to facilitate improved practice. The art of management depends on a reasonable success rate for actions in a probabilistic environment. Our hope is that systems concepts and contingency views, while continually being refined by scientists/researchers/theorists, will also be made more applicable.

NOTE

1. An entire article could be devoted to a discussion of ingenious ways in which the term *systems approach* has been used in the literature pertinent to organization theory and management practice.

REFERENCES

1. Ackoff, Russell L. "Towards a System of Systems Concepts." *Management Science,* July 1971.
2. Back, Kurt W. "Biological Models of Social Change." *American Sociological Review,* August 1971.
3. Barnard, Chester I. *The Functions of the Executive.* Cambridge, Mass.: Harvard University Press, 1938.
4. Berrien, F. Kenneth. *General and Social Systems.* New Brunswick, N.J.: Rutgers University Press, 1968.
5. Blau, Peter M. "The Comparative Study of Organizations." *Industrial and Labor Relations Review,* April 1965.
6. Boulding, Kenneth E. "General Systems Theory: The Skeleton of Science." *Management Science,* April 1956.
7. Buckley, Walter, ed. *Modern Systems Research for the Behavioral Scientist.* Chicago: Aldine, 1968.
8. Burns, Tom, and G. M. Stalker. *The Management of Innovation.* London: Tavistock Publications, 1961.
9. Chamberlain, Neil W. *Enterprise and Environment: The Firm in Time and Place.* New York: McGraw-Hill, 1968.
10. Churchman, C. West. *The Systems Approach.* New York: Dell, 1968.
11. DeGreene, Kenyon, ed. *Systems Psychology.* New York: McGraw-Hill, 1970.
12. Deutsch, Karl W. "Toward A Cybernetic Model of Man and Society." In *Modern Systems Research for the Behavioral Scientist,* ed. Walter Buckley. Chicago: Aldine, 1968.
13. Easton, David. *A Systems Analysis of Political Life.* New York: John Wiley & Sons, 1965.
14. Emery, F. E., and E. L. Trist. "Socio-technical Systems." In *Management Sciences: Models and Techniques,* ed. C. West Churchman and Michele Verhulst. New York: Pergamon, 1960.
15. Emshoff, James R. *Analysis of Behavioral Systems.* New York: Macmillan, 1971.
16. Gross, Bertram M. "The Coming General Systems Models of Social Systems." *Human Relations,* November 1967.
17. Hall, A. D., and R. E. Eagen. "Definition of System." *General Systems, Yearbook for the Society for the Advancement of General Systems Theory.* Vol. 1, 1956.
18. Kast, Fremont E., and James E. Rosenzweig. *Organization and Management Theory: A Systems Approach.* New York: McGraw-Hill, 1970.
19. Katz, Daniel, and Robert L. Kahn. *The Social Psychology of Organizations.* New York: John Wiley & Sons, 1966.
20. Kuhn, Thomas S. *The Structure of Scientific Revolutions.* Chicago: University of Chicago Press, 1962.
21. Litterer, Joseph A. *Organizations: Structure and Behavior.* Vol. 1. New York: John Wiley & Sons, 1969.

22. _____ . *Organizations: Systems, Control and Adaptation*. Vol. 2. New York: John Wiley & Sons, 1969.

23. Lorsch, Jay W., and Paul R. Lawrence. *Studies in Organizational Design*. Homewood, Ill.: Irwin-Dorsey, 1970.

24. Miller, E. J., and A. K. Rice. *Systems of Organizations*. London: Tavistock Publications, 1967.

25. Miller, James G. "Living Systems: Basic Concepts." *Behavioral Science,* July 1965.

26. Miller, Robert F. "The New Science of Administration in the USSR." *Administrative Science Quarterly,* September 1971.

27. Murray, Henry A. "Preparation for the Scaffold of a Comprehensive System." In *Psychology: A Study of a Science*. Vol. 3, ed. Sigmund Koch. New York: McGraw-Hill, 1959.

28. Parsons, Talcott. *The Social System*. New York: Free Press of Glencoe, 1951.

29. Phillips, D. C. "Systems Theory—A Discredited Philosophy." In *Management Systems,* ed. Peter P. Schoderbek. New York: John Wiley & Sons, 1971.

30. Rapoport, Anatol, and William J. Horvath. "Thoughts on Organization Theory." In *Modern Systems Research for the Behavioral Scientist,* ed. Walter Buckley. Chicago: Aldine, 1968.

31. Rice, A. K. *The Modern University*. London: Tavistock Publications, 1970.

32. Schein, Edgar. *Organizational Psychology*. Rev. ed. Englewood Cliffs, N.J.: Prentice-Hall, 1970.

33. Scott, William G. "Organization Theory: An Overview and an Appraisal." *Academy of Management Journal,* April 1961.

34. Silverman, David. *The Theory of Organizations*. New York: Basic Books, 1971.

35. Simon, Herbert A. "The Architecture of Complexity." In *Organizations: Systems, Control and Adaptation*. Vol. 2, ed. Joseph A. Litterer. New York: John Wiley & Sons, 1969.

36. Springer, Michael. "Social Indicators, Reports, and Accounts: Toward the Management of Society." *The Annals of the American Academy of Political and Social Science,* March 1970.

37. Terreberry, Shirley. "The Evolution of Organizational Environments." *Administrative Science Quarterly,* March 1968.

38. Thompson, James D. *Organizations in Action*. New York: McGraw-Hill, 1967.

39. von Bertalanffy, Ludwig. *General System Theory*. New York: George Braziller, 1968.

40. _____ . "The Theory of Open Systems in Physics and Biology." *Science,* January 13, 1950.

41. Yuchtman, Ephraim, and Stanley E. Seashore. "A System Resource Approach to Organizational Effectiveness." *American Sociological Review,* December 1967.

PART TWO

Classical Management Processes

The management processes of planning, organizing, and controlling are among those functions universally recognized as central components of the manager's role. Whether one is a classicist, neoclassicist, or behaviorist, the importance of these managerial functions is not debated. This section of the text presents nine articles that address these three processes.

It has been said that poor managers work on yesterday's problems, good managers work on today's problems, and the truly outstanding managers focus on tomorrow's problems. Focusing on tomorrow's problems clearly requires *planning*. Planning is an essential function of the management process and involves the application of thought, analysis, imagination, and judgment to future activities.

One of the themes of the classical school of management is that there is a distinct difference between planning and executing. Fayol and others argued that managers should plan and nonmanagers should execute. The behaviorists, on the other hand, would counter with the argument that managers and nonmanagers together should be active participants in both planning and executing. Both groups, however, would agree that the planning function includes those activities that result in a definition of goals and the determination of appropriate means to achieve these goals. Simply stated, planning is advance thinking as the basis for doing.

Whenever goals and tasks require the efforts of two or more people, the need for *organizing* arises. For example, when an object is too heavy for one person to lift, the efforts of others must be used. If more than one person is involved in the lifting, the effort must be coordinated. Organizing refers to the process of achieving coordinated effort. The organizing function in management is the means by which managers seek to achieve a coordinated effort through the design of a structure of tasks and authority relationships.

The organizing function is often discussed in terms of dividing tasks, departmentalizing tasks, and delegating authority. The principles of specialization, departmentalization, span of control, and unity of command provide the basic elements for discussing the organizing function. These principles are not ironclad laws or facts but are guidelines that serve to aid the manager faced with organizing decisions. Regardless of what those decisions are, all organizing efforts share a common goal of channelling individual and group behavior into patterns that contribute to effective organizational performance.

For many students of management, the *control* processes are both the least understood and least appreciated managerial functions. Simply stated, control processes are those activities involved in setting standards, measuring performance against these standards, and correcting or adjusting for deviations from the standards. An important implication of this definition is that *plans* have been made and work has been *organized* —very important management activities also addressed in this section. Control, then, is what is necessary to insure that plans and organizations are executed in a manner consistent with achieving the desired results.

A. Planning

7

Planning

Henri Fayol

Written well over 60 years ago by a true pioneer in discussing planning, this short essay is as current as if it were written yesterday. Fayol identifies the features of a good plan of action and outlines the method of drawing up a plan. Note also the emphasis Fayol places on the human element of planning.—Eds.

The maxim, "managing means looking ahead," gives some idea of the importance attached to planning in the business world and it is true that if foresight is not the whole of management at least it is an essential part of it. To foresee, in this context, means both to assess the future and make provision for it; that is, foreseeing is itself action already. Planning is manifested on a variety of occasions and in a variety of ways, its chief manifestation, apparent sign, and most effective instrument being the plan of action. The plan of action is, at one and the same time, the result envisaged, the line of action to be followed, the stages to go through, and methods to use. It is a kind of future picture wherein proximate events are outlined with some distinctness, whilst remote events appear progressively less distinct, and it entails the running of the business as foreseen and provided against over a definite period.

The plan of action rests: (1) On the firm's resources (buildings, tools, raw materials, personnel, productive capacity, sales outlets, public relations, etc.). (2) On the nature and importance of work in progress. (3) On future trends which depend partly on technical, commercial, financial, and other conditions, all subject to change, whose importance and occurrence cannot be predetermined. The preparation of the plan of action is one of the

SOURCE: Reprinted by permission of Pitman Publishing Limited from Chapter V of *General and Industrial Management* by Henri Fayol (London: Sir Isaac Pitman and Sons, Ltd., 1949), pp. 43–52.

most difficult and most important matters of every business and brings into plan all departments and all functions, especially the management function. It is, in effect, in order to carry out his managerial function that the manager takes the initiative for the plan of action, that he indicates its objective and scope, fixes the share of each department in the communal task, coordinates the parts and harmonizes the whole; that he decides, in fine, the line of conduct to be followed. In this line of conduct it is not only imperative that nothing should clash with principles and rules of good management, but also that the arrangement adopted should facilitate application of these principles and rules. Therefore, to the divers technical, commercial, financial, and other abilities necessary on the part of a business head and his assistants, there must be added considerable managerial ability.

GENERAL FEATURES OF A GOOD PLAN OF ACTION

No one disputes the usefulness of a plan of action. Before taking action it is most necessary to know what is possible and what is wanted. It is known that absence of plan entails hesitation, false steps, untimely changes of direction, which are so many causes of weakness, if not of disaster, in business. The question of and necessity for a plan of action, then, does not arise and I think that I am voicing the general opinion in saying that a plan of action is indispensable. But there are plans and plans, there are simple ones, complex ones, concise ones, detailed ones, long- or short-term ones; there are those studied with meticulous attention, those treated lightly; there are good, bad, and indifferent ones. How are the good ones to be singled out from among the others? Experience is the only thing that finally determines the true value of a plan; that is, on the services it can render to the firm, and even then the manner of its application must be taken into account. There is both instrument and player. Nevertheless, there are certain broad characteristics on which general agreement may be reached beforehand without waiting for the verdict of experience.

Unity of plan is an instance. Only one plan can be put into operation at a time; two different plans would mean duality, confusion, disorder. But a plan may be divided into several parts. In large concerns, there is found alongside the general plan a technical, commercial, and a financial one, or else an overall one with a specific one for each department. But all these plans are linked, welded, so as to make up one only, and every modification brought to bear on any one of them is given expression in the whole plan. The guiding action of the plan must be continuous. Now the limitations of human foresight necessarily set bounds to the duration of plans, so, in order to have no break in the guiding action, a second plan must follow immediately upon the first, a third upon the second, and so on. In large businesses the annual plan is more or less in current use. Other plans of shorter or longer term, always in close accord with the annual plan, operate simultaneously with this latter. The plan should be flexible enough to bend before such adjustments, as it is considered well to introduce, whether from pressure or circumstances or from any other reason. First as last, it is the law to which one bows. Another good point about a plan is to have as much accuracy as is compatible with the unknown factors bearing on the fate of the concern. Usually it is possible to mark out the line of proximate action fairly accurately, while a simple general indication does for remote activities, for before the moment for their execution has arrived sufficient enlightenment will have been forthcoming to settle the line of action more precisely. When the unknown factor occupies a relatively very large place there can be no preciseness in the plan, and then the concern takes on the name of venture.

Unity, continuity, flexibility, precision: such are the broad features of a good plan of action.

As for other specific points which it should have, and which turn on the nature, importance, and condition of the business for which the plan is drawn up, there could be no possibility of settling them beforehand save by comparison with other plans already recognized as effective in similar businesses. In each case, then, comparable elements and models must be sought in business practice, after the fashion of the architect with a building to construct. But the architect, better served than the manager, can call upon books, courses in architecture, whereas there are no books on plans of action, no lessons in foresight, for management theory has yet to be formulated.

There is no lack of good plans; they can be guessed at from the externals of a business but not seen at sufficiently close quarters to be known and judged. Nevertheless, it would be most useful for those whose concern is management to know how experienced managers go about drawing up their plans. By way of information or sample, I am going to set out the method which has long been followed in a great mining and metallurgical concern with which I am well acquainted.

Method of Drawing Up the Plan of Action in a Large Mining and Metallurgical Firm

This company includes several separate establishments and employs about 10,000 personnel. The entire plan is made up of a series of separate plans called forecasts; and there are yearly forecasts, ten-yearly forecasts, monthly, weekly, daily forecasts, long-term forecasts, special forecasts, and all merge into a single program which operates as a guide for the whole concern.

(1) **Yearly Forecasts.** Each year, two months after the end of the budgetary period, a general report is drawn up of the work and results of this period. The report deals especially with production, sales, technical,

commercial, financial position, personnel, economic consequences, etc. The report is accompanied by forecasts dealing with those same matters, the forecasts being a kind of anticipatory summary of the activities and results of the new budgetary period. The two months of the new plan which have elapsed are not left without plan, because of provisional forecasts drawn up 15 days before the end of the previous period. In a large mining and metallurgical firm not many activities are quite completed during the course of one year. Cooperative projects of a technical, commercial, and financial nature, which provide the business with its activities, need more time for their preparation and execution. From another aspect, account must be taken of the repercussions which proximate activities must have on ultimate ones and of the obligation to prepare far ahead sometimes for a requisite state of affairs.

Finally, thought must be given to constant modifications operating on the technical, commercial, financial, and social condition of the industrial world in general and of the business in particular, to avoid being overtaken by circumstances. These various circumstances come outside the framework of yearly forecasts and lead on to longer-term ones. (See Table 1.)

(2) **Ten-Yearly Forecasts.** Ten-yearly forecasts deal with the same matters as yearly ones. At the outset, these two types of forecasts are identical, the yearly forecast merging into the first year of the ten-yearly one, but from the second year onwards notable divergences make their appearance. To maintain unity of plan each year the ten-yearly forecasts must be reconciled with annual ones so that at the end of some years the ten-yearly forecasts are generally so modified and transformed as to be no longer clear and need redrafting. In effect, the custom of redrafting every five years has become established. It is the rule that ten-yearly forecasts always embrace a decade, and that they are revised every five years. Thus, there is always a line of action marked out in advance for five years at least.

(3) **Special Forecasts.** There are some activities whose full cycle exceeds one or even several ten-yearly periods; there are others which, occurring suddenly, must sensibly affect the conditions of the business. Both the one and the other are the object of special forecasts whose findings necessarily have a place in the yearly and ten-yearly forecasts. But it must never be lost sight of that there is one plan only.

These three sorts of forecasts, yearly, ten-yearly, and special, merged and harmonized, constitute the firm's general plan.

So, having been prepared with meticulous care by each regional management, with the help of departmental management, and then revised, modified, and completed by general management and then submitted for scrutiny and approval to the board of directors, these forecasts become the plan which, so long as no other has been put in its place, shall serve as guide, directive, and law for the whole staff.

TABLE 1   Yearly and Ten-Yearly Forecasts

Contents

Technical Section
   Mining rights. Premises. Plant.
   Extraction. Manufacture. Output.
   New workings. Improvements.
   Maintenance of plant and buildings.
   Production costs.
Commercial Section
   Sales outlets.
   Marketable goods.
   Agencies. Contracts.
   Customer importance. Credit standing.
   Selling price.
Financial Section
   Capital. Loans. Deposits.

   Circulating assets $\begin{cases} \text{Supplies in hand.} \\ \text{Finished goods.} \\ \text{Debtors.} \\ \text{Liquid assets.} \end{cases}$

   Available assets.
   Reserves and sundry appropriations.

   Creditors $\begin{cases} \text{Wages.} \\ \text{Suppliers.} \\ \text{Sundry.} \end{cases}$

   Sinking funds. Dividends. Bankers.
Accounting
   Balance sheet. Profit and loss account.
   Statistics.
Security
   Accident precautions.
   Works police. Claims. Health service.
   Insurance.
Management
   Plan of action.
   Organization of personnel. Selection.
   Command.
   Coordination. Conferences.
   Control.

Fifty years ago I began to use this system of forecasts, when I was engaged in managing a colliery, and it rendered me such good service that I had no hesitation in subsequently applying it to various industries whose running was entrusted to me. I look upon it as a precious managerial instrument and have no hesitation in recommending its use to those who have no better instrument available. It has necessarily some shortcomings, but its shortcomings are very slight compared with the advantages it offers. Let us glance at these advantages and shortcomings.

Advantages and Shortcomings of Forecasts

1. The study of resources, future possibilities, and means to be used for attaining the objective call for contributions from all departmental heads within the framework of their mandate: each one brings to this study the contribution of his experience together with recognition of the responsibility which will fall upon him in executing the plan.

Those are excellent conditions for ensuring that no resource shall be neglected and that future possibilities shall be prudently and courageously assessed and that means shall be appropriate to ends. Knowing what are its capabilities and its intentions, the concern goes boldly on, confidently tackles current problems and is prepared to align all its forces against accidents and surprises of all kinds which may occur.

2. Compiling the annual plan is always a delicate operation and especially lengthy and laborious when done for the first time, but each repetition brings some simplification and when the plan has become a habit the toil and difficulties are largely reduced. Conversely, the interest it offers increases. The attention demanded for executing the plan, the indispensable comparison between predicted and actual facts, the recognition of mistakes made and successes attained, the search for means of repeating the one and avoiding the other—all go to make the new plan a work of increasing interest and increasing usefulness.

Also, by doing this work the personnel increases in usefulness from year to year, and at the end is considerably superior to what it was in the beginning. In truth, this result is not due solely to the use of planning but everything goes together; a well-thought-out plan is rarely found apart from sound organizational, command, coordination, and control practices. This management element exerts an influence on all the rest.

3. Lack of sequence in activity and unwarranted changes of course are dangers constantly threatening businesses without a plan. The slightest contrary wind can turn from its course a boat which is unfitted to resist. When serious happenings occur, regrettable changes of course may be decided upon under the influence of profound but transitory disturbance. Only a program carefully pondered at an undisturbed time permits of maintaining a clear view of the future and of concentrating maximum possible intellectual ability and material resources upon the danger.

It is in difficult moments above all that a plan is necessary. The best of plans cannot anticipate all unexpected occurrences which may arise, but it does include a place for these events and the means by which to prepare the weapons which may be needed at the moment of being surprised. The plan protects the business not only against undesirable changes of course which may be produced by grave events, but also against those arising simply from changes on the part of higher authority. Also, it protects against deviations, imperceptible at first, which end by deflecting it from its objective.

Conditions and Qualities Essential for Drawing Up a Good Plan of Action

To sum up: The plan of action facilitates the utilization of the firm's resources and the choice of best methods to use for attaining the objective. It suppresses or reduces hesitancy, false steps, unwarranted changes of course, and helps to improve personnel. It is a precious managerial instrument.

The question may be asked about why such an instrument is not in general use and everywhere developed to the farthest extent. The reason is that its compilation demands of managerial personnel a certain number of qualities and conditions rarely to be found in combination. The compilation of a good plan demands for the personnel in charge:

1. The art of handling men.
2. Considerable energy.
3. A measure of moral courage.
4. Some continuity of tenure.
5. A given degree of competence in the specialized requirements of the business.
6. A certain general business experience.

(1) **The Art of Handling Men.**   In a large firm the majority of departmental managers take part in the compiling of the working arrangements. The execution of this task from time to time is in addition to ordinary everyday work and includes a certain responsibility and does not normally carry any special remuneration. So, to have in such conditions loyal and active cooperation from departmental heads an able manager of men is needed who fears neither trouble nor responsibility. The art of handling men is apparent from keenness of subordinates and confidence of superiors.

(2) **Energy.**   Yearly and ten-yearly forecasts and special forecasts demand constant vigilance on the part of management.

(3) **Moral Courage.**   It is well known that the best-thought-out plan is never exactly carried out. Forecasts are not prophecies; their function is to minimize the unknown factor. Nevertheless, the public generally, and even shareholders best informed about the running of a business, are not

kindly disposed toward a manager who has raised unfulfilled hopes, or allowed them to be raised. Whence the need for a certain prudence which has to be reconciled with the obligation of making every preparation and seeking out optimum possible results.

The timid are tempted to suppress the plan or else whittle it down to nothing in order not to expose themselves to criticism, but it is a bad policy even from the point of view of self-interest. Lack of plan, which compromises smooth running, also exposes the manager to infinitely graver charges than that of having to explain away imperfectly executed forecasts.

(4) Continuity of Tenure. Some time goes by before a new manager is able to take sufficient cognizance of the course of affairs, its general setup, and future possibilities, so as usefully to undertake the compiling of the plan. If, at such a moment, he feels that he will not have enough time to complete the work or only enough to start putting it into execution, or if, on the other hand, he is convinced that such work, condemned to bear no fruit, will only draw criticism upon him, is it to be thought that he will carry it out enthusiastically or even undertake it unless obliged? Human nature must be reckoned with. Without continuity of tenure on the part of management personnel there can be no good plan of action.

(5 and 6) Professional Competence and General Business Knowledge. These are abilities just as necessary for drawing up a plan as for carrying it out.

Such are the conditions essential for compiling a good plan. They presuppose intelligent and experienced management. Lack of plan or a bad plan is a sign of managerial incompetence. To safeguard business against such incompetence:

1. A plan must be compulsory.
2. Good specimen plans must be made generally available. (Successful businesses could be asked to furnish such specimens. Experience and general discussion would single out the best.)
3. Planning (as a subject) must be introduced into education. Thus could general opinion be better informed and react upon management personnel, so that the latter's inefficiency would be less to be feared—a state of affairs which would in no wise detract from the importance of men of proven worth.

8

Long-Range Planning: Challenge to Management Science

Peter F. Drucker

In this article, one of the most widely read contributors to the practice of management starts off by identifying what long-range planning is not. From there he defines the proper role of management science in the planning process, stressing that planning is a continuous, ongoing process. Drucker's perspective on planning is a little different from the usual and is well worth examining.—Eds.

I

It is easier to define long-range planning by what it is not, rather than by what it is. Three things in particular, which it is commonly believed to be, it emphatically is not.

1. *First it is not "forecasting."* It is not masterminding the future, in other words. Any attempt to do so is foolish; human beings can neither predict nor control the future.

If anyone still suffers from the delusion that the ability to forecast beyond the shortest time span is given to us, let him look at the headlines in yesterday's paper, and then ask himself which of them he could possibly have predicted 10 years ago.

- Could he have forecast that by today the Russians would have drawn even with us in the most advanced branches of physical sciences and of engineering?

- Could he have forecast that West Germany in complete ruins and chaos then would have become the most conservative country in the

SOURCE: Reprinted by permission of the author and publisher from "Long-Range Planning: Challenge to Management Science," *Management Science* 5, no. 3 (1959), pp. 238–49.

world and one of the most productive ones, let alone that it would
become very stable politically?

- Could he have forecast that the Near East would become a central
trouble spot, or would he have had to assume that the oil revenues
there would take care of all problems?

This is the way the future always behaves. To try to mastermind it is
therefore childish; we can only discredit what we are doing by attempting it.
We must start out with the conclusion that forecasting is not respectable and
not worthwhile beyond the shortest of periods. *Long-range planning is necessary precisely because we cannot forecast.*

But there is another, and even more compelling reason why forecasting
is not long-range planning. Forecasting attempts to find the most probable
course of events, or, at best, a range of probabilities. But the entrepreneurial
problem is the unique event that will change the possibilities, for the entrepreneurial universe is not a physical but a value universe. Indeed, the
central entrepreneurial contribution, and the one which alone is rewarded
with a profit, is to bring about the unique event, the *innovation* that changes
the probabilities.

Let me give an example—a very elementary one which has nothing to
do with innovation but which illustrates the importance of the improbable
even for purely adaptive business behavior.

A large coffee distributor has for many years struggled with the problem of the location and capacity of its processing plants throughout the
country. It had long been known that coffee prices were as important a factor
in this, as location of market, volume, or transportation and delivery strategy. Now if we can forecast anything, it is single-commodity prices; and the
price forecasts of the company economists have been remarkably accurate.
Yet the decisions on plant location and capacity based on these forecasts
have again and again proven costly blunders. Extreme pricing events, the
probability of which at any one time was exceedingly low, had, even if they
lasted only for a week at a time, impact on the economics of the system that
were vastly greater than that of the accurately forecast "averages." Forecasting, in other words, obscured economic reality. What was needed (as the
Theory of Games could have proven) was to look at the extreme possibilities,
and to ask, "Which of these can we not afford to disregard?"

The only thing atypical in this example is that it is so simple. Usually
things are quite a bit more complex. But despite its (deceptive) simplicity it
shows why forecasting is not an adequate basis even for purely adaptive
behavior, let alone for the entrepreneurial decisions of long-range planning.

2. The next thing to be said about what long-range planning is not,
is that it does not deal with future decisions. It deals with the *futurity
of present decisions.*

Decisions exist only in the present. The question that faces the long-
range planner is not what we should do tomorrow. It is what do we have to

do today to be ready for an uncertain tomorrow. The question is not what will happen in the future. It is: What futurity do we have to factor into our present thinking and doing, what time spans do we have to consider, and how do we converge them to a simultaneous decision in the present?

Decision making is essentially a time machine which synchronizes into one present a great number of divergent time spans. This is, I think, something which we are only learning now. Our approach today still tends toward the making of plans for something we will decide to do in the future. This may be a very entertaining exercise, but it is a futile one.

Again, long-range planning is necessary because we can make decisions only in the present; the rest are pious intentions. And yet we cannot make decisions for the present alone; the most expedient, most opportunist decision—let alone the decision not to decide—may commit us on a long-range basis, if not permanently and irrevocably.

3. Finally, the most common misconception of all, *long-range planning is not an attempt to eliminate risk*. It is not even an attempt to minimize risk. Indeed, any such attempt can only lead to irrational and unlimited risk and to certain disaster.

The central fact about economic activity is that, by definition, it commits present resources to future and therefore highly uncertain expectations. To take risk is therefore the essence of economic activity. Indeed one of the most rigorous theorems of economics (Boehm-Bawerk's Law) proves that existing means of production will yield greater economic performance only through greater uncertainty, that is, through greater risk.

But while it is futile to try to eliminate risk, and questionable to try to minimize it, it is essential that the risks taken be the *right risks*. The end result of successful long-range planning must be a capacity to take a greater risk; for this is the only way to improve *entrepreneurial* performance. To do this, however, we must know and understand the risks we take. We must be able to rationally choose among risk-taking courses of action rather than plunge into uncertainty on the basis of hunch, hearsay, or experience (no matter how meticulously quantified).

Now I think we can attempt to define what long-range planning is. It is the continuous process of making *present entrepreneurial (risk-taking) decisions* systematically and with the best possible knowledge of their futurity, organizing systematically *the efforts* needed to carry out these decisions, and measuring the results of these decisions against the expectations through *organized, systematic feedback*.

II

"This is all very well," many experienced businessmen might say (and do say). "But why make a production out of it? Isn't this what the entrepreneur has been doing all along, and doing quite successfully? Why then should it need all this elaborate mumbo jumbo? Why should it be an organized, perhaps even a separate, activity? Why in other words, should we even talk about 'long-range planning,' let alone do it?"

It is perfectly true that there is nothing very new to entrepreneurial decisions. They have been made as long as we have had entrepreneurs. There is nothing new in here regarding the essentials of economic activity. It has always been the commitment of present resources to future expectations; and for the last 300 years this has been done in contemplation of change. (This was not true earlier. Earlier economic activity was based on the assumption that there would be no change, which assumption was institutionally guarded and defended. Altogether up to the 17th century it was the purpose of all human institutions to prevent change. The business enterprise is a significant and rather amazing novelty in that it is the first human institution having the purpose of bringing about change.)

But there are several things which are new; and they have created the need for the organized, systematic, and above all, specific process that we call "long-range planning."[1]

1. The time span of entrepreneurial and managerial decisions has been lengthening so fast and so much as to make necessary systematic exploration of the uncertainty and risk of decisions.

In 1888 or thereabouts, an old and perhaps apocryphal story goes, the great Thomas Edison, already a world figure, went to one of the big banks in New York for a loan on something he was working on. He had plenty of collateral and he was a great man; so the vice presidents all bowed and said "Certainly, Mr. Edison, how much do you need?" But one of them, out of idle curiosity asked, "Tell me, Mr. Edison, how long will it be before you have this new product?" Edison looked him in the eye and said, "Son, judging from past experience, it will be about 18 months before I even know whether I'll have a product or not." Whereupon the vice presidents collapsed in a body, and, despite the collateral, turned down the loan application. The man was obviously mad; 18 months of uncertainty was surely not a risk a sane businessman would take!

Today practically every manager takes 10- or 20-year risks without wincing. He takes them in product development, in research, in market development, in the development of a sales organization, and in almost anything. This lengthening of the time span of commitment is one of the most significant features of our age. It underlies our economic advances. But while quantitative in itself, it has changed the qualitative character of entrepreneurial decisions. It has, so to speak, converted time from being a dimension in which business decisions are being made into an essential element of the decisions themselves.

2. Another new feature is the speed and risk of innovation. To define what we mean by this term would go far beyond the scope of this paper.[2]

But we do not need to know more than that industrial research expenditures (i.e., business expenditures aimed at innovating primarily peacetime products and processes) have increased in this country from less than $100 million in 1928 to $7 or $8 billion in 1958. Clearly, a technologically slow-moving, if not essentially stable, economy has become one of violent technological flux, rapid obsolescence, and great uncertainty.

3. Then there is the growing complexity both of the business enterprise internally and of the economy and society in which it exists. There is the growing specialization of work, which creates increasing need for common vision, common understanding, and common language, without which top management decisions, however right, will never become effective action.

4. Finally—a subtle, but perhaps the most important point—the typical businessman's concept of the basis of entrepreneurial decision is, after all, a misconception.

Most businessmen still believe that these decisions are made by "top management." Indeed, practically all text books lay down the dictum that "basic policy decisions" are the "prerogative of top management." At most, top management "delegates" certain decisions.

But this reflects yesterday's rather than today's reality, let alone that of tomorrow. It is perfectly true that top management must have the final say, the final responsibility. But the business enterprise of today is no longer an organization in which there are a handful of "bosses" at the top who make all the decisions while the "workers" carry out orders. It is primarily an organization[3] of professionals of highly specialized knowledge exercising autonomous, responsible judgment. And every one of them—whether manager or individual expert contributor—constantly makes truly entrepreneurial decisions, that is, decisions which affect the economic characteristics and risks of the entire enterprise. He makes them not by "delegation from above" but inevitably in the performance of his own job and work.

For this organization to be functioning, two things are needed: knowledge by the entire organization of what the direction, the goals, the expectations are; and knowledge by top management of what the decisions, commitments, and efforts of the people in the organization are. The needed focus—one might call it a *model of the relevants in internal and external environment*—only a "long-range plan" can provide.

One way to summarize what is new and different in the process of entrepreneurial decision making is in terms of information. The amount, diversity, and ambiguity of the information that is beating in on the decision maker have all been increasing so much that the built-in experience reaction that a good manager has cannot handle it. He breaks down; and his breakdown will take either of the two forms known to any experimental psychologist. One is withdrawal from reality (i.e., "I know what I know and

I only go by it; the rest is quite irrelevant and I won't even look at it)." Or there is a feeling that the universe has become so completely irrational that one decision is as good as the other, resulting in paralysis. We see both in executives who have to make decisions today. Neither is likely to result in rational or in successful decisions.

There is something else managers and management scientists might learn from the psychologists. Organization of information is often more important to the ability to perceive and act than analysis and understanding of the information. I recall one experience with the organization of research planning in a pharmaceutical company. The attempt to analyze the research decisions—even to define alternatives of decisions—was a dismal failure. In the attempt, however, the decisions were classified to the point where the research people could know what kind of a decision was possible at what stage. They still did not know what factors should or should not be considered in a given decision, nor what its risks were. They could not explain why they made this decision, rather than another one, nor spell out what they expected. But the mere organization of this information enabled them again to apply their experience and to "play hunches"—with measurable and very significant improvement in the performance of the entire research group.

"Long-range planning" is more than organization and analysis of information; it is a decision-making process. But even the information job cannot be done except as part of an organized planning effort—otherwise there is no way of determining which information is relevant.

III

What then are the requirements of long-range planning? We cannot satisfy all of them as yet with any degree of competence; but we can specify them.

Indeed, we can—and should—give two sets of specifications: one in terms of the characteristics of the process itself; another in terms of its major and specific new-knowledge content.

1. Risk-taking entrepreneurial decisions, no matter whether made rationally or by tea-leaf reading, always embody the same eight elements:

a. *Objectives.* This is, admittedly, an elusive term, perhaps even a metaphysical one. It may be as difficult for Management Science to define "objectives" as it is for biology to define "life." Yet, we will be as unable to do without "objectives" as the biologists are unable to do without "life." Any entrepreneurial decision, let alone the integrated decision system we call a "long-range plan," has objectives, consciously or not.

b. *Assumptions.* These are what is believed by the people who make and carry out decisions to be "real" in the internal and external universe of the business.

c. *Expectations.* The future events or results considered likely or attainable. These three elements can be said to *define the decision.*

d. *Alternative courses of action.* There never is—indeed, in a true uncertainty situation there never can be—"one right decision." There cannot even be "one best decision." There are always "wrong decisions," that is, decisions inadequate to the objectives, incompatible with the assumptions, or grossly improbable in the light of the expectations. But once these have been eliminated, there will still be alternatives left—each a different configuration of objectives, assumptions, and expectations, each with its own risks and its own ratio between risks and rewards, each with its own impact, its specific efforts, and its own results. Every decision is thus a value judgment—it is not the "facts that decide"; people have to choose between imperfect alternatives on the basis of uncertain knowledge and fragmentary understanding.

Two alternatives deserve special mention, if only because they have to be considered in almost every case. One is the alternative of no action (which is, of course, what postponing a decision often amounts to); the other is the very important choice between adaptive and innovating action—each having risks that differ greatly in character though not necessarily in magnitude.

e. The next element in the decision-making process is the *decision itself.*

f. But there is no such thing as one isolated decision; every decision is, of necessity, part of a *decision structure.*

Every financial man knows, for instance, that the original capital appropriation on a new investment implies a commitment to future and usually larger capital appropriations which, however, are almost never as much as mentioned in the proposal submitted. Few of them seem to realize, however, that this implies not only a positive commitment but also, by mortgaging future capital resources, limits future freedom of action. The structuring impact of a decision is even greater in respect to allocations of scarce manpower, such as research people.

g. A decision is only pious intention unless it leads to action. Every decision, therefore, has an *impact stage.*

This impact always follows Newton's Second Law, so to speak; it consists of action and reaction. It requires effort. But it also dislocates. There is, therefore, always the question: what effort is required, by whom, and where? What must people know, what must they do, and what must they achieve? But there is also the question—generally neglected—what does this decision do to other areas? Where does it shift the burden, the weaknesses, and the . stress points; and what impact does it have on the outside; in the market, in the supply structure, in the community, and so on?

h. And, finally, there are *results*.

Each of these elements of the process deserves an entire book by itself. But I think I have said enough to show that both, the process itself and each element in it, are *rational*, no matter how irrational and arbitrary they may appear. Both the process and all its elements can therefore be defined, can be studied, and can be analyzed. And both can be improved through systematic and organized work. In particular, as in all rational processes, the entire process is improved and strengthened as we define, clarify, and analyze each of its constituent elements.

2. We can also, as said above, describe long-range planning in terms of its specific new-knowledge content. Among the areas where such new knowledge is particularly cogent, might be mentioned:

a. *The time dimensions of planning.* To say "long-range" or "short-range" planning implies that a given time span defines the planning; and this is actually how businesses look at it when they speak of a "five-year plan" or a "ten-year plan." But the essence of planning is to make present decisions with knowledge of their futurity. It is the futurity that determines the time span, and not vice versa.

Strictly speaking, short range and long range do not describe time spans but stages in every decision. "Short-range" is the stage before the decision has become fully effective, the stage during which it is only "costs" and not yet "results." The short-range of a decision to build a steel mill are the five years or so until the mill is in production. And the "long-range" of any decision is the period of expected performance needed to make the decision a successful one—the 20 or more years above break-even point operations in the case of the steel mill, for instance.

There are limitations on futurity. In business decisions the most precise mathematical statement is often that of my eighth grade teacher that parallels are two lines which do not meet this side of the school yard. Certainly, in the expectations and anticipations of a business the old rule of statistics usually applies that anything beyond 20 years equals infinity; and since expectations more than 20 years hence have normally a present value of zero, they should receive normally only a minimal allocation of present efforts and resources.

Yet it is also true that, if future results require a long gestation period, they will be obtained only if initiated early enough. Hence, long-range planning requires knowledge of futurity: What do we have to do today if we want to be some place in the future? What will not get done at all if we do not commit resources to it today? If we know that it takes 99 years to grow Douglas firs in the Northwest to pulping size, planting seedlings today is the only way we can provide for pulp supply in 99 years. Someone may well develop some speeding-up hormone; but we cannot bank on it if we are in the paper industry. It is quite conceivable, may indeed be highly probable, that we will use trees primarily as a source of chemicals long before these trees grow to maturity. We may even get the bulk of paper supply 30 years hence from less precious, less highly structured sources of cellulose than a tree, which is the most advanced chemical factory in the plant kingdom. This simply means, however, that our forests may put us into the chemical industry some time within the next 30 years; and we had better learn now something about chemistry. If our paper plants depend on Douglas fir, our planning cannot confine itself to 20 years but must consider 99 years. For we must be able to say whether we have to plant trees today, or whether we can postpone this expensive job.

But on other decisions even five years would be absurdly long. If our business is buying up distress merchandise and selling it at auction, then next week's clearance sale is "long-range future"; and anything beyond is largely irrelevant to us.

It is the nature of the business and the nature of the decision which determine the time spans of planning.

Yet the time spans are not static or "given." The time decision itself is the first and a highly important risk-taking decision in the planning process. It largely determines the allocation of resources and efforts. It largely determines the risks taken (and one cannot repeat too often that to postpone a decision is in itself a risk-taking and often irrevocable decision). Indeed, the time decision largely determines the character and nature of the business.

b. *Decision structure and configuration.*   The problem of the time dimension is closely tied in with that of decision structure.

Underlying the whole concept of long-range planning are two simple insights. We need an integrated decision structure for the business as a whole. There are really no isolated decisions on a product, or on markets, or on people. Each major risk-taking decision has impact throughout the whole; and no decision is isolated in time. Every decision is a move in a chess game, except that the rules of enterprise are by no means as clearly defined. There is no finite "board," and the pieces are neither as neatly distinguished nor as few in number. Every move opens some future opportunities for decision, and forecloses others. Every move, therefore, commits positively and negatively.

Let me illustrate these insights with a simple example, that of a major steel company today.

I posit that it is reasonably clear to any student of technology (not of steel technology but of technology in general) that steel-making is on the threshold of major technological change. *What* they are perhaps the steelmaker knows; but *that* they are I think any study of the pattern, rhythm, and I would say morphology of technological development, might indicate. A logical—rather than metallurgical—analysis of the process would even indicate *where* the changes are likely to occur. At the same time, the steel company faces the need of building new capacity if it wants to keep its share of the market, assuming that steel consumption will continue to increase. A decision to build a plant today, when there is nothing but the old technology available, means in effect that for 15 to 20 years the company cannot go into the new technology except at prohibitive cost. It is very unlikely, looking at the technological pattern, that these changes will be satisfied by minor modifications in existing facilities; they are likely to require new facilities to a large extent. By building today the company closes certain opportunities to itself, or at least it very greatly raises the future entrance price. At the same time, by making the decision to postpone building, it may foreclose other opportunities, such as market position, perhaps irrevocably. Management, therefore, has to understand—without perhaps too much detail—the location of this decision in the continuing process of entrepreneurial decision.

At the same time, entrepreneurial decisions must be fundamentally expedient decisions. It is not only impossible to know all the contingent effects of a decision, even for the shortest time period ahead. The very attempt to know them would lead to complete paralysis.

But the determination of what should be considered and what should be ignored, is in itself a difficult and consequential decision. We need knowledge to make it—I might say that we need a theory of entrepreneurial inference.

c. *The characteristics of risks.* It is not only magnitude of risk that we need to be able to appraise in entrepreneurial decisions. It is above all the character of the risk. Is it, for instance, the kind of risk we can afford to take, or the kind of risk we cannot afford to take? Or is it that rare but singularly important risk, the risk we cannot afford not to take—sometimes regardless of the odds?

The best General Electric scientists, we are told, advised their management in 1945 that it would be at least 40 years before nuclear energy could be used to produce electric power commercially. Yet General Electric—rightly—decided that it had to get into the atomic energy field. It could not afford not to take the risk as long as there was the remotest possibility that atomic energy would, after all, become a feasible source of electric power.

We know from experience that the risk we cannot afford not to take is like a "high-low" poker game. A middle hand will inevitably lose out. But we do not know why this is so. And the other, and much more common, kinds of risk we do not really understand at all.

d. *Finally, there is the area of measurements.* I do not have to explain . . . why measurements are needed in management, and especially for the organized entrepreneurial decisions we call "long-range planning."

But it should be said that in human institutions, such as a business enterprise, measurements, strictly speaking, do not and cannot exist. It is the definition of a measurement that it be impersonal and objective, that is, extraneous to the event measured. A child's growth is not dependent on the yardstick or influenced by being recorded. But any measurement in a business enterprise determines action—both on the part of the measurer and the measured—and thereby directs, limits, and causes behavior and performance of the enterprise. Measurement in the enterprise is always motivation, that is, moral force, as much as it is *ratio cognoscendi*.

In addition, in long-range planning we do not deal with observable events. We deal with future events, that is, with expectations. And expectations, being incapable of being observed, are never "facts" and cannot be measured.

Measurements, in long-range planning, thus present very real problems, especially conceptual ones. Yet precisely because what we measure and how we measure determines what will be considered relevant, and determines thereby not just what we see, but what we—and others—do, measurements are all-important in the planning process. Above all, unless we build expectations into the planning decision in such a way that we can very early realize whether they are actually fulfilled or not—including a fair understanding of what are significant deviations both in time and in scale—we cannot plan; and we have no feedback, no way of self-control in management.

We obviously also need for long-range planning *managerial* knowledge—the knowledge with respect to the operations of a business. We need such knowledge as that of the resources available, especially the human resources; their capacities and their limitations. We need to know how to "translate" from business needs, business results, and business decisions into functional capacity and specialized effort. There is, after all, no functional decision, there is not even functional data, just as there is no functional profit, no functional loss, no functional investment, no functional risk, no functional customer, no functional product, and no functional image of a company. There is only a unified company product, risk, investment, and so on, hence only company performance and company results. Yet at the same time the work obviously has to be done by people each of whom has to be specialized. Hence for a decision to be possible, we must be able to integrate divergent individual knowledges and capacities into one organization potential; and for a decision to be effective, we must be able to translate it into a diversity of individual and expert, yet focused efforts.

There are also big problems of knowledge in the entrepreneurial task that I have not mentioned—the problems of growth and change, for instance, or those of the moral values of a society and their meaning to business. But these are problems that exist for many areas and disciplines other than management.

And in this paper I have confined myself intentionally to knowledge that is specific to the process of long-range planning. Even so I have barely mentioned the main areas. But I think I have said enough to substantiate three conclusions:

1. Here are areas of genuine knowledge, not just areas in which we need data. What we need above all are basic theory and conceptual thinking.

2. The knowledge we need is new knowledge. It is not to be found in the traditional disciplines of business, such as accounting or economics. It is also not available, by and large, in the physical or life sciences. From the existing disciplines we can get a great deal of help, of course, especially in tools and techniques. And we need all we can get. But the knowledge we need is distinct and specific. It pertains not to the physical, the biological, or the psychological universe, though it partakes of them all. It pertains to the specific institution, the enterprise, which is a social institution existing in contemplation of human values. What is "knowledge" in respect to this institution, let alone what is "scientific," must therefore always be determined by reference to the nature, function, and purposes of this specific (and very peculiar) institution.

3. It is not within the decision of the entrepreneur whether he wants to make risk-taking decisions with long futurity; he makes them by definition. All that is within his power is to decide whether he wants to make them responsibly or irresponsibly, with a rational chance of effectiveness and success, or as blind gamble against all odds. And both because the process is essentially a rational process, and because the effectiveness of the entrepreneurial decisions depends on the understanding and voluntary efforts of others, the process will be the more responsible and the more likely to be effective, the more it is a rational, organized process based on knowledge.

IV

Long-range planning is risk-taking decision making. As such it is the responsibility of the policy maker, whether we call him entrepreneur or manager. To do the job rationally and systematically does not change this. Long-range planning does not "substitute facts for judgment," does not "substitute science for the manager." It does not even lessen the importance and role of managerial ability, courage, experience, intuition, or even hunch just as scientific biology and systematic medicine have not lessened the importance of these qualities in the individual physician. On the contrary, the systematic organization of the planning job and the supply of knowledge to it, should make more effective individual managerial qualities of personality and vision.

But at the same time long-range planning offers major opportunity and major challenge to Management Science and to the Management Scientist.[4] We need systematic study of the process itself and of every one of its elements. We need systematic work in a number of big areas of new knowledge—at least we need to know enough to organize our ignorance.

At the same time, long-range planning is the crucial area; it deals with the decisions which, in the last analysis, determine the character and the survival of the enterprise.

So far, it must be said, Management Science has not made much contribution to long-range planning. Sometimes one wonders whether those who call themselves "Management Scientists" are even aware of the risk-taking character of economic activity and of the resultant entrepreneurial job of long-range planning. Yet, in the long run, Management Science and Management Scientists may well, and justly, be judged by their ability to supply the knowledge and thinking needed to make long-range planning possible, simple, and effective.

NOTES AND REFERENCES

1. *Long-range planning* is not a term I like or would have picked myself. It is a misnomer—as are so many of our terms in economics and management, such as *capitalism, automation, operations research, industrial engineering,* or *depreciation.* But it is too late to do anything about the term; it has become common usage.
2. For a discussion see my book, *The Landmarks of Tomorrow* (New York: Harper & Row, 1958).
3. For a discussion of this "new organization," see again my *The Landmarks of Tomorrow,* mentioned above.
4. I would like to say here that I do not believe that the world is divided into "managers" and "management scientists." One man may well be both. Certainly, management scientists must understand the work and job of the manager, and vice versa. But conceptually and as a kind of work, the two are distinct.

9

Making Long-Range Company Planning Pay Off

George A. Steiner

This article makes a strong case for the importance of long-range planning to American companies. For those interested in prescriptions, the article outlines a series of "how to" steps designed to lead to effective plan development. Note particularly his first step—planning to plan.—Eds.

This article is devoted to a thumbnail sketch of two major aspects of long-range planning. First is the methodology or procedure for long-range planning. The second concerns the payoff to a company that does long-range planning.

I have chosen to dwell on these two points for several reasons. First, while long-range planning has grown rapidly in recent years and has paid off handsomely for many companies, there still are questions raised about its value. Second, while important progress has been made in the techniques of long-range planning, there are comparatively few detailed case studies and principles which are available for those who wish to initiate the process or improve their planning.

These two factors are related. I suspect, although solid proof is not available, that the major reason for the fact that more companies do not engage in long-range planning is that they do not know precisely how to go about it. Not wishing to admit this even to themselves, other reasons are given for the lack of long-range planning.[1]

WHAT IS LONG-RANGE PLANNING?

Planning, in general, is the conscious determination of courses of action to achieve preconceived objectives. It is deciding in advance what is to be done, when it is to be done, by whom it is to be done, and how it is to be done.

SOURCE: © 1962 by the Regents of the University of California. Reprinted from *California Management Review* IV, no. 2, pp. 28–41, by permission of the Regents.

It can range from the detailed, specific, and rigid to the broad, general, and flexible design.

Long-range planning does this for extended periods of time. Long-range planning is a process for establishing long-range goals; working out strategies, programs, and policies to achieve these goals; and setting up the necessary machinery to insure that the company gets where it wants to go.

It is a process of choosing from among alternative courses of action and charting the use of time, resources, and effort to achieve the objective sought. The further into the future the plan stretches the less detailed are its specific parts. The subject matter of long-range plans should cover products, services, facilities, manpower, research and development, organization, marketing, financial matters, and various aspects of management itself.[2]

HOW LONG IS LONG-RANGE?

How long a time should a long-range plan cover? The answer to this question is much like the response of Abraham Lincoln when asked how long a man's legs ought to be. "Long enough to reach the ground," said the President.

Similarly, the length of a planning period will vary considerably from company to company and subject to subject. It is not fixed or rigid. The time span of a plan should cover the period encompassing important financial commitments and their payoff.

For example, depending upon subject matter, coverage should embrace product development time and period of major financial impact following development; resource development time (e.g., sources of supply, management talent, or labor skills); and time required to develop physical facilities plus payoff period for major capital investments. For most businesses such factors will establish a minimum long-range planning period of from 5 to 10 years.

FORMAL LONG-RANGE PLANNING
IN INDUSTRY

All managers engage in long-range planning—if only to increase their own salaries. If they do not plan they are not doing their jobs. In the past, when top managers needed help in planning they often hired an assistant or created a vice president for administration.

Large and complex organizations centuries ago had staff positions for planning. Long-range planning, therefore, is not new. What is new is charging someone with full-time responsibility for planning and giving him a staff to do the job. It is the growth of planning departments and staff specialists at the top levels of corporations and major divisions that is new.

Pressures on American companies to establish such formal organizations have been most strong during the past 10 years. Among the major pressures are the following:

1. Business has become increasingly complex because of expanding enterprise size, decentralization of authority, diversification of product lines, mergers, and the growing sensitivity of internal operations to uncontrollable environmental forces.
2. Technological rates of change are increasing and placing a premium on those organizations which can foresee and adapt to them.
3. A variety of forces are squeezing profit margins.
4. End-use markets (domestic) are altering significantly and rapidly with geographic population shifts, changes in population composition, new social trends influencing market behavior of consumers, and growing competition for consumer savings.
5. End-use markets (abroad) are changing rapidly with new commercial alignments and efforts to industrialize the underdeveloped countries of the world.
6. There has been a rapid development of tools for planning and a growing recognition of the need for skilled technical competence to apply them to long-range planning. This trend promises to accelerate. In mind are not alone the new powerful mathematical tools which have been adapted to business decision making (e.g., linear programming, game theory, probability theory, etc.); but the application of computers, simulation and systems concepts, and new developments in economics, psychology, and other social sciences.
7. Competitors are devoting more attention to long-range planning.[3]

Under such pressures more and more companies in the past 10 years have been developing long-range planning programs and extending the field of inquiry further into the future. I believe, however, that effective long-range planning in industry is not as widespread as it ought to be.

Facts about the growth of formalized long-range planning are not plentiful nor reliable. *Nation's Business* concluded that about 20 percent of businesses had long-range planning in 1953, compared to about 50 percent in 1958.[4] The National Industrial Conference Board concluded in 1956 that of 189 manufacturing companies participating in its survey only one out of four had no formalized forward planning or failed to plan ahead beyond one year. About half of those having long-range plans said they included all the major elements of the enterprise in their planning. Only half said they placed much reliance on the plans.[5]

A survey made by *Management Methods* in 1958 revealed that, among its respondents, only 18 percent had formal advanced plans while another 52 percent had informal advanced plans. No advanced plans were made in

30 percent of the companies covered. When asked whether respondents felt they were doing as much advanced planning as they should, 72 percent replied in the negative. Practically all planning in companies in this survey was for five years or less.

Professors Sord and Welsch found in a study published in the same year that two thirds of the number surveyed had long-range plans, but the subject matter varied greatly. Two thirds had long-range sales plans, but only about one third had long-range research or expense plans. Only about half had long-range profit or cash plans. Practically all plans were for five years or less.[6]

These data, while not conclusive, are helpful. My own empirical observations, together with the data cited, lead me to conclude that, while formal long-range corporate planning has grown by leaps and bounds in the past 10 years, the practice is heavily concentrated in larger enterprises, and it is centered there on a few major problem areas (capital expenditures, product development, and sales) for periods less than 5 years. The coverage, time span, and usage is not great enough in light of potential value.

HOW TO MAKE A LONG-RANGE PLAN

In developing long-range plans it is helpful to think in terms of a series of steps. But, since the planner must always think in terms of retracing his thinking, allowance must also be made for some overlapping of these steps.

The sequence of steps presented in the next few paragraphs illustrates one concrete framework upon which a company may plan. It is flexible and has been used successfully. This particular sequence has the virtue of focusing attention on product which is usually, although not always, the principal theme of a business long-range plan.

The specific methodology of planning may vary much from one company to another whether or not the steps presented here are followed. This arises because the process must be flexible to accommodate an unusually complex intermeshing of variables which are subject to constant change. In mind are such factors as the technical knowledge and wisdom of the planners, the particular needs of the enterprise, the organization for planning, availability of strategic facts, subject-matter of the plans, and uses to be made of the results.[7]

First: Plan to Plan

First is *planning to plan.* As the Cleveland Electric Illuminating Company has so well documented, company planning must be planned.[8] This may seem as redundant as Cole Porter's "Begin the Beguine." But planning does not just happen. It must be planned!

A suitable planning climate must be established, and the organization made planning conscious. Policy decisions must be made about who will do what in planning. And, step-by-step procedures must be worked out. In one major planning program of a large corporation in which I participated, the first thing we did was to prepare a detailed letter covering the entire planning procedure for signature by the president. The letter was addressed to all parties involved. In this way everyone knew what was the plan to plan. The newer the plan the more important the thoroughness with which this step should be taken. But even where planning is well established the procedures should be carefully spelled out, as in, for example, the *Westinghouse Planning Guide*.[9]

On the other hand, care should be taken to avoid overdoing this step. It is easily possible to preplan too long, in too much detail, and to spend too much time on clarification of procedures. There is too much feedback in going through the sequences of planning to warrant more than just enough detail in this step to get the process moving.

Basic assumptions must be made at various stages in the planning process. At the outset, however, some of the overall assumptions upon which planning rests should be set forth. In mind, for example, are premises which provide a framework for planning, such as the course of the cold war, population movements, or competitors' activities.

Purely methodological premises may also be established, such as plans will be based upon constant, rather than actual anticipated, prices. But, whatever the premises determined, the point is that standards must be developed to guide the planning program. Otherwise, lack of coordination, unnecessary emphasis and study on less important subjects, excessive planning costs, and confusion in drawing conclusions are predictive consequences of poorly devised or neglected premises.

Second: Define Objectives

Second, *objectives of planning must be clearly specified*. The purpose of the plan, the objectives to be sought in the planning process, and the relation of planning goals to other goals and objectives in the enterprise must be clarified. Setting objectives provides the key to how planning will be done, the strategic factors to be emphasized in plan development, and methods by which planning will become the basis for action.

The objective of every business, of course, is to make a profit. Otherwise the business will not survive. But saying this is far from developing a set of goals which will best serve a company and its long-range planning program.

Be Specific.   Goals should be established as concretely as possible. What does this mean? Is the goal to be an aggregate absolute volume of profits? Is the goal to be expressed in terms of a percentage of sales? Is it to be in terms of percentage of investment? If it is return of investment, how is this to be calculated? Is it the E. I. du Pont de Nemours & Company or the

Monsanto Chemical Company formula? Will a rising rate of return on investment be accepted even if sales do not increase?

Is sales growth in itself a goal? Is sales stability a goal? How are conflicts among goals to be resolved? Are there other objectives which need to be expressed as a guide to the planning program?

Defining Corporate Goals. There has recently been a growing interest in defining corporate goals, probably in part as an outgrowth of long-range planning needs. Often-stated economic-type objectives, besides those mentioned in preceding paragraphs, are: growth, expressed in terms of sales, assets, employees, profits, or product line; stability, usually expressed in terms of sales, manpower, and profits; flexibility, expressed in numerous ways, such as ability to innovate, speed of response to new environment, especially competition; diversity in preparedness to compete; sensitivity to technological and market changes; and acquisition of a given status of technical skill.

Very frequently, goals express ethical or moral considerations. These are generally described in such terms as leadership of the firm in the industry, integrity and honesty in dealing with others, maintenance of amicable community relations, and assumption of social responsibilities with respect to community problems.[10]

Must Be Realistic. Long-range company goals should be given the greatest thought and formulated as realistically as possible. The validity of goals for planning should be tested upon the basis of past experience of the company and its industry, and future prospects for both. Unrealistic goals are not very helpful.

Sometimes an immediate problem will serve as the focal point for planning. If, for example, rate of return on stockholders' investment for a company has been well below the industry average for the past five years, the prime goal for the company planning may be to achieve the industry average or better.

Similarly, actual or anticipated trouble with a product may provide the basis for a concrete goal (e.g., "eliminate the product and substitute others," "undertake new research on the product to improve its salability," or "cut costs of the product by X percent of sales so it will attract a new level of demand").

Realistic projections of company operations must be placed against any goals established for the future. The difference between the two sets of numbers will reveal the magnitude of the tasks that lie ahead for the corporation. If, for example, a sales objective of 1,000,000 units is established for 5 years in the future, and 1,500,000 for 10 years ahead, and a realistic forecast shows 750,000 units in 1967 and 1,150,000 in 1972, the magnitude of the problem for the company is revealed.

Through this process long-range company goals should be established for sales, profits, capital requirements, new and old product requirements. Then, for each of these, the gap between aspirations and projections on present plans and trends must be measured or defined.

Third: Explore Possible Strategies

The third step is to *develop strategies to fill the major gaps*. The problem here is to bring to the foreground and examine the principal alternatives open to the company in filling the gaps and then to choose from among them those most acceptable. There obviously are many ways to do this.

In this step, companies must come face to face with major questions of policy. If there is a sales gap, for example, to what extent will it be filled with old products, by further penetration of old markets, or entrance into new markets? If this is not enough, to what extent should the old product be importantly modified by research? Where can and should costs be reduced or increased? Should new products be introduced? If so, should they be developed by the present company or acquired through merger? Should all new acquisitions have an affinity with present product lines, or is this not necessary?

While the central focus of planning is naturally on products, the question of strategies is not exclusively concerned with products. Strategies may be developed, for example, for management training, management succession, organization, investments of surplus cash, dividend policy, or public relations.

The precise steps to be followed in developing strategies to answer the kinds of questions given above obviously vary from case to case. One illustrative approach is as follows.

To begin, tentative alternative courses of action may be set forth for testing in the planning process. These may be suggested by managers at different levels. A planning group itself may, and probably will, think up alternative strategies. The planning process will apply several screenings to the suggestions, the sifting measures which will become more rigorous in successive planning stages.

It is also healthy and often indispensable to undertake an objective and honest appraisal of company strengths and weaknesses in relevant areas. For example, if a company is planning a diversification program, analysis is important in the following areas—management competence to digest proposed mergers; financial capability; marketing abilities for the new product; and, if stock is used to acquire a new company, the ability of the present management to continue control of the enterprise. Other areas of review might include basic research and engineering competence, advertising and promotion skills, labor relations, quality of management, capacity to control costs and production, and product and service acceptability.

Elemental, of course, is the build-up of information important in choosing between alternative courses of action. This is a critical stage in planning because it is frequently difficult to acquire reliable information about the most crucial strategic factors in decision making. It is most important at this stage to concentrate on the strategic data, or those which will have the most significance in choice conclusions.

The range of phenomena about which data should be collected is very wide. For a new product possibility, for example, the analysis may cover technological matters, ranging from projection of prospective scientific advances affecting the product to costs and timing of research, development, tests, and engineering for the product. There are many economic matters of interest, including market changes, possible demand at different pricing levels, estimated fixed and variable costs, break-even volume, prospective return on investment, and probabilities of profit amounts at different price-volume-cost ranges. Where applicable, there are also, of course, social, political, military, and internal administrative matters demanding attention.

The next step is to *select strategies from among alternative possibilities.* More or less simultaneously, four analytical processes merge at this point.

The first is the application, where appropriate, of new mathematical techniques to get a quantitative optimization of objectives.

The second is a modification of quantitative conclusions by a broad range of qualitative factors which will have a determining impact on final choices. Included in the latter, for example, would be estimates of what competitors are likely to do under given circumstances.

Break-even Calculations. Third, to the extent practicable, the financial impact of decisions should be measured individually and in their entirety. This should be done by the preparation of break-even calculations, cash flow analyses, and balance sheet and profit and loss statements. The detail of analysis should naturally be tailored to fit the need and importance of the data to the reliability of conclusions. Computer simulation, while not now used very extensively in this step, is a fourth process which promises to grow in importance.

The net results of this stage should be the development of strategies to fill the gaps apparent in step two. These broad plans of action should be either the best possible solutions to the problems or, at the very least, suitable ones. They should be tested for feasibility in terms of management, manpower, finances, competitor actions, technical expectations, and market acceptability. Broad magnitudes and timing should be established.

Resulting strategies can be broad or relatively narrow. One important aerospace company in the United States recently matched a frank appraisal of its strengths and weaknesses in various disciplines of knowledge used in the industry against prospective new product developments. It reasoned that it could not maintain strength in all the areas of knowledge which it now covered. The result was an increase in strength in some areas and an elimination of many other areas.

Some companies have decided to expand through merger, even though the resulting product line is heterogeneous. Other companies feel it a better strategy to acquire new products through merger only when there is a close relationship with present product line. Some companies mix these two strategies. Certain companies have decided to lead their industry in research and development. Others are content to follow.

A manufacturer of ceramics ware recently decided to concentrate only on products requiring advanced scientific and engineering skills and to abandon mass production of dinnerware. One electronics producer recently decided, following an agonizing appraisal, to abandon his computer line.

A medium-sized California food processor worked out a completely new detailed strategy for timing of annual sales promotion and new product development. A large oil company recently completed a detailed strategy covering its foreign investment program. These are illustrations of results from this step.

Fourth: Subplan to Fit Strategy

The fourth step in long-range planning is to *develop derivative operational plans*. A planning process is not complete until subsidiary plans are made to put into effect the strategies developed in step three. This seems elementary but is not always followed in practice. Decisions made without methods to carry them out are ineffective. The following cover the most important functional areas where derivative plans must be made.

Research and development programs should be supported, timed, and controlled to achieve the new product or other requirements needed to reach goals. These other requirements may, for example, include improving old products, reducing production costs, hiring new scientific skills, or increasing basic research.

Production programs should reflect digestion of new equipment, scheduling, new quality controls and inspection methods, and associated activities.

Marketing and promotion plans would, of course, include new selling efforts, advertising programs, reorganization of sales territories, pricing, and perhaps packaging.

Organizational changes may be required as a result of the new program which in turn, of course, needs detailed planning before implementation. Included here might be new management training programs.

Financial plans would include preparations for new equity financing or borrowing, budgeting of capital, and detailed financial forecasts to support the feasibility of the operational plans.

Parallel Planning.   An important feature of long-range planning is parallel planning. It would be a waste of time and resources to insist that production await engineering before beginning its derivative plans, or that marketing await production, or that organization await all of them. It is true that what is decided in one functional area will have a determining impact on other areas. But planning in all areas must proceed in parallel to the fullest extent practicable to save time. This can be accomplished by good communications in planning and sharpening of abilities to guess correctly what is going on in other functional areas that will affect planning in another area.

Naturally, the nearer-term plans should be sufficiently detailed to permit operations and control. For this purpose, detailed budgets or other planning and control techniques should be prepared. The further away in time the less detail should be needed or justified in terms of cost.

Fifth: Integrate Plans

The fifth and final step is to *assure the integration of long-range and short-range plans and to introduce the necessary controls to be sure operations take place in conformance with plans.*

Sequential Stages.   Short-range plans must, of course, be prepared in light of longer-range goals. Meshing the two can be accomplished by developing sequential stages to meet long-range goals, as, for example, promotion plans, the near-term aspects of which would be included in specific budgetary items. Where long-range plans are not specified in concrete terms, as, for example, outlines to improve the quality of management, the connection is looser.

In such instances, short-range plans should reflect the longer-range goals and policies set to achieve them. In some companies the problem of meshing short-range and long-range plans is accomplished by developing five-year plans in which the first year is the current operating budget.

The control process designed to insure that operations take place in conformance with plans extends too far beyond the planning function discussed in this paper and will not be treated here. It is perhaps unnecessary to say that plans which are not executed are only exercises. They may be important as exercises but they are not plans in the sense the term is used here. Reciprocally, efficient control of operations is rather difficult without the goals and standards of performance which plans establish.

Organization for Planning.   Too large a field of inquiry for extended treatment here is the subject of business practices and principles in organizing for long-range planning. But, since it has a direct bearing upon the way planning steps such as the above are performed, a few observations are in order.

First of all, organization for planning is not a simple matter of working out procedural or data flows. It must face the fundamental question of who is going to do what about basic decision making in an organization.

Boards of directors have superior authority, but there is great variation in the extent to which they choose to use this power. At E. I. du Pont de Nemours & Company, for example, the board has delegated great power to subcommittees of the board, principally the executive committee. Long-range planning at Du Pont centers in this group. In other companies, the board has delegated its planning powers to the president. In some, the president in turn has delegated his powers in varying degrees to committees, departments, or individuals.

Top Management Support.   Second, and closely associated with the above issue, long-range planning will be most useful and effective if the top executives of the company have confidence and faith in it. A long-range planning program is not likely to be of much value if the chief executives do not support it actively.

Third, rather widespread participation in the process should be encouraged, but not to the extent that timetables cannot be met, objectivity in analyzing facts is lost, or strategic decisions become known to too many people. Long-range plans are usually rather important to a great many people in an enterprise. Their participation in and execution of the plan will be enhanced if they can point to some contribution of theirs in it, or if they can find in it a goal worth striving for.

Effective planning requires decentralization. It is true that top management itself may define basic long-range planning strategies. But the execution of these programs requires effective coordination of many people. As Peter Drucker has pointed out, planning and doing are separate parts of the same job. They are not separate jobs. Planning proceeds best when both top management and operating people participate fully in it.

DOES PLANNING PAY OFF?

Determining payoff is a matter of relating the value of planning results to the costs of planning. Every planning program should be examined to determine the margin between value and cost. On the whole, payoff calculations are probably more easily determined for short-range than for long-range plans.

Long-range planning may not pay off for 5, 10, or more years. It is because of the difficulties in making cost-value calculations, together with the length of time needed to draw conclusions, that questions often arise about payoff for long-range planning.

"Extinct by Instinct"

Two extreme approaches seem to be taken by companies that either ignore or improperly face the question of payoff. One approach is to minimize costs by ignoring basic steps in planning. This method depends upon conclusions derived without encumbrances of carefully developed facts or lines of reasoning. For this approach the practitioner feels little need for a conscious and deliberate assessment of relevant considerations upon which judgments can be developed. In common parlance this is called "flying by the seat of your pants." I prefer to call it the road to becoming extinct by instinct.

"Paralysis by Analysis"

At the other extreme is overemphasis of value in relation to cost. With this approach there is recognition of the need for planning. An assignment is made to a dedicated hard-working soul with a reputation for thoroughness. Work is begun without much reference to the complexities of the task and before long a large number of people are involved at substantial cost.

Somewhere along the line, usually later than sooner, a voluminous report is prepared and promptly filed away "for future reference." Either the need for decision has long since passed or the report is too complex and bulky for busy people to read and digest. This I call the road to paralysis by analysis.[11]

Cost-Value Equation

For planning to pay off, a happy balance between the two extremes must be struck. The precise payoff for any particular planning operation is difficult to determine. No one can do this without examining the cost-value equation for that program. But planning has paid off for companies that have considered this equation and achieved the balance required.

The Stanford Research Institute studied the question "Why Companies Grow." One major conclusion of the study was that: "In the cases of both high-growth and low-growth companies, those that now support planning programs have shown a superior growth rate in recent years."[12]

The Stanford study observed that most companies with formalized planning programs were enthusiastic about their value. Well might they be if, partly as a result of planning, their growth rates have been exceptional. For these companies planning has clearly paid off.

Ford's Experience

Ernest Breech, former chairman of the board of the Ford Motor Company, has observed: "We believe it is our business, and that of other large companies, to make trends, not to follow them. A confident aggressive spirit, backed up by intelligent planning and hard-hitting management, can be contagious."[13] For Ford, planning has paid off handsomely as the last 10 years of that company's history will testify.

On the other hand, the path to bankruptcy is strewn with corpses who failed to plan or planned poorly. A study by the Bureau of Business Research at the University of Pittsburgh concluded that, among the 10 companies chosen for intensive study, every one was guilty of poor planning, and this shortcoming was the major cause of failure in the majority of cases.[14]

It is probably true that the only certainty about long-range planning is that the conclusions will prove to be in error. There is no such thing as 20/20 foresight. But, one great advantage of forward planning is that coming to grips with uncertainty by analysis and study should result in a reduction of the margin of doubt about the future. Despite the fog enshrouding the future, many companies have planned ahead and hit goals surprisingly accurately.

FORWARD PLANNING

Ralph Cordiner, commenting on this point in his book *New Frontiers for Professional Managers,* has observed that one of the three principal new horizons ahead for managers lies in the area of long-range planning. As he put it, "In a time of radical worldwide change, when every day introduces new elements of uncertainty, forward planning may seem to be nearly impossible—an exercise in futility. Yet there never was a more urgent need for long-range planning on the part of every business, and indeed every other important element of our national life."[15]

The argument is often presented that for large companies the choices for investing funds are many and necessitate advance planning. But, since a range of choice in investment of funds in a small single-product company does not exist for it, advance planning is a waste of time.

This idea is most erroneous. Small companies have just as great a need for long-range planning as large ones. They may not have the cash to support technical specialists, but there are other means to acquire the needed expertise. Many small companies, through long-range planning, have opened the door to successful expansion, new products, and new markets by multiplying ranges of desirable choices.

In considering payoff for long-range planning, value is generally considered to lie in the areas of improved profit stability, growth, more efficient sales, capital expenditure, inventory, research and development, or cost reduction programs. Or long-range planning may prove its worth in better management replacement and improvement programs; or some other tangible and concrete activities of the enterprise.

ANCILLARY BENEFITS

It should also be pointed out that a number of important ancillary and intangible benefits have accrued to companies having formal long-range planning programs. A brief list of them would include the following points. The planning process constitutes an excellent channel of communication throughout the organization. It identifies problems ahead for a firm long before they become acute. It focuses attention on the principal determinants of the business. It provides an organized mechanism for testing value judgments.

It opens new horizons for profitable study. It prevents piecemeal solutions to problems. It is a good training ground for future managers, and it brings to those responsible for running the business a comprehensive, coordinated, and uniform picture of present and future business.

CONCLUSIONS

Despite the phenomenal growth of formal long-range planning, and its important payoff to many companies, there are still too many companies that do not employ the process effectively. The reasons are often anchored in their lack of knowledge about how to do it, misunderstanding of its cost-value calculation, or both.

Five operational steps for long-range planning have been set forth and examined. They are recapitulated in graphic form (Table 1).

For long-range planning to pay off, a balance must be struck between minimizing cost by ignoring basic steps and principles of effective planning and incurring overly heavy cost by excessive analysis. While full benefits may not be derived for many years, efforts should be made to measure them and offset them against costs. This article has been devoted to the proposition that available knowledge about how to undertake long-range planning is quite sufficient, and full understanding of the cost-value equation is so pervasive, that all businesses, large and small, should have a more or less formal long-range planning program and reap rich rewards from it.

TABLE 1   Five Steps for Long-Range Planning

1—PLANNING TO PLAN

2—SPECIFYING OBJECTIVES OF ENTERPRISE
  • Forecasting future prospects.
  • Measuring the gaps between aspirations and projections.

3—DEVELOPING STRATEGIES
  • To fill in the major gaps.

4—DEVELOPING DERIVATIVE OR DETAILED PLANS IN MAJOR FUNCTIONAL AREAS TO FIT THE STRATEGIES
  • Research and development.
  • Production.
  • Marketing and promotion.

5—INTEGRATION OF LONG-RANGE AND SHORT-RANGE PLANS
  • Introducing necessary controls.

NOTES AND REFERENCES

(This article, translated into Italian, appeared abroad under the title "II rendimento della Programmazione d'impresa a lungo termine" in a recent issue of the *Rivista Internazionale di Scienze Economiche e Commerciali,* a periodical published by the Universita Bocconi in Milan. G.A.S.)

1. For example, other reasons given are: Our business is too cyclical. Our customers do not know their plans, so how can we know ours? Long-range planning is too vague. Not enough time exists for short-range planning, let alone long-range planning. We cannot afford specialists needed to do the job. It costs more than it is worth.

2. For other definitions, see George A. Steiner, "What Do We Know about Using Long-Range Plans?" *California Management Review,* Fall 1959; Peter F. Drucker, "Long-Range Planning, Challenge to Management Science," *Management Science,* April 1959; Bruce Payne and James H. Kennedy, "Making Long-Range Planning Work," *The Management Review,* February 1959; and William H. Newman and Charles E. Summer, Jr., *The Process of Management* (Englewood Cliffs, N.J.: Prentice-Hall, 1961), pp. 430–36.

3. See Charles E. Summer, Jr., "The Future Role of the Corporate Planner," *California Management Review,* Winter 1961.

4. "Planning Tomorrow's Profits," *Nation's Business,* August 1958.

5. "Long-Range Planning Pays Off," *Business Record,* October 1956.

6. Burnard H. Sord and Glenn A. Welsch, *Business Budgeting* (New York: Controllership Foundation, 1958).

7. For other operational planning sequences, see David W. Ewing, *Long-Range Planning for Management* (New York: Harper & Row, 1958); William E. Hill, "Planning for Profits: A Four-Stage Method," *California Management Review,* Spring 1959, which is a method much like that presented here; Bruce Payne and James H. Kennedy, "Making Long-Range Planning Work," *The Management Review,* February 1959; *Westinghouse Planning Guide,* Westinghouse Electric Corporation, 1959; *Guide to Profit Improvement Program,* American Brake Shoe Company, 1959; and Arthur W. Lucas and William G. Livingston, "Long-Range Planning and the Capital Appropriations Program," in *Financial Planning for Greater Profits,* American Management Association Report No. 44, 1960. For a detailed analytical planning sequence see Preston P. Le Breton and Dale A. Henning, *Planning Theory* (Englewood Cliffs, N.J.: Prentice-Hall, 1961).

8. Ralph M. Besse, "Company Planning Must Be Planned!" *Dun's Review,* April 1957.

9. See note 7.

10. See, for example, Stewart Thompson, *Management Creeds and Philosophies,* Research Study No. 32, American Management Association, New York, 1958; Richard Fells, *The Meaning of Modern Business,* chapter 6, "Corporate Goals" (New York: Columbia University Press, 1960); Peter Drucker, *The Practice of Management,* chapter 7, "The Objectives of a Business" (New York: Harper & Row, 1954); and George R. Terry, *Principles of Management,* chapter 9, "Management Objectives and Ethics" (Homewood, Ill.: Richard D. Irwin, 1956).

11. From Charles R. Schwartz, "The Return-on-Investment Concept as a Tool for Decision Making" in *Improving the Caliber of Company Management,* General Management Series, no. 183, American Management Association, 1956, p. 46.
12. N. R. Maines, *Why Companies Grow* (Palo Alto, Calif.: Stanford Research Institute, 1957), p. 4.
13. Ernest R. Breech, "Planning the Basic Strategy of a Large Business," in *Planning the Future Strategy of Your Business,* ed. Edward C. Bursk and Dan H. Fenn (New York: McGraw-Hill, 1956), p. 17.
14. A. M. Woodruff and T. G. Alexander, *Success and Failure in Small Manufacturing* (Pittsburgh: University of Pittsburgh Press, 1958), pp. 48 and 100.
15. Ralph Cordiner, *New Frontiers for Professional Managers* (New York: McGraw-Hill, 1956), p. 82.

B. Organizing

10

Of the Division of Labour

Adam Smith

Written at the beginnings of the Industrial Revolution, this selection, which details the organizations of a pin factory, is the best-known statement on the economic rationale for the factory system.—Eds.

The greatest improvement in the productive powers of labour, and the greater part of the skill, dexterity, and judgment with which it is any where directed, or applied, seem to have been the effects of the division of labour.

The effects of the division of labour, in the general business of society, will be more easily understood, by considering in what manner it operates in some particular manufactures. It is commonly supposed to be carried furthest in some very trifling ones; not perhaps that it really is carried further in them than in others of more importance: but in those trifling manufactures which are destined to supply the small wants of but a small number of people, the whole number of workmen must necessarily be small; and those employed in every different branch of the work can often be collected into the same workhouse, and placed at once under the view of the spectator. In those great manufactures, on the contrary, which are destined to supply the great wants of the great body of the people, every different branch of the work employs so great a number of workmen, that it is impossible to collect them all into the same workhouse. We can seldom see more, at one time, than those employed in one single branch. Though in such manufactures, therefore, the work may really be divided into a much greater number of parts, than in those of a more trifling nature, the division is not near so obvious, and has accordingly been much less observed.

To take an example, therefore, from a very trifling manufacture; but one in which the division of labour has been very often taken notice of, the trade of the pin-maker; a workman not educated to this business (which the

---

SOURCE: Adam Smith, *The Wealth of Nations* (1776), chapter 1.

division of labour has rendered a distinct trade), nor acquainted with the use of the machinery employed in it (to the invention of which the same division of labour has probably given occasion), could scarce, perhaps, with his utmost industry, make one pin in a day, and certainly could not make twenty. But in the way in which this business is now carried on, not only the whole work is a peculiar trade, but it is divided into a number of branches, of which the greater part are likewise peculiar trades. One man draws out the wire, another straights it, a third cuts it, a fourth points it, a fifth grinds it at the top for receiving the head; to make the head requires two or three distinct operations; to put it on, is a peculiar business, to whiten the pins is another; it is even a trade by itself to put them into the paper; and the important business of making a pin is, in this manner, divided into about eighteen distinct operations, which, in some manufactories, are all performed by distinct hands, though in others the same man will sometimes perform two or three of them. I have seen a small manufactory of this kind where ten men only were employed, and where some of them consequently performed two or three distinct operations. But though they were very poor, and therefore but indifferently accommodated with the necessary machinery, they could, when they exerted themselves, make among them about twelve pounds of pins in a day. There are in a pound upwards of four thousand pins of a middling size. Those ten persons, therefore, could make among them upwards of forty-eight thousand pins in a day. Each person, therefore, making a tenth part of forty-eight thousand pins, might be considered as making four thousand eight hundred pins in a day. But if they had all wrought separately and independently, and without any of them having been educated to this peculiar business, they certainly could not each of them have made twenty, perhaps not one pin in a day; that is, certainly, not the two hundred and fortieth, perhaps not the four thousand eight hundredth part of what they are at present capable of performing, in consequence of a proper division and combination of their different operations.

In every other art and manufacture, the effects of the division of labour are similar to what they are in this very trifling one; though, in many of them, the labour can neither be so much subdivided, nor reduced to so great a simplicity of operation. The division of labour, however, so far as it can be introduced, occasions, in every art, a proportionable increase of the productive powers of labour. The separation of different trades and employments from one another, seems to have taken place, in consequence of this advantage. This separation too is generally carried furthest in those countries which enjoy the highest degree of industry and improvement; what is the work of one man in a rude state of society, being generally that of several in an improved one. In every improved society, the farmer is generally nothing but a farmer; the manufacturer, nothing but a manufacturer. The labour too which is necessary to produce any one complete manufacture, is almost always divided among a great number of hands. How many different trades are employed in each branch of the linen and woollen manufactures, from the growers of the flax and the wool, to the bleachers and smoothers of the linen, or to the dyers and dressers of the cloth! The nature of agriculture, indeed, does not admit of so many subdivisions of labour, nor of so complete a separation of one business from another, as manufactures. It is impossible to separate so entirely, the business of the grazier from that of the corn-farmer, as the trade of the carpenter is commonly separated from that of the smith. The spinner is almost always a distinct person from the weaver; but the ploughman, the harrower, the sower of the seed, and the reaper of the corn, are often the same. The occasions for those different sorts of labour returning with the different seasons of the year, it is impossible that one man should be constantly employed in any one of them. This impossibility of making so complete and entire a separation of all the different branches of labour employed in agriculture, is perhaps the reason why the improvement of the productive powers of labour in this art, does not always keep pace with their improvement in manufactures. The most opulent nations, indeed, generally excel all their neighbours in agriculture as well as in manufactures; but they are commonly more distinguished by their superiority in the latter than in the former. Their lands are in general better cultivated, and having more labour and expence bestowed upon them, produce more in proportion to the extent and natural fertility of the ground. But this superiority of produce is seldom much more than in proportion to the superiority of labour and expence. In agriculture, the labour of the rich country is not always much more productive than that of the poor; or, at least, it is never so much more productive, as it commonly is in manufactures. The corn of the rich country, therefore, will not always, in the same degree of goodness, come cheaper to market than that of the poor. The corn of Poland, in the same degree of goodness, is as cheap as that of France, notwithstanding the superior opulence and improvement of the latter country. The corn of France is, in the corn provinces, fully as good, and in most years nearly about the same price with the corn of England, though, in opulence and improvement, France is perhaps inferior to England. The corn-lands of England, however, are better cultivated than those of France, and the corn-lands of France are said to be much better cultivated than those of Poland. But though the poor country, notwithstanding the inferiority of its cultivation, can, in some measure, rival the rich in the cheapness and goodness of its corn, it can pretend to no such competition in its manufactures; at least if those manufactures suit the soil, climate, and situation of the rich country. The silks of France are better and cheaper than those of England, because the silk manufacture, at least under the present high duties upon the importation of raw silk, does not so well suit the climate of England as that of France. But the hard-ware and the coarse woollens of England are beyond all comparison superior to those of France, and much cheaper too in the same degree of goodness. In Poland there are said to be scarce any manufactures of any kind, a few of those coarser household manufactures excepted, without which no country can well subsist.

This great increase of the quantity of work, which, in consequence of the division of labour, the same number of people are capable of performing, is owing to three different circumstances; first, to the increase of dexterity in every particular workman; secondly, to the saving of the time which is commonly lost in passing from one species of work to another; and lastly, to the invention of a great number of machines which facilitate and abridge labour, and enable one man to do the work of many.

First, the improvement of the dexterity of the workman necessarily increases the quantity of the work he can perform; and the division of labour, by reducing every man's business to some one simple operation, and by making this operation the sole employment of his life, necessarily increases very much the dexterity of the workman. A common smith, who, though accustomed to handle the hammer, has never been used to make nails, if upon some particular occasion he is obliged to attempt it, will scarce, I am assured, be able to make above two or three hundred nails in a day, and those too very bad ones. A smith who has been accustomed to make nails, but whose sole or principal business has not been that of a nailer, can seldom with his utmost diligence make more than eight hundred or a thousand nails in a day. I have seen several boys under twenty years of age who had never exercised any other trade but that of making nails, and who, when they exerted themselves, could make, each of them, upwards of two thousand three hundred nails in a day. The making of a nail, however, is by no means one of the simplest operations. The same person blows the bellows, stirs or mends the fire as there is occasion, heats the iron, and forges every part of the nail: In forging the head too he is obliged to change his tools. The different operations into which the making of a pin, or of a metal button, is subdivided, are all of them much more simple, and the dexterity of the person, of whose life it has been the sole business to perform them, is usually much greater. The rapidity with which some of the operations of those manufactures are performed, exceeds what the human hand could, by those who had never seen them, be supposed capable of acquiring.

Secondly, the advantage which is gained by saving the time commonly lost in passing from one sort of work to another, is much greater than we should at first view be apt to imagine it. It is impossible to pass very quickly from one kind of work to another, that is carried on in a different place, and with quite different tools. A country weaver, who cultivates a small farm, must lose a good deal of time in passing from his loom to the field, and from the field to his loom. When the two trades can be carried on in the same workhouse, the loss of time is no doubt much less. It is even in this case, however, very considerable. A man commonly saunters a little in turning his hand from one sort of employment to another. When he first begins the new work he is seldom very keen and hearty; his mind, as they say, does not go to it, and for some time he rather trifles than applies to good purpose. The habit of sauntering and of indolent careless application, which is naturally, or rather necessarily acquired by every country workman who is obliged to change his work and his tools every half hour, and to apply his hand in twenty different ways almost every day of his life; renders him almost always slothful and lazy, and incapable of any vigorous application even on the most pressing occasions. Independent, therefore, of his deficiency in point of dexterity, this cause alone must always reduce considerably the quantity of work which he is capable of performing.

Thirdly, and lastly, every body must be sensible how much labour is facilitated and abridged by the application of proper machinery. It is unnecessary to give any example. I shall only observe, therefore, that the invention of all those machines by which labour is so much facilitated and abridged, seems to have been originally owing to the division of labour. Men are much more likely to discover easier and readier methods of attaining any object, when the whole attention of their minds is directed towards that single object, than when it is dissipated among a great variety of things. But in consequence of the division of labour, the whole of every man's attention comes naturally to be directed towards some one very simple object. It is naturally to be expected, therefore, that some one or other of those who are employed in each particular branch of labour should soon find out easier and readier methods of performing their own particular work, wherever the nature of it admits of such improvement. A great part of the machines made use of in those manufactures in which labour is most subdivided, were originally the inventions of common workmen, who, being each of them employed in some very simple operation, naturally turned their thoughts towards finding out easier and readier methods of performing it. Whoever has been much accustomed to visit such manufactures, must frequently have been shewn very pretty machines, which were the inventions of such workmen, in order to facilitate and quicken their own particular part of the work. In the first fire-engines, a boy was constantly employed to open and shut alternately the communication between the boiler and the cylinder, according as the piston either ascended or descended. One of those boys, who loved to play with his companions, observed that, by tying a string from the handle of the valve which opened this communication to another part of the machine, the valve would open and shut without his assistance, and leave him at liberty to divert himself with his play-fellows. One of the greatest improvements that has been made upon this machine, since it was first invented, was in this manner the discovery of a boy who wanted to save his own labour.

All the improvements in machinery, however, have by no means been the inventions of those who had occasion to use the machines. Many improvements have been made by the ingenuity of the makers of the machines, when to make them become the business of a peculiar trade; and some by that of those who are called philosophers or men of speculation, whose trade it is not to do any thing, but to observe every thing; and who, upon that account, are often capable of combining together the powers of the most distant and dissimilar objects. In the progress of society, philosophy or speculation becomes, like every other employment, the principal or sole trade and occupation of a particular class of citizens. Like every other employment too, it is subdivided into a great number of different branches, each of which affords occupation to a peculiar tribe or class of philosophers; and this subdivision of employment in philosophy, as well as in every other business, improves dexterity, and saves time. Each individual becomes more expert in his own peculiar branch, more work is done upon the whole, and the quantity of science is considerably increased by it.

It is the great multiplication of the productions of all the different arts, in consequence of the division of labour, which occasions, in a well-governed society, that universal opulence which extends itself to the lowest ranks of the people. Every workman has a great quantity of his own work to dispose of beyond what he himself has occasion for; and every other workman being exactly in the same situation, he is enabled to exchange a great quantity of his own goods for a great quantity, or, what comes to the same thing, for the price of a great quantity of theirs. He supplies them abundantly with what they have occasion for, and they accommodate him as amply with what he has occasion for, and a general plenty diffuses itself through all the different ranks of the society.

Observe the accommodation of the most common artificer or day-labourer in a civilized and thriving country, and you will perceive that the number of people of whose industry a part, though but a small part, has been employed in procuring him this accommodation, exceeds all computation. The woollen coat, for example, which covers the day-labourer, as course and rough as it may appear, is the produce of the joint labour of a great multitude of workmen. The shepherd, the sorter of the wool, the wool-comber or carder, the dyer, the scribbler, the spinner, the weaver, the fuller, the dresser, with many others, must all join their different arts in order to complete even this homely production. How many merchants and carriers, besides, must have been employed in transporting the materials from some of those workmen to others who often live in a very distant part of the country! how much commerce and navigation in particular, how many ship-builders, sailors, sail-makers, rope-makers, must have been employed in order to bring together the different drugs made use of by the dyer, which often come from the remotest corners of the world! What a variety of labour too is necessary in order to produce the tools of the meanest of those workmen! To say nothing of such complicated machines as the ship of the sailor, the mill of the fuller, or even the loom of the weaver, let us consider only what a variety of labour is requisite in order to form that very simple machine, the shears with which the shepherd clips the wool. The miner, the builder of the furnace for smelting the ore, the feller of the timber, the burner of the charcoal to be made use of in the smelting-house, the brick-maker, the brick-layer, the workmen who attend the furnace, the mill-wright, the forger, the smith, must all of them join their different arts in order to produce them. Were we to examine, in the same manner, all the different parts of his dress and household furniture, the coarse linen shirt which he wears next his skin, the shoes which cover his feet, the bed which he lies on, and all the different parts which compose it, the kitchen-grate at which he prepares his victuals, the coals which he makes use of for that purpose, dug from the bowels of the earth, and brought to him perhaps by a long sea and a long land carriage, all the other utensils of his kitchen, all the furniture of his table, the knives and forks, the earthen or pewter plates upon which he serves up and divides his victuals, the different hands employed in preparing his bread and his beer, the glass window which lets in the heat and the light, and keeps out the wind and the rain, with all the knowledge and art requisite for preparing that beautiful and happy invention, without which these northern parts of the world could scarce have afforded a very comfortable habitation, together with the tools of all the different workmen employed in producing those different conveniencies; if we examine, I say, all these things, and consider what a variety of labour is employed about each of them, we shall be sensible that without the assistance and co-operation of many thousands, the very meanest person in a civilized country could not be provided, even according to, what we very falsely imagine, the easy and simple manner in which he is commonly accommodated. Compared, indeed, with the more extravagant luxury of the great, his accommodation must no doubt appear extremely simple and easy; and yet it may be true, perhaps, that the accommodation of an European prince does not always so much exceed that of an industrious and frugal peasant, as the accommodation of the latter exceeds that of many an African king. . . .

11

Organization Theory: An Overview and an Appraisal

William G. Scott

Organizing the organization is what organization theory is all about. In this article William Scott identifies three theories of organization which have had considerable impact on management thought and practice: classical, neoclassical, and modern. The article makes a cogent argument for unification of elements of all three theories.—Eds.

Man is intent on drawing himself into a web of collectivized patterns. "Modern man has learned to accommodate himself to a world increasingly organized. The trend toward ever more explicit and consciously drawn relationships is profound and sweeping; it is marked by depth no less than by extension."[1] This comment by Seidenberg nicely summarizes the pervasive influence of organization in many forms of human activity.

Some of the reasons for intense organizational activity are found in the fundamental transitions which revolutionized our society, changing it from a rural culture to a culture based on technology, industry, and the city. From these changes, a way of life emerged characterized by the *proximity* and *dependency* of people on each other. Proximity and dependency, as conditions of social life, harbor the threats of human conflict, capricious antisocial behavior, instability of human relationships, and uncertainty about the nature of the social structure with its concomitant roles.

Of course, these threats to social integrity are present to some degree in all societies, ranging from the primitive to the modern. But, these threats become dangerous when the harmonious functioning of a society rests on the maintenance of a highly intricate, delicately balanced form of human collaboration. The civilization we have created depends on the preservation of a precarious balance. Hence, disrupting forces impinging on this shaky form of collaboration must be eliminated or minimized.

SOURCE: Reprinted by permission of the author and publisher from "Organization Theory: An Overview and an Appraisal," *The Academy of Management Journal*, April 1961, pp. 7–26.

Traditionally, organization is viewed as a vehicle for accomplishing goals and objectives. While this approach is useful, it tends to obscure the inner workings and internal purposes of organization itself. Another fruitful way of treating organization is as a mechanism having the ultimate purpose of offsetting those forces which undermine human collaboration. In this sense, organization tends to minimize conflict, and to lessen the significance of individual behavior which deviates from values that the organization has established as worthwhile. Further, organization increases stability in human relationships by reducing uncertainty regarding the nature of the system's structure and the human roles which are inherent to it. Corollary to this point, organization enhances the predictability of human action, because it limits the number of behavioral alternatives available to an individual. As Presthus points out:

> Organization is defined as a system of structural interpersonal relations. . . . individuals are differentiated in terms of authority, status, and role with the result that personal interaction is prescribed. . . . Anticipated reactions tend to occur, while ambiguity and spontaneity are decreased.[2]

In addition to all of this, organization has built-in safeguards. Besides prescribing acceptable forms of behavior for those who elect to submit to it, organization is also able to counterbalance the influence of human action which transcends its established patterns.[3]

Few segments of society have engaged in organizing more intensively than business.[4] The reason is clear. Business depends on what organization offers. Business needs a system of relationships among functions; it needs stability, continuity, and predictability in its internal activities and external contacts. Business also appears to need harmonious relationships among the people and processes which make it up. Put another way, a business organization has to be free, relatively, from destructive tendencies which may be caused by divergent interests.

As a foundation for meeting these needs rests administrative science. A major element of this science is organization theory, which provides the grounds for management activities in a number of significant areas of business endeavor. Organization theory, however, is not a homogeneous science based on generally accepted principles. Various theories of organization have been, and are being evolved. For example, something called "modern organization theory" has recently emerged, raising the wrath of some traditionalists, but also capturing the imagination of a rather elite avant-garde.

The thesis of this paper is that modern organization theory, when stripped of its irrelevancies, redundancies, and "speech defects," is a logical and vital evolution in management thought. In order for this thesis to be supported, the reader must endure a review and appraisal of more traditional forms of organization theory which may seem elementary to him.

In any event, three theories of organization are having considerable influence on management thought and practice. They are arbitrarily labeled in this paper as the classical, the neoclassical, and the modern. Each of these is fairly distinct; but they are not unrelated. Also, these theories are ongoing, being actively supported by several schools of management thought.

THE CLASSICAL DOCTRINE

For lack of a better method of identification, it will be said that the classical doctrine deals almost exclusively with the _anatomy of formal organization._ This doctrine can be traced back to Frederick W. Taylor's interest in functional foremanship and planning staffs. But most students of management thought would agree that in the United States, the first systematic approach to organization, and the first comprehensive attempt to find organizational universals, is dated 1931 when Mooney and Reiley published _Onward Industry._[5] Subsequently, numerous books, following the classical vein, have appeared. Two of the more recent are Brech's _Organization_[6] and Allen's _Management and Organization._[7]

Classical organization theory is built around four key pillars. They are the division of labor, the scalar and functional processes, structure, and span of control. Given these major elements just about all of classical organization theory can be derived.

1. _The division of labor_ is without doubt the cornerstone among the four elements.[8] From it the other elements flow as corollaries. For example, _scalar_ and _functional_ growth requires specialization and departmentalization of functions. Organization _structure_ is naturally dependent upon the direction which specialization of activities travels in company development. Finally, _span of control_ problems result from the number of specialized functions under the jurisdiction of a manager.

2. _The scalar and functional processes_ deal with the vertical and horizontal growth of the organization, respectively.[9] The scalar process refers to the growth of the chain of command, the delegation of authority and responsibility, unity of command, and the obligation to report.

The division of the organization into specialized parts and the regrouping of the parts into compatible units are matters pertaining to the functional process. This process focuses on the horizontal evolution of the line and staff in a formal organization.

3. _Structure_ is the logical relationships of functions in an organization, arranged to accomplish the objectives of the company efficiently. Structure implies system and pattern. Classical organization theory usually works with two basic structures, the line and the staff. However, such activities as committee and liaison functions fall quite

readily into the purview of structural considerations. Again, structure is the vehicle for introducing logical and consistent relationships among the diverse functions which comprise the organization.[10]

4. *The span of control* concept relates to the number of subordinates a manager can effectively supervise. Graicunas has been credited with first elaborating the point that there are numerical limitations to the subordinates one man can control.[11] In a recent statement on the subject, Brech points out, "span" refers to ". . . the number of persons, themselves carrying managerial and supervisory responsibilities, for whom the senior manager retains his overembracing responsibility of direction and planning, coordination, motivation, and control."[12] Regardless of interpretation, span of control has significance, in part, for the shape of the organization which evolves through growth. Wide span yields a flat structure; short span results in a tall structure. Further, the span concept directs attention to the complexity of human and functional interrelationships in an organization.

It would not be fair to say that the classical school is unaware of the day-to-day administrative problems of the organization. Paramount among these problems are those stemming from human interactions. But the interplay of individual personality, informal groups, intraorganizational conflict, and the decision-making processes in the formal structure appears largely to be neglected by classical organization theory. Additionally, the classical theory overlooks the contributions of the behavioral sciences by failing to incorporate them in its doctrine in any systematic way. In summary, classical organization theory has relevant insights into the nature of organization, but the value of this theory is limited by its narrow concentration on the formal anatomy of organization.

NEOCLASSICAL THEORY OF ORGANIZATION

The neoclassical theory of organization embarked on the task of compensating for some of the deficiencies in classical doctrine. The neoclassical school is commonly identified with the human relations movement. Generally, the neoclassical approach takes the postulates of the classical school, regarding the pillars of organization as givens. But these postulates are regarded as modified by people, acting independently or within the context of the informal organization.

One of the main contributions of the neoclassical school is the introduction of behavioral sciences in an integrated fashion into the theory of organization. Through the use of these sciences, the human relationists demonstrate how the pillars of the classical doctrine are affected by the impact of human actions. Further, the neoclassical approach includes a systematic treatment of the informal organization, showing its influence on the formal structure.

Thus, the neoclassical approach to organization theory gives evidence of accepting classical doctrine, but superimposing on it modifications resulting from individual behavior, and the influence of the informal group. The inspiration of the neoclassical school was the Hawthorne studies.[13] Current examples of the neoclassical approach are found in human relations books like Gardner and Moore, *Human Relations in Industry,*[14] and Davis, *Human Relations in Business.*[15] To a more limited extent, work in industrial sociology also reflects a neoclassical point of view.[16]

It would be useful to look briefly at some of the contributions made to organization theory by the neoclassicists. First to be considered are modifications of the pillars of classical doctrine; second is the informal organization.

Examples of the Neoclassical Approach to the Pillars of Formal Organization Theory

1. The *division of labor* has been a long-standing subject of comment in the field of human relations. Very early in the history of industrial psychology, a study was made of industrial fatigue and monotony caused by the specialization of the work.[17] Later, attention shifted to the isolation of the worker, and his feeling of anonymity resulting from insignificant jobs which contributed negligibly to the final product.[18]

Also, specialization influences the work of management. As an organization expands, the need concomitantly arises for managerial motivation and coordination of the activities of others. Both motivation and coordination in turn relate to executive leadership. Thus, in part, stemming from the growth of industrial specialization, the neoclassical school has developed a large body of theory relating to motivation, coordination, and leadership. Much of this theory is derived from the social sciences.

2. Two aspects of the *scalar and functional* processes which have been treated with some degree of intensity by the neoclassical school are the delegation of authority and responsibility, and gaps in or overlapping of functional jurisdictions. The classical theory assumes something of perfection in the delegation and functionalization processes. The neoclassical school points out that human problems are caused by imperfections in the way these processes are handled.

For example, too much or insufficient delegation may render an executive incapable of action. The failure to delegate authority and responsibility equally may result in frustration for the delegatee. Overlapping of authorities often causes clashes in personality. Gaps in authority cause failures in getting jobs done, with one party blaming the other for shortcomings in performance.[19]

The neoclassical school says that the scalar and functional processes are theoretically valid, but tend to deteriorate in practice. The ways in which they break down are described, and some of the human causes are pointed out. In addition the neoclassicists make recommendations, suggesting various "human tools" which will facilitate the operation of these processes.

3. *Structure* provides endless avenues of analysis for the neoclassical theory of organization. The theme is that human behavior disrupts the best laid organizational plans and thwarts the cleanness of the logical relationships founded in the structure. The neoclassical critique of structure centers on frictions which appear internally among people performing different functions.

Line and staff relations is a problem area, much discussed, in this respect. Many companies seem to have difficulty keeping the line and staff working together harmoniously. Both Dalton[20] and Juran[21] have engaged in research to discover the causes of friction, and to suggest remedies.

Of course, line-staff relations represent only one of the many problems of structural frictions described by the neoclassicists. As often as not, the neoclassicists will offer prescriptions for the elimination of conflict in structure. Among the more important harmony-rendering formulae are participation, junior boards, bottom-up management, joint committees, recognition of human dignity, and "better" communication.

4. An executive's *span of control* is a function of human determinants, and the reduction of span to a precise, universally applicable ratio is silly, according to the neoclassicists. Some of the determinants of span are individual differences in managerial abilities, the type of people and functions supervised, and the extent of communication effectiveness.

Coupled with the span of control question are the human implications of the type of structure which emerges. That is, is a tall structure with a short span or a flat structure with a wide span more conducive to good human relations and high morale? The answer is situational. Short span results in tight supervision; wide span requires a good deal of delegation with looser controls. Because of individual and organizational differences, sometimes one is better than the other. There is a tendency to favor the looser form of organization, however, for the reason that tall structures breed autocratic leadership, which is often pointed out as a cause of low morale.[22]

The Neoclassical View of the Informal Organization

Nothing more than the barest mention of the informal organization is given even in the most recent classical treatises on organization theory.[23] Systematic discussion of this form of organization has been left to the neoclassicists. The informal organization refers to people in group associations at work, but these associations are not specified in the "blueprint" of the formal organization. The informal organization means natural groupings of people in the work situation.

In a general way, the informal organization appears in response to the social need—the need of people to associate with others. However, for analytical purposes, this explanation is not particularly satisfying. Research has produced the following, more specific determinants underlying the appearance of informal organizations.

1. The *location* determinant simply states that in order to form into groups of any lasting nature, people have to have frequent face-to-face contact. Thus, the geography of physical location in a plant or office is an important factor in predicting who will be in what group.[24]

2. *Occupation* is a key factor determining the rise and composition of informal groups. There is a tendency for people performing similar jobs to group together.[25]

3. *Interests* are another determinant for informal group formation. Even though people might be in the same location, performing similar jobs, differences of interest among them explain why several small, instead of one large, informal organizations emerge.

4. *Special issues* often result in the formation of informal groups, but this determinant is set apart from the three previously mentioned. In this case, people who do not necessarily have similar interests, occupations, or locations may join together for a common cause. Once the issue is resolved, then the tendency is to revert to the more "natural" group forms.[26] Thus, special issues give rise to a rather impermanent informal association; groups based on the other three determinants tend to be more lasting.

When informal organizations come into being they assume certain characteristics. Since understanding these characteristics is important for management practice, they are noted below:

1. Informal organizations act as agencies of *social control.* They generate a culture based on certain norms of conduct which, in turn, demands conformity from group members. These standards may be at odds with the values set by the formal organization. So an individual may very well find himself in a situation of conflicting demands.

2. The form of human interrelationships in the informal organization requires *techniques of analysis* different from those used to plot the relationships of people in a formal organization. The method used for determining the structure of the informal group is called sociometric analysis. Sociometry reveals the complex structure of interpersonal relations which is based on premises fundamentally unlike the logic of the formal organization.

3. Informal organizations have *status and communication* systems peculiar to themselves, not necessarily derived from the formal systems. For example, the grapevine is the subject of much neoclassical study.

4. Survival of the informal organization requires stable continuing relationships among the people in them. Thus, it has been observed that the informal organization *resists change*.[27] Considerable attention is given by the neoclassicists to overcoming informal resistance to change.

5. The last aspect of analysis which appears to be central to the neoclassical view of the informal organization is the study of the *informal leader*. Discussion revolves around who the informal leader is, how he assumes this role, what characteristics are peculiar to him, and how he can help the manager accomplish his objectives in the formal organization.[28]

This brief sketch of some of the major facets of informal organization theory has neglected, so far, one important topic treated by the neoclassical school. It is the way in which the formal and informal organizations interact.

A conventional way of looking at the interaction of the two is the "live and let live" point of view. Management should recognize that the informal organization exists, nothing can destroy it, and so the executive might just as well work with it. Working with the informal organization involves not threatening its existence unnecessarily, listening to opinions expressed for the group by the leader, allowing group participation in decision-making situations, and controlling the grapevine by prompt release of accurate information.[29]

While this approach is management centered, it is not unreasonable to expect that informal group standards and norms could make themselves felt on formal organizational policy. An honestly conceived effort by managers to establish a working relationship with the informal organization could result in an association where both formal and informal views would be reciprocally modified. The danger which at all costs should be avoided is that "working with the informal organization" does not degenerate into a shallow disguise for human manipulation.

Some neoclassical writing in organization theory, especially that coming from the management-oriented segment of this school, gives the impression that the formal and informal organizations are distinct, and, at times, quite irreconcilable factors in a company. The interaction which takes place between the two is something akin to the interaction between the company and a labor union, or a government agency, or another company.

The concept of the social system is another approach to the interactional climate. While this concept can be properly classified as neoclassical, it borders on the modern theories of organization. The phrase "social system" means that an organization is a complex of mutually interdependent, but variable, factors.

These factors include individuals and their attitudes and motives, jobs, the physical work setting, the formal organization, and the informal organizations. These factors, and many others, are woven into an overall pattern of interdependency. From this point of view, the formal and informal organizations lose their distinctiveness, but find real meaning, in terms of human behavior, in the operation of the system as a whole. Thus, the study of organization turns away from descriptions of its component parts, and is refocused on the system of interrelationships among the parts.

One of the major contributions of the Hawthorne studies was the integration of Pareto's idea of the social system into a meaningful method of analysis for the study of behavior in human organizations.[30] This concept is still vitally important. But unfortunately some work in the field of human relations undertaken by the neoclassicists has overlooked, or perhaps discounted, the significance of this consideration.[31]

The fundamental insight regarding the social system, developed and applied to the industrial scene by the Hawthorne researchers, did not find much extension in subsequent work in the neoclassical vein. Indeed, the neoclassical school after the Hawthorne studies generally seemed content to engage in descriptive generalizations, or particularized empirical research studies which did not have much meaning outside their own context.

The neoclassical school of organization theory has been called bankrupt. Criticisms range from, "human relations is a tool for cynical puppeteering of people," to "human relations is nothing more than a trifling body of empirical and descriptive information." There is a good deal of truth in both criticisms, but another appraisal of the neoclassical school of organization theory is offered here. The neoclassical approach has provided valuable contributions to lore of organization. But, like the classical theory, the neoclassical doctrine suffers from incompleteness, a shortsighted perspective, and lack of integration among the many facets of human behavior studied by it. Modern organization theory has made a move to cover the shortcomings of the current body of theoretical knowledge.

MODERN ORGANIZATION THEORY

The distinctive qualities of modern organization theory are its conceptual-analytical base, its reliance on empirical research data, and, above all, its integrating nature. These qualities are framed in a philosophy which accepts the premise that the only meaningful way to study organization is to study it as a system. As Henderson put it, the study of a system must rely on a method of analysis, ". . . involving the simultaneous variations of mutually dependent variables."[32] Human systems, of course, contain a huge number of dependent variables which defy the most complex simultaneous equations to solve.

Nevertheless, system analysis has its own peculiar point of view which aims to study organization in the way Henderson suggests. It treats organization as a system of mutually dependent variables. As a result, modern organization theory, which accepts system analysis, shifts the conceptual level of organization study above the classical and neoclassical theories. Modern organization theory asks a range of interrelated questions which are not seriously considered by the two other theories.

Key among these questions are: (1) What are the strategic parts of the system? (2) What is the nature of their mutual dependency? (3) What are the main processes in the system which link the parts together, and facilitate their adjustment to each other? (4) What are the goals sought by systems?[33]

Modern organization theory is in no way a unified body of thought. Each writer and researcher has his special emphasis when he considers the system. Perhaps the most evident unifying thread in the study of systems is the effort to look at the organization in its totality. Representative books in this field are March and Simon, *Organizations,*[34] and Haire's anthology, *Modern Organization Theory.*[35]

Instead of attempting a review of different writers' contributions to modern organization theory, it will be more useful to discuss the various ingredients involved in system analysis. They are the parts, the interactions, the processes, and the goals of systems.

The Parts of the System and Their Interdependency

The first basic part of the system is the *individual,* and the personality structure he brings to the organization. Elementary to an individual's personality are motives and attitudes which condition the range of expectancies he hopes to satisfy by participating in the system.

The second part of the system is the formal arrangement of functions, usually called the *formal organization.* The formal organization is the interrelated pattern of jobs which make up the structure of a system. Certain writers, like Argyris, see a fundamental conflict resulting from the demands made by the system, and the structure of the mature, normal personality. In any event, the individual has expectancies regarding the job he is to perform; and, conversely, the job makes demands on, or has expectancies relating to, the performance of the individual. Considerable attention has been given by writers in modern organization theory to incongruencies resulting from the interaction of organizational and individual demands.[36]

The third part in the organization system is the *informal organization.* Enough has been said already about the nature of this organization. But it must be noted that an interactional pattern exists between the individual and the informal group. This interactional arrangement can be conveniently discussed as the mutual modification of expectancies. The informal organization has demands which it makes on members in terms of anticipated forms of behavior, and the individual has expectancies of satisfaction he hopes to derive from association with people on the job. Both these sets of expectancies interact, resulting in the individual modifying his behavior to accord with the demands of the group, and the group, perhaps, modifying what it expects from an individual because of the impact of his personality on group norms.[37]

Much of what has been said about the various expectancy systems in an organization can also be treated using status and role concepts. Part of modern organization theory rests on research findings in social psychology relative to reciprocal patterns of behavior stemming from role demands generated by both the formal and informal organizations, and role perceptions peculiar to the individual. Bakke's *fusion process* is largely concerned with the modification of role expectancies. The fusion process is a force, according to Bakke, which acts to weld divergent elements together for the preservation of organizational integrity.[38]

The fifth part of system analysis is the *physical setting* in which the job is performed. Although this element of the system may be implicit in what has been said already about the formal organization and its functions, it is well to separate it. In the physical surroundings of work, interactions are present in complex man-machine systems. The human "engineer" cannot approach the problems posed by such interrelationships in a purely technical, engineering fashion. As Haire says, these problems lie in the domain of the social theorist.[39] Attention must be centered on responses demanded from a logically ordered production function, often with the view of minimizing the error in the system. From this standpoint, work cannot be effectively organized unless the psychological, social, and physiological characteristics of people participating in the work environment are considered. Machines and processes should be designed to fit certain generally observed psychological and physiological properties of men, rather than hiring men to fit machines.

In summary, the parts of the system which appear to be of strategic importance are the individual, the formal structure, the informal organization, status and role patterns, and the physical environment of work. Again, these parts are woven into a configuration called the organizational system. The processes which link the parts are taken up next.

The Linking Processes

One can say, with a good deal of glibness, that all the parts mentioned above are interrelated. Although this observation is quite correct, it does not mean too much in terms of system theory unless some attempt is made to analyze the processes by which the interaction is achieved. Role theory is devoted to certain types of interactional processes. In addition, modern organization theorists point to three other linking activities which appear to be universal to human systems of organized behavior. These processes are communication, balance, and decision making.

1. Communication is mentioned often in neoclassical theory, but the emphasis is on description of forms of communication activity (i.e., formal-informal, vertical-horizontal, line-staff). Communication, as a mechanism which links the segments of the system together, is overlooked by way of much considered analysis.

One aspect of modern organization theory is study of the communication network in the system. Communication is viewed as the method by which action is evoked from the parts of the system. Communication acts not only as stimuli resulting in action but also as a control and coordination mechanism linking the decision centers in the system into a synchronized pattern. Deutsch points out that organizations are composed of parts which communicate with each other, receive messages from the outside world, and store information. Taken together, these communication functions of the parts comprise a configuration representing the total system.[40] More is to be said about communication later in the discussion of the cybernetic model.

2. The concept of *balance* as a linking process involves a series of some rather complex ideas. Balance refers to an equilibrating mechanism whereby the various parts of the system are maintained in a harmoniously structured relationship to each other.

The necessity for the balance concept logically flows from the nature of systems themselves. It is impossible to conceive of an ordered relationship among the parts of a system without also introducing the idea of a stabilizing or an adapting mechanism.

Balance appears in two varieties—quasi-automatic and innovative. Both forms of balance act to insure system integrity in the face of changing conditions, either internal or external to the system. The first form of balance, quasi-automatic, refers to what some think are "homeostatic" properties of systems. That is, systems seem to exhibit built-in propensities to maintain steady states.

If human organizations are open, self-maintaining systems, then control and regulatory processes are necessary. The issue hinges on the degree to which stabilizing processes in systems, when adapting to change, are automatic. March and Simon have an interesting answer to this problem, which in part is based on the type of change and the adjustment necessary to adapt to the change. Systems have programs of action which are put into effect when a change is perceived. If the change is relatively minor, and if the change comes within the purview of established programs of action, then it might be fairly confidently predicted that the adaptation made by the system will be quasi-automatic.[41]

The role of innovative, creative balancing efforts now needs to be examined. The need for innovation arises when adaptation to a change is outside the scope of existing programs designed for the purpose of keeping the system in balance. New programs have to be evolved in order for the system to maintain internal harmony.

New programs are created by trial-and-error search for feasible action alternatives to cope with a given change. But innovation is subject to the limitations and possibilities inherent in the quantity and variety of information present in a system at a particular time. New combinations of alternatives for innovative purposes depend on:

(a) The possible range of output of the system, or the capacity of the system to supply information.

(b) The range of available information in the memory of the system.

(c) The operating rules (program) governing the analysis and flow of information within the system.

(d) The ability of the system to "forget" previously learned solutions to change problems.[42] A system with too good a memory might narrow its behavioral choices to such an extent as to stifle innovation. In simpler language, old learned programs might be used to adapt to change, when newly innovated programs are necessary.[43]

Much of what has been said about communication and balance brings to mind a cybernetic model in which both these processes have vital roles. Cybernetics has to do with feedback and control in all kinds of systems. Its purpose is to maintain system stability in the face of change. Cybernetics cannot be studied without considering communication networks, information flow, and some kind of balancing process aimed at preserving the integrity of the system.

Cybernetics directs attention to key questions regarding the system. These questions are: How are communication centers connected, and how are they maintained? Corollary to this question: What is the structure of the feedback system? Next, what information is stored in the organization, and at what points? And as a corollary: How accessible is this information to decision-making centers? Third, How conscious is the organization of the operation of its own parts? That is, to what extent do the policy centers receive control information with sufficient frequency and relevancy to create a real awareness of the operation of the segments of the system? Finally, What are the learning (innovating) capabilities of the system?[44]

Answers to the questions posed by cybernetics are crucial to understanding both the balancing and communication processes in systems.[45] Although cybernetics has been applied largely to technical-engineering problems of automation, the model of feedback, control, and regulation in all systems has a good deal of generality. Cybernetics is a fruitful area which can be used to synthesize the processes of communication and balance.

3. A wide spectrum of topics dealing with types of decisions in human systems makes up the core of analysis of another important process in organizations. Decision analysis is one of the major contributions of March and Simon in their book *Organizations*. The two major

classes of decisions they discuss are decisions to produce and decisions to participate in the system.[46]

Decisions to produce are largely a result of an interaction between individual attitudes and the demands of organization. Motivation analysis becomes central to studying the nature and results of the interaction. Individual decisions to participate in the organization reflect on such issues as the relationship between organizational rewards versus the demands made by the organization. Participation decisions also focus attention on the reasons why individuals remain in or leave organizations.

March and Simon treat decisions as internal variables in an organization which depend on jobs, individual expectations and motivations, and organizational structure. Marschak[47] looks on the decision process as an independent variable upon which the survival of the organization is based. In this case, the organization is viewed as having, inherent to its structure, the ability to maximize survival requisites through its established decision processes.

The Goals of Organization

Organization has three goals which may be either intermeshed or independent ends in themselves. They are growth, stability, and interaction. The last goal refers to organizations which exist primarily to provide a medium for association of its members with others. Interestingly enough, these goals seem to apply to different forms of organization at varying levels of complexity, ranging from simple clockwork mechanisms to social systems.

These similarities in organizational purposes have been observed by a number of people, and a field of thought and research called "general system theory" has developed, dedicated to the task of discovering organizational universals. The dream of general system theory is to create a science of organizational universals, or, if you will, a universal science using common organizational elements found in all systems as a starting point.

Modern organization theory is on the periphery of general system theory. Both general system theory and modern organization theory study:

(1) The parts (individuals) in aggregates, and the movement of individuals into and out of the system.
(2) The interaction of individuals with the environment found in the system.
(3) The interactions among individuals in the system.
(4) General growth and stability problems of systems.[48]

Modern organization theory and general system theory are similar in that they look at organization as an integrated whole. They differ, however, in terms of their generality. General system theory is concerned with every level of system, whereas modern organizational theory focuses primarily on human organization.

The question might be asked, What can the science of administration gain by the study of system levels other than human? Before attempting an answer, note should be made of what these other levels are. Boulding presents a convenient method of classification:

(1) The static structure—a level of framework, the anatomy of a system; for example, the structure of the universe.

(2) The simple dynamic system—the level of clockworks, predetermined necessary motions.

(3) The cybernetic system—the level of the thermostat, the system moves to maintain a given equilibrium through a process of self-regulation.

(4) The open system—level of self-maintaining systems, moves toward and includes living organisms.

(5) The genetic-societal system—level of cell society, characterized by a division of labor among cells.

(6) Animal systems—level of mobility, evidence of goal-directed behavior.

(7) Human systems—level of symbol interpretation and idea communication.

(8) Social system—level of human organization.

(9) Transcendental systems—level of ultimates and absolutes which exhibit systematic structure but are unknowable in essence.[49]

This approach to the study of systems by finding universals common at all levels of organization offers intriguing possibilities for administrative organization theory. A good deal of light could be thrown on social systems if structurally analogous elements could be found in the simpler types of systems. For example, cybernetic systems have characteristics which seem to be similar to feedback, regulation, and control phenomena in human organizations. Thus, certain facets of cybernetic models could be generalized to human organization. Considerable danger, however, lies in poorly founded analogies. Superficial similarities between simpler system forms and social systems are apparent everywhere. Instinctually based ant societies, for example, do not yield particularly instructive lessons for understanding rationally conceived human organizations. Thus, care should be taken that analogies used to bridge system levels are not mere devices for literary enrichment. For analogies to have usefulness and validity, they must exhibit inherent structural similarities or implicitly identical operational principles.[50]

Modern organization theory leads, as it has been shown, almost inevitably into a discussion of general system theory. A science of organizational universals has some strong advocates, particularly among biologists.[51] Organization theorists in administrative science cannot afford to overlook the contributions of general system theory. Indeed, modern organization concepts could offer a great deal to those working with general system theory. But the ideas dealt with in the general theory are exceedingly elusive.

Speaking of the concept of equilibrium as a unifying element in all systems, Easton says, "It [equilibrium] leaves the impression that we have a useful general theory when in fact, lacking measurability, it is a mere pretence for knowledge."[52] The inability to quantify and measure universal organization elements undermines the success of pragmatic tests to which general system theory might be put.

Organization Theory: Quo Vadis?

Most sciences have a vision of the universe to which they are applied, and administrative science is not an exception. This universe is composed of parts. One purpose of science is to synthesize the parts into an organized conception of its field of study. As a science matures, its theorems about the configuration of its universe change. The direction of change in three sciences, physics, economics, and sociology, are noted briefly for comparison with the development of an administrative view of human organization.

The first comprehensive and empirically verifiable outlook of the physical universe was presented by Newton in his *Principia*. Classical physics, founded on Newton's work, constitutes a grand scheme in which a wide range of physical phenomena could be organized and predicted. Newtonian physics may rightfully be regarded as "macro" in nature, because its system of organization was concerned largely with gross events of which the movement of celestial bodies, waves, energy forms, and strain are examples. For years classical physics was supreme, being applied continuously to smaller and smaller classes of phenomena in the physical universe. Physicists at one time adopted the view that everything in their realm could be discovered by simply subdividing problems. Physics thus moved into the "micro" order.

But in the 19th century a revolution took place motivated largely because events were being noted which could not be explained adequately by the conceptual framework supplied by the classical school. The consequences of this revolution are brilliantly described by Eddington:

> From the point of view of philosophy of science the conception associated with entropy must I think be ranked as the great contribution of the 19th century to scientific thought. It marked a reaction from the view that everything to which science need pay attention is discovered by microscopic dissection of objects. It provided an alternative standpoint in which the centre of interest is shifted from the entities reached by the customary analysis (atoms, electric potentials, etc.) to qualities possessed by the system as a whole, which cannot be split up and located—a little bit here, and a little bit there. . . .
>
> We often think that when we have completed our study of *one* we know all about *two*, because "two" is "one and one." We forget that we have still to make a study of "and." Secondary physics is the study of "and"—that is to say, of organization.[53]

Although modern physics often deals in minute quantities and oscillations, the conception of the physicist is on the "macro" scale. He is concerned with the "and," or the organization of the world in which the events occur. These developments did not invalidate classical physics as to its usefulness for explaining a certain range of phenomena. But classical physics is no longer the undisputed law of the universe. It is a special case.

Early economic theory, and Adam Smith's *Wealth of Nations* comes to mind, examined economic problems in the macro order. The *Wealth of Nations* is mainly concerned with matters of national income and welfare. Later, the economics of the firm, micro-economics, dominated the theoretical scene in this science. And, finally, with Keynes's *The General Theory of Employment, Interest and Money,* a systematic approach to the economic universe was reintroduced on the macro level.

The first era of the developing science of sociology was occupied by the great social "system builders." Comte, the so-called father of sociology, had a macro view of society in that his chief works are devoted to social reorganization. Comte was concerned with the interrelationships among social, political, religious, and educational institutions. As sociology progressed, the science of society compressed. Emphasis shifted from the macro approach of the pioneers to detailed, empirical study of small social units. The compression of sociological analysis was accompanied by study of social pathology or disorganization.

In general, physics, economics, and sociology appear to have two things in common. First, they offered a macro point of view as their initial systematic comprehension of their area of study. Second, as the science developed, attention fragmented into analysis of the parts of the organization, rather than attending to the system as a whole. This is the micro phase.

In physics and economics, discontent was evidenced by some scientists at the continual atomization of the universe. The reaction to the micro approach was a new theory or theories dealing with the total system, on the macro level again. This third phase of scientific development seems to be more evident in physics and economics than in sociology.

The reason for the "macro-micro-macro" order of scientific progress lies, perhaps, in the hypothesis that usually the things which strike man first are of great magnitude. The scientist attempts to discover order in the vastness. But after macro laws or models of systems are postulated, variations appear which demand analysis, not so much in terms of the entire system, but more in terms of the specific parts which make it up. Then, intense study of microcosm may result in new general laws, replacing the old models of organization. Or, the old and the new models may stand together, each explaining a different class of phenomenon. Or, the old and the new concepts of organization may be welded to produce a single creative synthesis.

Now, what does all this have to do with the problem of organization in administrative science? Organization concepts seem to have gone through the same order of development in this field as in the three just mentioned. It is evident that the classical theory of organization, particularly as in the work of Mooney and Reiley, is concerned with principles common to all organizations. It is a macro-organizational view. The classical approach to organization, however, dealt with the gross anatomical parts and processes of the formal organization. Like classical physics, the classical theory of organization is a special case. Neither is especially well equipped to account for variation from its established framework.

Many variations in the classical administrative model result from human behavior. The only way these variations could be understood was by a microscopic examination of particularized, situational aspects of human behavior. The mission of the neoclassical school thus is "micro-analysis."

It was observed earlier, that somewhere along the line the concept of the social system, which is the key to understanding the Hawthorne studies, faded into the background. Maybe the idea is so obvious that it was lost to the view of researchers and writers in human relations. In any event, the press of research in the microcosmic universes of the informal organization, morale and productivity, leadership, participation, and the like forced the notion of the social system into limbo. Now, with the advent of modern organization theory, the social system has been resurrected.

Modern organization theory appears to be concerned with Eddington's "and." This school claims that its operational hypothesis is based on a macro point of view; that is, the study of organization as a whole. This nobility of purpose should not obscure, however, certain difficulties faced by this field as it is presently constituted. Modern organization theory raises two questions which should be explored further. First, Would it not be more accurate to speak of modern organization theories? Second, Just how much of modern organization theory is modern?

The first question can be answered with a quick affirmative. Aside from the notion of the system, there are few, if any, other ideas of a unifying nature. Except for several important exceptions,[54] modern organization theorists tend to pursue their pet points of view,[55] suggesting they are part of system theory, but not troubling to show by what mystical means they arrive at this conclusion.

The irony of it all is that a field dealing with systems has, indeed, little system. Modern organization theory needs a framework, and it needs an integration of issues into a common conception of organization. Admittedly, this is a large order. But it is curious not to find serious analytical treatment of subjects like cybernetics or general system theory in Haire's *Modern Organization Theory*, which claims to be a representative example of work in this field. Beer has ample evidence in his book *Cybernetics and Management* that cybernetics, if imaginatively approached, provides a valuable conceptual base for the study of systems.

The second question suggests an ambiguous answer. Modern organization theory is in part a product of the past; system analysis is not a new idea. Further, modern organization theory relies for supporting data on microcosmic research studies, generally drawn from the journals of the last 10 years. The newness of modern organization theory, perhaps, is its effort to synthesize recent research contributions of many fields into a system theory characterized by a reoriented conception of organization.

One might ask, But what is the modern theorist reorienting? A clue is found in the almost snobbish disdain assumed by some authors of the neoclassical human relations school, and particularly, the classical school. Reevaluation of the classical school of organization is overdue. However, this does not mean that its contributions to organization theory are irrelevant and should be overlooked in the rush to get on the "behavioral science bandwagon."

Haire announces that the papers appearing in *Modern Organization Theory* constitute "the ragged leading edge of a wave of theoretical development."[56] Ragged, yes; but leading, no! The papers appearing in this book do not represent a theoretical breakthrough in the concept of organization. Haire's collection is an interesting potpourri, with several contributions of considerable significance. But readers should beware that they will not find vastly new insights into organizational behavior in this book, if they have kept up with the literature of the social sciences, and have dabbled to some extent in the esoterica of biological theories of growth, information theory, and mathematical model building. For those who have not maintained the pace, *Modern Organization Theory* serves the admirable purpose of bringing them up to date on a rather diversified number of subjects.

Some work in modern organization theory is pioneering, making its appraisal difficult and future uncertain. While the direction of this endeavor is unclear, one thing is patently true. Human behavior in organizations, and indeed, organization itself, cannot be adequately understood within the ground rules of classical and neoclassical doctrines. Appreciation of human organization requires a *creative* synthesis of massive amounts of empirical data, a high order of deductive reasoning, imaginative research studies, and a taste for individual and social values. Accomplishment of all these objectives, and the inclusion of them into a framework of the concept of the system, appears to be the goal of modern organization theory. The vitality of administrative science rests on the advances modern theorists make along this line.

Modern organization theory, 1960 style, is an amorphous aggregation of synthesizers and restaters, with a few extending leadership on the frontier. For the sake of these few, it is well to admonish that pouring old wine into new bottles may make the spirits cloudy. Unfortunately, modern organization theory has almost succeeded in achieving the status of a fad. Popularization and exploitation contributed to the disrepute into which human relations has fallen. It would be a great waste if modern organization theory yields to the same fate, particularly since both modern organization theory and human relations draw from the same promising source of inspiration—system analysis.

Modern organization theory needs tools of analysis and a conceptual framework uniquely its own, but it must also allow for the incorporation of relevant contributions of many fields. It may be that the framework will come from general system theory. New areas of research, such as decision theory, information theory, and cybernetics, also offer reasonable expectations of analytical and conceptual tools. Modern organization theory represents a frontier of research which has great significance for management. [The potential is great, because it offers the opportunity for uniting what is valuable in classical theory with the social and natural sciences into a systematic and integrated conception of human organization.]

NOTES AND REFERENCES

1. Roderick Seidenberg, *Post Historic Man* (Boston: Beacon Press, 1951), p. 1.
2. Robert V. Presthus, "Toward a Theory of Organizational Behavior," *Administrative Science Quarterly*, June 1958, p. 50.
3. Regulation and predictability of human behavior are matters of degree, varying with different organizations on something of a continuum. At one extreme are bureaucratic type organizations with tight bonds of regulation. At the other extreme are voluntary associations, and informal organizations with relatively loose bonds of regulation.

    This point has an interesting sidelight. A bureaucracy with tight controls and a high degree of predictability of human action appears to be unable to distinguish between destructive and creative deviations from established values. Thus, the only thing which is safeguarded is the status quo.
4. The monolithic institutions of the military and government are other cases of organizational preoccupation.
5. James D. Mooney and Alan C. Reiley, *Onward Industry* (New York: Harper & Row, 1931). Later published by James D. Mooney under the title *Principles of Organization.*
6. E. F. L. Brech, *Organization* (London: Longmans, Green, 1957).
7. Louis A. Allen, *Management and Organization* (New York: McGraw-Hill, 1958).
8. Usually the division of labor is treated under a topical heading of departmentation; see, for example: Harold Koontz and Cyril O'Donnell, *Principles of Management.* (New York: McGraw-Hill, 1959), chap. 7.
9. These processes are discussed at length in Ralph Currier Davis, *The Fundamentals of Top Management* (New York: Harper & Row, 1951), chap. 7.
10. For a discussion of structure see: William H. Newman, *Administrative Action* (Englewood Cliffs, N.J.: Prentice-Hall, 1951), chap. 16.
11. V. A. Graicunas, "Relationships in Organization," *Papers on the Science of Administration* (New York: Columbia University, 1937).
12. Brech, p. 78 (see note 6).
13. See: F. J. Roethlisberger and William J. Dickson, *Management and the Worker* (Cambridge, Mass.: Harvard University Press, 1939).
14. Burleigh B. Gardner and David G. Moore, *Human Relations in Industry* (Homewood, Ill.: Richard D. Irwin, 1955).
15. Keith Davis, *Human Relations in Business* (New York: McGraw-Hill, 1957).
16. For example see: Delbert C. Miller and William H. Form, *Industrial Sociology* (New York: Harper & Row, 1951).
17. See: Hugo Munsterberg, *Psychology and Industrial Efficiency* (Boston: Houghton Mifflin, 1913).

18. Probably the classic work is Elton Mayo, *The Human Problems of an Industrial Civilization* (Cambridge, Mass.: Harvard University Press, 1946, first printed 1933).

19. For further discussion of the human relations implications of the scalar and functional processes see: Keith Davis, pp. 60–66 (see note 15).

20. Melville Dalton, "Conflicts between Staff and Line Managerial Officers," *American Sociological Review,* June 1950, pp. 342–51.

21. J. M. Juran, "Improving the Relationship between Staff and Line," *Personnel,* May 1956, pp. 515–24.

22. Gardner and Moore, pp. 237–43 (see note 14).

23. For example: Brech, pp. 27–29 (see note 6); and Allen, pp. 61–62 (see note 7).

24. See: Leon Festinger, Stanley Schachter, and Kurt Back, *Social Pressures in Informal Groups* (New York: Harper & Row, 1950), pp. 153–63.

25. For example see: W. Fred Cottrell, *The Railroader* (Palo Alto, Calif.: Stanford University Press, 1940), chap. 3.

26. Except in cases where the existence of an organization is necessary for the continued maintenance of employee interest. Under these conditions the previously informal association may emerge as a formal group, such as a union.

27. Probably the classic study of resistance to change is Lester Coch and John R. P. French, Jr., "Overcoming Resistance to Change," in *Human Factors in Management,* ed. Schuyler Dean Hoslett (New York: Harper & Row, 1951), pp. 242–68.

28. For example see: Robert Saltonstall, *Human Relations in Administration* (New York: McGraw-Hill, 1959), pp. 330–31;   and Keith Davis, pp. 99–101 (see note 15).

29. For an example of this approach see: John T. Doutt, "Management Must Manage the Informal Group, Too," *Advanced Management,* May 1959, pp. 26–28.

30. See: Roethlisberger and Dickson, chap. 24 (see note 13).

31. A check of management human relations texts, the organization and human relations chapters of principles of management texts, and texts on conventional organization theory for management courses reveals little or no treatment of the concept of the social system.

32. Lawrence J. Henderson, *Pareto's General Sociology* (Cambridge, Mass.: Harvard University Press, 1935), p. 13.

33. There is another question which cannot be treated in the scope of this paper. It asks: What research tools should be used for the study of the system?

34. James G. March and Herbert A. Simon, *Organizations* (New York: John Wiley & Sons, 1958).

35. Mason Haire, ed., *Modern Organization Theory* (New York: John Wiley & Sons, 1959).

36. See: Chris Argyris, *Personality and Organization* (New York: Harper & Row, 1957), especially chaps. 2, 3, 7.

37. For a larger treatment of this subject see: George C. Homans, *The Human Group* (New York: Harcourt Brace Jovanovich, 1950), chap. 5.

38. E. Wight Bakke, "Concept of the Social Organization," *Modern Organization Theory,* ed. Mason Haire (New York: John Wiley & Sons, 1959), pp. 60–61.

39. Mason Haire, "Psychology and the Study of Business: Joint Behavioral Sciences," *Social Science Research on Business: Product and Potential* (New York: Columbia University Press, 1959), pp. 53–59.

40. Karl W. Deutsch, "On Communication Models in the Social Sciences," *Public Opinion Quarterly* 16 (1952), pp. 356–80.

41. March and Simon, pp. 139–40 (see note 34).
42. Mervyn L. Cadwallader, "The Cybernetic Analysis of Change in Complex Social Organization," *The American Journal of Sociology,* September 1959, p. 156.
43. It is conceivable for innovative behavior to be programmed into the system.
44. These are questions adapted from Deutsch, pp. 368–70 (see note 40).
45. Answers to these questions would require a comprehensive volume. One of the best approaches currently available is Stafford Beer, *Cybernetics and Management* (New York: John Wiley & Sons, 1959).
46. March and Simon, chaps. 3 and 4 (see note 34).
47. Jacob Marschak, "Efficient and Viable Organizational Forms," *Modern Organization Theory,* ed. Mason Haire (New York: John Wiley & Sons, 1959), pp. 307–20.
48. Kenneth E. Boulding, "General System Theory—The Skeleton of a Science," *Management Science,* April 1956, pp. 200–02.
49. Ibid., pp. 202–05.
50. Seidenberg, p. 136 (see note 1). The fruitful use of the type of analogies spoken of by Seidenberg is evident in the application of thermodynamic principles, particularly the entropy concept, to communication theory. See: Claude E. Shannon and Warren Weaver, *The Mathematical Theory of Communication* (Urbana: University of Illinois Press, 1949). Further, the existence of a complete analogy between the operational behavior of thermodynamic systems, electrical communications systems, and biological systems has been noted by Y. S. Touloukian, *The Concept of Entropy in Communication, Living Organisms, and Thermodynamics,* Research Bulletin 130, Purdue Engineering Experiment Station.
51. For example see: Ludwig von Bertalanffy, *Problem of Life* (London: Watts, 1952).
52. David Easton, "Limits of the Equilibrium Model in Social Research," *Profits and Problems of Homeostatic Models in the Behavioral Sciences,* Publication 1, Chicago Behavioral Sciences, 1953, p. 39.
53. Sir Arthur Eddington, *The Nature of the Physical World* (Ann Arbor: University of Michigan Press, 1958), pp. 103–04.
54. For example, E. Wight Bakke, pp. 18–75 (see note 38).
55. There is a large selection including decision theory, individual-organization interaction, motivation, vitality, stability, growth, and graph theory, to mention a few.
56. Mason Haire, "General Issues," in *Modern Organization Theory,* ed. Mason Haire (New York: John Wiley & Sons, 1959), p. 2.

12

Parkinson's Law

C. Northcote Parkinson

One of the most famous articles on management, "Parkinson's Law," focuses on a specific aspect of organizing, namely staff size, and demonstrates how work expands to fill the time available for its completion. Many would argue that the Law of Multiplication of Subordinates and the Law of Multiplication of Work are validated constantly in organizations throughout the world.—Eds.

It is a commonplace observation that work expands so as to fill the time available for its completion. Thus, an elderly lady of leisure can spend an entire day in writing and despatching a postcard to her niece at Bognor Regis. An hour will be spent in finding the postcard, another in hunting for spectacles, half-an-hour in a search for the address, an hour and a quarter in composition, and twenty minutes in deciding whether or not to take an umbrella when going to the pillar-box in the next street. The total effort which would occupy a busy man for three minutes all told may in this fashion leave another person prostrate after a day of doubt, anxiety, and toil.

Granted that work (and especially paper work) is thus elastic in its demands of time, it is manifest that there need be little or no relationship between the work to be done and the size of the staff to which it may be assigned. Before the discovery of a new scientific law—herewith presented to the public for the first time, and to be called Parkinson's Law—there has, however, been insufficient recognition of the implication of this fact in the field of public administration. Politicians and taxpayers have assumed (with occasional phases of doubt) that a rising total in the number of civil servants must reflect a growing volume of work to be done. Cynics, in questioning this belief, have imagined that the multiplication of officials must have left some of them idle or all of them able to work for shorter hours. But this is a matter in which faith and doubt seem equally misplaced. The fact is that the number of the officials and the quantity of the work to be done are not related to each other at all. The rise in the total of those employed is governed by Parkinson's Law, and would be much the same whether the volume of the work were to increase, diminish, or even disappear. The importance of Parkinson's Law lies in the fact that it is a law of growth based upon an analysis of the factors by which the growth is controlled.

The validity of this recently discovered law must rely mainly on statistical proofs, which will follow. Of more interest to the general reader is the explanation of the factors that underlie the general tendency to which this law gives definition. Omitting technicalities (which are numerous) we may distinguish, at the outset, two motive forces. They can be represented for the present purpose by two almost axiomatic statements, thus:

Factor I.   An official wants to multiply subordinates, not rivals; and

Factor II. Officials make work for each other. We must now examine these motive forces in turn.

THE LAW OF MULTIPLICATION OF SUBORDINATES

To comprehend Factor I, we must picture a civil servant called A who finds himself overworked. Whether this overwork is real or imaginary is immaterial; but we should observe, in passing, that A's sensation (or illusion) might easily result from his own decreasing energy—a normal symptom of middle-age. For this real or imagined overwork there are, broadly speaking, three possible remedies:

1. He may resign.
2. He may ask to halve the work with a colleague called B.
3. He may demand the assistance of two subordinates to be called C and D.

There is probably no instance in civil service history of A choosing any but the third alternative. By resignation he would lose his pension rights. By having B appointed, on his own level in the hierarchy, he would merely bring in a rival for promotion to W's vacancy when W (at long last) retires. So A would rather have C and D, junior men, below him. They will add to his consequence; and, by dividing the work into two categories, as between C and D, he will have the merit of being the only man who comprehends them both.

It is essential to realize, at this point, that C and D are, as it were, inseparable. To appoint C alone would have been impossible. Why? Because C, if by himself, would divide the work with A and so assume almost the equal status which has been refused in the first instance to B: a status the more emphasized if C is A's only possible successor. Subordinates must thus number two or more, each being kept in order by fear of the other's promotion. When C complains in turn of being overworked (as he certainly will), A will, with the concurrence of C, advise the appointment of two assistants to help C. But he can then avert internal friction only by advising the appointment of two more assistants to help D, whose position is much the same. With this recruitment of E, F, G and H, the promotion of A is now practically certain.

THE LAW OF MULTIPLICATION OF WORK

Seven officials are now doing what one did before. This is where Factor II comes into operation. For these seven make so much work for each other that all are fully occupied and A is actually working harder than ever. An incoming document may well come before each of them in turn. Official E decides that it falls within the province of F, who places a draft reply before C, who amends it drastically before consulting D, who asks G to deal with it. But G goes on leave at this point, handing the file over to H, who drafts a minute, which is signed by D and returned to C, who revises his draft accordingly and lays the new version before A.

What does A do? He would have every excuse for signing the thing unread, for he has many other matters on his mind. Knowing now that he is to succeed W next year, he has to decide whether C or D should succeed to his own office. He had to agree to G going on leave, although not yet strictly entitled to it. He is worried whether H should not have gone instead, for reasons of health. He has looked pale recently—partly but not solely because of his domestic troubles. Then there is the business of F's special increment of salary for the period of the conference, and E's application for transfer to the Ministry of Pensions. A has heard that D is in love with a married typist and that G and F are no longer on speaking terms—no one seems to know why. So A might be tempted to sign C's draft and have done with it.

But A is a conscientious man. Beset as he is with problems created by his colleagues for themselves and for him—created by the mere fact of these officials' existence—he is not the man to shirk his duty. He reads through the draft with care, deletes the fussy paragraphs added by C and H, and restores the thing back to the form preferred in the first instance by the able (if quarrelsome) F. He corrects the English—none of these young men can write grammatically—and finally produces the same reply he would have written if officials C to H have never been born. Far more people have taken far longer to produce the same result. No one has been idle. All have done their best. And it is late in the evening before A finally quits his office and begins the return journey to Ealing. The last of the office lights are being turned off in the gathering dusk which marks the end of another day's administrative toil. Among the last to leave, A reflects, with bowed shoulders and a wry smile, that late hours, like grey hairs, are among the penalties of success.

THE SCIENTIFIC PROOFS

From this description of the factors at work, the student of political science will recognize that administrators are more or less bound to multiply. Nothing has yet been said, however, about the period of time likely to elapse between the date of A's appointment and the date from which we can calculate the pensionable service of H. Vast masses of statistical evidence have been collected and it is from a study of this data that Parkinson' s Law has been deduced. Space will not allow of detailed analysis, but research began in the British Navy Estimates. These were chosen because the Admiralty's responsibilities are more easily measurable than those of (say) the Board of Trade.

The accompanying table is derived from Admiralty statistics for 1914 and 1928. The criticism voiced at the time centered on the comparison between the sharp fall in numbers of those available for fighting and the sharp rise in those available only for administration, the creation, it was said, of "a magnificent Navy on land." But that comparison is not to the present purpose. What we have to note is that the 2,000 Admiralty officials of 1914 had become the 3,569 of 1928; and that this growth was unrelated to any possible increase in their work. The Navy during that period had diminished, in point of fact, by a third in men and two thirds in ships. Nor, from 1922 onwards, was its strength even expected to increase, for its total of ships (unlike its total of officials) was limited by the Washington Naval Agreement of that year. Yet in these circumstances we had a 78.45 percent increase in Admiralty officials over a period of 14 years, an average increase of 5.6 percent a year on the earlier total. In fact, as we shall see, the rate of increase was not as regular as that. All we have to consider, at this stage, is the percentage rise over a given period.

Can this rise in the total number of civil servants be accounted for except on the assumption that such a total must always rise by a law governing its growth? It might be urged, at this point, that the period under discussion was one of rapid development in naval technique. The use of the flying machine was no longer confined to the eccentric. Submarines were

	1914	1928	Percentage Increase or Decrease
Capital ships in commission	62	20	− 67.74%
Officers and men in Royal Navy	146,000	100,000	− 31.50
Dockyard workers	57,000	62,439	+ 9.54
Dockyard officials and clerks	3,249	4,558	+ 40.28
Admiralty officials	2,000	3,569	+ 78.45

tolerated if not approved. Engineer officers were beginning to be regarded as almost human. In so revolutionary an age we might expect the storekeepers would have more elaborate inventories to compile. We might not wonder to see more draughtsmen on the payroll, more designers, more technicians and scientists. But these, the dockyard officials, increased only by 40 percent in number, while the men of Whitehall increased by nearly 80 percent. For every new foreman or electrical engineer at Portsmouth there had to be two or more clerks at Charing Cross. From this we might be tempted to conclude, provisionally, that the rate of increase in administrative staff is likely to be double that of the technical staff at a time when the actually useful strength (in this case, of seamen) is being reduced by 31.5 percent. It has been proved, however, statistically, that this last percentage is irrelevant. *The Officials would have multiplied at the same rate had there been no actual seamen at all.*

It would be interesting to follow the further progress by which the 8,118 Admiralty staff of 1935 came to number 33,788 by 1954. But the staff of the Colonial Office affords a better field of study during a period of Imperial decline. The relevant statistics are set down below. Before showing what the rate of increase is, we must observe that the extent of this department's responsibilities was far from constant during these 20 years. The colonial territories were not much altered in area or population between 1935 and 1939. They were considerably diminished by 1943, certain areas being in enemy hands. They were increased again in 1947, but have since then shrunk steadily from year to year as successive colonies achieve self-government.

It would be rational, prior to the discovery of Parkinson's Law, to suppose that these changes in the scope of Empire would be reflected in the size of its central administration. But a glance at the figures shows that the staff totals represent automatic stages in an inevitable increase. And this increase, while related to that observed in other departments, has nothing to do with the size—or even the existence—of the Empire. What are the percentages of increase? We must ignore, for this purpose, the rapid increase in staff which accompanied the diminution of responsibility during World War II. We should note rather the peacetime rates of increase over 5.24 percent between 1935 and 1939, and 6.55 percent between 1947 and 1954. This gives an average increase of 5.89 percent each year, a percentage markedly similar to that already found in the Admiralty staff increase between 1914 and 1928.

Colonial Office Officials

1935	1939	1943	1947	1954
372	450	817	1,135	1,661

Further and detailed statistical analysis of departmental staffs would be inappropriate in such an article as this. It is hoped, however, to reach a tentative conclusion regarding the time likely to elapse between a given official's first appointment and the later appointment of his two or more assistants. Dealing with the problem of pure staff accumulation, all the researches so far completed point to average increase of about 5.75 percent per year. This fact established, it now becomes possible to state Parkinson's Law in mathematical form, thus:

In any public administrative department not actually at war the staff increase may be expected to follow this formula:

$$x = \frac{2k^m + p}{n}$$

where k is the number of staff seeking promotion through the appointment of subordinates; p represents the difference between the ages of appointment and retirement; m is the number of man-hours devoted to answering minutes within the department; and n is the number of effective units being administered. Then x will be the number of new staff required each year.

Mathematicians will, of course, realize that to find the percentage increase they must multiply x by 100 and divide by the total of the previous year, thus:

$$\frac{100(2k^m + p)}{yn}\%$$

where y represents the total original staff. And this figure will invariably prove to be between 5.17 percent and 6.56 percent, irrespective of any variation in the amount of work (if any) to be done.

The discovery of this formula and of the general principles upon which it is based has, of course, no emotive value. No attempt has been made to inquire whether departments ought to grow in size. Those who hold that this growth is essential to gain full employment are fully entitled to their opinion. Those who doubt the stability of an economy based upon reading each other's minutes are equally entitled to theirs. Parkinson's Law is a purely scientific discovery, inapplicable except in theory to the politics of the day. It is not the business of the botanist to eradicate the weeds. Enough for him if he can tell us just how fast they grow.

13

The Ideal Bureaucracy

Max Weber

To Max Weber, control is an essential element in the efficient functioning of any enterprise, and the best control is that which is attained in a bureaucratic form of organizational arrangement. If you are one of those people who associate bureaucracy with inefficiency and red tape, this article should convince you that that is not Weber's definition of an ideal bureaucracy at all. Rather, he sees it as the best known means of carrying out imperative control of human beings.—Eds.

The purest type of exercise of legal authority is that which employs a bureaucratic administrative staff. Only the supreme chief of the organization occupies his position of authority by virtue of appropriation, of election, or of having been designated for the succession. But even his authority consists in a sphere of legal "competence." The whole administrative staff under the supreme authority then consists, in the purest type, of individual officials who are appointed and function according to the following criteria:

1. They are personally free and subject to authority only with respect to their impersonal official obligations.
2. They are organized in a clearly defined hierarchy of offices.
3. Each office has a clearly defined sphere of competence in the legal sense.
4. The office is filled by a free contractual relationship. Thus, in principle, there is free selection.
5. Candidates are selected on the basis of technical qualifications. In the most rational case, this is tested by examination or guaranteed by diplomas certifying technical training, or both. They are appointed, not elected.

SOURCE: Reprinted with permission of Macmillan Publishing Company, Inc., from *The Theory of Social and Economic Organizations* by Max Weber, translated by Talcott Parsons and A. M. Henderson. Copyright © 1947, 1975 by Talcott Parsons.

6. They are remunerated by fixed salaries in money, for the most part with a right to pensions. Only under certain circumstances does the employing authority, especially in private organizations, have a right to terminate the appointment, but the official is always free to resign. The salary scale is primarily graded according to rank in the hierarchy; but, in addition to this criterion, the responsibility of the position and the requirements of the incumbent's social status may be taken into account.

7. The office is treated as the sole, or at least the primary, occupation of the incumbent.

8. It constitutes a career. There is a system of "promotion" according to seniority or to achievement, or both. Promotion is dependent on the judgment of superiors.

9. The official works entirely separated from ownership of the means of administration and without appropriation of his position.

10. He is subject to strict and systematic discipline and control in the conduct of the office.

This type of organization is in principle applicable with equal facility to a wide variety of different fields. It may be applied in profit-making business or in charitable organizations, or in any number of other types of private enterprises serving ideal or material ends. It is equally applicable to political and to religious organizations. With varying degrees of approximation to a pure type, its historical existence can be demonstrated in all these fields.

1. For example, this type of bureaucracy is found in private clinics as well as in endowed hospitals or the hospitals maintained by religious orders. Bureaucratic organization has played a major role in the Catholic Church. It is well illustrated by the administrative role of the priesthood in the modern church, which has expropriated almost all the old church benefices which were in former days to a large extent subject to private appropriation. It is also illustrated by the conception of the universal Episcopate, which is thought of as formally constituting a universal legal competence in religious matters. Similarly, the doctrine of papal infallibility is thought of as in fact involving a universal competence, but only one which functions ex cathedra in the sphere of the office, thus implying the typical distinction between the sphere of office and that of the private affairs of the incumbent. The same phenomena are found in the large-scale capitalistic enterprise; and the larger it is, the greater their role. And this is not less true of political parties, which will be discussed separately. Finally, the modern army is essentially a bureaucratic organization administered by that peculiar type of military functionary, the "officer."

2. Bureaucratic authority is carried out in its purest form where it is most clearly dominated by the principle of appointment. There is no such thing as a hierarchy of elected officials in the same sense as there is a hierarchical organization of appointed officials. In the first place, election makes it impossible to attain a stringency of discipline even approaching that in the appointed type; for it is open to a subordinate official to compete for elective honors on the same terms as his superiors, and his prospects are not dependent on the superior's judgment.

3. Appointment by free contract, which makes free selection possible, is essential to modern bureaucracy. Where there is a hierarchical organization with impersonal spheres of competence but occupied by unfree officials—like slaves or dependents, who, however, function in a formally bureaucratic manner—the term *patrimonial bureaucracy* will be used.

4. The role of technical qualifications in bureaucratic organizations is continually increasing. Even an official in a party or a trade union organization is in need of specialized knowledge, though it is usually of an empirical character, developed by experience, rather than by formal training. In the modern state, the only "offices" for which no technical qualifications are required are those of ministers and presidents. This only goes to prove that they are "officials" only in a formal sense and not substantively, as is true of the managing director or president of a large business corporation. Thus, at the top of a bureaucratic organization, there is necessarily an element which is at least not purely bureaucratic. The category of bureaucracy is one applying only to the exercise of control by means of a particular kind of administrative staff.

5. The bureaucratic official normally receives a fixed salary. By contrast, sources of income which are privately appropriated will be called "benefices." Bureaucratic salaries are also normally paid in money. Though this is not essential to the concept of bureaucracy, it is the arrangement which best fits the pure type. Payments in kind are apt to have the character of benefices, and the receipt of a benefice normally implies the appropriation of opportunities for earnings and of positions. There are, however, gradual transitions in this field, with many intermediate types. Appropriation by virtue of leasing or sale of offices or the pledge of income from office are phenomena foreign to the pure type of bureaucracy.

6. "Offices" which do not constitute the incumbent's principal occupation, in particular "honorary" offices, belong in other categories. The typical "bureaucratic" official occupies the office as his principal occupation.

7. With respect to the separation of the official from ownership of the means of administration, the situation is essentially the same in the

field of public administration and in private bureaucratic organizations, such as the large-scale capitalistic enterprise.

8. Collegial bodies are rapidly decreasing in importance in favor of types of organization which are in fact, and for the most part formally as well, subject to the authority of a single head. For example, the collegial "governments" in Prussia have long since given way to the monocratic "district president." The decisive factor in this development has been the need for rapid, clear decisions, free of the necessity of compromise between different opinions and also free of shifting majorities.

9. The modern army officer is a type of appointed official who is clearly marked off by certain class distinctions. In this respect such officers differ radically from elected military leaders, from charismatic condottieri, from the type of officers who recruit and lead mercenary armies as a capitalistic enterprise, and, finally, from the incumbents of commissions which have been purchased. There may be gradual transitions between these types. The patrimonial "retainer," who is separated from the means of carrying out his function and the proprietor of a mercenary army for capitalistic purposes have, along with the private capitalistic entrepreneur, been pioneers in the organization of the modern type of bureaucracy.

THE MONOCRATIC TYPE OF BUREAUCRATIC ADMINISTRATION

Experience tends universally to show that the purely bureaucratic type of administrative organization—that is, the monocratic variety of bureaucracy—is, from a purely technical point of view, capable of attaining the highest degree of efficiency and is in this sense formally the most rational known means of carrying out imperative control over human beings. It is superior to any other form in precision, in stability, in the stringency of its discipline, and in its reliability. It thus makes possible a particularly high degree of calculability of results for the heads of the organization and for those acting in relation to it. It is finally superior both in intensive efficiency and in the scope of its operations and is formally capable of application to all kinds of administrative tasks.

The development of the modern form of the organization of corporate groups in all fields is nothing less than identical with the development and continual spread of bureaucratic administration. This is true of church and state, of armies, political parties, economic enterprises, organizations to promote all kinds of causes, private associations, clubs, and many others. Its development is, to take the most striking case, the most crucial phenomenon of the modern Western state. However many forms there may be which do not appear to fit this pattern—such as collegial representative bodies, parliamentary committees, soviets, honorary officers, lay judges, and what not—and however much people may complain about the "evils of bureaucracy," it would be sheer illusion to think for a moment that continuous administrative work could be carried out in any field except by means of officials working in offices. The whole pattern of everyday life is cut to fit this framework. For bureaucratic administration is, other things being equal, always, from a formal, technical point of view, the most rational type. For the needs of mass administration today, it is completely indispensable. The choice is only that between bureaucracy and dilettantism in the field of administration.

The primary source of the superiority of bureaucratic administration lies in the role of technical knowledge which, through the development of modern technology and business methods in the production of goods, has become completely indispensable. In this respect, it makes no difference whether the economic system is organized on a capitalistic or a socialistic basis. Indeed, if in the latter case a comparable level of technical efficiency were to be achieved, it would mean a tremendous increase in the importance of specialized bureaucracy.

When those subject to bureaucratic control seek to escape the influence of the existing bureaucratic apparatus, this is normally possible only by creating an organization of their own which is equally subject to the process of bureaucratization. Similarly, the existing bureaucratic apparatus is driven to continue functioning by the most powerful interests which are material and objective, but also ideal in character. Without it, a society like our own—with a separation of officials, employees, and workers from ownership of the means of administration, dependent on discipline and on technical training—could no longer function. The only exception would be those groups, such as the peasantry, who are still in possession of their own means of subsistence. Even in case of revolution by force or of occupation by an enemy, the bureaucratic machinery will normally continue to function just as it had for the previous legal government.

The question is always who controls the existing bureaucratic machinery. And such control is possible only to a very limited degree for persons who are not technical specialists. Generally speaking, in the long run the trained permanent official is more likely to get his way than his nominal superior, the Cabinet minister, who is not a specialist.

Though by no means alone, the capitalistic system has undeniably played a major role in the development of bureaucracy. Indeed, without it capitalistic production could not continue, and any rational type of socialism would have simply to take it over and increase its importance. Its development, largely under capitalistic auspices, has created an urgent need for stable, strict, intensive, and calculable administration. It is this need which gives bureaucracy a crucial role in our society as the central element in any kind of large-scale administration. Only by reversion in every field—political, religious, economic, and so forth—to small-scale organization would it be possible to any considerable extent to escape its influence. On the one hand, capitalism in its modern stages of development strongly tends to foster the development of bureaucracy, although both capitalism and bureaucracy have arisen from many different historical sources. Conversely, capitalism is the most rational economic basis for bureaucratic administration and enables it to develop in the most rational form, especially because, from a fiscal point of view, it supplies the necessary money resources.

Along with these fiscal conditions of efficient bureaucratic administration, there are certain extremely important conditions in the field of communication and transportation. The precision of its functioning requires the services of the railway, the telegraph, and the telephone and becomes increasingly dependent on them. A socialistic form of organization would not alter this fact. It would be a question whether in a socialistic system it would be possible to provide conditions for carrying out as stringent bureaucratic organization as has been possible in a capitalistic order. For socialism would, in fact, require a still higher degree of formal bureaucratization than capitalism. If this should prove not to be possible, it would demonstrate the existence of another of those fundamental elements of irrationality in social systems—a conflict between formal and substantive rationality of the sort which sociology so often encounters.

Bureaucratic administration means fundamentally the exercise of control on the basis of knowledge. This is the feature of it which makes it specifically rational. This consists on the one hand in technical knowledge which, by itself, is sufficient to ensure it a position of extraordinary power. But in addition to this, bureaucratic organizations, or the holders of power who make use of them, have the tendency to increase their power still further by the knowledge growing out of experience in the service; for they acquire through the conduct of office a special knowledge of facts and have available a store of documentary material peculiar to themselves. While not peculiar to bureaucratic organizations, the concept of "official secrets" is certainly typical of them. It stands in relation to technical knowledge in somewhat the same position as commercial secrets do to technological training. It is a product of the striving for power.

Bureaucracy is superior in knowledge, including both technical knowledge and knowledge of the concrete fact within its own sphere of interest, which is usually confined to the interests of a private business—a capitalistic enterprise. The capitalistic entrepreneur is, in our society, the only type who has been able to maintain at least relative immunity from subjection to the control of rational bureaucratic knowledge. All the rest of the population have tended to be organized in large-scale corporate groups which are inevitably subject to bureaucratic control. This is as inevitable as the dominance of precision machinery in the mass production of goods.

The following are the principal more general social consequences of bureaucratic control:

1. The tendency to "leveling" in the interest of the broadest possible basis of recruitment in terms of technical competence.

2. The tendency to plutocracy growing out of the interest in the greatest possible length of technical training. Today this often lasts up to the age of 30.

3. The dominance of a spirit of formalistic impersonality, without hatred or passion, and hence without affection or enthusiasm. The dominant norms are concepts of straightforward duty without regard for personal considerations. Everyone is subject to formal equality of treatment—that is, everyone in the same empirical situation. This is the spirit in which the ideal official conducts his office.

The development of bureaucracy greatly favors the leveling of social classes, and this can be shown historically to be the normal tendency. Conversely, every process of social leveling creates a favorable situation for the development of bureaucracy; for it tends to eliminate class privileges, which include the appropriation of means of administration and the appropriation of authority as well as the occupation of offices on an honorary basis or as an avocation by virtue of wealth. This combination everywhere inevitably foreshadows the development of mass democracy.

The "spirit" of rational bureaucracy normally has the following general characteristics:

1. Formalism, which is promoted by all the interests which are concerned with the security of their own personal situation, whatever this may consist in. Otherwise the door would be open to arbitrariness, and hence formalism in the line of least resistance.

2. There is another tendency, which is apparently in contradiction to the above—a contradiction which is in part genuine. It is the tendency of officials to treat their official function from what is substantively a utilitarian point of view in the interest of the welfare of those under their authority. But this utilitarian tendency is generally expressed in the enactment of corresponding regulatory measures which themselves have a formal character and tend to be treated in a formalistic spirit. This tendency to substantive rationality is supported by all those subject to authority who are not included in the class mentioned above as interested in the security of advantages already controlled. The problems which open up at this point belong in the theory of "democracy."

14

Leaders' Control and Members' Compliance

Amitai Etzioni

Etzioni suggests that organizations can be categorized in terms of how their leaders exercise control through the use of coercive, remunerative, or normative power. This classification may be developed further by examining how organizational members respond to these control attempts. He suggests three categories of response: involvement, commitment, and alienation. It is the discussion of the relationship between types of control and responses to them that makes this article such a significant one.—Eds.

A CLASSIFICATION OF POWER

Power is an actor's ability to induce or influence another actor to carry out his directives or any other norms he supports.[1] Goldhamer and Shils state that "a person may be said to have power to the extent that he influences the behavior of others in accordance with his own intentions."[2] Of course, "his own intentions" might be to influence a person to follow others' "intentions" or those of a collectivity. In organizations, enforcing the collectivity norms is likely to be a condition determining the powerholder's access to the means of power.

Power positions are positions whose incumbents regularly have access to means of power. Statements about power positions imply a particular group (or groups) who are subject to this power. For instance, to state that prison guards have a power position implies the subordination of inmates. In the following analysis we focus on power relations in organizations between those higher and those lower in rank. We refer to those in power positions, who are higher in rank, as *elites* or as organizational *representatives*. We refer to those in subject positions, who are lower in rank, as *lower participants*.

SOURCE: Reprinted with permission of Macmillan Publishing Company, Inc., from *A Comparative Analysis of Complex Organizations* by Amitai Etzioni. Copyright © 1961 by Free Press of Glencoe, Inc.

Power differs according to the means employed to make the subjects comply. These means may be physical, material, or symbolic.[3]

Coercive power rests on the application, or the threat of application, of physical sanctions, such as infliction of pain, deformity, or death; generation of frustration through restriction of movement; or controlling through force the satisfaction of needs, such as those for food, sex, comfort, and the like.

Remunerative power is based on control over material resources and rewards through allocation of salaries and wages, commissions and contributions, "fringe benefits," services, and commodities.

Normative power rests on the allocation and manipulation of symbolic rewards and deprivations through employment of leaders, manipulation of mass media, allocation of esteem and prestige symbols, administration of ritual, and influence over the distribution of "acceptance" and "positive response." (A more eloquent name for this power would be persuasive, or manipulative, or suggestive power. But all these terms have negative value connotations, which we wish to avoid.)

There are two kinds of normative power. One is based on the manipulation of esteem, prestige, and ritualistic symbols (such as a flag or a benediction); the other, on allocation and manipulation of acceptance and positive response.[4] Although both powers are found both in vertical and in horizontal relationships, the first is more frequent in vertical relations, between actors who have different ranks, whereas the second is more common in horizontal relations, among actors equal in rank—in particular, in the power of an "informal" or primary group over its members. Lacking better terms, we refer to the first kind as *pure normative power* and to the second as *social power*.[5] Social power could be treated as a distinct kind of power. But since powers are here classed according to the means of control employed, and since both social and pure normative power rest on the same set of means—manipulation of symbolic rewards—we treat these two powers as belonging to the same category.

From the viewpoint of the organization, pure normative power is more useful, since it can be exercised directly down the hierarchy. Social power becomes organizational power only when the organization can influence the group's powers, as when a teacher uses the class climate to control a deviant child or a union steward agitates the members to use their informal power to bring a deviant into line.

Organizations can be ordered according to their power structure, taking into account which power is predominant, how strongly it is stressed compared with other organizations in which the same power is predominant, and which power constitutes the secondary source of control. . . .

NEUTRALIZATION OF POWER

Most organizations employ all three kinds of power, but the degree to which they rely on each differs from organization to organization. Most organizations tend to emphasize only one means of power, relying less on the other two.[6] Evidence to this effect is presented below in the analysis of the compliance structures of various organizations. The major reason for power specialization seems to be that, when two kinds of power are emphasized at the same time, over the same subject group, they tend to neutralize each other.

Applying force, for instance, usually creates such a high degree of alienation that it becomes impossible to apply normative power successfully. This is one of the reasons that rehabilitation is rarely achieved in traditional prisons, that custodial measures are considered as blocking therapy in mental hospitals, and that teachers in progressive schools tend to oppose corporal punishment.

Similarly, the application of remunerative powers makes appeal to "idealistic" (pure normative) motives less fruitful. In a study of the motives which lead to purchase of war bonds, Merton pointed out that in one particularly effective drive (the campaign of Kate Smith), all "secular" topics were omitted and the appeal was centered on patriotic, "sacred" themes. Merton asked a sample of 978 people: "Do you think that it is a good idea to give things to people who buy bonds?"

> Fifty percent were definitely opposed in principle to premiums, bonuses, and other such inducements, and many of the remainder thought it a good idea only for "other people" who might not buy otherwise.[7]
> By omitting this [secular] argument, the authors of her scripts were able to avoid the strain and incompatibility between the two main lines of motivation: unselfish, sacrificing love of country and economic motives of sound investment.[8]

It is possible to make an argument for the opposite position. It might be claimed that, the larger the number of personal needs whose satisfaction the organization controls, the more power it has over the participants. For example, labor unions that cater to and have control over the social as well as the economic needs of their members have more power over those members than do unions that focus only on economic needs. There may be some tension between the two modes of control, some ambivalence and uneasy feeling among members about the combinations, but undoubtedly the total control is larger. Similarly, it is obvious that the church has more power over the priest than over the average parishioner. The parishioner is exposed to normative power, whereas the priest is controlled by both normative and remunerative powers.

The issue is complicated by the fact that the *amount* of each kind of power applied must be taken into account. If a labor union with social powers has economic power which is much greater than that of another union, this fact may explain why the first union has greater power in sum, despite some "waste" due to neutralization. A further complication follows from the fact that neutralization may also occur through application of the "wrong" power in terms of the cultural definition of what is appropriate to the particular organization and activity. For example, application of economic power in religious organizations may be less effective than in industries, not because two kinds of power are mixed, but because it is considered illegitimate to use economic pressures to attain religious goals. Finally, some organizations manage to apply two kinds of power abundantly and without much waste through neutralization, because they segregate the application of one power from that of the other. The examination below of combat armies and labor unions supplies an illustration of this point.

We have discussed some of the factors related to the tendency of organizations to specialize their power application. In conclusion, it seems that, although there can be little doubt that such a tendency exists, its scope and a satisfactory explanation for it have yet to be established.

THREE KINDS OF INVOLVEMENT: A COMPARATIVE DIMENSION

Involvement, Commitment, and Alienation

Organizations must continually recruit means if they are to realize their goals. One of the most important of these means is the positive orientation of the participants to the organizational power. *Involvement*[9] refers to the cathectic-evaluative orientation of an actor to an object, characterized in terms of intensity and direction.

The intensity of involvement ranges from high to low. The direction is either positive or negative. We refer to positive involvement as *commitment*[10] and to negative involvement as *alienation*.[11] (The advantage of having a third term, *involvement,* is that it enables us to refer to the continuum in a neutral way.[12]) Actors can accordingly be placed on an involvement continuum which ranges from a highly intense negative zone through mild negative and mild positive zones to a highly positive zone.[13]

Three Kinds of Involvement

We have found it helpful to name three zones of the involvement continuum, as follows: *alienative,* for the high alienation zone; *moral,* for the high commitment zone; and *calculative,* for the two mild zones. This classification of involvement can be applied to the orientations of actors in all social units and to all kinds of objects. Hence, the definitions and illustrations presented below are not limited to organizations but are applicable to orientations in general.

Alienative Involvement.   Alienative involvement designates an intense negative orientation; it is predominant in relations among hostile foreigners. Similar orientations exist among merchants in "adventure" capitalism, where trade is built on isolated acts of exchange, each side trying to maximize immediate profit.[14] Such an orientation seems to dominate the approach of prostitutes to transient clients.[15] Some slaves seem to have held similar attitudes to their masters and to their work. Inmates in prisons, prisoners of war, people in concentration camps, enlisted men in basic training, all tend to be alienated from their respective organizations.[16]

Calculative Involvement. Calculative involvement designates either a negative or a positive orientation of low intensity. Calculative orientations are predominant in relationships of merchants who have continuous business contacts. Attitudes of (and toward) permanent customers are often predominantly calculative, as are relationships among entrepreneurs in modern (rational) capitalism. Inmates in prisons who have established contact with prison authorities, such as "rats" and "peddlers," often have predominantly calculative attitudes toward those in power.[17]

Moral Involvement.[18] Moral involvement designates a positive orientation of high intensity. The involvement of the parishioner in his church, the devoted member in his party, and the loyal follower in his leader are all "moral."

There are two kinds of moral involvement, pure and social. They differ in the same way pure normative power differs from social power. Both are intensive modes of commitment, but they differ in their foci of orientation and in the structural conditions under which they develop. Pure moral commitments are based on internalization of norms and identification with authority (like Riesman's inner-directed "mode of conformity"); social commitment rests on sensitivity to pressures of primary groups and their members (Riesman's "other-directed"). Pure moral involvement tends to develop in vertical relationships, such as those between teachers and students, priests and parishioners, leaders and followers. Social involvement tends to develop in horizontal relationships like those in various types of primary groups. Both pure moral and social orientations might be found in the same relationships, but, as a rule, one orientation predominates.

Actors are means to each other in alienative and in calculative relations; but they are ends to each other in "social" relationships. In pure moral relationships the means-orientation tends to predominate; hence, for example, the willingness of devoted members of totalitarian parties or religious orders to use each other. But unlike the means-orientation of calculative relationships, the means-orientation here is expected to be geared to needs of the collectivity in serving its goals, and not to those of an individual.

NOTES AND REFERENCES

1. T. Parsons, *The Social System* (New York: Free Press of Glencoe, 1951), p. 121.
2. H. Goldhamer and E. A. Shils, "Types of Power and Status," *American Journal of Sociology* 45 (1939), p. 171.

3. We suggest that this typology is exhaustive, although the only way we can demonstrate this is by pointing out that every type of power we have encountered so far can be classified as belonging to one of the categories or to a combination of them.

4. Parsons, *The Social System,* p. 108.

5. This distinction draws on the difference between social and normative integration, referred to by T. Parsons, R. F. Bales, and E. A. Shils, *Working Papers in the Theory of Action* (New York: Free Press of Glencoe, 1953), p. 182, as the distinction between the "integrative" and the "latent pattern maintenance" phases. . . . Shils distinguishes between social and ideological primary groups (private communication). J. S. Coleman, "Multidimensional Scale Analysis," *American Journal of Sociology* 63 (1957), p. 255, has pointed to the difference between group-oriented and idea-oriented attachments.

6. In more technical language, one can say that the three continua of power constitute a three-dimensional property space. If we collapse each dimension into high, medium, and low segments, there are 27 possible combinations or cells. Our hypothesis reads that most organizations fall into cells which are high on one dimension and low or medium on the others; this excludes 18 cells (not counting three types of dual structures discussed below).

7. R. K. Merton, *Mass Persuasion: The Social Psychology of a War Bond Drive* (New York: Harper & Row, 1946), p. 47.

8. Ibid., p. 45.

9. *Involvement* has been used in a similar manner by Nancy C. Morse, *Satisfactions in the White-Collar Job* (Survey Research Center, University of Michigan, 1953), pp. 76–96. The term is used in a somewhat different way by students of voting, who refer by it to the psychological investment in the outcome of an election, rather than in the party, which would be parallel to Morse's usage and ours. See, for example, A. Campbell, G. Gurin, and W. E. Miller, *The Voter Decides* (New York: Harper & Row, 1954), pp. 33–40.

10. Mishler defined *commitment* in a similar though more psychological way: "An individual is committed to an organization to the extent that central tensions are integrated through organizationally relevant instrumental acts." Cited by C. Argyris, *Personality and Organization* (New York: Harper & Row, 1957), p. 202.

11. We draw deliberately on the associations this term has acquired from its usage by Marx and others. For a good analysis of the idea of alienation in Marxism, and of its more recent development, see D. Bell, "The 'Rediscovery' of Alienation," *Journal of Philosophy* 56 (1959), pp. 933–52; and D. Bell, *The End of Ideology* (New York: Free Press of Glencoe, 1960), pp. 335–68. See also D. G. Dean, "Alienation and Political Apathy," *Social Forces* 38 (1960), pp. 185–89.

12. An example of empirical indicators which can be used to translate the involvement continuum into directly observable terms is offered by E. A. Shils and M. Janowits, "Cohesion and Disintegration in the Wehrmacht in World War II," *Public Opinion Quarterly* 12, no. 2 (1948), pp. 282–83. They classify "modes of social disintegration" in the armed forces as follows: desertion, active surrender, passive surrender, routine resistance, "last-ditch" resistance. In the terms used here, these measures indicate varying degrees of involvement, from highest alienation (desertion) to highest commitment (last-ditch resistance).

Nettler (1958) has developed a 17-item unidimensional scale which measures alienation from society. It seems that a similar scale could be constructed for measuring alienation from or commitment to organizational power without undue difficulties. A. Kornhauser, H. L. Sheppard, and A. J. Mayer, *When Labor Votes* (New York: University Books, 1956), pp. 147–48, have developed a six-item scale, measuring the orientation of union members to their organization, which supplies another illustration of the wide use and measurability of these concepts, which are central to our analysis.

13. Several sociologists have pointed out that the relationship between intensity and direction of involvement is a curvilinear one: the more positive or negative the orientation, the more intensely it is held. L. Guttman, "The Cornell Technique for Scale and Intensity Analysis," *Education and Psychology Measurement* 7 (1947), pp. 247–79.

14. H. H. Gerth and C. W. Mills, *From Max Weber: Essays in Sociology* (New York: Oxford University Press, 1946), p. 67.

15. K. Davis, "The Sociology of Prostitution," *American Sociological Review* 2 (1937), pp. 748–49.

16. For a description of this orientation in prisons, see D. Clemmer, *The Prison Community* (New York: Holt, Rinehart & Winston, 1958), p. 152ff. Attitudes toward the police, particularly on the part of members of the lower class, are often strictly alienative. See, for example, E. Banfield, *The Moral Basis of a Backward Society* (New York: Free Press of Glencoe, 1958).

17. G. M. Sykes, *The Society of Captives* (Princeton: Princeton University Press, 1958), pp. 87–95.

18. The term *moral* is used here . . . to refer to an orientation of the actor; it does not involve a value-position of the observer. See T. Parsons et al., *Toward a General Theory of Action* (Cambridge, Mass.: Harvard University Press, 1952), pp. 170ff.

15

Human Organizational Measurements: Key to Financial Success

Rensis Likert

A significant objective of the control process is to identify deviations from planned objectives. Clearly the sooner a deviation is identified the more rapidly a correction can be made. In this article, Rensis Likert suggests that we need no longer rely on "after-the-fact" measurements to tell us of problems. By measuring certain aspects of the human part of the organization, it may be possible to identify future problems in advance and greatly improve upon our control processes.—Eds.

Managers and administrators need no longer wait until "after-the-fact" measurements tell them that they are in trouble before taking corrective steps. All performance, accounting, and financial data are after-the-fact measurements. They reveal the state of a department or organization as it was *yesterday*. As a consequence, often before a problem becomes sufficiently clear to be recognized, it has reached serious proportions.

Recent research developments in the social sciences, however, now can enable any administrator to have data one or more years in advance of trouble. These data can reveal the operating and performance problems which his organization is likely to encounter, the probable causes of these problems, and the steps which if taken now will correct the situation and prevent the problem from developing.

These *lead time data* are measurements of the state of the human organization of an agency or department. They include such measurements as the leadership behavior of administrators and reveal the extent to which the agency is capable of performing in a highly efficient, productive manner.

SOURCE: Reprinted by permission from the May 1971 issue of the *Michigan Business Review*, published by the Graduate School of Business Administration, The University of Michigan.

These measurements of the human organization are objective, impartial, and replicable. They can be used to:

1. Reveal the extent to which the organization as a whole and each of its administrators and supervisors are using managerial principles and practices which yield the highest productivity and the best performance. They will show how well each manager or administrator is building his subordinates into a highly motivated, highly effective unit.

2. Provide evidence concerning the condition for each firm, department, or subordinate unit of such variables as communication, decision making, attitudes and loyalty, motivation, performance goals, and commitment to the organization's success.

3. Increase the lead time by one to three years concerning awareness of operational and performance problems caused by deterioration of the human organization and its productive capability. Lead time measurements will reveal problems at their early stages, point to the major causes of each incipient problem, provide clues to the course of action most likely to correct the situation, show at an early stage how effective each attempt to solve a problem is proving to be, and indicate the further steps likely to bring additional improvement.

4. Reveal the extent to which greater productivity and better performance represent true improvement, in contrast to that achieved by costly liquidation of the human organization.

5. Establish the basis for improving the compensation of managers and supervisors by providing more objective and more accurate data concerning the effectiveness of each administrator's managerial practices.

6. Improve labor relations by facilitating early awareness of problem situations, more accurate diagnosis of these causes, and early action of a remedial character.

7. Detect at an early stage new innovative improvements in organizational structure or in managerial or supervisory behavior. This early detection of better principles and methods of administration will enable the more rapid dissemination of these principles and methods to other parts of the organization. In this manner, all managers and supervisors in the organization can be aided in rapidly adopting better practices.

MANAGEMENT AND ACHIEVEMENT

These and similar uses of lead time measurements are based on the capacity of these measurements to describe correctly the condition of the human organization of a firm and to predict the trends in the performance capability of that firm. A large number of studies of business firms and governmental agencies by the Institute for Social Research, involving thousands of managers and tens of thousands of employees, reveal a relatively consistent relationship between the leadership style and management system of a business firm and the extent to which the organization is able to achieve its objectives fully and efficiently. In widely different kinds of organizations, the managers who are achieving the greatest productivity, lowest cost, best quality of operation, and best labor relations are using the same basic principles of management. These principles differ significantly from those used by managers who achieve average or below average information.

The kind of organization created by the most successful managers can be described briefly: This human system is made up of interlocking work groups, with a high degree of group loyalty among members and favorable attitudes and trust between supervisors and subordinates. Sensitivity to others and relatively high levels of skill in personal interaction and the functioning of groups also are present. These skills permit effective participation in decisions on common problems. Participation is used, for example, to establish organizational objectives, which are a satisfactory integration of the needs and desires of all members of the organization and of persons functionally related to it. High levels of reciprocal influence occur, and high levels of total coordinated influence are achieved in the organization. Responsibility for the organization's success is felt individually by the members and each initiates action, when necessary, to assure that the organization accomplishes its objectives. Communication is efficient and effective. There is a flow from one part of the organization to another of all relevant information important for each decision and action. The leadership in the organization has developed what might well be called a highly effective social system for interaction and mutual influence.

The system of management based on this theory has been labelled "System 4" for convenient reference. Prevailing systems of management and administration, which are more authoritarian in character, will be referred to as "System 2." System 4 is an appreciably more effective management system than is System 2.

SIGNIFICANCE OF TRENDS

These relationships between the management systems of an organization and the excellence of its performance are, however, *much more marked if trends and relationships over time* are examined, instead of using measurements made only at one point in time.

In a recent study of a continuous process plant, for example, the relationship was examined between managerial behavior and cost performance of 40 departments. When both measurements were obtained at the same point in time, the relationships were so slight as to be not statistically significant. But when these measurements of managerial behavior obtained in 1966 were related to cost performance by departments in 1967 (i.e., one year later) one fourth of the variation in costs among departments was accounted for by the behavior of the managers one year earlier. When the time interval was two years, one half of the variation in costs among departments could be attributed to managerial behavior two years earlier.

These findings and other recent studies reveal that measurements of such causal variables as the behavior of administrators and supervisors can be used to predict subsequent trends in organizational performance. As a consequence, these measurements are highly valuable for the uses suggested for lead time purposes.

Any business firm, governmental agency, or educational institution that wishes to do so can use both lead time human organizational measurements and System 4 to achieve excellent performance at low cost. A number of studies show that, when an organization does this, productivity is higher and costs lower by 15 to 30 percent or more. The use of System 4 and human organizational measurements can pay off handsomely.

PLANNING-PROGRAMMING-BUDGETING

There are, moreover, other valuable uses of these human organizational measurements which reveal the productive capability of an agency and the probable trends in this capability. For example, these data can be used in conjunction with P.P.B. (Planning-Programming-Budgeting).

P.P.B. is a powerful administrative management tool, but it can be effective only in situations where objectives and progress toward their achievement can be expressed in quantitative dimensions. For many governmental operations, it is very difficult, if not impossible, to so state organizational objectives that the extent to which they are being achieved can be measured quantitatively and at a reasonable cost. When this condition exists, it is still possible to make effective use of the powerful resources of P.P.B. This involves shifting the P.P.B. activity from focusing on end-result variables to dealing with human organizational variables. For this purpose, all of the major human organizational variables should be used, including both *causal*—such as managerial behavior—and *intervening*—such as communication, motivation, and control.

This application of the human organizational variables as the fundamental dimension for P.P.B. is based on the substantial body of research findings which show that, when an organization is functioning well, as revealed by measurements of its human organizational variables, it is, or soon will be, achieving its performance, service, and other end-result objectives well. This application of P.P.B. requires that objectives be stated and progress toward their achievement measured in terms of human organizational variables. To date, this combined use of P.P.B. and human organizational variables has not been tried. It is, however, perfectly feasible and is likely to yield highly profitable results.

P.P.B. is used commonly in situations where some, but not all, of the objectives of an organization can be dealt with quantitatively. In some of these situations, P.P.B. may work well. In many, however, it may give the appearance of working well when its use is actually producing costly adverse consequences. This occurs when P.P.B. causes an agency to focus its efforts on activities which, when carried out, may achieve the quantitatively stated subobjective, but with considerable adverse consequences so far as the total objectives of the organization are concerned.

IMPACTS OF COST REDUCTION PROGRAM

The typical cost reduction program can be used to illustrate this point. These cost reduction programs, like P.P.B., focused on a quantitatively defined subobjective, usually accomplish their immediate cost reduction goals, but with serious financial losses to the agency or firm. A study was made recently of a typical cost reduction program in a plant of about 700 persons. This cost reduction program employed the usual methods of "tightening up." The work was analyzed with the aid of outside consultants to see whether the work could be reorganized so as to require less labor. This analysis revealed that in some departments savings in labor could be achieved. For each of these departments, teams consisting of persons from other departments, staff, and outside consultants were established to study the department and recommend how the estimated labor savings could be achieved. The manager of each affected department was ordered to introduce the specific changes and achieve the designated labor savings. The total annual savings amounted to approximately $250,000.

This saving, viewed by itself, was a nice reduction in costs. But measurements of the human organizational variables for this plant, and especially for the departments most affected by the cost reduction effort, showed an appreciable drop. Leadership behavior, motivation, communication, control, coordination, and similar variables all showed an adverse shift. When scores on these variables worsen, research findings show that productivity and earnings drop subsequently. The unfavorable shift in these variables for this plant indicate that an annual drop in earnings of approximately one million dollars is likely to occur in each of the next several years.

Recent data from this plant concerning production, costs, quality, and labor relations indicate that the poorer results forecast by the adverse shift in the human organizational variables are occurring. Moreover, the estimated loss mentioned above understates the total drop, since it ignores all losses due to downtime and any losses caused by customer dissatisfaction due to poor quality.

Long-range survival and financial success are more important in this company's total objectives than are short-range cash flows erroneously labelled "savings." This cash flow was accompanied in this plant by a liquidation of the firm's human assets far greater in amount than the increased cash flow reported as savings. This cost reduction program illustrates the unfavorable consequences to an organization of concentrating on those subobjectives which can be measured with traditional methods, ignoring the extent to which the total objectives are, or are not, being realized.

PROMISE AND PROBLEMS IN P.P.B.

Education is a good example of a situation where it is possible to deal with subobjectives quantitatively, but where it is virtually impossible at any reasonable cost to measure the extent to which each teacher, class, school, and school system is performing efficiently as an educational institution. It is extremely difficult to eliminate or partial out from measurements of educational achievement such influences as each student's native ability and the environment of his home. It is extremely difficult, consequently, and would be prohibitively costly to attempt to measure the overall effectiveness of a school system in achieving its total educational objectives efficiently. For these reasons, P.P.B. cannot be applied to the overall operation of a school system.

P.P.B. is used at present, however, for such specific educational subobjectives as teaching students to read or having a designated proportion of students achieve a specified score on a standardized achievement test. The danger of this use of P.P.B., when only a fractional part of an agency's total objectives is dealt with in quantitative dimensions, is that the subobjective may be accomplished but, often, serious adverse consequences for the organization's total objectives may ensue. The cost of teaching youngsters to read might be reduced, for example, by focusing intensive effort on it and by putting pressure on each teacher to achieve specified results and on each pupil to learn. Such a program could achieve the P.P.B. objective in reducing the costs of teaching students to read, but it could simultaneously create resentful attitudes in teachers and develop hostile attitudes among students toward reading, school, and education. Hostile attitudes toward schools and education lead to dropouts. If the least costly way of teaching reading led to dropouts years later, it would be a high cost to pay for a 5 percent reduction in the cost of learning to read. This would be as inefficient and undesirable as the typical cost reduction programs which yield immediate cash flows accompanied by financial losses over many subsequent years.

It is perfectly feasible for an organization to use P.P.B. to gain the benefit of achieving some of its subobjectives efficiently, without suffering overall adverse consequences. This requires measurements of both the causal and intervening human organizational variables and their use in conjunction with the P.P.B. effort focused on achieving the subobjective. If these human organizational variables are measured and examined regularly, trends in these variables can be used to prevent costly overall consequences while achieving the subobjective. Thus, when P.P.B. is used to reduce the costs of teaching students to read, measurements of the human organizational variables of the school system should be obtained. If the latter measurements reveal an adverse shift in the motivation, values, attitudes, and behavior of teachers and students, the effort to achieve the specified subobjective should be modified appropriately.

These are a few examples of the use of human organizational variables to improve the capacity of any agency or organization to achieve its objectives efficiently.

PART THREE

Managing Individual Behavior

The individual employee is the basic building block of the organization. To a very large degree, overall organizational performance is a function of the individual performance of all organizational members. Although the link between individual level effectiveness and total organizational effectiveness is not simply an additive one, it is clear that successful performance at the individual level is necessary (although perhaps not sufficient) for organizational success.

It has been said that the two basic questions which the field of organizational behavior attempts to answer are, Why do people in organizational settings behave the way they do? and How can we get them to behave differently? It is not oversimplifying too much to say that it was not until the famous Hawthorne studies conducted at Western Electric over 60 years ago that we realized the importance of even asking the first question.

To successfully manage individual behavior in organizations requires that various aspects of what shapes and energizes behavior be recognized, and, when feasible, taken into consideration while carrying out the job of managing organizational behavior. These variables that are so critical in determining individual behavior include individual abilities and skills, personality makeup, psychological variables of perception, attitudes, and needs, socialization experiences, and even such demographic variables as age, gender, and race.

Effective management of individual behavior also requires recognition of the need to obtain the best possible fit between the individual and the larger organization. Aspects of such fit include matching individual needs with organizational rewards, and matching individual skills, abilities, and expertise with job requirements and expectations. The potential dysfunctional consequences of a lack of fit have been both speculated upon and studied by numerous writers and researchers. Such consequences include increases in absenteeism, turnover, waste, sabotage, goldbricking, rate setting, and errors. Similarly, decreases in quantity and quality of output, morale, willingness to take initiatives and accept responsibilities, and commitment to organizational goals and objectives may also occur.

The readings in this part touch upon a variety of individual behavior considerations relevant to managers, including a look at the cause and effects of role conflict and ambiguity in work settings, an overview of the benefits of increasing an individual's level of participation in making decisions, a discussion of why organizations frequently *mis*manage individuals by rewarding the wrong kinds of behaviors, and a classical essay on humanizing the management of individuals in organizations.

16

Role Conflict and Ambiguity in Organizations

Robert L. Kahn

Each individual organizational member has numerous roles to play. These roles, the relationships between and among them, and, particularly, the conflict that can result from them, is the focus of this article. The dynamics of several different types of role conflict are discussed in the context of what the author calls "role episodes."—Eds.

Our studies of role conflict and ambiguity in industry are among a number of researches which share a common and distant goal: to make understandable the effects of the contemporary environment on the person, including his physical and mental health. We begin by thinking of the environment of any individual as consisting very largely of formal organizations and groups. From this point of view the life of the person can be seen as an array of roles which he plays in the particular set of organizations and groups to which he belongs. These groups and organizations, or rather the subparts of each which affect the person directly, together make up his objective environment. Characteristics of these organizations and groups (company, union, church, family, and others) affect the physical and emotional state of the person and are major determinants of his behavior.

The first requirement for linking the individual and the organization is to locate the individual in the total set of ongoing relationships and behaviors comprised by the organization. The key concept for doing this is office, by which we mean a unique point in organizational space, where space is defined in terms of a structure of interrelated offices and the pattern of activities associated with them. Associated with each office is a set of activities or potential behaviors. These activities constitute the role to be performed by any person who occupies that office. Each office in an organization is directly related to certain others, less directly to still others, and,

---

SOURCE: Reprinted with permission from *The Personnel Administrator* 9 (March–April 1964), pp. 8–13.

perhaps only remotely, to the remaining offices included in the organization. Consider the office oi press foreman in a factory manufacturing external trim parts for automobiles. The offices most directly related to that of press foreman might include general foreman and superintendent, from which press foreman's work assignments emanate and to which he turns for approval of work done. Also directly related to the office of press foreman will be the foreman of the sheet metal shop, which provides stock for the presses, the inspector who must pass or reject the completed stampings, the shipping foreman who receives and packages the stampings, and, of course, the 14 press operators for whose work press foreman is responsible. We can imagine the organizational chart spread before us like a vast fish net, in which each knot represents an office and each string a functional relationship between offices. If we pick up the net by seizing any office, we see immediately the other offices to which it is directly attached. Thus, when we pick the office of press foreman, we find it attached directly to 19 others—general foreman, superintendent, sheet metal foreman, inspector, shipping room foreman, and 14 press operators. These 19 offices make up the role-set for the office of press foreman.

In similar fashion each member of an organization is directly associated with a relatively small number of others, usually the occupants of offices adjacent to his in the work flow structure. They constitute his role-set and usually include his immediate supervisor (and perhaps his supervisor's direct superior), his immediate subordinates, and certain members of his own and other departments with whom he must work closely. These offices are defined into his role-set by virtue of his work flow, technology, and authority structure of the organization. Also included in a person's role-set may be people who are related to him in other ways—close friends, respected "identification models," and others within or outside the organization who for one reason or another are concerned with his behavior in his organization role (Figure 1).

All members of a person's role-set depend upon his performance in some fashion; they are rewarded by it, or they require it in order to perform their own tasks. Because they have a stake in his performance, they develop beliefs and attitudes about what he should and should not do as his role. These preferences, which we will refer to as "role expectations," are by no means restricted to the job description as it might be given by the head of the organization or prepared by some specialist in personnel.

For each person in an organization, then, there is a pattern of role expectations, which exists in the minds of members of his role-set, and represent standards in terms of which they evaluate his performance. The expectations do not remain in the minds of members of the role-set, however. They are communicated in many ways—sometimes directly, as when a supervisor instructs a subordinate in the requirements of his job; sometimes indirectly, as when a colleague expresses admiration or disappointment in some behavior. The crucial point is that the activities which define a role

FIGURE 1   Focal Person and Role-Set

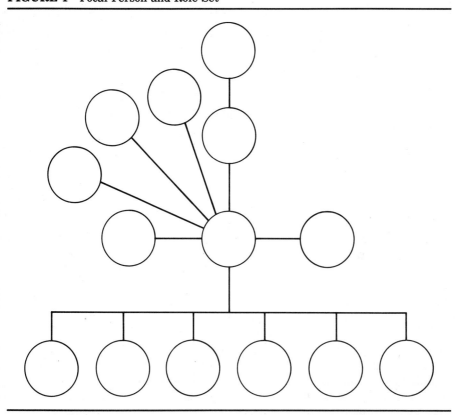

consist of the expectations of members of the role-set, and that these expectations are communicated or sent to the focal person (the person occupying the role being studied).

It is apparent from the approach to social role described above that various members of the role-set for a given office may hold quite different role expectations toward the focal person. At any given time, they may impose pressures on him toward different kinds of behavior. To the extent that these role pressures are felt by him, he experiences psychological conflict. In the objective sense, then, role conflict may be defined as the simultaneous occurrence of two or more sets of pressures, such that compliance with one would make more difficult or render impossible compliance with the other. For example, a person's superior may make it clear to him that he is expected to hold his subordinates strictly to company rules and to high production schedules. At the same time, his subordinates may indicate in various ways that they would like loose, relaxed supervision, and that they will make things difficult if they are pushed too hard. The pressures from above and below in this case are incompatible, since the style of supervision which satisfies one set of pressures violates the other set. Cases of this kind are so common that a whole literature has been created on the problem of the first line supervisor as the man in the middle, or the master and victim of double-talk.

Several types of role conflict can be identified. One might be termed intra-sender conflict: different prescriptions and proscriptions from a given member of the role-set may be incompatible, as for example when a supervisor requests a man to acquire material which is unavailable through normal channels and at the same time prohibits violations of normal channels.

A second type might be termed inter-sender conflict: pressures from one role sender oppose pressures from another sender. The pressures for close versus loose supervisory styles cited above constitute an example of this type of conflict.

A third type of conflict we refer to as inter-role conflict. In this case the role pressure is associated with membership in one organization and in conflict with pressures which stem from membership in other groups. For example, demands on the job for overtime or take-home work may conflict with pressures from one's wife to give undivided attention to family affairs during evening hours. The conflict arises between the role of the person as worker and his role as husband and father.

All three of these types of role conflict begin in the objective environment, although they will regularly result in psychological conflicts for the focal person. Other types of conflict, however, are generated directly by a combination of environmental pressures and internal forces. A major example is the conflict which may exist between the needs and values of a person and the demands of others in his role-set. This fourth type of conflict we will call person-role conflict. It can occur when role requirements violate moral values—for example, when pressures on an executive to enter price- fixing conspiracies are opposed by his personal code of ethics. In other cases, a person's needs and aspirations may lead to behaviors which are unacceptable to members of his role-set; for example, an ambitious young man may be called up short by his associates for stepping on their toes while trying to advance in the organization.

All the types of role conflict discussed above have in common one major characteristic—members of a role-set exerting pressure to change the behavior of a focal person. When such pressures are generated and sent, they do not enter an otherwise empty field; the focal person is already in role, already behaving, already maintaining some kind of equilibrium among the disparate forces and motives which he experiences. Pressures to change, therefore, represent new and additional forces with which he must cope; by definition, they threaten an existing equilibrium. Moreover, the stronger the pressures from role senders toward change in the behavior of the focal person, the greater the conflict created for him.

This approach to the understanding of behavior in organizations in general and the understanding of role conflict in particular is summarized in Figure 2, which illustrates a role episode: that is, a complete cycle of role sending, response by the focal person, and the effects of that response on the role senders.

The four boxes in Figure 2 represent events that constitute a role episode. The arrows connecting them imply a causal sequence. Role pressures are assumed to originate in the expectations held by members of the role-set. Role senders have expectations regarding the way in which the focal role should be performed. They also have perceptions regarding the way in which the focal person is actually performing. They correlate the two and exert pressures to make his performance congruent with their expectations. These pressures induce in the focal person an experience which has both perceptual and cognitive properties, and which leads in turn to certain adjustive (or maladjustive) responses. The responses of the focal person are typically perceived by those exerting the pressures, and their expectations are correspondingly adjusted. Thus, for both the role senders and the focal person the episode involves experience and the response to experience. Let us look in more detail at the contents of the four boxes in Figure 2 and at the relations among them.

A role episode starts with the existence of a set of role expectations held by other persons about a focal person and his behavior on the job. Speaking of the members of a person's role-set as a group is a matter of convenience. In fact, each member of the role-set behaves toward the focal person in ways determined by his own expectations and his own anticipations of the focal person's responses. Under certain circumstances a member of the role-set, responding to his own immediate experience, expresses his expectations overtly; he attempts to influence the focal person in the direction of greater conformity with his expectations. Arrow 1 indicates that the total set of such influence attempts affects the immediate experience of the focal person in a given situation (Box III in Figure 2). This experience includes, for example, the focal person's perception of the demands and requirements placed on

FIGURE 2   A Model of the Role Episode

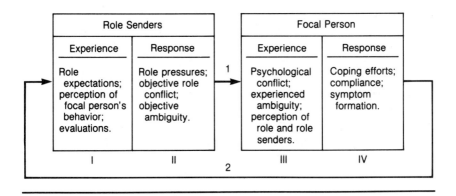

him by members of his role-set, and his awareness or experience of psychological conflict. The specific reactions of each focal person to a situation are immediately determined by the nature of his experience in that situation. Any person who is confronted with a situation of role conflict, however, must respond to it in some fashion. One or more members of his role-set are exerting pressure on him to change his behavior, and he must cope somehow with the pressure they are exerting. Whatever pattern of response he adopts may be regarded as an attempt to attain or regain an adequately gratifying experience in the work situation. He may attempt a direct solution of the objective problem by compliance or by persuading others to modify their incompatible demands. He may attempt to avoid the sources of stress, perhaps by using defense mechanisms which distort the reality of a conflictful or ambiguous situation. There is also the possibility that coping with the pressures of the work will involve the formation of affective or physiological symptoms. Regardless of which of these, singly or in combination, the focal person uses, his behavior can be assessed in relation to the expectations of each of his role senders.

The degree to which the focal person's behavior conforms to the expectations held for him will affect the state of those expectations at the next moment. If his response is essentially a hostile counterattack, members of his role-set are apt to think of him and behave toward him in ways quite different than if he were submissively compliant. If he complies partially under pressure, they may increase the pressure; if he is obviously overcome with tension and anxiety, they may "lay off." In some, the role episode is abstracted from a process which is cyclic and ongoing; the response of the focal person to role pressure feeds back on the senders of those pressures in ways that alter or reinforce them. The next role sendings of each member of the set depend on his evaluations of the response to his last sendings, and thus a new episode begins.

In order to understand more fully the causal dynamics of such episodes and their consequences for the person's adjustment, the model must be extended to include three additional classes of variables—organizational factors, personality factors, and the character of inter-personal relations between the focal person and other members of his role-set. Taken in combination, these factors represent the context within which the episode occurs. In Figure 3 the role episode is shown in the context of these three additional classes of variables. Figure 2 forms the core of Figure 3. However, the circles in Figure 3 represent not momentary events but enduring states of the organization, the person, and the inter-personal relations between focal person and other members of his role set. An analysis of these factors makes more understandable the sequence of events in a role episode. Figure 3 provides a convenient framework within which to summarize the major research findings obtained from an intensive study of 54 role sets in a number of different industries, and from a national survey of approximately 1,500 households.

FIGURE 3   A Theoretical Model of Factors Involved in Adjustment to Role
Conflict and Ambiguity

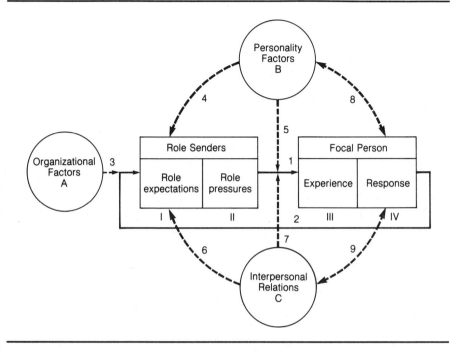

EFFECTS OF CONFLICT AND AMBIGUITY

Role Conflict

The experience of role conflict is common indeed in the work situation. Almost half of our respondents reported being caught "in the middle" between two conflicting persons or factions. These conflicts are usually hierarchical; 88 percent of the people involved in them report at least one party to the conflict as being above them in the organization. Somewhat less than half report that one of the conflicting parties is outside the organization. One of the dominant forms of role conflict is overload, which can be thought of as a conflict among legitimate tasks, or a problem in the setting of priorities; almost half of all respondents reported this problem.

The intensive study, in which role senders and focal persons were interviewed independently, deals more directly with the causal sequences initiated by conditions of conflict. Measures of objective conflict, as derived from the expectations of individual role senders, are strongly associated with the subjective experience of conflict, as reported by the focal person, who is target of incompatible expectations. These, in turn, are linked to affective and behavioral responses of that person.

For the focal person, the emotional costs of role conflict include low job satisfaction, low confidence in the organization, and high scores on the multi-item index of tension. The most frequent behavioral response to role conflict is withdrawal or avoidance of those who are seen as creating the conflict. Symptomatic of this is the attempt of the conflicted person to reduce communication with his co-workers and to assert (sometimes unrealistically) that they lack power over him. Case material indicates that such withdrawal, while a mechanism of defense is not a mechanism of solution. It appears to reduce the possibility of subsequent collaborative solutions to role conflict.

Role Ambiguity

The prevalence of role ambiguity appears to be approximately comparable to that of role conflict. Four specific subjects of ambiguity are cited as disturbing and troublesome in approximately equal numbers of respondents. These include uncertainty about the way in which one's supervisor evaluates one's work, about opportunities for advancement, about scope of responsibility, and about the expectations of others regarding one's performance. Each of these areas of ambiguity was mentioned by approximately one third of the respondents. In all, about two persons out of five considered that they were given insufficient information to perform their jobs adequately.

Among the major sources of role ambiguity about which we speculated were complexity of task and technology, rapidity of organizational change, interconnectedness of organizational positions, and that managerial philosophy which advocates restriction of information on the assumption that the division of labor makes broad information unnecessary for most positions.

The individual consequences of ambiguity conditions are in general comparable to the individual effects of role conflict. These include, for ambiguity: low job satisfaction, low self-confidence, a high sense of futility, and a high score on the tension index. There is evidence, however, that the response of the person to ambiguity is highly selective. For example, ambiguity regarding the evaluations of others does not decrease the intrinsic satisfaction of the employee with the job, although it does decrease his self-confidence and weaken his positive effect for co-workers.

Determinants of Conflict and Ambiguity. The major organizational determinants of conflict and ambiguity include three kinds of role requirements—the requirement for crossing organizational boundaries, the requirement for producing innovative solutions to nonroutine problems, and the requirement for being responsible for the work of others (Arrow 3).

Let us consider first the requirement for crossing a company boundary. Both the frequency and the importance of making contacts outside one's company are associated with the experience of role conflict. Crossing the company boundary is associated also with experienced tension, but the relationship is curvilinear; greatest tension is experienced by those who have discontinuous contacts outside the organization. We propose the hypothesis that, in positions which require extra-company contacts on a continuous basis, there are special facilities or some other organizational acknowledgment of boundary difficulties which renders them less painful.

Hypothetical explanations for the stressfulness of boundary crossing are available primarily from case materials. It appears that the person who must frequently deal with people outside the company usually has limited control over these outsiders. He cannot strongly influence their demands and the resources which they supply to him. Moreover, a person in a boundary position is likely to be blamed by people in his own company for what his outside contacts do or fail to do. They in turn may blame him for shortcomings in his own company. The difficulties of living at the boundary of an organization are intensified when the boundary-dweller must coordinate his extra-organizational activities with people in other departments within the company.

In general, living "near" a departmental or other intra-organizational boundary has effects very like those just remarked for boundaries of the organization itself. Nearness to a departmental boundary and frequency of dealing across such boundaries are associated with felt conflict and with experienced tension.

Roles which demand creative problem solving are associated with high role conflict and with tension. The occupants of such roles appear to become engaged in conflict primarily with older and often more powerful individuals in the organization, who want to maintain the status quo. Among the major role conflicts which persons in innovative jobs complain of is the conflict of priority between the nonroutine activities which are at the core of the creative job and the routine activities of administration or paper work. These latter, according to the people who fill innovative positions, are unduly time consuming, disrupt the continuity of their creative work, and are generally unpalatable.

There is considerable evidence that organizations exercise selective effort in choosing people for innovative positions. People in such positions tend to be characterized by high self-confidence, high mobility aspirations, high job involvement, low apathy, and a tendency to rate the importance of a job extremely high compared to the importance of other areas of their lives.

Supervisory responsibility emerges as a major organizational determinant of role conflict. Either the supervision of rank-and-file employees or the supervision of people who are themselves supervisors appears to have substantial effects on the degree of objective conflict and the amount of experienced conflict. In combination, direct and indirect supervisory responsibility produce very substantial role conflict and tension. There is a systematic relationship also between rank and role conflict, as there is between rank and tension. The often heard assertion that the lowest levels of supervision are subjected to the greatest conflict is not borne out by these data. Rather, there is a curvilinear relationship in which the maximum of conflict and conflict experience occurs at what might be called the "upper middle" levels of management. We interpret this in part as a consequence of the still unfulfilled mobility aspirations of middle management, in contrast to the better actualized aspirations of top management people.

Inter-personal Relations and Role Conflict.   The sources of pressure and conflict for a person can be expressed rather fully in terms of his inter-personal relations with these pressure sources. The greatest pressure is directed to a person from other people who are in the same department as he is, who are his superiors in the hierarchy, and who are sufficiently dependent on his performance to care about his adequacy without being so completely dependent as to be inhibited in making their demands known (Arrow 6). The people who are least likely to apply such pressures are a person's peers and role senders outside his own department.

The kinds of pressure which people are prepared to apply, as well as the degree of that pressure, vary considerably with their formal inter-personal relationship to the potential target of their pressures. Thus, supervisors seem to refrain from exerting coercive power where it might impede the performance of the focal person and perhaps reflect upon the supervisor himself. On the other hand, the techniques used by subordinates to apply coercive power are precisely those which threaten the efficiency of the organization. They include the withholding of aid and information.

When a person is surrounded by others who are highly dependent on him and who have high power over him and exert high pressure on him, his response is typically one of apathy and withdrawal (Arrow 7). Moreover, under such circumstances, his experience of role conflict is very high and his job satisfaction correspondingly reduced. Emotionally he experiences a sense of futility and attempts a hopeless withdrawal from his co-workers.

There is significant evidence that close and positive inter-personal relations between a focal person and members of his role set can mediate substantially the effects of role conflict (Arrow 7). A given degree of objective role conflict is experienced as less stressful in the context of positive affective relations with others. Nevertheless, experienced conflict and ambiguity appear to cause deterioration in inter-personal relations (Arrow 9). Thus, a consequence of role conflict is decreased trust, respect, and liking for co-workers, and in the presence of experienced ambiguity there is a similar attempt on the part of the focal person to weaken inter-personal relations. As with conflict, this weakening of inter-personal relations is self-defeating, since he finds himself withdrawing in the face of ambiguity from the very persons from whom he requires information.

Personality Variables in Conflict and Ambiguity.   Several personality dimensions mediate significantly (Arrow 8) the degree to which a given intensity of objective conflict is experienced as strain by the focal person. These personality dimensions include emotional sensitivity, sociability, and flexibility-rigidity. With respect to sociability, we find that the effects of objective role conflict on inter-personal bonds and on tension are more pronounced for people who are unsociable (independent). The independent person, in other words, develops social relations which, while often congenial and trusting, are easily undermined by conditions of stress. The preference of such people for autonomy becomes manifest primarily when social contacts are stressful; that is, when others are exerting strong pressures and thereby creating conflict for the persons. In similar fashion, emotional sensitivity conditions very sharply the relationship between objective conflict and tension, with emotionally sensitive persons showing substantially higher tension scores for any given degree of objective conflict. There is also a tendency for people of different personality characteristics to be exposed by their senders to differing degrees of objective conflict (Arrow 4). Thus, people who are relatively flexible are subjected to stronger pressures than those who have already demonstrated by their rigidity the futility of applying such pressures.

CONCLUSION

Much of the role conflict in industry takes the form of overload, especially in managerial positions. The focal person has more demands flooding in on him than he can possibly satisfy. He may try to deal with such pressures by exporting his work-induced tensions to outside groups, such as his family, but this is a form of industrial drainage which the community can ill afford. Some persons shut off communication from others in the work situation and thus reduce their own pressures—at the same time reducing the effectiveness of the organization and increasing the pressures of those people who try in vain to communicate with them.

It is not exaggeration to say that most of the responses which we have observed for coping with conflict, ambiguity, and overload are less than satisfactory for individual and for organization. It seems that more constructive resolution of pressure situations ought to be possible. For example, why should the person who experiences role conflict or ambiguity not convene the members of his role-set, who have in effect created the situation which he finds stressful, so they can make a joint attack on the problem? None of the people in the set knows the totality of the focal person's job requirements (any more than he knows theirs), but this is something he can explain to them. Each person in an organization is the ultimate expert in this single respect: He knows better than anyone else the combination of demands which are being made upon him and what their immediate sources are.

A ceremony of confrontation and joint problem solving would seem to be a useful mode of conflict resolution. Why does it not happen? Two factors may work to prevent it. The first is subjective, a feeling that such an approach is unorthodox, unlikely to work, or even downright dangerous. The second may be inherent in the structure of hierarchical organizations.

Regarding the subjective factor, it is indeed difficult to find people who are willing and able to undertake such a confrontation of superiors, subordinates, and peers. A person may have deliberately created overload, conflict, or ambiguity in order to further his own organizational ambitions or to increase his power. More often, his feelings of insecurity and embarrassment prevent him from attempting such a group solution to his problems. Regarding the organizational factor, the risks and rewards of industrial life often cause individuals to keep their information sources private and hold as much power as possible in their own hands. Confrontation under such circumstances could be viewed as a giving away of precious power and information, or even as an admission of incompetence. More frequently, perhaps, the person in conflict feels that he lacks the power to convene the members of his role-set in the first place. How many people in industry can recall taking the initiative in bringing together their subordinates, supervisors, and peers to consider the incompatibilities in their various expectations?

Nevertheless, there is in many managements a growing interest in solving the human problems of large-scale organizations, a growing realization that the solutions will involve structural changes as well as gains in interpersonal skills, and a growing willingness to innovate and evaluate in the effort to put organizations more fully into the service of human needs. These attitudes of management, in combination with research, offer new possibilities for understanding organized human behavior. We know of no goal more deserving of our effort.

17

Participation by Subordinates in the Managerial Decision-Making Process

Robert Tannenbaum
and
Fred Massarik

Issues relating to the extent and means of individual participation in a variety of organizational contexts have long been debated. This article examines three major approaches to dealing with participation in decision making. The possible advantages of participation are analyzed, as are the psychological conditions necessary for effective participation. —Eds.

I. INTRODUCTION

The role of "participation" by individuals or groups in American culture in general and in industrial organizations specifically has been treated by many writers. Its implications for political theory as well as for a theory of human relations in formal organizations are numerous. However, in spite of this academic and extra-academic interest, a clear-cut, operational definition of the concept, or a precise set of hypotheses regarding its dynamics, has not been developed. While to do so will be the object of this paper, the treatment will not be completely operational. The development of appropriate methods of measurement is conceived as a next step that should follow the preliminary one of conceptual clarification undertaken in this paper.

A review of the literature indicates that three major approaches have been taken in dealing with "participation":

(1) The Experiential Approach. This approach is exemplified by writers who in the course of their experience in enterprise work have obtained a "feel" for the role of participation in the decision-making process and have put down their experiences in article or book form.[1] Writings such

---

SOURCE: From *The Canadian Journal of Economics and Political Science* 16, no. 3 (August 1950), pp. 408–18. Reprinted with permission.

as these provide a set of insights and hunches whose verification in any systematic fashion has not been attempted. The actual referents from which these formulations are derived often are single sets of observations in a single or in a few enterprises—observations generally made in an uncontrolled fashion.

The experiential approach, operating outside the bounds of scientific method, nonetheless adds to scientific knowledge indirectly by providing the raw material from which hypotheses may be moulded. The precise structure of these hypotheses is not stated neatly by the experiential writers, but rather remains to be formulated.

(2)   The Conceptual, Nonexperimental Approach.   This approach characterizes the writings of authors who are, essentially, academicians with strong theoretical backgrounds. It is typified by writings that deal with "conditions," "functions," and other abstractions, generally of a sociopsychological nature, that attempt to explain the dynamics of participation.[2] The conceptual, nonexperimental approach at its best is the process of theory or hypothesis formulation. Ideally it lays the groundwork for actual testing and experimental work, but much of this type of technical literature so far published on participation lacks the clarity of conceptual definition necessary to make it useful as a basis for experimental work.

(3)   The Experimental Approach.   This approach is found in the writings of authors who have seen fit to apply experimental techniques either to especially constructed social situations involving participation, or else in natural settings in which participational activities prevail.[3] With adequate controls and with a meaningful theoretical structure within which individual findings may be placed, this approach is doubtless the most fruitful. Ideally it indicates what will happen under specified sets of conditions and with what degree of probability. Unfortunately, up to now, experimental work on the dynamics of participation in the decision-making process has been sporadic.[4]

The present paper is of the conceptual, nonexperimental type. Participation in the decision-making process is conceived here as an instrument that may be used by the formal leadership of an enterprise in the pursuit of its goals. No attempt will be made to examine it from an ethical standpoint or in terms of its consistency within the frame of a democratic society, although it is by no means assumed that such considerations are less important than the ones set forward here.

II.   DEFINITION OF PARTICIPATION

It is essential, in dealing with participation, to make clear the meaning which is to be attached to the concept. One must specify both who the participators are and in what they are participating. Too frequently in the available literature on the subject the reader must determine these matters for himself, since no explicit statements bearing on them are made by the writers.

As already indicated, this paper is primarily concerned with participation as a managerial device. Attention, therefore, is focused on the subordinates of managers in enterprises as the participators. It is important to note that these subordinates may be either nonmanagers or managers.[5] If they are managers, they are subordinates of superior managers in the formal organization of the enterprise in addition to having subordinates who are responsible to them.

Because of space limitations, consideration of the participation of individuals as union members in specific activities of an enterprise is excluded from the scope of this paper. Suffice it to say here that, in those cases where the participation of union members is direct and personal, the benefits to be derived by the enterprise are similar to those derived from participation within the superior-subordinate relationship. However, in those cases (which are the greatest in number) where the participation of the union member is indirect and impersonal, it is doubtful if such is the result. It is our conclusion that most of the statements which follow are relevant to the former cases.[6]

What then is the meaning of participation, and with what type of participation by subordinates are we here concerned? An individual participates in something when he takes a part or share in that thing. Since taking a part or sharing is always involved, participation takes place in a social context. Managerial subordinates in formal enterprises are responsible to their superiors for the performance of designated tasks. In such performance, they are participating in the production of the good or service of the enterprise. They also participate (share), through the receipt of wages or salaries, in the distribution of the total revenue received by the enterprise. These types of participation are common to all enterprises. But there is another type of participation which is much less frequently encountered, although its use as a managerial device has, of recent years, grown rapidly in importance. This type involves participation by subordinates with their superiors in the managerial decision-making process.

Decisions are made by managers in order to organize, direct, or control responsible subordinates to the end that all service contributions be coordinated in the attainment of an enterprise purpose.[7] Since managers are those who accomplish results through subordinates, the latter are always directly and intimately affected by managerial decisions and, therefore, may have a considerable interest in them. Because of this possible interest, subordinates may have a strong desire, particularly in a nation with deeply ingrained democratic traditions, to participate in the determination of matters affecting them. It is of importance, therefore, to consider the form which such participation might assume.

Decision making involves a conscious choice or selection of one behavior alternative from among a group of two or more behavior alternatives.[8] Three steps are involved in the decision-making process. First, an individual must become aware of as many as possible of those behavior alternatives which are relevant to the decision to be made. Second, he must define each of these alternatives, a definition which involves a determination of as many as possible of the consequences related to each alternative under consideration. Third, the individual must exercise a choice between the alternatives, that is, make a decision.

In enterprises, managerial subordinates, as subordinates, can participate in the first two steps of the managerial decision-making process. They cannot participate in the third step. The actual choice between relevant alternatives must be made or accepted by the manager who is responsible to his superior for the decision.[9] However, subordinates can provide and discuss with their manager information with respect both to relevant alternatives and to the consequences attendant upon specific alternatives. In so doing they are participating in the managerial decision-making process.[10]

The participation with which we are here concerned may take place in two different ways. First, it may involve interaction solely between a subordinate and his manager.[11] This would be the case where a worker originates a suggestion which he transmits to his boss. Secondly, it may involve interaction between a group of subordinates and their manager. This would be the case where a manager calls his subordinates together to discuss a common problem or to formulate a recommendation.[12]

III. POSSIBLE ADVANTAGES OF PARTICIPATION AS A MANAGERIAL DEVICE

It becomes useful to inquire why managers might find it advantageous to use this device. In other words, what are the possible benefits which might accrue to an enterprise whose managers made it possible for subordinates to participate in the decision-making process? In providing an answer to this question, it is first necessary to indicate the criterion which would guide the managerial choice relating to the use of participation.

A manager of an enterprise (profit or nonprofit) who behaves rationally will attempt to make a selection from among alternatives related to any problem which will maximize results (the degree of attainment of a given end) at a given cost or which will attain given results at the lowest cost.[13] This is the criterion of rationality. Guided by this criterion, rational managers will find it advantageous to use participation whenever such use will lead to increased results at a given cost or to the attainment of given results at a lower cost.

There are many advantages which *may* stem from the use of participation as a managerial device. The following are the principal ones:

1. A higher rate of output and increased quality of product (including reduced spoilage and wastage) as a result of greater personal effort and attention on the part of subordinates.[14]

2. A reduction in turnover, absenteeism, and tardiness.

3. A reduction in the number of grievances and more peaceful manager-subordinate and manager-union relations.

4. A greater readiness to accept change.[15] When changes are arbitrarily introduced from above without explanation, subordinates tend to feel insecure and to take countermeasures aimed at a sabotage of the innovations. But when they have participated in the process leading to the decision, they have had an opportunity to be heard. They know what to expect and why, and they may desire the change. Blind resistance tends to become intelligent adaptation as insecurity is replaced by security.

5. Greater ease in the management of subordinates.[16] Fewer managers may be necessary, the need for close supervision may be reduced, and less disciplinary action may be called for. Subordinates who have participated in the process leading toward a determination of matters directly affecting them may have a greater sense of responsibility with respect to the performance of their assigned tasks and may be more willing to accept the authority of their superiors. All managers possess a given amount of formal authority delegated to them by their superiors. But formal authority is not necessarily the equivalent of effective authority. The real source of the authority possessed by an individual lies in the acceptance of its exercise by those who are subject to it. It is the subordinates of an individual who determine the authority which he may wield. Formal authority is, in effect, nominal authority. It becomes real only when it is accepted. Thus, to be effective, formal authority must coincide with authority determined by its acceptance. The latter defines the useful limits of the former.[17] The use of participation as a managerial device may result in a widening of these limits, reducing the amount of resistance to the exercise of formal authority and increasing the positive responses of subordinates to managerial directives.

6. The improved quality of managerial decisions. It is seldom, if ever, possible for managers to have knowledge of *all* alternatives and *all* consequences related to the decisions which they must make. Because of the existence of barriers to the upward flow of information in most enterprises, much valuable information possessed by subordinates never reaches their managers. Participation tends to break down the barriers, making the information available to managers. To the extent that such information alters the decisions which managers make, the quality of their decisions may thereby be improved.

These, then, are the principal advantages which *may* stem from the use of participation as a managerial device.[18] The conditions under which it *will* accomplish them—under which participation will lead to motivation—is the concern of the section which follows.

IV. THE PSYCHOLOGICAL CONDITIONS OF EFFECTIVE PARTICIPATION

All managers of an enterprise are faced with the problem of eliciting services—contributions from their subordinates at a high level of quality and intensity. These service contributions are essential if the formal goals of the enterprise are to be attained. What induces subordinates to contribute their services? What motivates them?

A motivated individual is one who is striving to achieve a goal; his activity is goal-oriented.[19] But it should be stressed that motivation is only *potential* motion towards a goal. Whether or not the goal is reached depends not only upon the strength of the force in the direction of the goal but also upon other forces (both driving and restraining) in the given situation.[20] To illustrate, a person may be motivated to produce 200 units of an item per day, while the restraining force in the form of machine failure or a quarrel with the next man may lead him to attain an output of only 150 units.

In enterprises, the goals toward which individuals strive may be of two kinds. They may be the formal goals of the enterprise, or they may be goals which are complementary to the formal goals. The latter is the typical case. Individuals may strive for monetary reward, prestige, power, security and the like, or they may strive for certain psychological gratifications through the very act of doing the job (i.e., they work because they like their work). The primary reason why they contribute their services is to attain these latter goals. In attaining these desired goals, they make possible the attainment of the formal goals of the enterprise which to them are simply means to their own ends. In this sense, the desired goals and the formal goals are complementary.

In the former case, the goals desired by the individual and the formal goals are the same. The individual contributes his services primarily because such contribution makes possible the attainment of the formal goals of the enterprise which coincide with his own personal goals. To the extent that this coincidence of goals exists, the necessity for managers to provide complementary goals for subordinates is thereby lessened, and related costs are reduced. It is suggested that participation tends to bring about a coincidence of formal and personal goals.[21] It may be that, through participation, the subordinate who formerly was moved to contribute his services only because he sought, for example, security and financial rewards, now comes to be moved additionally because he recognizes that the success of the enterprise in turn will enhance his own ability to satisfy his needs.[22]

Whether one conceives of participation as involving separate subordinates with their superiors or subordinates in groups with their superiors, in the final analysis one must not lose sight of the fact that the subordinate is a unique human being with a given personality. This implies that whether or not participation will bring forth the restructuring of his goal pattern (incorporating the formal goals within the scope of the personal goals) will depend upon a set of dynamic psychological conditions, the primary ones of which are outlined below:

1. The subordinate must be capable of becoming psychologically involved in the participational activities. He must be free from "blockages" which may prevent him from rearranging his particular goal pattern in the light of new experience. He must possess some minimum amount of intelligence so that he may grasp the meaning and implications of the thing being considered. He must be in touch with reality. If he responds to a dream world, any "real" developments, such as opportunities to take part in certain decision-making processes, may not penetrate without gross distortion and as a result miss their point.

2. The subordinate must favor participational activity. In other words, the person who believes that "the boss knows best" and that the decision-making process is none of his business is not likely to become strongly motivated if given an opportunity to participate. It is apparent that, for personality types shaped intensely by an authoritarian system, opportunities for participation may be regarded as signs of weakness and leadership incompetence and, on that basis, may be rejected unequivocally.[23]

3. The subordinate must see the relevance to his personal life pattern of the thing being considered. When he realizes that through participation he may affect the course of his future in such a fashion as to increase its positive goal elements and to diminish the negative ones, he will become motivated. For example, a person who can see the relationship between "putting his two bits" into a discussion of a new way of using a stitching machine and the fact that this may mean greater job security and increased pay for himself may be motivated.

4. The subordinate must be able to express himself to his own satisfaction with respect to the thing being considered. He must be psychologically able to communicate; and, further, he must feel that he is making some sort of contribution. Of course, if he cannot communicate (owing to mental blocks—fear of being conspicuous, etc.), by definition he is not participating. If he does not feel that he is contributing, he may, instead of becoming motivated, come to feel inadequate and frustrated. This presupposes that not only is he articulate but that he has a certain fund of knowledge on which to draw. Participation may fail if it involves considering matters that are quite outside the scope of experience of the participators.

All of the above conditions must be satisfied to some minimum extent. Beyond this requirement, however, the conditions may be mutually compensating, and a relatively low degree of one (although necessarily above the minimum) may be offset somewhat by an extremely high degree of another. For example, if a subordinate is unusually anxious to take part in participational activity (perhaps for reasons of prestige desires), he may come to be quite involved in the process of restructuring his goal pattern so it will include some of the formal goals, even though he is not always certain whether he is really contributing anything worthwhile. Further, the relationships specified by the conditions are essentially dynamic. Opportunities for participation, reluctantly used at first, ultimately may lead to a change of mind and to their enthusiastic acceptance.[24]

It is apparent that individual differences are highly important in considering the effectiveness of participation as a motivational device; however, the "amount of participation opportunities" made possible by the managers is also a variable quantity. Thus, it is necessary to inquire what the limits to opportunities to participate are in terms of maximum results.

Common-sense experience indicates that, when some subordinates are given too many opportunities for participation, or too much leeway in participating, they may tend to flounder; they may find themselves unable to assimilate effectively the range of "thinking opportunities" with which they are faced.[25] On the other hand, if they are given little or no opportunity to take part in the decision-making process, by definition they will not come to be motivated by participational activity. For each individual, an amount of participation opportunities lying somewhere between these two extremes will result in a maximum amount of motivation. A hypothesis stemming from this formulation is that, for effective operation of participation as a motivational device in a group situation, the members of the group must respond similarly to given amounts of participation, for wide divergences of response may bring forth social tensions and lack of team work within the group.

Of course, many factors act together to motivate an individual. Therefore, the usefulness of the conceptualization advanced depends upon the possibility of breaking down the total of motivational forces into those owing to participation and those owing to other factors. Experimental control methods, matching of cases, and similar devices may have to be utilized to make such an analysis possible. Whether the increment of motivation owing to participation is worthwhile depends to an important extent upon the level of intensity of motivation that prevailed previous to introduction of the device of participation. No doubt, there are upper limits to intensity of motivation, and, if motivation has been strong all along, the effect of participation may not be very great.

V. EXTRAPARTICIPATIONAL CONDITIONS FOR EFFECTIVE PARTICIPATION

Beyond the factors governing the relationship between participation and possible resultant motivation, certain conditions "outside" the individual must be considered by the managers in deciding whether this particular device is applicable.[26] It would be possible to distinguish a great number of such outside conditions that may determine whether the use of participation is feasible in a given situation. Those here indicated are suggestive, rather than fully definitive. All are viewed with this question in mind: "Granting that participation may have certain beneficial effects, is it useful in a given instance if the ends of the enterprise are to be achieved?"

To answer this question affirmatively, the following conditions must be met:

(1) *Time Availability.* The final decision must not be of a too urgent nature.[27] If it is necessary to arrive at some sort of emergency decision rapidly, it is obvious that, even though participation in the decision-making process may have a beneficial effect in some areas, slowness of decision may result in thwarting other goals of the enterprise or even may threaten the existence of the enterprise. Military decisions frequently are of this type.

(2) *Rational Economics.* The cost of participation in the decision-making process must not be so high that it will outweigh any positive values directly brought about by it. If it should require outlays which could be used more fruitfully in alternative activities (for example, buying more productive though expensive equipment), then investment in it would be ill-advised.

(3) *Intraplant Strategy.*

    (a) *Subordinate Security.* Giving the subordinates an opportunity to participate in the decision-making process must not bring with it any awareness on their part of unavoidable catastrophic events. For example, a subordinate who is made aware in the participation process that he will lose his job *regardless* of any decisions towards which he might contribute may experience a drop in motivation. Furthermore, to make it possible for the subordinate to be willing to participate, he must be given the feeling that no matter what he says or thinks his status or role in the plant setting will not be affected adversely. This point has been made effectively in the available literature.[28]

    (b) *Manager-subordinate Stability.* Giving subordinates an opportunity to participate in the decision-making process must not threaten seriously to undermine the formal authority of the managers of the enterprise. For example, in some cases managers may have good reasons to assume that participation may lead nonmanagers to doubt the competence of the formal leadership, or that serious crises would result were it to develop that the subordinates were right while the final managerial decision turned out to be in disagreement with them and incorrect.

(4) *Interplant Strategy.* Providing opportunities for participation must not open channels of communication to competing enterprises. "Leaks" of information to a competitor from subordinates who have participated in a given decision-making process must be avoided if participation is to be applicable.

(5) *Provision for Communication Channels.* For participation to be effective, channels must be provided through which the employee may take part in the decision-making process. These channels must be available continuously and their use must be convenient and practical.[29]

(6) *Education for Participation.* For participation to be effective, efforts must be made to educate subordinates regarding its function and purpose in the overall functioning of the enterprise.[30]

It must be stressed that the conditions stipulated in this section are dynamic in their own right and may be affected by the very process of participation as well as by other factors.

VI. EFFECTS OF PARTICIPATION AS A FUNCTION OF TIME

An area of research that still remains relatively unexplored is that relating to the variation of the effects of participation with time. Some experimental studies have examined these effects in terms of increased productivity over a period of several weeks or months and found no appreciable reductions in productivity with time; while other evidence indicates that in some cases participation may have a sort of "shock" effect, leading to a surge of interest and increased motivation, with a subsequent decline.[31] Inadequate attention seems to have been given to this rather crucial question, and the present writers know of no studies that have traced the effects of participation (or other motivational devices) over periods as long as a year. However, on a priori grounds, and on the basis of experiential evidence, it would seem that, after an initial spurt, a plateau of beneficial effects will be attained, which finally will dissolve into a decline, unless additional managerial devices are skillfully employed.

NOTES AND REFERENCES

1. For example: H. H. Carey, "Consultative Supervision and Management," *Personnel,* March 1942; Alexander R. Heron, *Why Men Work* (Palo Alto, 1948); Eric A. Nicol, "Management through Consultative Supervision," *Personnel Journal,* November 1948; James C. Worthy, "Changing Concepts of the Personnel Function," *Personnel,* November 1948.

2. For example: Douglas McGregor, "Conditions for Effective Leadership in the Industrial Situation," *Journal of Consulting Psychology* 8 (March–April 1944); Gordon W. Allport, "The Psychology of Participation," *Psychological Review,* May 1945.

3. For the concept of the "natural experiment," see F. Stuart Chapin, *Experimental Designs in Sociological Research* (New York 1947), and Ernest Greenwood, *Experimental Sociology* (New York 1945).

4. For a good summary of relevant experimental work, see Ronald Lippitt, "A Program of Experimentation on Group Functioning and Productivity," *Current Trends in Social Psychology* (Pittsburgh 1948).

5. For definitions of these terms as used here, see Robert Tannenbaum, "The Manager Concept: A Rational Synthesis," *Journal of Business,* October 1949.
6. In connection with this discussion, it should be noted that, when participation takes place within the superior-subordinate relationship, managers have primary control over the nature of the activity; when it takes place as a part of the manager-union relationship, they may or may not, depending upon the relative power of the two parties.
7. See Tannenbaum, "The Manager Concept: A Rational Synthesis."
8. This discussion of the decision-making process is based upon Robert Tannenbaum, "Managerial Decision-Making," *Journal of Business,* January 1950.
9. In a democratic group, the choice can be made through a vote participated in by the rank and file. But, in such a case, the leader is organizationally responsible to the rank and file, and the members of the rank and file are not properly, insofar as the decision is concerned, subordinates of the leader.

   Members of a democratic group, making the final choice in matters directly affecting them, may be more highly motivated as a result thereof than managerial subordinates who are granted the right to participate only in the first two steps of the managerial decision-making process. For evidence of the motivational effects of group decision, see Kurt Lewin, "Group Decision and Social Change," *Readings in Social Psychology,* eds. T. M. Newcomb and E. L. Hartley (New York 1947).
10. It is this type of participation that most writers who deal with human relations in enterprises have in mind when they use the concept. The following examples illustrate this contention: "One of the most important conditions of the subordinate's growth and development centers around his opportunities to express his ideas and to contribute his suggestions before his superiors take action on matters which involve him. Through participation of this kind he becomes more and more aware of his superiors' problems, and he obtains genuine satisfaction in knowing that his opinions and ideas are given consideration in the search for solutions" (D. McGregor, "Conditions for Effective Leadership in the Industrial Situation," p. 60); "I am not suggesting that we take over intact the apparatus of the democratic state. Business cannot be run by the ballot box. . . . We must develop other inventions, adapted to the special circumstances of business, which will give employees at all levels of our organizations a greater sense of personal participation and 'belonging' " (J. Worthy, "Changing Concepts of the Personnel Function," p. 175); "Action initiated by the responsible head to bring his subordinates into the picture on matters of mutual concern is not a sharing of prerogatives of authority. Rather, it is an extension of the opportunity of participation in the development of points of view and the assembly of facts upon which decisions are made" (H. Carey, "Consultative Supervision and Management," p. 288).
11. The concept of interaction as used here is not restricted to direct person-to-person, two-way communication (as in the process of superior-subordinate discussion), but encompasses more indirect forms (such as, for example, written communication) as well.
12. It may be observed that participation in the latter way, where there is communication between participators and where the act of participation is carried out through the medium of the group (as in cases of "group decision"), may often yield the more useful results. The level of derivable benefits may be higher than if participation had proceeded through channels in which there had been no

interparticipator communication. Some factors important in this context are the following: *(a)* the feeling of "group belongingness" obtained by means of "action together" and *(b)* the role of norms, set as a result of group discussion, toward which behavior will tend to gravitate.

13. The term *cost* is here used in its highly precise form to refer to whatever must be given or sacrificed to attain an end. See "Price," *Webster's Dictionary of Synonyms.* The term *end* is broadly conceived to embrace whatever factors (monetary or nonmonetary) the managers themselves define as the formal ends of the enterprise.

14. For examples, see Lippitt, "A Program of Experimentation on Group Functioning and Productivity"; John R. P. French, Jr., Arthur Kornhauser, and Alfred Marrow, "Conflict and Cooperation in Industry," *Journal of Social Issues,* February 1946; *Productivity, Supervision and Morale,* Survey Research Center Study no. 6, Ann Arbor, 1948.

15. See, for example, Alex Bavelas, "Some Problems of Organizational Change," *Journal of Social Issues,* Summer 1948; Elliott Jacques, "Interpretive Group Discussion as a Method of Facilitating Social Change," *Human Relations,* August 1948; Lewin, "Group Decision and Social Change."

16. See, for example, L. P. Bradford and R. Lippitt, "Building a Democratic Work Group," *Personnel,* November 1945; O. H. Mowrer, "Authoritarianism vs. 'Self-Government' in the Management of Children's Aggressive (Antisocial) Reactions as a Preparation for Citizenship in a Democracy," *Journal of Social Psychology,* February 1939, pp. 121–26.

17. This concept of effective authority is expanded on in Tannenbaum, "Managerial Decision Making."

18. These advantages will henceforth be referred to as "enterprise advantages."

19. A goal is defined as a result which, when achieved, has the power to reduce the tension of the organism that has caused the organism to seek it.

20. Thus, motion in the direction of goals may be achieved not only by adding forces in the goal direction but also by reducing forces impeding such motion. See K. Lewin, "Frontiers in Group Dynamics," *Human Relations* 1, no. 1 (1947), pp. 26–27.

21. It must be noted that participation as used in this context is only one device which may lead to additional motivation by bringing about a coincidence of formal and personal goals. For example, some other devices that under certain conditions may result in motivational increases and their derivative benefits to the enterprise are permitting personal discretion to the person to be motivated and stimulation of a sense of pride of workmanship. In the former context, managers in all enterprises must always decide the amount of discretion to permit to subordinates. Many considerations naturally underlie this decision. For present purposes, it is important to emphasize that, in many circumstances, the granting of considerable discretion may lead to substantial increases in motivation. Several devices may be used concurrently, and the dynamics of the devices themselves are interrelated. For example, use of discretion may bring about an enhanced pride-of-workmanship feeling.

22. It must be recognized that typically goal configurations, rather than single goals, act as motivating agents.

23. For example, see A. H. Maslow, "The Authoritarian Character Structure," *Twentieth Century Psychology,* ed. P. L. Harriman (New York 1946). For more detailed treatments, see the major works of Erich Fromm and Abram Kardiner.

24. It should be stressed that "life spaces" of individuals (i.e., their conceptions of themselves in relation to the totality of a physical and psychological environment) and their readiness for action in the light of these conceptions are never static. Constant change and "restructuring" take place, making for an essentially dynamic patterning of behavior. For alternative definitions of the concept "life space," see Robert W. Leeper, *Lewin's Topological and Vector Psychology* (Eugene 1943), p. 210.

25. For the belief that "thinking" as a solution for the industrial problem of motivation is usable more effectively on the supervisory level, but less applicable on the "lower levels" of the organizational hierarchy, see Willard Tomlison, "Review of A. R. Heron, *Why Men Work," Personnel Journal,* July–August 1948, p. 122.

26. For analytical purposes, this article differentiates between conditions regarding the dynamics of participation as a psychological process and all conditions outside this psychological participation-to-motivation link. The latter category of conditions is treated under the present heading.

27. See Chester I. Barnard, *Organization and Management* (Cambridge 1948), p. 48.

28. See McGregor, "Conditions for Effective Leadership in the Industrial Situation," passim.

29. For a rigorous mathematical treatment of channels of communication within groups, see Alex Bavelas, "A Mathematical Model for Group Structures," *Applied Anthropology,* Summer 1948, p. 16ff.

30. See French, Kornhauser, and Marrow, "Conflict and Cooperation in Industry," p. 30.

31. For evidence of no decline in the motivational effect of certain participational procedures in an industrial retraining situation after a relatively brief time period subsequent to initiation of participation had elapsed, see, for example, L. Coch and J. R. P. French, "Overcoming Resistance to Change," *Human Relations* 1, no. 4, pp. 522–23. Also Lewin, "Group Decision and Social Change," pp. 338 and 343. For the hypothesis that under certain conditions decline may occur with time, see Heron, *Why Men Work,* p. 180.

18

On the Folly of Rewarding A, while Hoping for B

Steven Kerr

Supposedly, we reward people for doing what we want them to and don't reward them when they do something else. While it sounds very simple and straightforward, this article by Steven Kerr suggests that it isn't that way at all. He notes that all too often organizations create motivational forces which lead to unwanted and unintended consequences by rewarding behaviors that are not desired and by discouraging behaviors that are desired.—Eds.

Whether dealing with monkeys, rats, or human beings, it is hardly controversial to state that most organisms seek information concerning what activities are rewarded, and then seek to do (or at least pretend to do) those things, often to the virtual exclusion of activities not rewarded. The extent to which this occurs of course will depend on the perceived attractiveness of the rewards offered, but neither operant nor expectancy theorists would quarrel with the essence of this notion.

Nevertheless, numerous examples exist of reward systems that are fouled up, in that behaviors which are rewarded are those which the rewarder is trying to *discourage,* while the behavior he desires is not being rewarded at all.

In an effort to understand and explain this phenomenon, this paper presents examples from society, from organizations in general, and from profit-making firms in particular. Data from a manufacturing company and information from an insurance firm are examined to demonstrate the consequences of such reward systems for the organizations involved, and possible reasons why such reward systems continue to exist are considered.

SOCIETAL EXAMPLES

Politics

Official goals are "purposely vague and general and do not indicate . . . the host of decisions that must be made among alternative ways of achiev-

SOURCE: Reprinted from *Academy of Management Journal* 18 (1975), pp. 769–83.

ing official goals and the priority of multiple goals . . ." (8, p. 66). They usually may be relied on to offend absolutely no one, and in this sense can be considered high-acceptance, low-quality goals. An example might be "build better schools." Operative goals are higher in quality but lower in acceptance, since they specify where the money will come from, what alternative goals will be ignored, etc.

The American citizenry supposedly wants its candidates for public office to set forth operative goals, making their proposed programs "perfectly clear," specifying sources and uses of funds, etc. However, since operative goals are lower in acceptance, and since aspirants to public office need acceptance (from at least 50.1 percent of the people), most politicians prefer to speak only of official goals, at least until after the election. They, of course, would agree to speak at the operative level if "punished" for not doing so. The electorate could do this by refusing to support candidates who do not speak at the operative level.

Instead, however, the American voter typically punishes (withholds support from) candidates who frankly discuss where the money will come from, rewards politicians who speak only of official goals, but hopes that candidates (despite the reward system) will discuss the issues operatively. It is academic whether it was moral for Nixon, for example, to refuse to discuss his 1968 "secret plan" to end the Vietnam war, his 1972 operative goals concerning the lifting of price controls, the reshuffling of his cabinet, etc. The point is that the reward system made such refusal rational.

It seems worth mentioning that no manuscript can adequately define what is "moral" and what is not. However, examination of costs and benefits, combined with knowledge of what motivates a particular individual, often will suffice to determine what for him is "rational."[1] If the reward system is so designed that it is irrational to be moral, this does not necessarily mean that immorality will result. But is this not asking for trouble?

War

If some oversimplification may be permitted, let it be assumed that the primary goal of the organization (Pentagon, Luftwaffe, or whatever) is to win. Let it be assumed further that the primary goal of most individuals on the front lines is to get home alive. Then there appears to be an important conflict in goals—personally rational behavior by those at the bottom will endanger goal attainment by those at the top.

But not necessarily! It depends on how the reward system is set up. The Vietnam war was indeed a study of disobedience and rebellion, with terms such as "fragging" (killing one's own commanding officer) and "search and evade" becoming part of the military vocabulary. The difference in subordinates' acceptance of authority between World War II and Vietnam is reported to be considerable, and veterans of the Second World War often have been quoted as being outraged at the mutinous actions of many American soldiers in Vietnam.

Consider, however, some critical differences in the reward system in use during the two conflicts. What did the GI in World War II want? To go home. And when did he get to go home? When the war was won! If he disobeyed the orders to clean out the trenches and take the hills, the war would not be won and he would not go home. Furthermore, what were his chances of attaining his goal (getting home alive) if he obeyed the orders compared to his chances if he did not? What is being suggested is that the rational soldier in World War II, *whether patriotic or not,* probably found it expedient to obey.

Consider the reward system in use in Vietnam. What did the man at the bottom want? To go home. And when did he get to go home? When his tour of duty was over! This was the case *whether or not* the war was won. Furthermore, concerning the relative chance of getting home alive by obeying orders compared to the chance if they were disobeyed, it is worth noting that a mutineer in Vietnam was far more likely to be assigned rest and rehabilitation (on the assumption that fatigue was the cause) than he was to suffer any negative consequence.

In his description of the "zone of difference," Barnard stated that "a person can and will accept a communication as authoritative only when . . . at the time of his decision, he believes it to be compatible with his personal interests as a whole" (1, p. 165). In light of the reward system used in Vietnam, would it not have been personally irrational for some orders to have been obeyed? Was not the military implementing a system which *rewarded* disobedience, while *hoping* that soldiers (despite the reward system) would obey orders?

Medicine

Theoretically, a physician can make either of two types of error, and intuitively one seems as bad as the other. A doctor can pronounce a patient sick when he is actually well, thus causing him needless anxiety and expense, curtailment of enjoyable foods and activities, and even physical danger by subjecting him to needless medication and surgery. Alternately, a doctor can label a sick person well, and thus avoid treating what may be a serious, even fatal ailment. It might be natural to conclude that physicians seek to minimize both types of error.

Such a conclusion would be wrong.[2] It is estimated that numerous Americans are presently afflicted with iatrogenic (physician-*caused*) illnesses (9). This occurs when the doctor is approached by someone complaining of a few stray symptoms. The doctor classifies and organizes these symptoms, gives them a name, and obligingly tells the patient what further symptoms may be expected. This information often acts as a self-fulfilling prophecy, with the result that from that day on the patient for all practical purposes is sick.

Why does this happen? Why are physicians so reluctant to sustain a type 2 error (pronouncing a sick person well) that they will tolerate many type 1 errors? Again, a look at the reward system is needed. The punishments for a type 2 error are real: guilt, embarrassment, and the threat of lawsuit and scandal. On the other hand, a type 1 error (labeling a well person sick) "is sometimes seen as sound clinical practice, indicating a healthy conservative approach to medicine" (9, p. 69). Type 1 errors also are likely to generate increased income and a stream of steady customers who, being well in a limited physiological sense, will not embarrass the doctor by dying abruptly.

Fellow physicians and the general public therefore are really *rewarding* type 1 errors and at the same time *hoping* fervently that doctors will try not to make them.

GENERAL ORGANIZATIONAL EXAMPLES

Rehabilitation Centers and Orphanages

In terms of the prime beneficiary classification (2, p. 42) organizations such as these are supposed to exist for the "public-in-contact," that is, clients. The orphanage, therefore, theoretically is interested in placing as many children as possible in good homes. However, often orphanages surround themselves with so many rules concerning adoption that it is nearly impossible to pry a child out of the place. Orphanages may deny adoption unless the applicants are a married couple, both of the same religion as the child, without history of emotional or vocational instability, with a specified minimum income and a private room for the child, etc.

If the primary goal is to place children in good homes, then the rules ought to constitute means toward that goal. Goal displacement results when these "means become ends-in-themselves that displace the original goals" (2, p. 229).

To some extent these rules are required by law. But the influence of the reward system on the orphanage's management should not be ignored. Consider, for example, that the:

1. Number of children enrolled often is the most important determinant of the size of the allocated budget.
2. Number of children under the director's care will also affect the size of his staff.
3. Total organizational size will determine largely the director's prestige at the annual conventions, in the community, etc.

Therefore, to the extent that staff size, total budget, and personal prestige are valued by the orphanage's executive personnel, it becomes rational for them to make it difficult for children to be adopted. After all, who wants to be the director of the smallest orphanage in the state?

If the reward system errs in the opposite direction, paying off only for placements, extensive goal displacement again is likely to result. A common example of vocational rehabilitation in many states, for example, consists of placing someone in a job for which he has little interest and few qualifications, for two months or so, and then "rehabilitating" him again in another position. Such behavior is quite consistent with the prevailing reward system, which pays off for the number of individuals placed in any position for 60 days or more. Rehabilitation counselors also confess to competing with one another to place relatively skilled clients, sometimes ignoring persons with few skills who would be harder to place. Extensively disabled clients find that counselors often prefer to work with those whose disabilities are less severe.[3]

Universities

Society *hopes* that teachers will not neglect their teaching responsibilities but *rewards* them almost entirely for research and publications. This is most true at the large and prestigious universities. Clichés, such as "good research and good teaching go together" notwithstanding, professors often find that they must choose between teaching and research-oriented activities when allocating their time. Rewards for good teaching usually are limited to outstanding teacher awards, which are given to only a small percentage of good teachers and which usually bestow little money and fleeting prestige. Punishments for poor teaching also are rare.

Rewards for research and publications, on the other hand, and punishments for failure to accomplish these, are commonly administered by universities at which teachers are employed. Furthermore, publication-oriented résumés usually will be well received at other universities, whereas teaching credentials, harder to document and quantify, are much less transferable. Consequently, it is rational for university teachers to concentrate on research, even if to the detriment of teaching and at the expense of their students.

By the same token, it is rational for students to act based upon the goal displacement which has occurred within universities concerning what they are rewarded for. If it is assumed that a primary goal of a university is to transfer knowledge from teacher to student, then grades become identifiable as a means toward that goal, serving as motivational, control, and feedback devices to expedite the knowledge transfer. Instead, however, the grades themselves have become much more important for entrance to graduate school, successful employment, tuition refunds, parental respect, etc., than the knowledge or lack of knowledge they are supposed to signify.

It, therefore, should come as no surprise that information has surfaced in recent years concerning fraternity files for examinations, term-paper writing services, organized cheating at the service academies, and the like. Such activities constitute a personally rational response to a reward system which pays off for grades, rather than knowledge.

BUSINESS-RELATED EXAMPLES

Ecology

Assume that the president of XYZ Corporation is confronted with the following alternatives:

1. Spend $11 million for antipollution equipment to keep from poisoning fish in the river adjacent to the plant; or
2. Do nothing, in violation of the law, and assume a 1-in-10 chance of being caught, with a resultant $1 million fine plus the necessity of buying the equipment.

Under this not unrealistic set of choices it requires no linear program to determine that XYZ Corporation can maximize its probabilities by flouting the law. Add the fact that XYZ's president is probably being rewarded (by creditors, stockholders, and other salient parts of his task environment) according to criteria totally unrelated to the number of fish poisoned, and his probable course of action becomes clear.

Evaluation of Training

It is axiomatic that those who care about a firm's well-being should insist that the organization get fair value for its expenditures. Yet it is commonly known that firms seldom bother to evaluate a new GRID, MBO, job enrichment program, or whatever, to see if the company is getting its money's worth. Why? Certainly it is not because people have not pointed out that this situation exists; numerous practitioner-oriented articles are written each year to just this point.

The individuals (whether in personnel, manpower planning, or wherever) who normally would be responsible for conducting such evaluations are the same ones often charged with introducing the change effort in the first place. Having convinced top management to spend the money, they usually are quite animated afterwards in collecting rigorous vignettes and anecdotes about how successful the program was. The last thing many desire is a formal, systematic, and revealing evaluation. Although members of top management may actually *hope* for such systematic evaluation, their reward systems continue to *reward* ignorance in this area. And if the personnel department abdicates its responsibility, who is to step into the breach? The change agent himself? Hardly! He is likely to be too busy collecting anecdotal "evidence" of his own, for use with his next client.

Miscellaneous

Many additional examples could be cited of systems which in fact are rewarding other behaviors than those supposedly desired by the rewarder. A few of these are described briefly below.

Most coaches disdain to discuss individual accomplishments, preferring to speak of teamwork, proper attitude, and a one-for-all spirit. Usually, however, rewards are distributed according to individual performance. The college basketball player who feeds his teammates instead of shooting will not compile impressive scoring statistics and is less likely to be drafted by the pros. The ballplayer who hits to right field to advance the runners will win neither the batting nor home run titles, and will be offered smaller raises. It, therefore, is rational for players to think of themselves first and the team second.

In business organizations where rewards are dispensed for unit performance or for individual goals achieved, without regard for overall effectiveness, similar attitudes often are observed. Under most Management by Objectives (MBO) systems, goals in areas where quantification is difficult often go unspecified. The organization, therefore, often is in a position where it *hopes* for employee effort in the areas of team building, interpersonal relations, creativity, etc., but it formally *rewards* none of these. In cases where promotions and raises are formally tied to MBO, the system itself contains a paradox in that it "asks employees to set challenging, risky goals, only to face smaller paychecks and possibly damaged careers if these goals are not accomplished" (5, p. 40).

It is *hoped* that administrators will pay attention to long-run costs and opportunities and will institute programs which will bear fruit later on. However, many organizational reward systems pay off for short-run sales and earnings only. Under such circumstances it is personally rational for officials to sacrifice long-term growth and profit (by selling off equipment and property, or by stifling research and development) for short-term advantages. This probably is most pertinent in the public sector, with the result that many public officials are unwilling to implement programs which will not show benefits by election time.

As a final, clear-cut example of a fouled-up reward system, consider the cost-plus contract or its next of kin, the allocation of next year's budget as a direct function of this year's expenditures. It probably is conceivable that those who award such budgets and contracts really hope for economy and prudence in spending. It is obvious, however, that adopting the proverb "to him who spends shall more be given," rewards not economy but spending itself.

TWO COMPANIES' EXPERIENCES

A Manufacturing Organization

A Midwest manufacturer of industrial goods had been troubled for some time by aspects of its organizational climate it believed dysfunctional. For research purposes, interviews were conducted with many employees and a questionnaire was administered on a company-wide basis, including plants and offices in several American and Canadian locations. The company strongly encouraged employee participation in the survey and made available time and space during the workday for completion of the instrument. All employees in attendance during the day of the survey completed the questionnaire. All instruments were collected directly by the researcher, who personally administered each session. Since no one employed by the firm handled the questionnaires, and since respondent names were not asked for, it seems likely that the pledge of anonymity given was believed.

A modified version of the Expect Approval scale (7) was included as part of the questionnaire. The instrument asked respondents to indicate the degree of approval or disapproval they could expect if they performed each of the described actions. A seven-point Likert scale was used, with 1 indicating that the action would probably bring strong disapproval and 7 signifying likely strong approval.

Although normative data for this scale from studies of other organizations are unavailable, it is possible to examine fruitfully the data obtained from this survey in several ways. First, it may be worth noting that the questionnaire data corresponded closely to information gathered through interviews. Furthermore, as can be seen from the results summarized in Table 1, sizable differences between various work units, and between employees at different job levels within the same work unit, were obtained. This suggests that response bias effects (social desirability in particular loomed as a potential concern) are not likely to be severe.

Most importantly, comparisons between scores obtained on the Expect Approval scale and a statement of problems which were the reason for the survey revealed that the same behaviors which managers in each division thought dysfunctional were those which lower level employees claimed were rewarded. As compared to job levels 1 to 8 in Division B (see Table 1), those in Division A claimed a much higher acceptance by management of "conforming" activities. Between 31 and 37 percent of Division A employees at levels 1–8 stated that going along with the majority, agreeing with the boss, and staying on everyone's good side brought approval; only once (level 5–8 responses to one of the three items) did a majority suggest that such actions would generate disapproval.

Furthermore, responses from Division A workers at levels 1–4 indicate that behaviors geared toward risk avoidance were as likely to be rewarded as to be punished. Only at job levels 9 and above was it apparent that the reward system was positively reinforcing behaviors desired by top management. Overall, the same "tendencies toward conservatism and applepolishing at the lower levels" which divisional management had complained about during the interviews were those claimed by subordinates to be the most rational course of action in light of the existing reward system. Management apparently was not getting the behaviors it was *hoping* for, but it certainly was getting the behaviors it was perceived by subordinates to be *rewarding*.

TABLE 1 Summary of Two Divisions' Data Relevant to Conforming and Risk-Avoidance Behaviors (extent to which subjects expect approval)

Dimension	Item	Division and Sample	Total Responses	*Percentage of Workers Responding*		
				1, 2, or 3 (Disapproval)	4	5, 6, or 7 (Approval)
Risk avoidance	Making a risky decision based on the best information available at the time, but which turns out wrong.	A, levels 1–4 (lowest)	127	61%	25%	14%
		A, levels 5–8	172	46	31	23
		A, levels 9 and above	17	41	30	30
		B, levels 1–4 (lowest)	31	58	26	16
		B, levels 5–8	19	42	42	16
		B, levels 9 and above	10	50	20	30
Risk	Setting extremely high and challenging standards and goals, and then narrowly failing to make them.	A, levels 1–4	122	47	28	25
		A, levels 5–8	168	33	26	41
		A, levels 9+	17	24	6	70
		B, levels 1–4	31	48%	23%	29%
		B, levels 5–8	18	17	33	50
		B, levels 9+	10	30	0	70

TABLE 1 (*continued*)

Dimension	Item	Division and Sample	Total Responses	Percentage of Workers Responding		
				1, 2, or 3 (Disapproval)	4	5, 6, or 7 (Approval)
	Settings goals which are extremely easy to make and then making them.	A, levels 1–4	124	35	30	35
		A, levels 5–8	171	47	27	26
		A, levels 9+	17	70	24	6
		B, levels 1–4	32	58	26	16
		B, levels 5–8	19	63	16	21
		B, levels 9+	10	80	0	20
	Being a "yes man" and always agreeing with the boss.	A, levels 1–4	126	46	17	37
		A, levels 5–8	180	54	14	31
		A, levels 9+	17	88	12	0
		B, levels 1–4	32	53	28	19
		B, levels 5–8	19	68	21	11
		B, levels 9+	10	80	10	10

TABLE 1 (*concluded*)

Dimension	Item	Division and Sample	Total Responses	Percentage of Workers Responding		
				1, 2, or 3 (Disapproval)	4	5, 6, or 7 (Approval)
	Always going along with the majority.	A, levels 1–4	125	40%	25%	35%
		A, levels 5–8	173	47	21	32
		A, levels 9+	17	70	12	18
		B, levels 1–4	31	61	23	16
		B, levels 5–8	19	68	11	21
		B, levels 9+	10	80	10	10
	Being careful to stay on the good side of everyone, so that everyone agrees that you are a great guy.	A, levels 1–4	124	45	18	37
		A, levels 5–8	173	45	22	33
		A, levels 9+	17	64	6	30
		B, levels 1–4	31	54	23	23
		B, levels 5–8	19	73	11	16
		B, levels 9+	10	80	10	10

An Insurance Firm

The Group Health Claims Division of a large eastern insurance company provides another rich illustration of a reward system which reinforces behaviors not desired by top management.

Attempting to measure and reward accuracy in paying surgical claims, the firm systematically keeps track of the number of returned checks and letters of complaint received from policyholders. However, underpayments are likely to provoke cries of outrage from the insured, while overpayments often are accepted in courteous silence. Since it often is impossible to tell from the physician's statement which of two surgical procedures, with different allowable benefits, was performed, and since writing for clarifications will interfere with other standards used by the firm concerning "percentage of claims paid within two days of receipt," the new hire in more than one claims section is soon acquainted with the informal norm: "When in doubt, pay it out!"

The situation would be even worse were it not for the fact that other features of the firm's reward system tend to neutralize those described. For example, annual "merit" increases are given to all employees, in one of the following three amounts:

1. If the worker is "outstanding" (a select category, into which no more than two employees per section may be placed): 5 percent

2. If the worker is "above average" (normally all workers not "outstanding" are so rated): 4 percent

3. If the worker commits gross acts of negligence and irresponsibility for which he might be discharged in many other companies: 3 percent.

Now, since (a) the difference between the 5 percent theoretically attainable through hard work and the 4 percent attainable merely by living until the review date is small and (b) since insurance firms seldom dispense much of a salary increase in cash (rather, the worker's insurance benefits increase, causing him to be further overinsured), many employees are rather indifferent to the possibility of obtaining the extra one percent reward and, therefore, tend to ignore the norm concerning indiscriminant payments.

However, most employees are not indifferent to the rule which states that, should absences or latenesses total three or more in any six-month period, the entire 4 or 5 percent due at the next "merit" review must be forfeited. In this sense the firm may be described as *hoping* for performance, while *rewarding* attendance. What it gets, of course, is attendance. (If the absence-lateness rule appears to the reader to be stringent, it really is not. The company counts "times," rather than "days" absent, and a 10-day absence, therefore, counts the same as one lasting 2 days. A worker in danger of accumulating a third absence within six months merely has to remain ill (away from work) during his second absence until his first absence is more than six months old. The limiting factor is that at some point his salary ceases, and his sickness benefits take over. This usually is sufficient to get the younger workers to return, but for those with 20 or more years' service, the company provides sickness benefits of 90 percent of normal salary, tax-free! Therefore . . .)

CAUSES

Extremely diverse instances of systems which reward behavior A although the rewarder apparently hopes for behavior B have been given. These are useful to illustrate the breadth and magnitude of the phenomenon, but the diversity increases the difficulty of determining commonalities and establishing causes. However, four general factors may be pertinent to an explanation of why fouled-up reward systems seem to be so prevalent.

Fascination with an "Objective" Criterion

It has been mentioned elsewhere that:

Most "objective" measures of productivity are objective only in that their subjective elements are (a) determined in advance, rather than coming into play at the time of the formal evaluation, and (b) well concealed on the rating instrument itself. Thus industrial firms seeking to devise objective rating systems first decide, in an arbitrary manner, what dimensions are to be rated, . . . usually including some items having little to do with organizational effectiveness while excluding others that do. Only then does Personnel Division churn out official-looking documents on which all dimensions chosen to be rated are assigned point values, categories, or whatever [6, p. 92].

Nonetheless, many individuals seek to establish simple, quantifiable standards against which to measure and reward performance. Such efforts may be successful in highly predictable areas within an organization, but are likely to cause goal displacement when applied anywhere else. Overconcern with attendance and lateness in the insurance firm and with number of people placed in the vocational rehabilitation division may have been largely responsible for the problems described in those organizations.

Overemphasis on Highly Visible Behaviors

Difficulties often stem from the fact that some parts of the task are highly visible while other parts are not. For example, publications are easier to demonstrate than teaching, and scoring baskets and hitting home runs are more readily observable than feeding teammates and advancing base runners. Similarly, the adverse consequences of pronouncing a sick person well are more visible than those sustained by labeling a well person sick. Team-building and creativity are other examples of behaviors which may not be rewarded simply because they are hard to observe.

Hypocrisy

In some of the instances described, the rewarder may have been getting the desired behavior, notwithstanding claims that the behavior was not desired. This may be true, for example, of management's attitude toward apple-polishing in the manufacturing firm (a behavior which subordinates felt was rewarded, despite management's avowed dislike of the practice). This also may explain politicians' unwillingness to revise the penalties for disobedience of ecology laws, and the failure of top management to devise reward systems which would cause systematic evaluation of training and development programs.

Emphasis on Morality or Equity, Rather than Efficiency

Some consideration of other factors prevents the establishment of a system which rewards behaviors desired by the rewarder. The felt obligation of many Americans to vote for one candidate or another, for example, may impair their ability to withhold support from politicians who refuse to discuss the issues. Similarly, the concern for spreading the risks and costs of wartime military service may outweigh the advantage to be obtained by committing personnel to combat until the war is over.

It should be noted that only with respect to the first two causes are reward systems really paying off for other than desired behaviors. In the case of the third and fourth causes, the system *is* rewarding behaviors desired by the rewarder, and the systems are fouled up only from the standpoints of those who believe the rewarder's public statements (cause 3), or those who seek to maximize efficiency, rather than other outcomes (cause 4).

CONCLUSIONS

Modern organization theory requires a recognition that the members of organizations and society possess divergent goals and motives. It, therefore, is unlikely that managers and their subordinates will seek the same outcomes. Three possible remedies for this potential problem are suggested.

Selection

It is theoretically possible for organizations to employ only those individuals whose goals and motives are wholly consonant with those of management. In such cases the same behaviors judged by subordinates to be rational would be perceived by management as desirable. State-of-the-art reviews of selection techniques, however, provide scant grounds for hope that such an approach would be successful (e.g., see 12).

Training

Another theoretical alternative is for the organization to admit those employees whose goals are not consonant with those of management and then, through training, socialization, or whatever, alter employee goals to make them consonant. However, research on the effectiveness of such training programs, though limited, provides further grounds for pessimism (e.g., see 3).

Altering the Reward System

What would have been the result if:

1. Nixon had been assured by his advisors that he could not win reelection except by discussing the issues in detail?
2. Physicians' conduct was subjected to regular examination by review boards for type 1 errors (calling healthy people ill) and to penalties (fines, censure, etc.) for errors of either type?
3. The president of XYZ Corporation had to choose between (a) spending $11 million for antipollution equipment and (b) incurring a 50-50 chance of going to jail for five years?

Managers who complain that their workers are not motivated might do well to consider the possibility that they have installed reward systems which are paying off for other behaviors than those they are seeking. This, in part, is what happened in Vietnam, and this is what regularly frustrates societal efforts to bring about honest politicians, civic-minded managers, etc. This certainly is what happened in both the manufacturing and the insurance companies.

A first step for such managers might be to find out what behaviors currently are being rewarded. Perhaps an instrument similar to that used in the manufacturing firm could be useful for this purpose. Chances are excellent that these managers will be surprised by what they find—that their firms are not rewarding what they assume they are. In fact, such undesirable behavior by organizational members as they have observed may be explained largely by the reward systems in use.

This is not to say that all organizational behavior is determined by formal rewards and punishments. Certainly it is true that in the absence of formal reinforcement some soldiers will be patriotic, some presidents will be ecology-minded, and some orphanage directors will care about children. The point, however, is that in such cases the rewarder is not *causing* the behaviors desired but is only a fortunate bystander. For an organization to *act* upon its members, the formal reward system should positively reinforce desired behaviors, not constitute an obstacle to be overcome.

It might be wise to underscore the obvious fact that there is nothing really new in what has been said. In both theory and practice these matters have been mentioned before. Thus, in many states good samaritan laws have been installed to protect doctors who stop to assist a stricken motorist. In states without such laws it is commonplace for doctors to refuse to stop, for fear of involvement in a subsequent lawsuit. In college basketball additional penalties have been instituted against players who foul their opponents deliberately. It has long been argued by Milton Friedman and others that penalties should be altered so as to make it irrational to disobey the ecology laws, and so on.

By altering the reward system the organization escapes the necessity of selecting only desirable people or of trying to alter undesirable ones. In Skinnerian terms (as described in 11, p. 704), "As for responsibility and goodness—as commonly defined—no one . . . would want or need them. They refer to a man's behaving well despite the absence of positive reinforcement that is obviously sufficient to explain it. Where such reinforcement exists, 'no one needs goodness.' "

NOTES

1. In Simon's (10, pp. 76–77) terms, a decision is "subjectively rational" if it maximizes an individual's valued outcomes so far as his knowledge permits. A decision is "personally rational" if it is oriented toward the individual's goals.
2. In one study (4) of 14,867 films for signs of tuberculosis, 1,216 positive readings turned out to be clinically negative; only 24 negative readings proved clinically active, a ratio of 50 to 1.
3. Personal interviews conducted during 1972–73.

REFERENCES

1. Barnard, Chester I. *The Functions of the Executive.* Cambridge, Mass.: Harvard University Press, 1968. (First published in 1936.)
2. Blau, Peter M., and W. Richard Scott. *Formal Organizations.* San Francisco: Chandler, 1962.
3. Fiedler, Fred E. "Predicting the Effects of Leadership Training and Experience from the Contingency Model." *Journal of Applied Psychology* 56 (1972), pp. 114–19.
4. Garland, L. H. "Studies of the Accuracy of Diagnostic Procedures." *American Journal Roentgenological, Radium Therapy Nuclear Medicine* 82 (1959), pp. 25–28.
5. Kerr, Steven. "Some Modifications in MBO as an OD Strategy." *Academy of Management Proceedings,* 1973, pp. 39–42.
6. Kerr, Steven. "What Price Objectivity?" *American Sociologist* 8 (1973), pp. 92–93.
7. Litwin, G. H., and R. A. Stringer, Jr. *Motivation and Organizational Climate.* Cambridge, Mass.: Harvard University Press, 1968.
8. Perrow, Charles. "The Analysis of Goals in Complex Organizations." In *Readings on Modern Organizations,* ed. A. Etzioni. Englewood Cliffs, N.J.: Prentice-Hall, 1969.

9. Scheff, Thomas J. "Decision Rules, Types of Error, and Their Consequences in Medical Diagnosis." In *Mathematical Explorations in Behavioral Science,* ed. F. Massarik and P. Ratoosh. Homewood, Ill.: Richard D. Irwin, 1965.

10. Simon, Herbert A. *Administrative Behavior.* New York: Free Press, 1957.

11. Swanson, G. E. "Review Symposium: Beyond Freedom and Dignity." *American Journal of Sociology* 78 (1972), pp. 702–5.

12. Webster, E. *Decision Making in the Employment Interview.* Montreal: Industrial Relations Center, McGill University, 1964.

19

The Human Side of Enterprise

Douglas M. McGregor

*In this, one of the most widely reprinted articles in the management litera-
ture, Douglas McGregor introduces the notion that, under proper conditions,
unimagined resources of creative human energy could become available
within organizational settings. Designating the conventional view of managing as Theory X and the social science based approach as Theory Y, McGregor discusses the advantages of decentralization, job enlargement, participation, and performance appraisal.—Eds.*

It has become trite to say that industry has the fundamental know-how to
utilize physical science and technology for the material benefit of mankind,
and that we must now learn how to utilize the social sciences to make our
human organizations truly effective.

To a degree, the social sciences today are in a position like that of the
physical sciences with respect to atomic energy in the thirties. We know that
past conceptions of the nature of man are inadequate and, in many ways,
incorrect. We are becoming quite certain that, under proper conditions, unimagined resources of creative human energy could become available
within the organizational setting.

We cannot tell industrial management how to apply this new knowledge in simple, economic ways. We know it will require years of exploration,
much costly development research, and a substantial amount of creative
imagination on the part of management to discover how to apply this growing knowledge to the organization of human effort in industry.

MANAGEMENT'S TASK: THE CONVENTIONAL VIEW

The conventional conception of management's task in harnessing human energy to organizational requirements can be stated broadly in terms

---

SOURCE: Reprinted by permission of the publisher from *Management Review,* November 1957,
© 1957 by American Management Association, Inc.

of three propositions. In order to avoid the complications introduced by a label, let us call this set of propositions "Theory X":

1. Management is responsible for organizing the elements of productive enterprise—money, materials, equipment, people—in the interest of economic ends.

2. With respect to people, this is a process of directing their efforts, motivating them, controlling their actions, modifying their behavior to fit the needs of the organization.

3. Without this active intervention by management, people would be passive—even resistant—to organizational needs. They must therefore be persuaded, rewarded, punished, controlled—their activities must be directed. This is management's task. We often sum it up by saying that management consists of getting things done through other people.

Behind this conventional theory there are several additional beliefs—less explicit, but widespread:

4. The average man is by nature indolent—he works as little as possible.

5. He lacks ambition, dislikes responsibility, prefers to be led.

6. He is inherently self-centered, indifferent to organizational needs.

7. He is by nature resistant to change.

8. He is gullible, not very bright, the ready dupe of the charlatan and the demagogue.

The human side of economic enterprise today is fashioned from propositions and beliefs such as these. Conventional organization structures and managerial policies, practices, and programs reflect these assumptions.

In accomplishing its task—with these assumptions as guides—management has conceived of a range of possibilities.

At one extreme, management can be "hard" or "strong." The methods for directing behavior involve coercion and threat (usually disguised), close supervision, tight controls over behavior. At the other extreme, management can be "soft" or "weak." The methods for directing behavior involve being permissive, satisfying people's demands, achieving harmony. Then they will be tractable, accept direction.

This range has been fairly completely explored during the past half century, and management has learned some things from the exploration. There are difficulties in the "hard" approach. Force breeds counterforce: restriction of output, antagonism, militant unionism, subtle but effective sabotage of management objectives. This hard approach is especially difficult during times of full employment.

There are also difficulties in the "soft" approach. It leads frequently to the abdication of management—to harmony, perhaps, but to indifferent performance. People take advantage of the soft approach. They continually expect more, but they give less and less.

Currently, the popular theme is "firm but fair." This is an attempt to gain the advantages of both the hard and the soft approaches. It is reminiscent of Teddy Roosevelt's "speak softly and carry a big stick."

IS THE CONVENTIONAL VIEW CORRECT?

The findings which are beginning to emerge from the social sciences challenge this whole set of beliefs about man and human nature and about the task of management. The evidence is far from conclusive, certainly, but it is suggestive. It comes from the laboratory, the clinic, the schoolroom, the home, and even to a limited extent from industry itself.

The social scientist does not deny that human behavior in industrial organization today is approximately what management perceives it to be. He has, in fact, observed it and studied it fairly extensively. But he is pretty sure that this behavior is *not* a consequence of man's inherent nature. It is a consequence, rather, of the nature of industrial organizations, of management philosophy, policy, and practice. The conventional approach of Theory X is based on mistaken notions of what is cause and what is effect.

Perhaps the best way to indicate why the conventional approach of management is inadequate is to consider the subject of motivation.

PHYSIOLOGICAL NEEDS

Man is a wanting animal—as soon as one of his needs is satisfied, another appears in its place. This process is unending. It continues from birth to death.

Man's needs are organized in a series of levels—a hierarchy of importance. At the lowest level, but preeminent in importance when they are thwarted, are his *physiological needs*. Man lives for bread alone, when there is no bread. Unless the circumstances are unusual, his needs for love, for status, for recognition are inoperative when his stomach has been empty for a while. But when he eats regularly and adequately, hunger ceases to be an important motivation. The same is true of the other physiological needs of man—for rest, exercise, shelter, protection from the elements.

A satisfied need is not a motivator of behavior! This is a fact of profound significance that is regularly ignored in the conventional approach to the management of people. Consider your own need for air: Except as you are deprived of it, it has no appreciable motivating effect upon your behavior.

SAFETY NEEDS

When the physiological needs are reasonably satisfied, needs at the next higher level begin to dominate man's behavior—to motivate him. These are called *safety needs*. They are needs for protection against danger, threat, deprivation. Some people mistakenly refer to these as needs for security. However, unless man is in a dependent relationship where he fears arbitrary deprivation, he does not demand security. The need is for the "fairest possible break." When he is confident of this, he is more than willing to take risks. But when he feels threatened or dependent, his greatest need is for guarantees, for protection, for security.

The fact needs little emphasis that, since every industrial employee is in a dependent relationship, safety needs may assume considerable importance. Arbitrary management actions, behavior which arouses uncertainty with respect to continued employment or which reflects favoritism or discrimination, unpredictable administration of policy—these can be powerful motivators of the safety needs in the employment relationship *at every level,* from worker to vice president.

SOCIAL NEEDS

When man's physiological needs are satisfied and he is no longer fearful about his physical welfare, his *social needs* become important motivators of his behavior—needs for belonging, for association, for acceptance by his fellows, for giving and receiving friendship and love.

Management knows today of the existence of these needs, but it often assumes quite wrongly that they represent a threat to the organization. Many studies have demonstrated that the tightly knit, cohesive work group may, under proper conditions, be far more effective than an equal number of separate individuals in achieving organizational goals.

Yet management, fearing group hostility to its own objectives, often goes to considerable lengths to control and direct human efforts in ways that are inimical to the natural "groupiness" of human beings. When man's social needs—and perhaps his safety needs, too—are thus thwarted, he behaves in ways which tend to defeat organizational objectives. He becomes resistant, antagonistic, uncooperative. But this behavior is a consequence, not a cause.

EGO NEEDS

Above the social needs—in the sense that they do not become motivators until lower needs are reasonably satisfied—are the needs of greatest significance to management and to man himself. They are the *egoistic needs,* and they are of two kinds:

1. Those needs that relate to one's self-esteem—needs for self-confidence, for independence, for achievement, for competence, for knowledge.
2. Those needs that relate to one's reputation—needs for status, for recognition, for appreciation, for the deserved respect of one's fellows.

Unlike the lower needs, these are rarely satisfied; man seeks indefinitely for more satisfaction of these needs once they have become important to him. But they do not appear in any significant way until physiological, safety, and social needs are all reasonably satisfied.

The typical industrial organization offers few opportunities for the satisfaction of these egoistic needs to people at lower levels in the hierarchy. The conventional methods of organizing work, particularly in mass production industries, give little heed to these aspects of human motivation. If the practices of scientific management were deliberately calculated to thwart these needs, they could hardly accomplish this purpose better than they do.

SELF-FULFILLMENT NEEDS

Finally—a capstone, as it were, on the hierarchy of man's needs—there are what we may call the *needs for self-fulfillment*. These are the needs for realizing one's own potentialities, for continued self-development, for being creative in the broadest sense of that term.

It is clear that the conditions of modern life give only limited opportunity for these relatively weak needs to obtain expression. The deprivation most people experience with respect to other lower level needs diverts their energies into the struggle to satisfy *those* needs, and the needs for self-fulfillment remain dormant.

MANAGEMENT AND MOTIVATION

We recognize readily enough that a man suffering from a severe dietary deficiency is sick. The deprivation of physiological needs has behavioral consequences. The same is true—although less well recognized—of deprivation of higher level needs. The man whose needs for safety, association, independence, or status are thwarted is sick just as surely as the man who has rickets. And his sickness will have behavioral consequences. We will be mistaken if we attribute his resultant passivity, his hostility, his refusal to accept responsibility to his inherent "human nature." These forms of behavior are *symptoms* of illness—of deprivation of his social and egoistic needs.

The man whose lower level needs are satisfied is not motivated to satisfy those needs any longer. For practical purposes they exist no longer. Management often asks, "Why aren't people more productive? We pay good wages, provide good working conditions, have excellent fringe benefits and steady employment. Yet people do not seem to be willing to put forth more than minimum effort."

The fact that management has provided for these physiological and safety needs has shifted the motivational emphasis to the social and perhaps to the egoistic needs. Unless there are opportunities *at work* to satisfy these higher level needs, people will be deprived; and their behavior will reflect this deprivation. Under such conditions, if management continues to focus its attention on physiological needs, its efforts are bound to be ineffective.

People *will* make insistent demands for more money under these conditions. It becomes more important than ever to buy the material goods and services which can provide limited satisfaction of the thwarted needs. Although money has only limited value in satisfying many higher level needs, it can become the focus of interest if it is the *only* means available.

THE CARROT-AND-STICK APPROACH

The carrot-and-stick theory of motivation (like Newtonian physical theory) works reasonably well under certain circumstances. The *means* for satisfying man's physiological and (within limits) his safety needs can be provided or withheld by management. Employment itself is such a means, and so are wages, working conditions, and benefits. By these means the individual can be controlled so long as he is struggling for subsistence.

But the carrot-and-stick theory does not work at all once man has reached an adequate subsistence level and is motivated primarily by higher needs. Management cannot provide a man with self-respect, or with the respect of his fellows, or with the satisfaction of needs for self-fulfillment. It can create such conditions that he is encouraged and enabled to seek such satisfactions for *himself*, or it can thwart him by failing to create those conditions.

But this creation of conditions is not "control." It is not a good device for directing behavior. And so management finds itself in an odd position. The high standard of living created by our modern technological know-how provides quite adequately for the satisfaction of physiological and safety needs. The only significant exception is where management practices have not created confidence in a "fair break"—and thus where safety needs are thwarted. But by making possible the satisfaction of low level needs, management has deprived itself of the ability to use as motivators the devices on which conventional theory has taught it to rely—rewards, promises, incentives, or threats and other coercive devices.

The philosophy of management by direction and control—*regardless of whether it is hard or soft*—is inadequate to motivate because the human needs on which this approach relies are today unimportant motivators of behavior. Direction and control are essentially useless in motivating people whose important needs are social and egoistic. Both the hard and the soft approach fail today because they are simply irrelevant to the situation.

People, deprived of opportunities to satisfy at work the needs which are now important to them, behave exactly as we might predict—with indolence, passivity, resistance to change, lack of responsibility, willingness to follow the demagogue, unreasonable demands for economic benefits. It would seem that we are caught in a web of our own weaving.

A NEW THEORY OF MANAGEMENT

For these and many other reasons, we require a different theory of the task of managing people based on more adequate assumptions about human nature and human motivation. I am going to be so bold as to suggest the broad dimensions of such a theory. Call it "Theory Y," if you will.

1. Management is responsible for organizing the elements of productive enterprise—money, materials, equipment, people—in the interest of economic ends.

2. People are *not* by nature passive or resistant to organizational needs. They have become so as a result of experience in organizations.

3. The motivation, the potential for development, the capacity for assuming responsibility, the readiness to direct behavior toward organizational goals are all present in people. Management does not put them there. It is a responsibility of management to make it possible for people to recognize and develop these human characteristics for themselves.

4. The essential task of management is to arrange organizational conditions and methods of operation so that people can achieve their own goals *best* by directing *their own* efforts toward organizational objectives.

This is a process primarily of creating opportunities, releasing potential, removing obstacles, encouraging growth, providing guidance. It is what Peter Drucker has called "management by objectives" in contrast to "management by control." It does *not* involve the abdication of management, the absence of leadership, the lowering of standards, or the other characteristics usually associated with the "soft" approach under Theory X.

SOME DIFFICULTIES

It is no more possible to create an organization today which will be a full, effective application of this theory than it was to build an atomic power plant in 1945. There are many formidable obstacles to overcome.

The conditions imposed by conventional organization theory and by the approach of scientific management for the past half century have tied men to limited jobs which do not utilize their capabilities, have discouraged the acceptance of responsibility, have encouraged passivity, have eliminated meaning from work. Man's habits, attitudes, expectations—his whole conception of membership in an industrial organization—have been conditioned by his experience under these circumstances.

People today are accustomed to being directed, manipulated, controlled in industrial organizations and to finding satisfaction for their social, egoistic, and self-fulfillment needs away from the job. This is true of much of management as well as of workers. Genuine "industrial citizenship"—to borrow again a term from Drucker—is a remote and unrealistic idea, the meaning of which has not even been considered by most members of industrial organizations.

Another way of saying this is that Theory X places exclusive reliance upon external control of human behavior, while Theory Y relies heavily on self-control and self-direction. It is worth noting that this difference is the difference between treating people as children and treating them as mature adults. After generations of the former, we cannot expect to shift to the latter overnight.

STEPS IN THE RIGHT DIRECTION

Before we are overwhelmed by the obstacles, let us remember that the application of theory is always slow. Progress is usually achieved in small steps. Some innovative ideas which are entirely consistent with Theory Y are today being applied with some success.

Decentralization and Delegation

These are ways of freeing people from the too-close control of conventional organization, giving them a degree of freedom to direct their own activities, to assume responsibility, and, importantly, to satisfy their egoistic needs. In this connection, the flat organization of Sears, Roebuck and Company provides an interesting example. It forces "management by objectives," since it enlarges the number of people reporting to a manager until he cannot direct and control them in the conventional manner.

Job Enlargement

This concept, pioneered by IBM and Detroit Edison, is quite consistent with Theory Y. It encourages the acceptance of responsibility at the bottom of the organization; it provides opportunities for satisfying social and egoistic needs. In fact, the reorganization of work at the factory level offers one of the more challenging opportunities for innovation consistent with Theory Y.

Participation and Consultative Management

Under proper conditions, participation and consultative management provide encouragement to people to direct their creative energies toward organizational objectives, give them some voice in decisions that affect them, provide significant opportunities for the satisfaction of social and egoistic needs. The Scanlon Plan is the outstanding embodiment of these ideas in practice.

Performance Appraisal

Even a cursory examination of conventional programs of performance appraisal within the ranks of management will reveal how completely consistent they are with Theory X. In fact, most such programs tend to treat the individual as though he were a product under inspection on the assembly line.

A few companies—among them General Mills, Ansul Chemical, and General Electric—have been experimenting with approaches which involve the individual in setting "targets" or objectives *for himself* and in a *self*-evaluation of performance semiannually or annually. Of course, the superior plays an important leadership role in this process—one, in fact, which demands substantially more competence than the conventional approach. The role is, however, considerably more congenial to many managers than the role of "judge" or "inspector" which is usually forced upon them. Above all, the individual is encouraged to take a greater responsibility for planning and appraising his own contribution to organizational objectives; and the accompanying effects on egoistic and self-fulfillment needs are substantial.

APPLYING THE IDEAS

The not infrequent failure of such ideas as these to work as well as expected is often attributable to the fact that a management has "bought the idea" but applied it within the framework of Theory X and its assumptions.

Delegation is not an effective way of exercising management by control. Participation becomes a farce when it is applied as a sales gimmick or as a device for kidding people into thinking they are important. Only the management that has confidence in human capacities and is itself directed toward organizational objectives, rather than toward the preservation of personal power, can grasp the implications of this emerging theory. Such management will find and apply successfully other innovative ideas as we move slowly toward the full implementation of a theory like Y.

THE HUMAN SIDE OF ENTERPRISE

It is quite possible for us to realize substantial improvements in the effectiveness of industrial organizations during the next decade or two. The social sciences can contribute much to such developments; we are only beginning to grasp the implications of the growing body of knowledge in these fields. But if this conviction is to become a reality instead of a pious hope, we will need to view the process much as we view the process of releasing the energy of the atom for constructive human ends—as a slow, costly, sometimes discouraging approach toward a goal which would seem to many to be quite unrealistic.

The ingenuity and the perseverance of industrial management in the pursuit of economic ends have changed many scientific and technological dreams into commonplace realities. It is now becoming clear that the application of these same talents to the human side of enterprise will not only enhance substantially these materialistic achievements but will bring us one step closer to "the good society."

PART FOUR

Managing Group Behavior

Groups form because of managerial action, but also because of individual efforts. An organization has technical requirements that arise from its stated goals. The accomplishment of these goals requires that certain tasks be performed and that employees be assigned to perform these tasks. As a result, most employees will be members of a group based on their position in the organization. Groups such as these, created by managerial decisions, are termed *formal* groups.

However, groups also form as a consequence of employees' actions. Such groups, termed *informal* groups, develop around common interests and friendships. Informal groups are natural groupings of people in the work situation in response to social needs. In other words, informal groups do not arise as a result of deliberate design but rather evolve naturally. Though not sanctioned by management, groups of this kind can most definitely affect organizational and individual performance.

Group behavior is more than simply the sum of the behavior of the individuals who comprise the group. The nature of groups is such that they exhibit behaviors which are a function of certain characteristics common to all groups. These characteristics include norms (generally agreed-upon standards of behavior for group members), cohesiveness (the field of forces operating to maintain group membership), roles (the position played by group members), and social control (the mechanisms employed by the group to insure member conformance with group norms.

For a manager to disregard or to underestimate the influence potential of groups in organizational settings is to seriously limit his or her effectiveness as a manager. Increasingly, the concern shown in recent years by United States corporations in the areas of quantity and quality of production are focusing on *group* factors. Quality circles, to use just one example, not only use groups (rather than individuals) as their basic building block for performance improvement but also deliberately attempt to strengthen group cohesion and identity precisely because of the recognition that groups are potent determinants of managerial and organizational success.

20

The Western Electric Researches

George C. Homans

Perhaps no single research study has had a greater impact on management theory and practice than that conducted at the Hawthorne Works of Western Electric. This article describes part of this multiyear project and the conclusions which flowed from it. No study of management is complete without a look at the "Hawthorne Research," credited by many as giving birth to the behavioral management thrust.—Eds.

Perhaps the most important program of research studied by the Committee on Work in Industry of the National Research Council is that which has been carried on at the Hawthorne (Chicago) Works of the Western Electric Company. This program was described by H. A. Wright and M. L. Putnam of the Western Electric Company and by F. J. Roethlisberger, now Professor of Human Relations, Graduate School of Business Administration, Harvard University, particularly at a meeting of the committee held on March 9, 1938. These men, together with Elton Mayo and G. A. Pennock, both members of the committee, had been intimately associated with the research.

A word about the Western Electric Company is a necessary introduction to what follows. This company is engaged in manufacturing equipment for the telephone industry. Besides doing this part of its work, it has always shown concern for the welfare of its employees. In the matter of wages and hours, it has maintained a high standard. It has provided good physical conditions for its employees; and it has tried to make use of every established method of vocational guidance in the effort to suit the worker to his work. The efforts of the company have been rewarded in good industrial relations: there has been no strike or other severe symptom of discontent for over 20 years. In short, there is no reason to doubt that, while these researches were being carried out, the morale of the company was high and

---

SOURCE: Reprinted from *Fatigue of Workers* by George C. Homans (Reinhold, 1941), pp. 56–65, by permission from the author.

that the employees, as a body, had confidence in the abilities and motives of the company management. These facts had an important bearing on the results achieved.

The program of research which will be described grew out of a study conducted at Hawthorne by the Western Electric Company in collaboration with the National Research Council, the aim of which was to determine the relation between intensity of illumination and efficiency of workers, measured in output. One of the experiments made was the following: Two groups of employees doing similar work under similar conditions were chosen, and records of output were kept for each group. The intensity of the light under which one group worked was varied, while that under which the other group worked was held constant. By this method the investigators hoped to isolate from the effect of other variables the effect of changes in the intensity of illumination on the rate of output.

In this hope they were disappointed. The experiment failed to show any simple relation between experimental changes in the intensity of illumination and observed changes in the rate of output. The investigators concluded that this result was obtained, not because such a relation did not exist, but because it was in fact impossible to isolate it from the other variables entering into any determination of productive efficiency. This kind of difficulty, of course, has been encountered in experimental work in many fields. Furthermore, the investigators were in agreement about the character of some of these other variables. They were convinced that one of the major factors which prevented their securing a satisfactory result was psychological. The employees being tested were reacting to changes in light intensity in the way in which they assumed that they were expected to react. That is, when light intensity was increased they were expected to produce more; when it was decreased they were expected to produce less. A further experiment was devised to demonstrate this point. The light bulbs were changed, as they had been changed before, and the workers were allowed to assume that as a result there would be more light. They commented favorably on the increased illumination. As a matter of fact, the bulbs had been replaced with others of just the same power. Other experiments of the sort were made, and in each case the results could be explained as a "psychological" reaction, rather than as a "physiological" one.

This discovery seemed to be important. It suggested that the relations between other physical conditions and the efficiency of workers might be obscured by similar psychological reactions. Nevertheless, the investigators were determined to continue in their course. They recognized the existence of the psychological factors, but they thought of them only as disturbing influences. They were not yet ready to turn their attention to the psychological factors themselves. Instead, they were concerned with devising a better way of eliminating them from the experiments, and the experiments they wanted to try by no means ended with illumination. For instance, there was the question of what was called "fatigue." Little information existed about the effect on efficiency of changes in the hours of work and the introduction of rest pauses. The investigators finally came to the conclusion that, if a small group of workers were isolated in a separate room and asked to cooperate, the psychological reaction would in time disappear, and they would work exactly as they felt. That is, changes in their rate of output would be the direct result of changes in their physical conditions of work and nothing else.

The decision to organize such a group was in fact taken. A small number of workers was to be selected and placed in a separate room, where experiments were to be made with different kinds of working conditions in order to see if more exact information could be secured. Six questions were asked by those setting up the experiment. They were the following:

1. Do employees actually get tired out?
2. Are rest pauses desirable?
3. Is a shorter working day desirable?
4. What is the attitude of employees toward their work and toward the company?
5. What is the effect of changing the type of working equipment?
6. Why does production fall off in the afternoon?

It is obvious that several of these questions could be answered only indirectly by the proposed experiment, and several of them touched upon the "psychological," rather than the "physiological," factors involved. Nevertheless, all of them arose out of the bewilderment of men of experience faced with the problem of dealing with fellow human beings in a large industrial organization. In fact, one of the executives of the company saw the purpose of the experiment in even simpler and more general terms. He said that the experiment grew out of a desire on the part of the management to "know more about our workers." In this way began the experiment which is referred to as the Relay Assembly Test Room. With this experiment and the others that followed, members of the Department of Industrial Research of the Graduate School of Business Administration, Harvard University, came to be closely associated.

In April 1927, six girls were selected from a large shop department of the Hawthorne Works. They were chosen as average workers, neither inexperienced nor expert, and their work consisted of the assembling of telephone relays. A coil, armature, contact springs, and insulators were put together on a fixture and secured in position by means of four machine screws. The operation at that time was being completed at the rate of about five relays in six minutes. This particular operation was chosen for the experiment because the relays were being assembled often enough so that even slight changes in output rate would show themselves at once on the output record. Five of the girls were to do the actual assembly work; the duty of the sixth was to keep the others supplied with parts.

The test room itself was an area divided from the main department by a wooden partition eight feet high. The girls sat in a row on one side of a long workbench. Their bench and assembly equipment was identical with that used in the regular department, except in one respect. At the right of each girl's place was a hole in the bench, and into this hole she dropped completed relays. It was the entrance to a chute, in which there was a flapper gate opened by the relay in its passage downward. The opening of the gate closed an electrical circuit which controlled a perforating device, and this in turn recorded the completion of the relay by punching a hole in a tape. The tape moved at the rate of one quarter of an inch a minute and had space for a separate row of holes for each operator. When punched, it thus constituted a complete output record for each girl for each instant of the day. Such records were kept for five years.

In this experiment then, as in the earlier illumination experiments, great emphasis was laid on the rate of output. A word of caution is needed here. The Western Electric Company was not immediately interested in increasing output. The experiments were not designed for that purpose. On the other hand, output is easily measured; that is, it yields precise quantitative data, and experience suggested that it was sensitive to at least some of the conditions under which the employees worked. Output was treated as an index. In short, the nature of the experimental conditions made the emphasis on output inevitable.

From their experience in the illumination experiments, the investigators were well aware that other factors than those experimentally varied might affect the output rate. Therefore, arrangements were made that a number of other records should be kept. Unsuitable parts supplied by the firm were noted down, as were assemblies rejected for any reason upon inspection. In this way the type of defect could be known and related to the time of day at which it occurred. Records were kept of weather conditions in general and of temperature and humidity in the test room. Every six weeks each operator was given a medical examination by the company doctor. Every day she was asked to tell how many hours she had spent in bed the night before and, during a part of the experiment, what food she had eaten. Besides all these records, which concerned the physical condition of the operators, a log was kept in which were recorded the principal events in the test room hour by hour, including among the entries snatches of conversation between the workers. At first these entries related largely to the physical condition of the operators: how they felt as they worked. Later the ground they covered somewhat widened, and the log ultimately became one of the most important of the test room records. Finally, when the so-called Interviewing Program was instituted at Hawthorne, each of the operators was interviewed several times by an experienced interviewer.

The girls had no supervisor in the ordinary sense, such as they would have had in a regular shop department, but a "test room observer" was placed in the room, whose duty it was to maintain the records, arrange the work, and secure a cooperative spirit on the part of the girls. Later, when the complexity of his work increased, several assistants were assigned to help him.

When the arrangements had been made for the test room, the operators who had been chosen to take part were called in for an interview in the office of the superintendent of the Inspection Branch, who was in general charge of the experiment and of the researches which grew out of it. The superintendent described this interview as follows:

> The nature of the test was carefully explained to these girls and they readily consented to take part in it, although they were very shy at the first conference. An invitation to six shop girls to come up to a superintendent's office was naturally rather startling. They were assured that the object of the test was to determine the effect of certain changes in working conditions, such as rest periods, midmorning lunches, and shorter working hours. They were expressly cautioned to work at a comfortable pace, and under no circumstances to try to make a race out of the test.

This conference was only the first of many. Whenever any experimental change was planned, the girls were called in, the purpose of the change was explained to them, and their comments were requested. Certain suggested changes which did not meet with their approval were abandoned. They were repeatedly asked, as they were asked in the first interview, not to strain but to work "as they felt."

The experiment was now ready to begin. Put in its simplest terms, the idea of those directing the experiment was that, if an output curve was studied for a long enough time under various changes in working conditions, it would be possible to determine which conditions were the most satisfactory. Accordingly, a number of so-called experimental periods were arranged. For two weeks before the operators were placed in the test room, a record was kept of the production of each one without her knowledge. In this way the investigators secured a measure of her productive ability while working in the regular department under the usual conditions. This constituted the first experimental period. And for five weeks after the girls entered the test room no change was made in working conditions. Hours remained what they had been before. The investigators felt that this period would be long enough to reveal any changes in output incidental merely to the transfer. This constituted the second experimental period.

The third period involved a change in the method of payment. In the regular department, the girls had been paid according to a scheme of group piecework, the group consisting of a hundred or more employees. Under these circumstances, variations in an individual's total output would not be immediately reflected in her pay, since such variations tended to cancel one another in a large group. In the test room, the six operators were made a group by themselves. In this way each girl received an amount more nearly in proportion to her individual effort, and her interests became more closely centered on the experiment. Eight weeks later, the directly experimental changes began. An outline will reveal their general character: Period IV: two rest pauses, each five minutes in length, were established, one occurring in midmorning and the other in the early afternoon. Period V: these rest pauses were lengthened to 10 minutes each. Period VI: six five-minute rests were established. Period VII: the company provided each member of the group with a light lunch in the midmorning and another in the midafternoon accompanied by rest pauses. This arrangement became standard for subsequent Periods VIII through XI. Period VIII: work stopped a half hour earlier every day—at 4:30 P.M. Period IX: work stopped at 4 P.M. Period X: conditions returned to what they were in Period VII. Period XI: a five-day work week was established. Each of these experimental periods lasted several weeks.

Period XI ran through the summer of 1928, a year after the beginning of the experiment. Already the results were not what had been expected. The output curve, which had risen on the whole slowly and steadily throughout the year, was obviously reflecting something other than the responses of the group to the imposed experimental conditions. Even when the total weekly output had fallen off, as it could hardly fail to do in such a period as Period XI, when the group was working only five days a week, daily output continued to rise. Therefore, in accordance with a sound experimental procedure, as a control on what had been done, it was agreed with the consent of the operators that in experimental Period XII a return should be made to the original conditions of work, with no rest pauses, no special lunches, and a full-length working week. This period lasted for 12 weeks. Both daily and weekly output rose to a higher point than ever before: the working day and the working week were both longer. The hourly output rate declined somewhat but it did not approach the level of Period III, when similar conditions were in effect.

The conclusions reached after Period XII may be expressed in terms of another observation. Identical conditions of work were repeated in three different experimental periods: Periods VII, X, and XII. If the assumptions on which the study was based had been correct—that is to say, if the output rate were directly related to the physical conditions of work—the expectation would be that in these three experimental periods there would be some similarity in output. Such was not the case. The only apparent uniformity was that in each experimental period output was higher than in the preceding one. In the Relay Assembly Test Room, as in the previous illumination experiments, something was happening which could not be explained by the experimentally controlled conditions of work.

There is no need here to go into the later history of the test room experiment, which came to an end in 1933. It is enough to say that the output of the group continued to rise until it established itself on a high plateau from which there was no descent until the time of discouragement and deepening economic depression which preceded the end of the test. The rough conclusions reached at the end of experimental Period XII were confirmed and sharpened by later research. T. N. Whitehead, Associate Professor of Business in the Graduate School of Business Administration, Harvard University, has made a careful statistical analysis of the output records. He shows that the changes which took place in the output of the group have no simple correlation with the experimental changes in working conditions. Nor can they be correlated with changes in other physical conditions of which records were kept, such as temperature, humidity, hours of rest, and changes of relay type. Even when the girls themselves complained of mugginess or heat, these conditions were not apparently affecting their output. This statement, of course, does not mean that there is never any relation between output rate and these physical conditions. There is such a thing as heat prostration. It means only that, within the limits in which these conditions were varying in the test room, they apparently did not affect the rate of work.

The question remains: With what facts, if any, can the changes in the output rate of the operators in the test room be correlated? Here the statements of the girls themselves are of first importance. Each girl knew that she was producing more in the test room than she ever had in the regular department, and each said that the increase had come about without any conscious effort on her part. It seemed easier to produce at the faster rate in the test room than at the slower rate in the regular department. When questioned further, each girl stated her reasons in slightly different words, but there was uniformity in the answers in two respects. First, the girls liked to work in the test room: "it was fun." Second, the new supervisory relation or, as they put it, the absence of the old supervisory control, made it possible for them to work freely without anxiety.

For instance, there was the matter of conversation. In the regular department, conversation was in principle not allowed. In practice it was tolerated if it was carried on in a low tone and did not interfere with work. In the test room an effort was made in the beginning to discourage conversation, though it was soon abandoned. The observer in charge of the experiment was afraid of losing the cooperation of the girls if he insisted too strongly on this point. Talk became common and was often loud and general. Indeed the conversation of the operators came to occupy an important place in the log. T. N. Whitehead has pointed out that the girls in the test room were far more thoroughly supervised than they ever had been in the regular department. They were watched by an observer of their own, an interested management, and outside experts. The point is that the character and purpose of the supervision were different and were felt to be so.

The operators knew that they were taking part in what was considered an important and interesting experiment. They knew that their work was expected to produce results—they were not sure what results—which would lead to the improvement of the working conditions of their fellow employees. They knew that the eyes of the company were upon them. Whitehead has further pointed out that, although the experimental changes might turn out to have no physical significance, their social significance was always favorable. They showed that the management of the company was still interested, that the girls were still part of a valuable piece of research. In the regular department, the girls, like the other employees, were in the position of responding to changes the source and purpose of which were beyond their knowledge. In the test room, they had frequent interviews with the superintendent, a high officer of the company. The reasons for the contemplated experimental changes were explained to them. Their views were consulted and in some instances they were allowed to veto what had been proposed. Professor Mayo has argued that it is idle to speak of an experimental period like Period XII as being in any sense what it purported to be—a return to the original conditions of work. In the meantime, the entire industrial situation of the girls had been reconstructed.

Another factor in what occurred can only be spoken of as the social development of the group itself. When the girls went for the first time to be given a physical examination by the company doctor, someone suggested as a joke that ice cream and cake ought to be served. The company provided them at the next examination, and the custom was kept up for the duration of the experiment. When one of the girls had a birthday, each of the others would bring her a present, and she would respond by offering the group a box of chocolates. Often one of the girls would have some good reason for feeling tired. Then the others would "carry" her. That is, they would agree to work especially fast to make up for the low output expected from her. It is doubtful whether this "carrying" did have any effect, but the important point is the existence of the practice, not its effectiveness. The girls made friends in the test room and went together socially after hours. One of the interesting facts which has appeared from Whitehead's analysis of the output records is that there were times when variations in the output rates of two friends were correlated to a high degree. Their rates varied simultaneously and in the same direction—something, of course, which the girls were not aware of and could not have planned. Also, these correlations were destroyed by such apparently trivial events as a change in the order in which the girls sat at the workbench.

Finally, the group developed leadership and a common purpose. The leader, self-appointed, was an ambitious young Italian girl who entered the test room as a replacement after two of the original members had left. She saw in the experiment a chance for personal distinction and advancement. The common purpose was an increase in the output rate. The girls had been told in the beginning and repeatedly thereafter that they were to work without straining, without trying to make a race of the test, and all the evidence shows that they kept this rule. In fact, they felt that they were working under less pressure than in the regular department. Nevertheless, they knew that the output record was considered the most important of the records of the experiment and was always closely scrutinized. Before long they had committed themselves to a continuous increase in production. In the long run, of course, this ideal was an impossible one, and when the girls found out that it was, the realization was an important element of the change of tone which was noticeable in the second half of the experiment. But for a time they felt that they could achieve the impossible. In brief, the increase in the output rate of the girls in the Relay Assembly Test Room could not be related to any changes in their physical conditions of work, whether experimentally induced or not. It could, however, be related to what can only be spoken of as the development of an organized social group in a peculiar and effective relation with its supervisors.

Many of these conclusions were not worked out in detail until long after the investigators at Hawthorne had lost interest in the Relay Assembly Test Room, but the general meaning of the experiment was clear at least as early as Period XII. A continuous increase in productivity had taken place irrespective of changing physical conditions of work. In the words of a company report made in January 1931, on all the research which had been done up to that date:

> Upon analysis, only one thing seemed to show a continuous relationship with this improved output. This was the mental attitude of the operators. From their conversations with each other and their comments to the test observers, it was not only clear that their attitudes were improving but it was evident that this area of employee reactions and feelings was a fruitful field for industrial research.

21

Overcoming Resistance
to Change

Lester Coch
and
John R. P. French, Jr.

Why do organizational work groups resist change and what can be done about it? This article describes a study wherein these were the central questions. The "pajama study," as this pioneering research is popularly known is as valid in its implications today as when it was originally carried out almost 50 years ago.—Eds.

INTRODUCTION

It has always been characteristic of American industry to change products and methods of doing jobs as often as competitive conditions or engineering progress dictates. This makes frequent changes in an individual's work necessary. In addition, the markedly greater turnover and absenteeism of recent years result in unbalanced production lines, which again makes for frequent shifting of individuals from one job to another. One of the most serious production problems faced at the Harwood Manufacturing Corporation has been the resistance of production workers to the necessary changes in methods and jobs. This resistance expressed itself in several ways, such as grievances about the piece rates that went with the new methods, high turnover, very low efficiency, restriction of output, and marked aggression against management. Despite these undesirable effects, it was necessary that changes in methods and jobs continue.

Efforts were made to solve this serious problem by the use of a special monetary allowance for transfers, by trying to enlist the cooperation and aid of the union, by making necessary lay-offs on the basis of efficiency, etc. In all cases, these actions did little or nothing to overcome the resistance to change. On the basis of these data, it was felt that the pressing problem of

SOURCE: Reprinted by permission of the authors and Plenum Publishing Company from "Overcoming Resistance to Change," *Human Relations,* August 1948, pp. 512–32.

resistance to change demanded further research for its solution. From the point of view of factory management, there were two purposes to the research: (1) Why do people resist change so strongly? and (2) What can be done to overcome this resistance?

Starting with a series of observations about the behavior of changed groups, the first step in the overall program was to devise a preliminary theory to account for the resistance to change. Then on the basis of the theory, a real life action experiment was devised and conducted within the context of the factory situation. Finally, the results of the experiment were interpreted in the light of the preliminary theory and the new data.

BACKGROUND

The main plant of the Harwood Manufacturing Corporation, where the present research was done, is located in the small town of Marion, Virginia. The plant produces pajamas and, like most sewing plants, employs mostly women. The plant's population is about 500 women and 100 men. The workers are recruited from the rural, mountainous areas surrounding the town and are usually employed without previous industrial experience. The average age of the workers is 23; the average education is eight years of grammar school.

The policies of the company in regard to labor relations are liberal and progressive. A high value has been placed on fair and open dealing with the employees, and they are encouraged to take up any problems or grievances with the management at any time. Every effort is made to help foremen find effective solutions to their problems in human relations, using conferences and role-playing methods. Carefully planned orientation, designed to help overcome the discouragement and frustrations attending entrance upon the new and unfamiliar situation, is used. Plantwide votes are conducted where possible to resolve problems affecting the whole working population. The company has invested both time and money in employee services, such as industrial music, health services, lunchroom, and recreation programs. In the same spirit, the management has been conscious of the importance of public relations in the local community; they have supported both financially and otherwise any activity which would build up good will for the company. As a result of these policies, the company has enjoyed good labor relations since the day it commenced operations.

Harwood employees work on an individual incentive system. Piece rates are set by time study and are expressed in terms of units. One unit is equal to one minute of standard work: 60 units per hour equal the standard efficiency rating. Thus, if on a particular operation the piece rate for one dozen is 10 units, the operator would have to produce 6 dozen per hour to achieve the standard efficiency rating of 60 units per hour. The skill required to reach 60 units per hour is great. On some jobs, an average trainee may take 34 weeks to reach the skill level necessary to perform at 60 units per hour. The first few weeks of work may be on an efficiency level of 5 to 20 units per hour.

The amount of pay received is directly proportional to the weekly average efficiency rating achieved. Thus, an operator with an average efficiency rating of 75 units per hour (25 percent more than standard) would receive 25 percent more than base pay. However there are two minimum wages below which no operator may fall. The first is the plantwide minimum, the hiring-in wage; the second is a minimum wage based on six months' employment and is 22 percent higher than the plantwide minimum wage. Both minima are smaller than the base pay for 60 units per hour efficiency rating.

The rating of every piece worker is computed every day and the results are published in a daily record of production which is shown to every operator. This daily record of production for each production line carries the names of all the operators on that line arranged in rank order of efficiency rating, with the highest rating girl at the top of the list. The supervisors speak to each operator each day about her unit ratings. Because of the above procedures, many operators do not claim credit for all work done in a given day. Instead, they save a few of the piece rate tickets as a "cushion" against a rainy day when they may not feel well or may have a great amount of machine trouble.

When it is necessary to change an operator from one type of work to another, a transfer bonus is given. The bonus is so designed that the changed operator who relearns at an average rate will suffer no loss in earnings after the change. Despite this allowance, the general attitudes toward job changes in the factory are markedly negative. Such expressions as, "When you make your units (standard production), they change your job," are all too frequent. Many operators refuse to change, preferring to quit.

THE TRANSFER LEARNING CURVE

An analysis of the after-change relearning curves of several hundred experienced operators rating standard or better prior to change showed that 38 percent of the changed operators recovered to the standard unit rating of 60 units per hour. The other 62 percent either became chronically substandard operators or quit during the relearning period.

The average relearning curve for those who recover to standard production on the simplest type job in the plant (Figure 1) is eight weeks long, and, when smoothed, provides the basis for the transfer bonus. The bonus is the percent difference between this expected efficiency rating and the standard of 60 units per hour. Progress is slow for the first two or three weeks, as the relearning curve shows, and then accelerates markedly to about 50 units per hour with an increase of 15 units in two weeks. Another slow

FIGURE 1   A Comparison of the Learning Curve for New, Inexperienced
Employees with the Relearning Curve for Only Those Transfers (38
percent) Who Eventually Recover to Standard Production

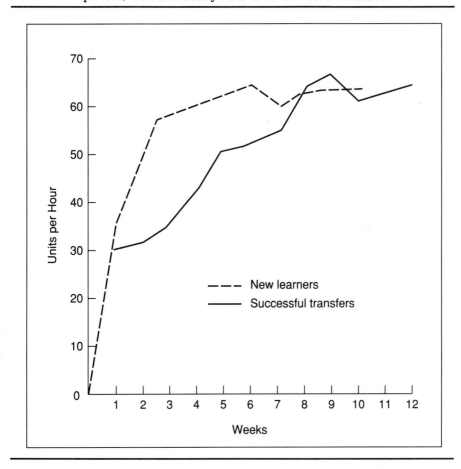

progress area is encountered at 50 units per hour, the operator improving
only 3 units in two weeks. The curve ends in a spurt of 10 units progress in
one week, a marked goal gradient behavior. The individual curves, of
course, vary widely in length according to the simplicity or difficulty of the
job to be relearned; but, in general, the successful curves are consistent with
the average curve in form.

It is interesting to note in Figure 1 that the relearning period for an
experienced operator is longer than the learning period for a new operator.
This is true despite the fact that the majority of transfers—the failures who
never recover to standard—are omitted from the curve. However, changed

FIGURE 2   The Drop in Production and the Rate of Recovery after Transfer for Skillful and for Substandard Operators

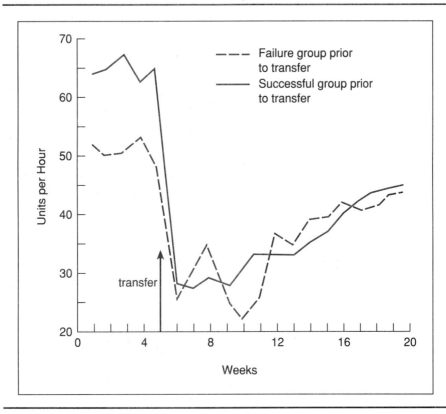

operators rarely complain of "wanting to do it the old way," etc., after the first week or two of change; and time and motion studies show few false moves after the first week of change. From this evidence it is deduced that proactive inhibition or the interference of previous habits in learning the new skill is either nonexistent or very slight after the first two weeks of change.

Figure 2, which presents the relearning curves for 41 experienced operators who were changed to very difficult jobs, gives a comparison between the recovery rates for operators making standard or better prior to change, and those below standard prior to change. Both classes of operators dropped to a little below 30 units per hour and recovered at a very slow but similar rate. These curves show a general (though by no means universal) phenomenon: that the efficiency rating prior to change does not indicate a faster or slower recovery rate after change.

A PRELIMINARY THEORY OF RESISTANCE TO CHANGE

The fact that relearning after transfer to a new job is so often slower than initial learning on first entering the factory would indicate, on the face of it, that the resistance to change and the slow relearning is primarily a motivational problem. The similar recovery rates of the skilled and unskilled operators shown in Figure 2 tend to confirm the hypothesis that skill is a minor factor and motivation is the major determinant of the rate of recovery. Earlier experiments at Harwood by Alex Bavelas demonstrated this point conclusively. He found that the use of group decision techniques on operators who had just been transferred resulted in very marked increases in the rate of relearning, even though no skill training was given and there were no other changes in working conditions.[1]

Interviews with operators who have been transferred to a new job reveal a common pattern of feelings and attitudes which are distinctly different from those of successful nontransfers. In addition to resentment against the management for transferring them, the employees typically show feelings of frustration, loss of hope of ever regaining their former level of production and status in the factory, feelings of failure, and a very low level of aspiration. In this respect these transferred operators are similar to the chronically slow workers studied previously.

Earlier unpublished research at Harwood has shown that the nontransferred employees generally have an explicit goal of reaching and maintaining an efficiency rating of 60 units per hour. A questionnaire administered to several groups of operators indicated that a large majority of them accept as their goal the management's quota of 60 units per hour. This standard of production is the level of aspiration according to which the operators measure their own success or failure; and those who fall below standard lose status in the eyes of their fellow employees. Relatively few operators set a goal appreciably above 60 units per hour.

The actual production records confirm the effectiveness of this goal of standard production. The distribution of the total population of operators in accordance with their production levels is by no means a normal curve. Instead, there is a very large number of operators who rate 60 to 63 units per hour and relatively few operators who rate just above or just below this range. Thus, we may conclude that:

1. There is a force acting on the operator in the direction of achieving a production level of 60 units per hour or more. It is assumed that the strength of this driving force (acting on an operator below standard) increases as she gets nearer the goal—a typical goal gradient (see Figure 1).

On the other hand restraining forces operate to hinder or prevent her from reaching this goal. These restraining forces consist among other things of the difficulty of the job in relation to the operator's level of skill. Other things being equal, the faster an operator is sewing the more difficult it is to increase her speed by a given amount. Thus, we may conclude that:

2. The strength of the restraining force hindering higher production increases with increasing level of production.

In line with previous studies, it is assumed that the conflict of these two opposing forces—the driving force corresponding to the goal of reaching 60 and the restraining force of the difficulty of the job—produces frustration. In such a conflict situation, the strength of frustration will depend on the strength of these forces. If the restraining force against increasing production is weak, then the frustration will be weak. But if the driving force toward higher production (i.e., the motivation) is weak, then the frustration will also be weak. Probably both of the conflicting forces must be above a certain minimum strength before any frustration is produced; for all goal-directed activity involves some degree of conflict of this type, yet a person is not usually frustrated so long as he is making satisfactory progress toward his goal. Consequently we assume that:

3. The strength of frustration is a function of the weaker of these two opposing forces, provided that the weaker force is stronger than a certain minimum necessary to produce frustration.[2]

An analysis of the effects of such frustration in the factory showed that it resulted, among other things, in high turnover and absenteeism. The rate of turnover for successful operators with efficiency ratings above standard was much lower than for unsuccessful operators. Likewise, operators on the more difficult jobs quit more frequently than those on the easier jobs. Presumably the effect of being transferred is a severe frustration which should result in similar attempts to escape from the field.

In line with this theory of frustration and the finding that job turnover is one resultant of frustration, an analysis was made of the turnover rate of transferred operators as compared with the rate among operators who had not been transferred recently. For the year September 1946 to September 1947 there were 198 operators who had not been transferred recently, that is, within the 34-week period allowed for relearning after transfer. There was a second group of 85 operators who had been transferred recently; that is, within the time allowed for relearning the new job. Each of the two groups was divided into several classifications according to their unit rating at the time of quitting. For each classification the percent turnover per month, based on the total number of employees in that classification, was computed.

The results are given in Figure 3. Both the levels of turnover and the form of the curves are strikingly different for the two groups. Among oper-

FIGURE 3   The Rate of Turnover at Various Levels of Production for Transfers
as Compared with Nontransfers

ators who have not been transferred recently the average turnover per
month is about 4½ percent; among recent transfers the monthly turnover is
nearly 12 percent. Consistent with the previous studies, both groups show a
very marked drop in the turnover curve after an operator becomes a success
reaching 60 units per hour or standard production. However, the form of
curves at lower unit ratings is markedly different for the two groups. The
nontransferred operators show a gradually increasing rate of turnover up to
a rating of 55 to 59 units per hour. The transferred operators, on the other
hand, show a high peak at the lowest unit rating of 30 to 34 units per hour,
decreasing sharply to a low point at 45 to 49 units per hour. Since most
changed operators drop to a unit rating of around 30 units per hour when
changed and then drop no further, it is obvious that the rate of turnover was
highest for these operators just after they were changed and again much
later just before they reached standard. Why?

It is assumed that the strength of frustration for an operator who has
not been transferred gradually increases because both the driving force

towards the goal of reaching 60 and the restraining force of the difficulty of the job increase with increasing unit rating. This is in line with hypotheses (1), (2), and (3) above. For the transferred operator, on the other hand, the frustration is greatest immediately after transfer when the contrast of her present status with her former status is most evident. At this point the strength of the restraining forces is at a maximum, because the difficulty is unusually great due to proactive inhibition. Then as she overcomes the interference effects between the two jobs and learns the new job, the difficulty and the frustration gradually decrease and the rate of turnover declines until the operator reaches 45–49 units per hour. Then at higher levels of production the difficulty starts to increase again, and the transferred operator shows the same peak in frustration and turnover at 55–59 units per hour.

Though our theory of frustration explains the forms of the two turnover curves in Figure 3, it hardly seems adequate to account for the markedly higher level of turnover for transfers as compared to nontransfers. On the basis of the difficulty of the job, it is especially difficult to explain the higher rate of turnover at 55–59 units per hour for transfers. Evidently, additional forces are operating.

Another factor which seems to affect recovery rates of changed operators is the amount of we-feeling. Observations seem to indicate that a strong psychological subgroup with negative attitudes toward management will display the strongest resistance to change. On the other hand, changed groups with high we-feeling and positive cooperative attitudes are the best relearners. Collections of individuals with little or no we-feeling display some resistance to change but not so strongly as the groups with high we-feeling and negative attitudes toward management. However, turnover for the individual transfers is much higher than in the latter groups. This phenomenon of the relationship between we-feeling and resistance to change is so overt that for years the general policy of the management of the plant was never to change a group as a group, but, rather, to scatter the individuals in different areas throughout the factory.

An analysis of turnover records for changed operators with high we-feeling showed a 4 percent turnover rate per month at 30 to 34 units per hour, not significantly higher than in unchanged operators but significantly lower than in changed operators with little or no we-feeling. However, the acts of aggression are far more numerous among operators with high we-feeling than among operators with little we-feeling. Since both types of operators experience the same frustration as individuals but react to it so differently, it is assumed that the effect of the in-group feeling is to set up a restraining force against leaving the group and perhaps even to set up driving forces toward staying in the group. In these circumstances, one would expect some alternative reaction to frustration, rather than escape from the field. This alternative is aggression. Strong we-feeling provides strength so that members dare to express aggression which would otherwise be suppressed.

One common result in a subgroup with strong we-feeling is the setting of a group standard concerning production. Where the attitudes toward management are antagonistic, this group standard may take the form of a definite restriction of production to a given level. This phenomenon of restriction is particularly likely to happen in a group that has been transferred to a job where a new piece rate has been set; for they have some hope that, if production never approaches the standard, the management may change the piece rate in their favor.

A group standard can exert extremely strong forces on an individual member of a small subgroup. That these forces can have a powerful effect on production is indicated in the production record of one presser during a period of 40 days (Table 1).

For the first 20 days she was working in a group of other pressers who were producing at the rate of about 50 units per hour. Starting on the 13th day, when she reached standard production and exceeded the production of the other members, she became a scapegoat of the group. During this time her production decreased toward the level of the remaining members of the group. After 20 days the group had to be broken up and all the other members were transferred to other jobs, leaving only the scapegoat operator. With the removal of the group, the group standard was no longer operative; and the production of the one remaining operator shot up from the level of about 45 to 96 units per hour in a period of four days. Her production stabilized at a level of about 92 and stayed there for the remainder of the 20 days. Thus, it is clear that the motivational forces induced in the individual by a strong subgroup may be more powerful than those induced by management.

TABLE 1

Days	Production per Day
In the Group	
1–3	46
4–6	52
7–9	53
10–12	56
Scapegoating Begins	
13–16	55
17–20	48
Becomes a Single Worker	
21–24	83
25–28	92
29–32	92
33–36	91
37–40	92

THE EXPERIMENT

On the basis of the preliminary theory that resistance to change is a combination of an individual reaction to frustration with strong group-induced forces, it seemed that the most appropriate methods for overcoming the resistance to change would be group methods. Consequently an experiment was designed employing two variations of democratic procedure in handling groups to be transferred. The first variation involved participation through representation of the workers in designing the changes to be made in the jobs. The second variation consisted of total participation by all members of the group in designing the changes. A third control group was also used. Two experimental groups received the total participation treatment. The three experimental groups and the control group were roughly matched with respect to: (1) the efficiency ratings of the groups before transfer, (2) the degree of change involved in the transfer, (3) the amount of we-feeling observed in the groups.

In no case was more than a minor change in the work routines and time allowances made. The control group, the 18 hand pressers, had formerly stacked their work in one-half dozen lots on a flat piece of cardboard the size of the finished product. The new job called for stacking their work in one-half dozen lots in a box the size of the finished product. The box was located in the same place the cardboard had been. An additional two minutes per dozen was allowed (by the time study) for this new part of the job. This represented a total job change of 8.8 percent.

Experimental group 1, the 13 pajama folders, had formerly folded coats with prefolded pants. The new job called for the folding of coats with unfolded pants. An additional 1.8 minutes per dozen was allowed (by time study) for this new part of the job. This represented a total job change of 9.4 percent.

Experimental groups 2 and 3, consisting of eight and seven pajama examiners, respectively, had formerly clipped threads from the entire garment and examined every seam. The new job called for pulling only certain threads off and examining every seam. An average of 1.2 minutes per dozen was subtracted (by time study) from the total time on these two jobs. This represented a total job change of 8 percent.

The control group of hand pressers went through the usual factory routine when they were changed. The production department modified the job, and a new piece rate was set. A group meeting was then held in which the control group was told that the change was necessary because of competitive conditions, and that a new piece rate had been set. The new piece rate was thoroughly explained by the time study man, questions were answered, and the meeting dismissed.

Experimental group 1 was changed in a different manner. Before any changes took place, a group meeting was held with all the operators to be changed. The need for the change was presented as dramatically as possible, showing two identical garments produced in the factory; one was produced in 1946 and had sold for 100 percent more than its fellow in 1947. The group was asked to identify the cheaper one and could not do it. This demonstration effectively shared with the group the entire problem of the necessity of cost reduction. A general agreement was reached that a savings could be effected by removing the "frills" and "fancy" work from the garment without affecting the folders' opportunity to achieve a high efficiency rating. Management then presented a plan to set the new job and piece rate:

1. Make a check study of the job as it was being done.
2. Eliminate all unnecessary work.
3. Train several operators in the correct methods.
4. Set the piece rate by time studies on these specially trained operators.
5. Explain the new job and rate to all the operators.
6. Train all operators in the new method so they can reach a high rate of production within a short time.

The group approved this plan (though no formal group decision was reached) and chose the operators to be specially trained. A submeeting with the "special" operators was held immediately following the meeting with the entire group. They displayed a cooperative and interested attitude and immediately presented many good suggestions. This attitude carried over into the working out of the details of the new job; and when the new job and piece rates were set, the "special" operators referred to the resultants as "our job," "our rate," etc. The new job and piece rates were presented at a second group meeting to all the operators involved. The "special" operators served to train the other operators on the new job.

Experimental groups 2 and 3 went through much the same kind of change meetings. The groups were smaller than experimental group 1, and a more intimate atmosphere was established. The need for a change was once again made dramatically clear; the same general plan was presented by management. However, since the groups were small, all operators were chosen as "special" operators; that is, all operators were to participate directly in the designing of the new jobs, and all operators would be studied by the time study man. It is interesting to note that, in the meetings with these two groups, suggestions were immediately made in such quantity that the stenographer had great difficulty in recording them. The group approved of the plans, but again no formal group decision was reached.

Results

The results of the experiment are summarized in graphic form in Figure 4. The gaps in the production curves occur because these groups were paid on a time-work basis for a day or two. The control group improved little beyond their early efficiency ratings. Resistance developed almost immedi-

FIGURE 4   The Effects of Participation through Representation (group 1) and of Total Participation (groups 2 and 3) on Recovery after an Easy Transfer

ately after the change occurred. Marked expressions of aggression against management occurred, such as conflict with the methods engineer, expression of hostility against the supervisor, deliberate restriction of production, and lack of cooperation with the supervisor. There were 17 percent quits in the first 40 days. Grievances were filed about the piece rate, but, when the rate was checked, it was found to be a little "loose."

Experimental group 1 showed an unusually good relearning curve. At the end of 14 days, the group averaged 61 units per hour. During the 14 days, the attitude was cooperative and permissive. They worked well with the methods engineer, the training staff, and the supervisor. (The supervisor was the same person in the cases of the control group and experimental group 1.) There were no quits in this group in the first 40 days. This group might have presented a better learning record if work had not been scarce during the first seven days. There was one act of aggression against the supervisor recorded in the first 40 days. It is interesting to note that the three special representative operators in experimental group 1 recovered at about the same rate as the rest of their group.

Experimental groups 2 and 3 recovered faster than experimental group 1. After a slight drop on the first day of change, the efficiency ratings returned to a prechange level and showed sustained progress thereafter to a level about 14 percent higher than the prechange level. No additional training was provided them after the second day. They worked well with their supervisors and no indications of aggression were observed from these groups. There were no quits in either of these groups in the first forty days.

A fourth experimental group, composed of only two sewing operators, was transferred by the total participation technique. Their new job was one of the most difficult jobs in the factory, in contrast to the easy jobs for the control group and the other three experimental groups. As expected, the total participation technique again resulted in an unusually fast recovery rate and a final level of production well above the level before transfer. Because of the difficulty of the new job, however, the rate of recovery was slower than for experimental groups 2 and 3, but faster than for experimental group 1.

In the first experiment, the control group made no progress after transfer for a period of 32 days. At the end of this period, the group was broken up and the individuals were reassigned to new jobs scattered throughout the factory. Two and a half months after their dispersal, the 13 remaining members of the original control group were again brought together as a group for a second experiment.

This second experiment consisted of transferring the control group to a new job, using the total participation technique in meetings which were similar to those held with experimental groups 2 and 3. The new job was a pressing job of comparable difficulty to the new job in the first experiment. On the average it involved about the same degree of change. In the meetings no reference was made to the previous behavior of the group on being transferred.

The results of the second experiment were in sharp contrast to the first (see Figure 5). With the total participation technique, the same control group now recovered rapidly to their previous efficiency rating, and, like the other groups under this treatment, continued on beyond it to a new high level of production. There was no aggression or turnover in the group for 19 days after change, a marked modification of their previous behavior after transfer. Some anxiety concerning their seniority status was expressed, but this was resolved in a meeting of their elected delegate, the union business agent, and a management representative. It should be noted in Figure 5 that the prechange level on the second experiment is just above 60 units per hour; thus, the individual transfers had progressed to just above standard during the two and a half months between the two experiments.

FIGURE 5   A Comparison of the Effect of the Control Procedure with the Total
Participation Procedure on the Same Group

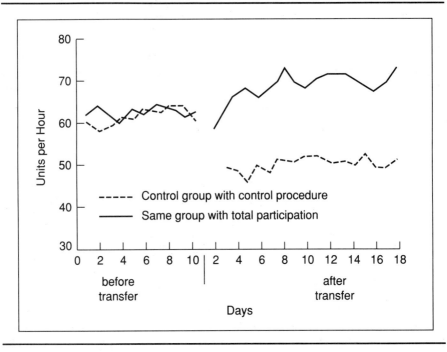

INTERPRETATION

The purpose of this section is to explain the drop in production resulting from transfer, the differential recovery rates of the control and the experimental groups, the increases beyond their former levels of production by the experimental groups, and the differential rates of turnover and aggression.

The first experiment showed that the rate of recovery is directly proportional to the amount of participation, and that the rates of turnover and aggression are inversely proportional to the amount of participation. The second experiment demonstrated more conclusively that the results obtained depended on the experimental treatment, rather than on personality factors like skill or aggressiveness, for identical individuals yielded markedly different results in the control treatment as contrasted with the total participation treatment.

Apparently total participation has the same type of effect as participation through representation, but the former has a stronger influence. In regard to recovery rates, this difference is not unequivocal, because the experiment was unfortunately confounded. Right after transfer, experimental group number 1 had insufficient material to work on for a period of seven days. Hence, their slower recovery during this period is at least in part due to insufficient work. In succeeding days, however, there was an adequate supply of work and the differential recovery rate still persisted. Therefore, we are inclined to believe that participation through representation results in slower recovery than does total participation.

Before discussing the details of why participation produces high morale, we will consider the nature of production levels. In examining the production records of hundreds of individuals and groups in this factory, one is struck by the constancy of the level of production. Though differences among individuals in efficiency rating are very large, nearly every experienced operator maintains a fairly steady level of production, given constant physical conditions. Frequently the given level will be maintained despite rather large changes in technical working conditions.

As Lewin has pointed out, this type of production can be viewed as a quasi-stationary process—in the ongoing work the operator is forever sewing new garments, yet the level of the process remains relatively stationary. Thus, there are constant characteristics of the production process permitting the establishment of general laws.

In studying production as a quasi-stationary equilibrium, we are concerned with two types of forces: (1) forces on production in a downward direction, (2) forces on production in an upward direction. In this situation we are dealing with a variety of both upward forces tending to increase the level of production and downward forces tending to decrease the level of production. However, in the present experiment we have no method of measuring independently all of the component forces either downward or upward. These various component forces upward are combined into one resultant force upward. Likewise, the several downward component forces combine into one resultant force downward. We can infer a good deal about the relative strengths of these resultant forces.

Where we are dealing with a quasi-stationary equilibrium, the resultant forces upward and the forces downward are opposite in direction and equal in strength at the equilibrium level. Of course, either resultant forces may fluctuate over a short period of time, so that the forces may not be equally balanced at a given moment. However over a longer period of time and on the average the forces balance out. Fluctuations from the average occur but there is a tendency to return to the average level.

Just before being transferred, all of the groups in both experiments had reached a stable equilibrium level at just above the standard production of 60 units per hour. This level was equal to the average efficiency rating for the entire factory during the period of the experiments. Since this production level remained constant, neither increasing nor decreasing, we may be sure that the strength of the resultant force upward was equal to the strength of the resultant force downward. This equilibrium of forces was maintained over the period of time when production was stationary at this level. But the forces changed markedly after transfer and these new constellations of forces were distinctly different for the control and the experimental groups.

For the control group, the period after transfer is a quasi-stationary equilibrium at a lower level, and the forces do not change during the period of 30 days. The resultant force upward remains equal to the resultant force downward and the level of production remains constant. The force field for this group is represented schematically in Figure 6. Only the resultant forces are shown. The length of the vector represents the strength of the force; and the point of the arrow represents the point of application of the force, that is, the production level and the time at which the force applies. Thus, the forces are equal and opposite only at the level of 50 units per hour. At higher levels of production the forces downward are greater than the forces upward; and at lower levels of production the forces upward are stronger than the forces downward. Thus, there is a tendency for the equilibrium to be maintained at an efficiency rating of 50.

The situation for the experimental groups after transfer can be viewed as a quasi-stationary equilibrium of a different type. Figure 7 gives a schematic diagram of the resultant forces for the experimental groups. At any given level of production, such as 50 units per hour or 60 units per hour, both the resultant forces upward and the resultant forces downward change over the period of 30 days. During this time the point of equilibrium, which starts at 50 units per hour, gradually rises until it reaches a level of over 70 units

FIGURE 6   A Schematic Diagram of the Quasi-stationary Equilibrium for the Control Group after Transfer

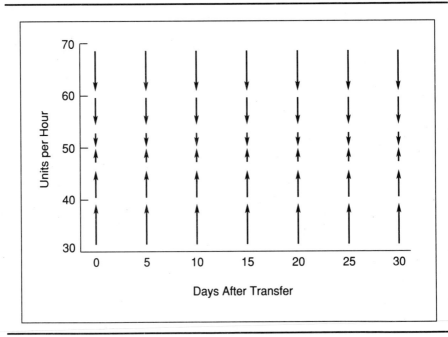

FIGURE 7   A Schematic Diagram of the Quasi-stationary Equilibrium for the Experimental Groups after Transfer

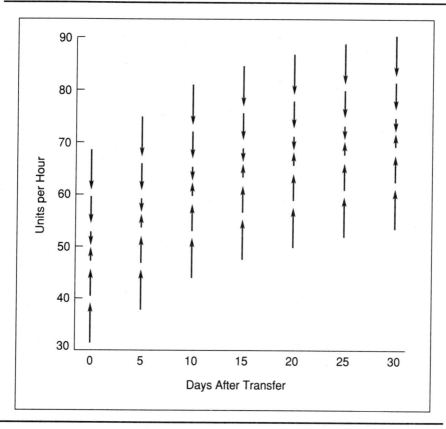

per hour after 30 days. Yet here again the equilibrium level has the character of a "central force field," where at any point in the total field the resultant of the upward and the downward forces is in the direction of the equilibrium level.

To understand how the difference between the experimental and the control treatments produced the differences in force fields represented in Figures 6 and 7, it is not sufficient to consider only the resultant forces. We must also look at the component forces for each resultant force.

There are three main component forces influencing production in a downward direction: (1) the difficulty of the job. . . ; (2) a force corresponding to avoidance of strain; (3) a force corresponding to a group standard to restrict production to a given level. The resultant force upward in the direction of greater production is composed of three additional component forces: (1) the force corresponding to the goal of standard production. . . ;

(2) a force corresponding to pressures induced by the management through supervision; (3) a force corresponding to a group standard of competition. Let us examine each of these six component forces.

1. Job Difficulty. For all operators the difficulty of the job is one of the forces downward on production. The difficulty of the job, of course, is relative to the skill of the operator. The given job may be very difficult for an unskilled operator but relatively easy for a highly skilled one. In the case of a transfer a new element of difficulty enters. For some time the new job is much more difficult, for the operator is unskilled at that particular job. In addition to the difficulty experienced by any learner, the transfer often encounters the added difficulty of proactive inhibition. Where the new job is similar to the old job there will be a period of interference between the two similar but different skills required. For this reason a very efficient operator whose skills have become almost unconscious may suffer just as great a drop as a much less efficient operator (see Figure 2). Except for group 4, the difficulty of these easy jobs does not explain the differential recovery rate, because both the initial difficulty and the amount of change were equated for these groups. The two operators in group 4 probably dropped further and recovered more slowly than any of the other three groups under total participation because of the greater difficulty of the job.

2. Strain Avoidance. The force toward lower production corresponding to the difficulty of the job (or the lack of skill of the person) has the character of a restraining force—that is, it acts to prevent locomotion, rather than as a driving force causing locomotion. However, in all production there is a closely related driving force toward lower production, namely "strain avoidance." We assume that working too hard and working too fast is an unpleasant strain; and corresponding to this negative valence there is a driving force in the opposite direction, namely toward taking it easy or working slower. The higher the level of production the greater will be the strain and, other things being equal, the stronger will be the downward force of strain avoidance. Likewise, the greater the difficulty of the job the stronger will be the force corresponding to strain avoidance. But the greater the operator's skill the smaller will be the strain and the strength of the force of strain avoidance. Therefore:

(4) The strength of the force of strain avoidance =

$$\frac{\text{Job difficulty} \times \text{Production level}}{\text{Skill of operator}}$$

The differential recovery rates of the control group in both experiments and the three experimental groups in Experiment I cannot be explained by strain avoidance, because job difficulty, production level, and operator skill were matched at the time immediately following transfer. Later, however, when the experimental treatments had produced a much higher level of production, these groups were subjected to an increased downward force of strain avoidance which was stronger than in the control group in Experiment I. Evidently other forces were strong enough to overcome this force of strain avoidance.

3. The Goal of Standard Production. In considering the negative attitudes toward transfer and the resistance to being transferred, there are several important aspects of the complex goal of reaching and maintaining a level of 60 units per hour. For an operator producing below standard, this goal is attractive, because it means success, high status in the eyes of her fellow employees, better pay, and job security. . . . On the other hand, there is a strong force against remaining below standard, because this lower level means failure, low status, low pay, and the danger of being fired. Thus, it is clear that the upward force corresponding to the goal of standard production will indeed be strong for the transfer who has dropped below standard.

It is equally clear why any operator, who accepts the stereotype about transfer, shows such strong resistance to being changed. She sees herself as becoming a failure and losing status, pay, and perhaps the job itself. The result is a lowered level of aspiration and a weakened force toward the goal of standard production.

Just such a weakening of the force toward 60 units per hour seems to have occurred in the control group in Experiment I. The participation treatments, on the other hand, seem to have involved the operators in designing the new job and setting the new piece rates in such a way that they did not lose hope of regaining the goal of standard production. Thus, the participation resulted in a stronger force toward higher production. However, this force alone can hardly account for the large differences in recovery rate between the control group and the experimental groups; certainly it does not explain why the latter increased to a level so high above standard.

4. Management Pressure. On all operators below standard the management exerts a pressure for higher production. This pressure is no harsh and autocratic treatment involving threats. Rather, it takes the form of persuasion and encouragement by the supervisors. They attempt to induce the low-rating operator to improve her performance and to attain standard production.

Such an attempt to induce a psychological force on another person may have several results. In the first place the person may ignore the attempt of the inducing agent, in which case there is no induced force acting on the person. On the other hand, the attempt may so succeed that an induced force on the person exists. Other things being equal, whenever there is an induced force acting on a person, the person will locomote in the direction of the force. An induced force, which depends on the power field of an inducing agent—some other individual or group—will cease to exist when the inducing power field is withdrawn. In this report it is different from an "own" force which stems from a person's own needs and goals.

The reaction of a person to an effective induced force will vary, depending, among other things, on the person's relation to the inducing agent. A force induced by a friend may be accepted in such a way that it acts more like an own force. An effective force induced by an enemy may be so resisted and rejected that the person complies unwillingly and shows signs of conflict and tension. Thus, in addition to what might be called a "neutral" induced force, we also distinguish an *accepted* induced force and a *rejected* induced force. Naturally, the acceptance and the rejection of an induced force can vary in degree from zero (i.e., a neutral induced force) to very strong acceptance or rejection. To account for the difference in character between the acceptance and the rejection of an induced force, we make the following assumptions:

(5) The acceptance of an induced force sets up additional own forces in the same direction.

(6) The rejection of an induced force sets up additional own forces in the opposite direction.

The grievances, aggression, and tension in the control group in Experiment I indicate that they rejected the force toward higher production induced by the management. The group accepted the stereotype that transfer is a calamity; but the control procedure did not convince them that the change was necessary, and they viewed the new job and the new piece rates set by management as arbitrary and unreasonable.

The experimental groups, on the contrary, participated in so designing the changes and setting the piece rates that they spoke of the new job as "our job" and the new piece rates as "our rates." Thus, they accepted the new situation and accepted the management induced force toward higher production.

From the acceptance by the experimental groups and the rejection by the control group of the management induced forces, we may derive [by (5) and (6) above] that the former had additional own forces toward higher production, whereas the latter had additional own forces toward lower production. This difference helps to explain the better recovery rate of experimental groups.

5.   Group Standards.   Probably the most important force affecting the recovery under the control procedure was a group standard, set by the group restricting the level of production to 50 units per hour. Evidently this explicit agreement to restrict production is related to the group's rejection of the change and of the new job as arbitrary and unreasonable. Perhaps they had faint hopes of demonstrating that standard production could not be attained and, thereby, obtain a more favorable piece rate. In any case, there was a definite group phenomenon which affected all the members of the group. We have already noted the striking example of the presser whose production was restricted in the group situation to about half the level she attained as an individual. . . . In the control group, too, we would expect the group to induce strong forces on the members. The more the member deviates above the standard the stronger would be the group induced force to conform to the standard, for such deviations both negate any possibility of managment increasing the piece rate and at the same time expose the other members to increased pressure from management. Thus, individual differences in levels of production should be sharply curtailed in the control group after transfer.

An analysis was made for all groups of the individual differences within the group in levels of production. In Experiment I the 40 days before change were compared with the 30 days after change; in Experiment II the 10 days before change were compared to the 17 days after change. As a measure of variability, the standard deviation was calculated each day for each group. The average daily standard deviations *before* and *after* change were as follows (Table 2):

There is indeed a marked decrease in individual differences within the control group after their first transfer. In fact, the restriction of production resulted in a lower variability than in any other group. Thus, we may conclude that the group standard at 60 units per hour set up strong group-induced forces, which were important components in the central force field shown in Figure 6. It is now evident that for the control group the quasi-stationary equilibrium after transfer has a steep gradient around the equilibrium level of 50 units per hour—the strength of the forces increases rapidly above and below this level. It is also clear that the group standard to restrict production is a major reason for the lack of recovery in the control group.

The table of variability also shows that the experimental treatments markedly reduced variability in the other four groups after transfer. In experimental group 1 (participation by representation) this smallest reduction of variability was produced by a group standard of individual competition. Competition among members of the group was reported by the supervisor soon after transfer. This competition was a force toward higher production, which resulted in good recovery to standard and continued progress beyond standard.

TABLE 2

Group	Variability	
	Before Change	*After Change*
Experiment I		
Control group	9.8	1.9
Experimental 1	9.7	3.8
Experimental 2	10.3	2.7
Experimental 3	9.9	2.4
Experiment II		
Control group	12.7	2.9

Experimental groups 2 and 3 showed a greater reduction in variability following transfer. These two groups under total participation were transferred on the same day. Group competition developed between the two groups. This group competition, which evidently resulted in stronger forces on the members than did the individual competition, was an effective group standard. The standard gradually moved to higher and higher levels of production, with the result that the groups not only reached but far exceeded their previous levels of production.

Turnover and Aggression

Returning now to our preliminary theory of frustration, we can see several revisions. The difficulty of the job and its relation to skill and strain avoidance has been clarified in proposition (4). It is now clear that the driving force toward 60 is a complex affair; it is partly a negative driving force corresponding to the negative valence of low pay, low status, failure, and job insecurity. Turnover results not only from the frustration produced by the conflict of these two forces but also as a direct attempt to escape from the region of these negative valences. For the members of the control group, the group standard to restrict production prevented escape by increasing production, so quitting their jobs was the only remaining escape. In the participation groups, on the contrary, both the group standards and the additional own forces resulting from the acceptance of management-induced forces combined to make increasing production the distinguished path of escape from this region of negative valence.

In considering turnover as a form of escape from the field, it is not enough to look only at the psychological present; one must also consider the psychological future. The employee's decision to quit the job is rarely made exclusively on the basis of a momentary frustration or an undesirable present situation; she usually quits when she also sees the future as equally hopeless. The operator transferred by the usual factory procedure (including the control group) has in fact a realistic view of the probability of continued failure because, as we have already noted, 62 percent of transfers do in fact fail to recover to standard production. Thus, the higher rate of quitting for transfers as compared to nontransfers results from a more pessimistic view of the future.

The control procedure had the effect for the members of setting up management as a hostile power field. They rejected the forces induced by this hostile power field, and group standards to restrict production developed within the group in opposition to management. In this conflict between the power field of management and the power field of the group, the control group attempted to reduce the strength of the hostile power field relative to the strength of their own power field. This change was accomplished in three ways: (1) the group increased its own power by developing a more cohesive and well-disciplined group, (2) they secured "allies" by getting the backing of the union in filing a formal grievance about the new piece rate, (3) they attacked the hostile power field directly in the form of aggression against the supervisor, the time study engineer, and the higher management. Thus, the aggression was derived not only from individual frustration but also from the conflict between two groups. Furthermore, this situation of group conflict both helped to define management as the frustration agent and gave the members strength to express any aggressive impulses produced by frustration.

CONCLUSIONS

It is possible for management to modify greatly or to remove completely group resistance to changes in methods of work and the ensuing piece rates. This change can be accomplished by the use of group meetings in which management effectively communicates the need for change and stimulates group participation in planning the changes.

For Harwood's management, and presumably for managements of other industries using an incentive system, this experiment has important implications in the field of labor relations. A majority of all grievances presented at Harwood have always stemmed from a change situation. By preventing or greatly modifying group resistance to change, this concomitant to change may well be greatly reduced. The reduction of such costly phenomena as turnover and slow relearning rates presents another distinct advantage.

Harwood's management has long felt that action research such as the present experiment is the only key to better labor-management relations. It is only by discovering the basic principles and applying them to the true causes of conflict that an intelligent, effective effort can be made to correct the undesirable effects of the conflict.

NOTES AND REFERENCES

1. John R. P. French, Jr., "The Behavior of Organized and Unorganized Groups under Conditions of Frustration and Fear, Studies in Topological and Vector Psychology, III," *University of Iowa Studies in Child Welfare* 20 (1944), pp. 229–308.
2. Kurt Lewin, "Frontiers in Group Dynamics," *Human Relations* 1, no. 1 (1947), pp. 5–41.

22

Participative Management: Time for a Second Look

Robert C. Albrook

Participative management might not be for everyone, cautions this article. Albrook calls for a reexamination of some of the notions we have about the democratic approach to management, noting that some assumptions about the utility of participation in decision making and the showing of authority are not always valid. Note particularly the discussion of the special difficulties involved in moving a traditionally authoritarian organization toward a participative style.—Eds.

The management of change has become a central preoccupation of U.S. business. When the directors have approved the record capital budget and congratulated themselves on "progress," when the banquet speaker has used his last superlative to describe the "world of tomorrow," the talk turns, inevitably, to the question: "Who will make it all work?" Some people resist change. Some hold the keys to it. Some admit the need for new ways but don't know how to begin. The question becomes what kind of management can ease the inevitable pains, unlock the talent, energy, and knowledge where they're needed, help valuable men to contribute to and shape change rather than be flattened by it.

The recipe is elusive, and increasingly business has turned to the academic world for help, particularly to the behavioral scientists—the psychologists, sociologists, and anthropologists whose studies have now become the showpieces of the better business schools. A number of major corporations, such as General Electric, Texas Instruments, and Standard Oil (N.J.), have brought social scientists onto their staffs. Some companies collaborate closely with university-based scholars and are contributing importantly to advanced theoretical work, just as industry's physicists, chemists, and engineers have become significant contributors of new knowledge in their

SOURCE: Reprinted by permission of the publisher from "Participative Management: Time for a Second Look," *Fortune*, May 1967, pp. 166–70, 197–200.

respective realms. Hundreds of companies, large and small, have tried one or another formulation of basic behavioral theory, such as the many schemes for sharing their savings with employees and actively soliciting their ideas for improved efficiency.

For 40 years the quantity and quality of academic expertise in this field have been steadily improving, and there has lately been a new burst of ideas which suggest that the researchers in the business schools and other centers of learning are really getting down to cases. The newest concepts already represent a considerable spin off from the appealingly simple notions on which the behavioral pioneers first concentrated. The essential message these outriders had for business was this: recognize the social needs of employees in their work, as well as their need for money; they will respond with a deeper commitment and better performance, help to shape the organization's changing goals, and make them their own. To blue-collar workers this meant such steps as organizing work around tasks large enough to have meaning and inviting workers' ideas; for middle and upper management it meant more participation in decision making, more sharing of authority and responsibility, more open and more candid communication, up, down, and sideways.

The new work suggests that neither the basic philosophy nor all of the early prescriptions of this management style were scientifically sound or universally workable. The word from the behavioral scientists is becoming more specific and "scientific," less simple and moralistic. At Harvard, M.I.T., the University of Michigan, Chicago, U.C.L.A., Stanford, and elsewhere, they are mounting bigger, longer, and more rigorous studies of the human factors in management than ever before undertaken.

One conclusion is that the "participative" or "group" approach doesn't seem to work with all people and in all situations. Research has shown that satisfied, happy workers are sometimes more productive—and sometimes merely happy. Some managers and workers are able to take only limited responsibility, however much the company tries to give them. Some people will recognize the need to delegate but "can't let go." In a profit squeeze the only way to get costs under control fast enough often seems to be with centralized, "get tough" management.

Few, if any, behaviorists espouse a general return to authoritarian management. Instead, they are seeking a more thorough, systematic way to apply participative principles on a sustained schedule that will give the theory a better chance to work. Others are insisting that management must be tailor-made, suited to the work or the people, rather than packaged in a standard mixture. Some people aren't and never will be suited for "democracy" on the job, according to one viewpoint, while others insist that new kinds of psychological training can fit most executives for the rugged give and take of successful group management.

As more variables are brought into their concepts, and as they look increasingly at the specifics of a management situation, the behaviorists are also being drawn toward collaboration with the systems designers and the theorists of data processing. Born in reaction to the cold scientism of the earlier "scientific management" experts with their stopwatches and measuring tapes, the "human relations" or behavioral school of today may be getting ready at last to bury that hatchet in a joint search for a broadly used "general theory" of management.

WHY EXECUTIVES DON'T PRACTICE WHAT THEY PREACH

Before any general theory can be evolved, a great deal more has to be known about the difficulty of putting theory into practice (i.e., of transforming a simple managerial attitude into an effective managerial style). "There are plenty of executives," observes Stanley Seashore, a social psychologist at the University of Michigan's Institute for Social Research, "who'll decide one morning they're going to be more participative and by the afternoon have concluded it doesn't work."

What's often lacking is an understanding of how deeply and specifically management style affects corporate operations. The executive who seeks a more effective approach needs a map of the whole terrain of management activity. Rensis Likert, director of the Michigan institute, has developed a chart to assist managers in gaining a deeper understanding of the way they operate. A simplified version appears in Table 1. By answering the questions in the left-hand column of the chart (e.g., "Are subordinates' ideas sought and used?"), an executive sketches a profile of the way his company is run and whether it leans to the "authoritative" or the "participative." Hundreds of businessmen have used the chart, under Likert's direction, and many have discovered a good deal they didn't realize about the way they were handling people.

Likert leads his subjects in deliberate steps to a conclusion that most of them do not practice what they say they believe. First, the executive is asked to think of the most successful company (or division of a company) he knows intimately. He then checks off on the chart his answers as they apply to that company. When the executive has finished this exercise, he has nearly always traced the profile of a strongly "participative" management system, well to the right on Likert's chart. He is next asked to repeat the procedure for the least successful company (or division) he knows well. Again, the profiles are nearly always the same, but this time they portray a strongly "authoritative" system, far to the left on the chart.

Then comes the point of the exercise. The executive is asked to describe his own company or division. Almost always, the resulting profile is that of a company somewhere in the middle, a blend of the "benevolent authoritative" and the "consultative"—well to the left of what the executive had previously identified as the most successful style. To check out the reliability of this self-analysis, Likert sometimes asks employees in the same com-

TABLE 1

	System 1 Exploitative Authoritative	System 2 Benevolent Authoritative	System 3 Consultative	System 4 Participative Group
Leadership				
How much confidence is shown in subordinates?	None	Condescending	Substantial	Complete
How free do they feel to talk to superiors about job?	Not at all	Not very	Rather free	Fully free
Are subordinates' ideas sought and used, if worthy?	Seldom	Sometimes	Usually	Always
Motivation				
Is predominant use made of (1) fear, (2) threats, (3) punishment, (4) rewards, (5) involvement?	1, 2, 3, occasionally 4	4, some 3	4, some 3 and 5	5, 4 based on group set goals
Where is responsibility felt for achieving organization's goals?	Mostly at top	Top and middle	Fairly general	At all levels
Communication				
How much communication is aimed at achieving organization's objectives?	Very little	Little	Quite a bit	A great deal
What is the direction of information flow?	Downward	Mostly downward	Down and up	Down, up, and sideways
How is downward communication accepted?	With suspicion	Possibly with suspicion	With caution	With an open mind
How accurate is upward communication?	Often wrong	Censored for the boss	Limited accuracy	Accurate

TABLE 1 (*concluded*)

	System 1 Exploitative Authoritative	System 2 Benevolent Authoritative	System 3 Consultative	System 4 Participative Group
How well do superiors know problems faced by subordinates?	Know little	Some knowledge	Quite well	Very well
Decisions				
At what level are decisions formally made?	Mostly at top	Policy at top, some delegation	Broad policy at top, more delegation	Throughout but well integrated
What is the origin of technical and professional knowledge used in decision making?	Top management	Upper and middle	To a certain extent, throughout	To a great extent, throughout
Are subordinates involved in decisions related to their work?	Not at all	Occasionally consulted	Generally consulted	Fully involved
What does decision-making process contribute to motivation?	Nothing, often weakens it	Relatively little	Some contribution	Substantial contribution
Goals				
How are organizational goals established?	Orders issued	Orders, some comment invited	After discussion, by orders	By group action (except in crisis)
How much covert resistance to goals is present?	Strong resistance	Moderate resistance	Some resistance at times	Little or none
Control				
How concentrated are review and control functions?	Highly at top	Relatively highly at top	Moderate delegation to lower levels	Quite widely shared
Is there an informal organization resisting the formal one?	Yes	Usually	Sometimes	No—same goals as formal
What are cost, productivity, and other control data used for?	Policing, punishment	Reward and punishment	Reward, some self-guidance	Self-guidance, problem solving

pany or division to draw its profile, too. They tend to rate it as slightly more "authoritative" than the boss does.

Likert believes that the predominant management style in U.S. industry today falls about in the middle of his chart, even though most managers seem to know from personal observation of other organizations that a more participative approach works better. What accounts for their consistent failure to emulate what they consider successful? Reaching for a general explanation, Likert asks his subjects one final question: "In your experience, what happens when the senior officer becomes concerned about earnings and takes steps to cut costs, increase productivity, and improve profits?" Most reply that the company's management profile shifts left, toward the authoritarian style. General orders to economize—and promptly—often result in quick, across-the-board budget cuts. Some programs with high potential are sacrificed along with obvious losers. Carefully laid, logical plans go down the drain. Some people are laid off—usually the least essential ones. But the best people in the organization sooner or later rebel at arbitrary decisions, and many of them leave.

At the outset, the arbitrary cost cutting produces a fairly prompt improvement in earnings, of course. But there is an unrecognized tradeoff in the subsequent loss of human capital, which shows up still later in loss of business. In due course, management has to "swing right" again, rebuilding its human assets at great expense in order to restore good performance. Yet the manager who puts his firm through this dreary cycle, Likert observes, is often rewarded with a bonus at the outset, when things still look good. Indeed, he may be sent off to work his magic in another division!

Likert acknowledges that there are emergencies when sharp and sudden belt-tightening is inescapable. The trouble, he says, is that it is frequently at the expense of human assets and relationships that have taken years to build. Often it would make more sense to sell off inventory or dispose of a plant. But such possibilities are overlooked because human assets do not show up in the traditional balance sheet the way physical assets do. A company can, of course, lose $100,000 worth of talent and look better on its statement than if it sells off $10,000 worth of inventory at half price.

A dollars-and-cents way of listing the value of a good engineering staff, an experienced shop crew, or an executive group with effective, established working relations might indeed steady the hand of a hard-pressed president whose banker is on the phone. Likert believes he is now on the trail of a way to assign such values—values that should be at least as realistic as the often arbitrary and outdated figures given for real estate and plant. It will take some doing to get the notion accepted by bankers and accountants, however sophisticated his method turns out to be. But today's executives are hardly unaware that their long payrolls of expensive scientific and managerial talent represent an asset as well as an expense. Indeed, it is an asset that is often bankable. A merely more regular, explicit recognition of human assets in cost-cutting decisions would help to ensure that human assets get at least an even break with plant and inventory in time of trouble.

Likert and his institute colleagues are negotiating with several corporations to enlist them in a systematic five-year study, in effect a controlled experiment, that should put a firmer footing under tentative conclusions and hypotheses. This study will test Likert's belief that across-the-board participative management, carefully developed, sustained through thick and thin, and supported by a balance sheet that somehow reckons the human factor, will show better long-run results than the cyclical swing between authoritarian and participative styles reflected in the typical middleground profile on his chart.

CONVERSION IN A PAJAMA FACTORY

Already there's enough evidence in industry experience to suggest that participative management gets in trouble when it is adopted too fast. In some cases, an authoritarian management has abruptly ordered junior executives or employees to start taking on more responsibility, not recognizing that the directive itself reasserted the fact of continuing centralized control. Sometimes, of course, a hard shove may be necessary, as in the recent experience of Harwood Manufacturing Corporation of Marion, Virginia, which has employed participative practices widely for many years. When it acquired a rival pajama maker, Weldon Manufacturing Company, the latter's long-held authoritarian traditions were hard to crack. With patient but firm prodding by outside consultants, who acknowledge an initial element of "coercion," the switch in style was finally accomplished.

Ideally, in the view of Likert and others, a move of this kind should begin with the patient education of top executives, followed by the development of the needed skills in internal communication, group leadership, and the other requisites of the new system. Given time, this will produce better employee attitudes and begin to harness personal motivation to corporate goals. Still later, there will be improved productivity, less waste, lower turnover and absence rates, fewer grievances and slow-downs, improved product quality, and, finally, better customer relations.

The transformation may take several years. A checkup too early in the game might prove that participative management, even when thoroughly understood and embraced at the top, doesn't produce better results. By the same token, a management that is retreating from the new style in a typical cost squeeze may still be nominally participative, yet may already have thrown away the fruits of the system. Some research findings do indicate that participation isn't producing the hoped-for results. In Likert's view, these were spot checks, made without regard to which way the company was tending and where it was in the cycle of change.

A growing number of behaviorists, however, have begun to question whether the participative style is an ideal toward which all management should strive. If they once believed it was, more as a matter of faith in their long struggle against the "scientific" manager's machine-like view of man than as a finding from any new science of their own, they are now ready to take a second look at the proposition.

It seems plain enough that a research scientist generally benefits from a good deal of freedom and autonomy, and that top executives, confronted every day by new problems that no routine can anticipate, operate better with maximum consultation and uninhibited contributions from every member of the team. If the vice president for finance can't talk candidly with the vice president for production about financing the new plant, a lot of time can be wasted. In sales, group effort—instead of the usual competition—can be highly productive. But in the accounting department, things must go by the book. "Creative accounting" sounds more like a formula for jail than for the old behaviorists' dream of personal self-fulfillment on the job. And so with quality control in the chemical plant. An inspired adjustment here and there isn't welcome, thank you; just follow the specifications.

In the production department, automation has washed out a lot of the old problem of man as a prisoner of the assembly line, the kind of problem that first brought the "human relations" experts into the factories in the 1920s and 1930s. If a shop is full of computer-controlled machine tools busily reproducing themselves, the boy with the broom who sweeps away the shavings may be the only one who can put a personal flourish into his work. The creativity is all upstairs in the engineering and programming departments. But then, so are most of the people.

"Look what's happened in the last 20 years," says Harold J. Leavitt, a social psychologist who recently moved to Stanford after some years at Carnegie Tech. "Originally the concern of the human relations people was with the blue-collar worker. Then the focus began to shift to foremen and to middle management. Now it's concentrated in special areas like research and development and in top management. Why? Because the 'group' style works best where nobody knows exactly and all the time what they're supposed to be doing, where there's a continuous need to change and adapt."

DEMOCRACY WORKS BETTER IN PLASTICS

One conclusion that has been drawn from this is that management style has to be custom designed to fit the particular characteristics of each industry. The participative approach will work best in those industries that are in the vanguard of change. A Harvard Business School study has compared high performance companies in three related, but subtly different, fields: plastics, packaged food, and standard containers. The plastics company faced the greatest uncertainties and change in research, new products, and market developments. The food company's business was somewhat more stable, while the container company encountered little or no requirement for innovation. The three achieved good results using markedly different management styles. The plastics firm provided for wide dispersal of responsibility for major decisions, the food company for moderate decentralization of authority, and the container company operated with highly centralized control.

Less-successful enterprises in each of the three industries were also examined, and their managements were compared with those of the high-performance companies. From this part of the study, Harvard researchers Paul Lawrence and Jay Lorsch drew another conclusion; not only may each industry have its own appropriate management style, but so may the individual operations within the same company. The companies that do best are those which allow for variations among their departments and know how to take these variations into account in coordinating the whole corporate effort.

Both the sales and the research departments in a fast-moving plastics company, for example, may adopt a style that encourages employees to participate actively in departmental decision making. But in special ways the two operations still need to differ. The research worker, for example, thinks in long-range terms, focusing on results expected in two or three years. The sales executive has his sights set on results next week or next month. This different sense of time may make it hard for the two departments to understand each other. But if top management recognizes the reasons and the need for such differences, each department will do its own job better, and they can be better coordinated. On the other hand, if top management ignores the differences and insists, for example, on rigidly uniform budgeting and planning timetables, there will be a loss of effectiveness.

It seems an obvious point that sales must be allowed to operate like sales, accounting like accounting, and production like production. But as Lawrence comments, "The mark of a good idea in this field is that, as soon as it is articulated, it does seem obvious. People forget that, five minutes before, it wasn't. One curse of the behavioral scientist is that anything he comes up with is going to seem that way, because anything that's good *is* obvious."

PEOPLE, TOO, HAVE THEIR STYLES

Other behavioral scientists take the view that management style should be determined not so much by the nature of the particular business operation involved but by the personality traits of the people themselves. There may be some tendency for certain kinds of jobs to attract certain kinds of people. But in nearly any shop or office a wide range of personality types may be observed. There is, for example, the outgoing, socially oriented scientist as well as the supposedly more typical introverted recluse. There are mature, confident managers, and there are those who somehow fill the job despite nagging self-doubt and a consuming need for reassurance.

For a long time, personality tests seemed to offer a way to steer people into the psychologically right kind of work. Whether such testing for placement is worthwhile is now a matter of some dispute. In any case, the whole question of individual differences is often reduced to little more than an office guessing game. Will Sue cooperate with Jane? Can Dorothy stand working for Jim? Will Harry take suggestions?

The participative approach to management may be based upon a greatly oversimplified notion about people, in the view of psychologist Clare Graves of Union College in Schenectady, New York. On the basis of limited samplings, he tentatively concludes that, as many as half the people in the northeastern United States, and a larger proportion nationwide, are not and many never will be the eager beaver workers on whom the late Douglas McGregor of M.I.T. based his "Theory Y." Only some variation of old-style authoritarian management will meet their psychological needs, Graves contends.

Graves believes he has identified seven fairly distinct personality types, although he acknowledges that many people are not "purebreds" who would fit his abstractions perfectly and that new and higher personality forms may still be evolving. At the bottom of his well-ordered hierarchy he places the childlike "autistic" personality, which requires "close care and nurturing." Next up the scale is the "animistic" type, which must be dealt with by sheer force or enticement; the "ordered" personality that responds best to a moralistic management; and the "materialistic" individual who calls for pragmatic, hard bargaining. None of these are suited for the participative kind of management.

At the top of Graves's personality ladder are the "sociocentric," the "cognitive," and the "apprehending" types of people. They are motivated, respectively, by a need for "belonging," for "information," and for an "understanding" of the total situation in which they are involved. For each of these levels some form of participative management will work. However, those at the very top, the unemotional "apprehending" individuals, must be allowed pretty much to set their own terms for work. Management can trust such people to contribute usefully only according to their own cool perception of what is needed. They will seldom take the trouble to fight authority when they disagree with it, but merely withdraw, do a passable but not excellent job, and wait for management to see things their way. In that sense, these highest-level people are probably not ideal participators.

Graves believes most adults are stuck at one level throughout their lifetimes or move up a single notch, at best. He finds, incidentally, that there can be bright or dull, mature or immature behavior at nearly all levels. The stages simply represent psychological growth toward a larger and larger awareness of the individual's relationship to society.

If a company has a mixture of personality types, as most do, it must somehow sort them out. One way would be to place participative-type managers in charge of some groups, and authoritarian managers in charge of others. Employees would then be encouraged to transfer into sections where the management style best suits them. This would hardly simplify corporate life. But companies pushing the group approach might at least avoid substituting harmful new rigidities—"participate, or else!"—for the old ones.

THE ANTHROPOLOGICAL VIEW

Behaviorists who have been studying management problems from an anthropological viewpoint naturally stress cultural, rather than individual, differences. Manning Nash, of the University of Chicago's business school, for example, observes that the American emphasis on egalitarianism and performance has always tempered management style in the United States. "No matter what your role is, if you don't perform, no one in this country will defer to you," he says. "Americans won't act unless they respect you. You couldn't have an American Charge of the Light Brigade." But try to export that attitude to a country with a more autocratic social tradition, and, in the words of Stanley Davis of Harvard, "it won't be bought and may not be workable."

Within the United States there are many cultural differences that might provide guides to managerial style if they could be successfully analyzed. Recent research by Lawrence and Arthur N. Turner at the Harvard Business School hints at important differences between blue-collar workers in cities and those in smaller towns, although religious and other factors fog the results. Town workers seem to seek "a relatively large amount of variety, autonomy, interaction, skill, and responsibility" in their work, whereas city workers "find more simple tasks less stress-producing and more satisfying."

In managerial areas where democratic techniques *are* likely to work, the problem is how to give managers skill and practice in participation. The National Education Association's National Training Laboratories 20 years ago pioneered a way of doing this called "sensitivity training" (see "Two Weeks in a T-Group," *Fortune*, August 1961). Small groups of men, commonly drawn from the executive ranks, sit down with a professional trainer but without agenda or rule book and "see what happens." The "vacuum" draws out first one and then another participant, in a way that tends to expose in fairly short order how he comes across to others.

The technique has had many critics, few more vocal than William Gomberg of the University of Pennsylvania's Wharton School. Renewing his assault recently, he called the "training" groups "titillating therapy, management development's most fashionable fad." When people from the same company are in the group, he argues, the whole exercise is an invasion of privacy, an abuse of the therapeutic technique to help the company, not the individual. For top executives in such groups, Gomberg and others contend, the technique offers mainly a catharsis for their loneliness or insecurity.

"PSYCHING OUT THE BOSS"

Undoubtedly the T-groups can be abused, intentionally or otherwise. But today's sensitivity trainers are trying to make sure the experience leads to useful results for both the individual and his firm. They realize that early groups, made up of total strangers gathered at some remote "cultural island," often gave the executive little notion of how to apply his new knowledge back on the job. To bring more realism to the exercise, the National Training Laboratories began 10 years ago to make up groups of executives and managers from the same company, but not men who had working relationships with one another. These "cousin labs" have led, in turn, to some training of actual management "families," a boss and his subordinates. At the West Coast headquarters of the T-group movement, the business school at U.C.L.A., some now call such training "task-group therapy."

Many businessmen insist T-groups have helped them. Forty-three presidents and chairmen and hundreds of lesser executives are National Training Laboratories alumni. U.C.L.A. is besieged by applicants, and many are turned away.

Sensitivity training is supposed to help most in business situations where there is a great deal of uncertainty, as there is in the training sessions themselves. In such situations in the corporate setting, there is sometimes a tendency for executives to withdraw, to defer action, to play a kind of game with other people in the organization to see who will climb out on a limb first. A chief ploy is "psyching out the boss," which means trying to anticipate the way the winds of ultimate decision will blow and to set course accordingly.

The aim of sensitivity training is to stop all this, to get the executive's nerve up so he faces facts, or, in the words of U.C.L.A.'s James V. Clark, to "lay bare the stress and strain faster and get a resolution of the problem." In that limited sense, such therapy could well serve any style of management. In Clark's view, this kind of training, early in the game, might save many a company a costly detour on the road to company-wide "democracy." He cites the experience of Non-Linear Systems, Inc., of Del Mar, California, a manufacturer of such electronic gear as digital voltmeters and data-logging equipment and an important supplier to aerospace contractors. The company is headed by Andrew Kay, a leading champion of the participative style. At the lower levels, Kay's application of participative concepts worked well. He gave workers responsibility for "the whole black box" instead of for pieces of his complex finished products. Because it was still a box, with some definite boundaries, the workers seized the new opportunity without fear or hesitation. The psychological magic of meaningful work, as opposed to the hopelessly specialized chore, took hold. Productivity rose.

VICE PRESIDENTS IN MIDAIR

But at the executive level, Kay moved too quickly, failing to prepare his executives for broad and undefined responsibilities—or failing to choose men better suited for the challenge. One vice president was put in charge of "innovation." Suspended in midair, without the support of departments or functional groups and lacking even so much as a job description, most of the VPs became passive and incapable of making decisions. "They lost touch with reality—including the reality of the market," recalls Clark. When the industry suffered a general slump and new competition entered the field, Non-Linear wasn't ready. Sales dropped 16 percent, according to Kay. In time he realized he was surrounded with dependent men, untrained to participate in the fashion he had peremptorily commanded. He trimmed his executive group and expects to set a new sales record this year.

Sheldon Davis of TRW Systems in Redondo Beach, California, blames the behavioral scientists themselves for breakdowns like Non-Linear's. Too often, he argues, "their messages come out sounding soft and easy, as if what we are trying to do is build happy teams of employees who feel 'good' about things, rather than saying we're trying to build effective organizations with groups that function well and that can zero in quickly on their problems and deal with them rationally."

To Davis, participation should mean "tough, open exchange," focused on the problem, not the organizational chart. Old-style managers who simply dictate a solution are wrong, he argues, and so are those new-style managers who think the idea is simply to go along with a subordinate's proposals if they're earnestly offered. Neither approach taps the full potential of the executive group. When problems are faced squarely, Davis believes, the boss—who should remain boss—gets the best solution because all relevant factors are thoroughly considered. And because everyone has contributed to the solution and feels responsible for it, it is also the solution most likely to be carried out.

One of the most useful new developments in the behavioral study of management is a fresh emphasis on collaboration with technology. In the early days of the human relations movement in industry, technology was often regarded as "the enemy," the source of the personal and social problems that the psychologists were trying to treat. But from the beginning, some social scientists wanted to move right in and help fashion machines and industrial processes so as to reduce or eliminate their supposedly antihuman effects. Today this concept is more than mere talk. The idea is to develop so-called sociotechnical systems that permit man and technology *together* to produce the best performance.

Some early experimentation in the British coal mines, by London's Tavistock Institute, as well as scattered work in this country and in Scandinavia, have already demonstrated practical results from such a collaboration. Tavistock found that an attempt to apply specialized factory-style technology to coal mining had isolated the miners from one another. They missed the sense of group support and self-direction that had helped them cope with uncertainty and danger deep in the coal faces. Productivity suffered. In this case, Tavistock's solution was to redesign the new system so men could still work in groups.

In the United States, a manufacturer of small household appliances installed some highly sophisticated new technical processes that put the company well in the front of its field. But the engineers had broken down the jobs to such an extent that workers were getting no satisfaction out of their performance and productivity declined. Costs went up and, in the end, some of the new machinery had to be scrapped.

Some technologists seem more than ready to welcome a partnership with the human relations expert. Louis Davis, a professor of engineering, has joined the U.C.L.A. business school faculty to lead a six-man sociotechnical research group that includes several behaviorists. Among them is Eric Trist, a highly respected psychologist from the Tavistock Institute. Davis hopes today's collaboration will lead in time to a new breed of experts knowledgeable in both the engineering and the social disciplines.

"IT'S TIME WE STOPPED BUILDING RIVAL DICTIONARIES"

The importance of time, the nature of the task, the differences within a large organization, the nature of the people, the cultural setting, the psychological preparation of management, the relationship to technology—all these and other variables are making the search for effective managerial style more and more complex. But the growing recognition of these complexities has drained the human-relations movement of much of its antagonism toward the "superrationalism" of management science. Humanists must be more systematic and rational if they are to make some useful sense of the scattered and half-tested concepts they have thus far developed, and put their new theories to a real test.

A number of behaviorists believe it is well past time to bury the hatchet and collaborate in earnest with the mathematicians and economists. Some business schools and commercial consulting groups are already realigning their staffs to encourage such work. It won't be easy. Most "systems" thinkers are preoccupied with bringing all the relevant knowledge to bear on a management problem in a systematic way, seeking the theoretically "best" solution. Most behaviorists have tended to assume that the solution which is *most likely to be carried out* is the best one, hence their focus on involving lots of people in the decision making so that they will follow through. Where the "experts" who shape decisions are also in charge of getting the job done, the two approaches sometimes blend, in practice. But in many organizations, it is a long, long road from a creative and imaginative decision to actual performance. A general theory of management must show how to build systematic expertise into a style that is also well suited to people.

The rapprochement among management theorists has a distinguished herald, Fritz J. Roethlisberger of Harvard Business School, one of the human relations pioneers who first disclosed the potential of the "small group" in industrial experiments 40 years ago. He laughs quickly at any suggestion that a unified approach will come easily. "But after all, we are all looking at the same thing," he says. "It's time we stopped building rival dictionaries and learned to make some sentences that really say something."

23

The Development and Enforcement of Group Norms

Daniel C. Feldman

Why group norms are enforced and how such norms develop are the focus of this article. The author suggests that groups will bring under normative control those behaviors that ensure group survival, increase the predictability of member behavior, or give expression to the central values of the group. The development of norms is the result of explicit statements by group members, past events, or primacy.—Eds.

Group norms are the informal rules that groups adopt to regulate and regularize group members' behavior. Although these norms are infrequently written down or openly discussed, they often have a powerful, and consistent, influence on group members' behavior (Hackman, 1976).

Most of the theoretical work on group norms has focused on identifying the types of group norms (March, 1954) or on describing their structural characteristics (Jackson, 1966). Empirically, most of the focus has been on examining the impact that norms have on other social phenomena. For example, Seashore (1954) and Schachter, Ellertson, McBride, and Gregory (1951) use the concept of group norms to discuss group cohesiveness; Trist and Bamforth (1951) and Whyte (1955a) use norms to examine production restriction; Janis (1972) and Longley and Pruitt (1980) use norms to illuminate group decision making; and Asch (1951) and Sherif (1936) use norms to examine conformity.

This paper focuses on two frequently overlooked aspects of the group norms literature. First, it examines *why* group norms are enforced. Why do groups desire conformity to these informal rules? Second, it examines *how* group norms develop. Why do some norms develop in one group but not in another? Much of what is known about group norms comes from post hoc examination of their impact on outcome variables; much less has been written about how these norms actually develop and why they regulate behavior so strongly.

SOURCE: Reprinted with permission from the publisher from "The Development and Enforcement of Group Norms," *Academy of Management Review*, January 1984, pp. 47–53.

Understanding how group norms develop and why they are enforced is important for two reasons. First, group norms can play a large role in determining whether the group will be productive or not. If the work group feels that management is supportive, groups norms will develop that facilitate—in fact, enhance—group productivity. In contrast, if the work group feels that management is antagonistic, group norms that inhibit and impair group performance are much more likely to develop. Second, managers can play a major role in setting and changing group norms. They can use their influence to set task-facilitative norms; they can monitor whether the group's norms are functional; they can explicitly address counterproductive norms with subordinates. By understanding how norms develop and why norms are enforced, managers can better diagnose the underlying tensions and problems their groups are facing, and they can help the group develop more effective behavior patterns.

WHY NORMS ARE ENFORCED

As Shaw (1981) suggests, a group does not establish or enforce norms about every conceivable situation. Norms are formed and enforced only with respect to behaviors that have some significance for the group. The frequent distinction between task maintenance duties and social maintenance duties helps explain why groups bring selected behaviors under normative control.

Groups, like individuals, try to operate in such a way that they maximize their chances for task success and minimize their chances of task failure. First of all, a group will enforce norms that facilitate its very survival. It will try to protect itself from interference from groups external to the organization or harassment from groups internal to the organization. Second, the group will want to increase the predictability of group members' behaviors. Norms provide a basis for predicting the behavior of others, thus enabling group members to anticipate each other's actions and to prepare quick and appropriate responses (Shaw, 1981; Kiesler and Kiesler, 1970).

In addition, groups want to ensure the satisfaction of their members and prevent as much interpersonal discomfort as possible. Thus, groups also will enforce norms that help the group avoid embarrassing interpersonal problems. Certain topics of conversation might be sanctioned, and certain types of social interaction might be openly discouraged. Moreover, norms serve an expressive function for groups (Katz and Kahn, 1978). Enforcing group norms gives group members a chance to express what their central values are and to clarify what is distinctive about the group and central to its identity (Hackman, 1976).

Each of these four conditions under which group norms are most likely to be enforced is discussed in more detail below.

1. *Norms are likely to be enforced if they facilitate group survival.* A group will enforce norms that protect it from interference or harassment by members of other groups. For instance, a group might develop

a norm not to discuss its salaries with members of other groups in the organization, so attention will not be brought to pay inequities in its favor. Groups might also have norms about not discussing internal problems with members of other units. Such discussions might boomerang at a later date if other groups use the information to develop a better competitive strategy against the group.

Enforcing group norms also makes clear what the "boundaries" of the group are. As a result of observation of deviant behavior and the consequences that ensue, other group members are reminded of the *range* of behavior that is acceptable to the group (Dentler and Erikson, 1959). The norms about productivity that frequently develop among piecerate workers are illustrative here. By observing a series of incidents (a person produces 50 widgets and is praised; a person produces 60 widgets and receives sharp teasing; a person produces 70 widgets and is ostracized), group members learn the limits of the group's patience: "This far, and no further." The group is less likely to be "successful" (i.e., continue to sustain the low productivity expectations of management) if it allows its jobs to be reevaluated.

The literature on conformity and deviance is consistent with this observation. The group is more likely to reject the person who violates group norms when the deviant has not been a "good" group member previously (Hollander, 1958, 1964). Individuals can generate "idiosyncrasy credits" with other group members by contributing effectively to the attainment of group goals. Individuals expend these credits when they perform poorly or dysfunctionally at work. When a group member no longer has a positive "balance" of credits to draw on when he or she deviates, the group is much more likely to reject that deviant (Hollander, 1961).

Moreover, the group is more likely to reject the deviant when the group is failing in meeting its goals successfully. When the group is successful it can afford to be charitable or tolerant towards deviant behavior. The group may disapprove, but it has some margin for error. When the group is faced with failure, the deviance is much more sharply punished. Any behavior that negatively influences the success of the group becomes much more salient and threatening to group members (Alvarez, 1968; Wiggins, Dill, and Schwartz, 1965).

2. *Norms are likely to be enforced if they simplify, or make predictable, what behavior is expected of group members.* If each member of the group had to decide individually how to behave in each interaction, much time would be lost performing routine activities. Moreover, individuals would have more trouble predicting the behaviors of others and responding correctly. Norms enable group members to anticipate each other's actions and to prepare the most appropriate response in the most timely manner (Hackman, 1976; Shaw, 1981).

For instance, when attending group meetings in which proposals are presented and suggestions are requested, do the presenters really want feedback or are they simply going through the motions? Groups may develop norms that reduce this uncertainty and provide a clearer course of action, for example, make suggestions in small, informal meetings but not in large, formal meetings.

Another example comes from norms that regulate social behavior. For instance, when colleagues go out for lunch together, there can be some awkwardness about how to split the bill at the end of the meal. A group may develop a norm that gives some highly predictable or simple way of behaving; for example, split evenly, take turns picking up the tab, or pay for what each ordered.

Norms also may reinforce specific individual members' roles. A number of different roles might emerge in groups. These roles are simply expectations that are shared by group members regarding who is to carry out what types of activities under what circumstances (Bales and Slater, 1955). Although groups obviously create pressure toward uniformity among members, there also is a tendency for groups to create and maintain *diversity* among members (Hackman, 1976). For instance, a group might have one person whom others expect to break the tension when tempers become too hot. Another group member might be expected to keep track of what is going on in other parts of the organization. A third member might be expected to take care of the "creature" needs of the group—making the coffee, making dinner reservations, and so on. A fourth member might be expected by others to take notes, keep minutes, or maintain files.

None of these roles are *formal* duties, but they are activities that the group needs accomplished and has somehow parcelled out among members. If the role expectations are not met, some important jobs might not get done, or other group members might have to take on additional responsibilities. Moreover, such role assignments reduce individual members' ambiguities about what is expected specifically of them. It is important to note, though, that who takes what role in a group also is highly influenced by individuals' personal needs. The person with a high need for structure often wants to be in the note-taking role to control the structuring activity in the group; the person who breaks the tension might dislike conflict and uses the role to circumvent it.

3. *Norms are likely to be enforced if they help the group avoid embarrassing interpersonal problems.* Goffman's work on "facework" gives some insight on this point. Goffman (1955) argues that each person in a group has a "face" he or she presents to other members of a group. This "face" is analogous to what one would call "self-image," the person's perceptions of himself or herself and how he or she would like to be seen by others. Groups want to insure that no one's self-image is damaged, called into question, or embarrassed. Consequently, the group will establish norms that discourage topics of conversation or situations

in which face is too likely to be inadvertantly broken. For instance, groups might develop norms about not discussing romantic involvements (so differences in moral values do not become salient) or about not getting together socially in people's homes (so differences in taste or income do not become salient).

A good illustration of Goffman's facework occurs in the classroom. There is always palpable tension in a room when either a class is totally unprepared to discuss a case or a professor is totally unprepared to lecture or lead the discussion. One part of the awkwardness stems from the inability of the other partner in the interaction to behave as he or she is prepared to or would like to behave. The professor cannot teach if the students are not prepared, and the students cannot learn if the professor is not teaching. Another part of the awkwardness, though, stems from self-images being called into question. Although faculty are aware that not all students are serious scholars, the situation is difficult to handle if the class as a group does not even show a pretense of wanting to learn. Although students are aware that many faculty are mainly interested in research and consulting, there is a problem if the professor does not even show a pretense of caring to teach. Norms almost always develop between professor and students about what level of preparation and interest is expected by the other, because both parties want to avoid awkward confrontations.

4. *Norms are likely to be enforced if they express the central values of the group and clarify what is distinctive about the group's identity.* Norms can provide the social justification for group activities to its members (Katz and Kahn, 1978). When the production group labels rate-busting deviant, it says: "We care more about maximizing group security than about individual profits." Group norms also convey what is distinctive about the groups to outsiders. When an advertising agency labels unstylish clothes deviant, it says: "We think of ourselves, personally and professionally, as trend-setters, and being fashionably dressed conveys that to our clients and our public."

One of the key expressive functions of group norms is to define and legitimate the power of the group itself over individual members (Katz and Kahn, 1978). When groups punish norm infraction, they reinforce in the minds of group members the authority of the group. Here, too, the literature on group deviance sheds some light on the issue at hand.

It has been noted frequently that the amount of deviance in a group is rather small (Erikson, 1966; Schur, 1965). The group uses norm enforcement to show the *strength* of the group. However, if a behavior becomes so widespread that it becomes impossible to control, then the labeling of the widespread behavior as deviance becomes problematic. It simply reminds members of the *weakness* of the group. At this point, the group will redefine what is deviant more narrowly, or it will define its job as that of keeping deviants *within bounds*, rather than that of obliterating it altogether. For example, though drug use is and always has been illegal, the widespread use of drugs has led to changes in law enforcement over time. A greater distinction now is made between "hard" drugs and other controlled substances; less penalty is given to those apprehended with small amounts than large amounts; greater attention is focused on capturing large-scale smugglers and traffickers than the occasional user. A group, unconsciously if not consciously, learns how much behavior it is capable of labeling deviant *and* punishing effectively.

Finally, this expressive function of group norms can be seen nicely in circumstances in which there is an inconsistency between what group members *say* is the group norm and how people actually *behave*. For instance, sometimes groups will engage in a lot of rhetoric about how much independence its managers are allowed and how much it values entrepreneurial effort; yet the harder data suggest that the more conservative, deferring, or dependent managers get rewarded. Such an inconsistency can reflect conflicts among the group's expressed values. First, the group can be ambivalent about independence; the group knows it needs to encourage more entrepreneurial efforts to flourish, but such efforts create competition and threaten the status quo. Second, the inconsistency can reveal major subgroup differences. Some people may value and encourage entrepreneurial behavior, but others do not—and the latter may control the group's rewards. Third, the inconsistency can reveal a source of the group's self-consciousness, a dichotomy between what the group is really like and how it would like to be perceived. The group may realize that it is too conservative, yet be unable or too frightened to address its problem. The expressed group norm allows the group members a chance to present a "face" to each other and to outsiders that is more socially desirable than reality.

HOW GROUP NORMS DEVELOP

Norms usually develop gradually and informally as group members learn what behaviors are necessary for the group to function more effectively. However, it also is possible for the norm development process to be short-cut by a critical event in the group or by conscious group decision (Hackman, 1976).

Most norms develop in one or more of the following four ways: explicit statements by supervisors or co-workers; critical events in the group's history; primacy; and carry-over behaviors from past situations.

1. *Explicit statements by supervisors or co-workers.* Norms that facilitate group survival or task success often are set by the leader of the group or powerful members (Whyte, 1955b). For instance, a group leader might explicitly set norms about not drinking at lunch, because subordinates who have been drinking are more likely to have problems dealing competently with clients and top management or they are more

likely to have accidents at work. The group leader might also set norms about lateness, personal phone calls, and long coffee breaks if too much productivity is lost as a result of time away from the work place.

Explicit statements by supervisors also can increase the predictability of group members' behavior. For instance, supervisors might have particular preferences for a way of analyzing problems or presenting reports. Strong norms will be set to ensure compliance with these preferences. Consequently, supervisors will have increased certainty about receiving work in the format requested, so they can plan accordingly; workers will have increased certainty about what is expected, so they will not have to outguess their boss or redo their projects.

Managers or important group members also can define the specific role expectations of individual group members. For instance, a supervisor or a co-worker might go up to a new recruit after a meeting to give the proverbial advice: "New recruits should be seen and not heard." The senior group member might be trying to prevent the new recruit from appearing brash or incompetent or from embarrassing other group members. Such interventions set specific role expectations for the new group member.

Norms that cater to supervisor preferences also are frequently established, even if they are not objectively necessary to task accomplishment. For example, although organizational norms may be very democratic in terms of everybody calling each other by their first names, some managers have strong preferences about being called Mr., Ms., or Mrs. Although the form of address used in the work group does not influence group effectiveness, complying with the norm bears little cost to the group member, whereas noncompliance could cause daily friction with the supervisor. Such norms help group members avoid embarrassing interpersonal interactions with their managers.

Fourth, norms set explicitly by the supervisor frequently express the central values of the group. For instance, a dean can set very strong norms about faculty keeping office hours and being on campus daily. Such norms reaffirm to members of the academic community their teaching and service obligations, and they send signals to individuals outside the college about what is valued in faculty behavior or distinctive about the school. A dean also could set norms that allow faculty to consult or do executive development two or three days a week. Such norms, too, legitimate other types of faculty behavior and send signals to both insiders and outsiders about some central values of the college.

2. *Critical events in the group's history.*   At times there is a critical event in the group's history that established an important precedent. For instance, a group member might have discussed hiring plans with members of other units in the organization, and as a result new positions were lost or there was increased competition for good applicants. Such indiscretion can substantially hinder the survival and task suc-

cess of the group; very likely the offender will be either formally censured or informally rebuked. As a result of such an incident, norms about secrecy might develop that will protect the group in similar situations in the future.

An example from Janis's *Victims of Groupthink* (1972) also illustrates this point nicely. One of President Kennedy's closest advisors, Arthur Schlesinger, Jr., had serious reservations about the Bay of Pigs invasion and presented his strong objections to the Bay of Pigs plan in a memorandum to Kennedy and Secretary of State Dean Rusk. However, Schlesinger was pressured by the President's brother, Attorney General Robert Kennedy, to keep his objections to himself. Remarked Robert Kennedy to Schlesinger: "You may be right or you may be wrong, but the President has made his mind up. Don't push it any further. Now is the time for everyone to help him all they can." Such critical events led group members to silence their views and set up group norms about the bounds of disagreeing with the president.

Sometimes group norms can be set by a conscious decision of a group after a particularly good or bad experience the group has had. To illustrate, a group might have had a particularly constructive meeting and be very pleased with how much it accomplished. Several people might say, "I think the reason we got so much accomplished today is that we met really early in the morning before the rest of the staff showed up and the phone started ringing. Let's try to continue to meet at 7:30 A.M." Others might agree, and the norm is set. On the other hand, if a group notices it accomplished way too little in a meeting, it might openly discuss setting norms to cut down on ineffective behavior (e.g., having an agenda, not interrupting others while they were talking). Such norms develop to facilitate task success and to reduce uncertainty about what is expected from each individual in the group.

Critical events also can identify awkward interpersonal situations that need to be avoided in the future. For instance, a divorce between two people working in the same group might have caused a lot of acrimony and hard feeling in a unit, not only between the husband and wife but also among various other group members who got involved in the marital problems. After the unpleasant divorce, a group might develop a norm about not hiring spouses to avoid having to deal with such interpersonal problems in the future.

Finally, critical events also can give rise to norms that express the central, or distinctive, values of the group. When a peer review panel finds a physician or lawyer guilty of malpractice or malfeasance, first it establishes (or reaffirms) the rights of professionals to evaluate and criticize the professional behavior of their colleagues. Moreover, it clarifies what behaviors are inconsistent with the group's self-image or its values. When a faculty committee votes on a candidate's tenure, it, too, asserts the legitimacy of influence of senior faculty over junior faculty.

In addition, it sends (hopefully) clear messages to junior faculty about its values in terms of quality of research, teaching, and service. There are important "announcement effects" of peer reviews; internal group members carefully reexamine the group's values, and outsiders draw inferences about the character of the group from such critical decisions.

3. *Primacy.* The first behavior pattern that emerges in a group often sets group expectations. If the first group meeting is marked by very formal interaction between supervisors and subordinates, then the group often expects future meetings to be conducted in the same way. Where people sit in meetings or rooms frequently is developed through primacy. People generally continue to sit in the same seats they sat in at their first meeting, even though those original seats are not assigned and people could change where they sit at every meeting. Most friendship groups of students develop their own "turf" in a lecture hall and are surprised/dismayed when an interloper takes "their" seats.

Norms that develop through primacy often do so to simplify, or make predictable, what behavior is expected of group members. There may be very little task impact from where people sit in meetings or how formal interactions are. However, norms develop about such behaviors to make life much more routine and predictable. Every time a group member enters a room, he or she does not have to "decide" where to sit or how formally to behave. Moreover, he or she also is much more certain about how other group members will behave.

4. *Carry-over behaviors from past situations.* Many group norms in organizations emerge because individual group members bring set expectations with them from other work groups in other organizations. Lawyers expect to behave towards clients in Organization I (e.g., confidentiality, setting fees) as they behaved towards those in Organization II. Doctors expect to behave toward patients in Hospital I (e.g., "bedside manner," professional distance) as they behaved in Hospital II. Accountants expect to behave towards colleagues at Firm I (e.g., dress code, adherence to statutes) as they behaved towards those at Firm II. In fact, much of what goes on in professional schools is giving new members of the profession the same standards and norms of behavior that practitioners in the field hold.

Such carry-over of individual behaviors from past situations can increase the predictability of group members' behaviors in new settings and facilitate task accomplishment. For instance, students and professors bring with them fairly constant sets of expectations from class to class. As a result, students do not have to relearn continually their roles from class to class; they know, for instance, if they come in late, to take a seat quietly at the back of the room without being told. Professors also do not have to relearn continually their roles; they know, for instance, not to mumble, scribble in small print on the blackboard, or be vague when making course assignments. In addition, presumably the most task-successful norms will be the ones carried over from organization to organization.

Moreover, such carry-over norms help avoid embarrassing interpersonal situations. Individuals are more likely to know which conversations and actions provoke annoyance, irritation, or embarrassment to their colleagues. Finally, when groups carry over norms from one organization to another, they also clarify what is distinctive about the occupational or professional role. When lawyers maintain strict rules of confidentiality, when doctors maintain a consistent professional distance with patients, when accountants present a very formal physical appearance, they all assert: "These are the standards we sustain *independent* of what we could 'get away with' in this organization. This is *our* self-concept."

SUMMARY

Norms generally are enforced only for behaviors that are viewed as important by most group members. Groups do not have the time or energy to regulate each and every action of individual members. Only those behaviors that ensure group survival, facilitate task accomplishment, contribute to group morale, or express the group's central values are likely to be brought under normative control. Norms that reflect these group needs will develop through explicit statements of supervisors, critical events in the group's history, primacy, or carry-over behaviors from past situations.

Empirical research on norm development and enforcement has substantially lagged descriptive and theoretical work. In large part, this may be due to the methodological problems of measuring norms and getting enough data points either across time or across groups. Until such time as empirical work progresses, however, the usefulness of group norms as a predictive concept, rather than as a post hoc explanatory device, will be severely limited. Moreover, until it is known more concretely why norms develop and why they are strongly enforced, attempts to *change* group norms will remain haphazard and difficult to accomplish.

REFERENCES

Alvarez, R. "Informal Reactions to Deviance in Simulated Work Organizations: A Laboratory Experiment." *American Sociological Review.* 1968, 33, 895–912.

Asch, S. "Effects of Group Pressure upon the Modification and Distortion of Judgment." In M. H. Guetzkow (ed.), *Groups, Leadership, and Men.* Pittsburgh: Carnegie, 1951, 117–90.

Bales, R. F., & Slater, P. E. "Role Differentiation in Small Groups." In T. Parsons, R. F. Bales, J. Olds, M. Zelditch, & P. E. Slater (eds.), *Family, Socialization, and Interaction Process.* Glencoe, Ill.: Free Press, 1955, 35–131.

Dentler, R. A., & Erikson, K. T. "The Functions of Deviance in Groups." *Social Problems,* 1959, 7, 98–107.

Erikson, K. T. *Wayward Puritans.* New York: John Wiley & Sons, 1966.

Goffman, E. "On Face-work: An Analysis of Ritual Elements in Social Interaction." *Psychiatry,* 1955, 18, 213–31.

Hackman, J. R. "Group Influences on Individuals." In M. Dunnette (ed.). *Handbook of Industrial and Organizational Psychology.* Chicago: Rand McNally, 1976, 1455–1525.

Hollander, E. P. "Conformity, Status, and Idiosyncrasy Credit." *Psychological Review,* 1958, 65, 117–27.

_____ . "Some Effects of Perceived Status on Responses to Innovative Behavior." *Journal of Abnormal and Social Psychology,* 1961, 63, 247–50.

_____ . *Leaders, Groups, and Influence.* New York: Oxford University Press, 1964.

Jackson, J. "A Conceptual and Measurement Model for Norms and Roles." *Pacific Sociological Review,* 1966, 9, 35–47.

Janis, I. *Victims of Groupthink: A Psychological Study of Foreign-policy Decisions and Fiascos.* New York: Houghton-Mifflin, 1972.

Katz, D., & Kahn, R. L. *The Social Psychology of Organizations.* 2nd ed. New York: John Wiley & Sons, 1978.

Kiesler, C. A., & Kiesler, S. B. *Conformity.* Reading, Mass.: Addison-Wesley, 1970.

Longley, J., & Pruitt, D. C. "Groupthink: A Critique of Janis' Theory." In Ladd Wheeler (ed.), *Review of Personality and Social Psychology.* Beverly Hills: Sage, 1980, 74–93.

March, J. "Group Norms and the Active Minority." *American Sociological Review,* 1954, 19, 733–41.

Schachter, S.; Ellertson, N.; McBride, D.; & Gregory, D. "An Experimental Study of Cohesiveness and Productivity." *Human Relations,* 1951, 4, 229–38.

Schur, E. M. *Crimes without Victims.* Englewood Cliffs, N.J.: Prentice-Hall, 1965.

Seashore, S. *Group Cohesiveness in the Industrial Work Group.* Ann Arbor: Institute for Social Research, University of Michigan, 1954.

Shaw, M. *Group Dynamics.* 3rd ed. New York: Harper & Row, 1936.

Trist, E. L., & Bamforth, K. W. "Some Social and Psychological Consequences of the Longwall Method of Coal-getting." *Human Relations,* 1951, 4, 1–38.

Whyte, W. F. *Money and Motivation.* New York: Harper & Row, 1955a.

_____ . *Street Corner Society.* Chicago: University of Chicago Press, 1955b.

Wiggins, J. A., Dill, F., & Schwartz, R. D. "On Status-liability." *Sociometry,* 1965, 28, 197–209.

PART FIVE

Managing Organizational Behavior

In this last part, our focus is on management processes that extend beyond simply an individual or group locus and encompass actions and behaviors at all levels of the organization. Managing behavior at the organizational level includes the topics of influence and leadership, motivation, decision making, and organizational change and development. Each of these comprises a portion of this section.

Probably no other area of managerial endeavor has received as much interest and emphasis for so long a time as leadership. The earliest writings bearing on leadership date back to around 1100 B.C. and the constitution of Chow, indicating the Chinese were cognizant of the importance of this process. Specific principles of leadership were addressed by Sun Tzu around 500 B.C. Since this time, numerous writers have studied leadership, resulting in a myriad of many times confusing and sometimes contradictory approaches, schools, theories, and styles. Nonetheless, significant strides have been made in understanding the dynamics of leadership.

Leadership is influence, and influence is what we are trying to exert when we talk about motivation. Motivation may be thought of as external (something we do to someone) and typified by the carrot-and-stick approach, or it may be conceived as internal (something someone does to himself or herself) and typified by the behavioral science approaches. A variety of perspectives are represented by the articles in this portion of Part Five.

Of all the management processes, decision making is in many respects the most complex. It has been said that management *is* decision making and, thus, the very essence of the entire managerial process is to be found in its study. The earliest managers made decisions on the basis of hunch, guesswork, intuition, and, in some cases, palmists and the phases of the moon. Today's managers have at their disposal a variety of decision-making tools and techniques their predecessors lacked, including the computer and a host of quantitative techniques, such as decision theory, linear programming, and simulation.

Organizations—and the environments in which they operate—are constantly changing. *Organizational development* is a term used to refer to the process of preparing for and managing change. Organizational development efforts are typically intended to affect people's beliefs, values, and attitudes or behaviors, or both. Regardless of the focus, the payoff is to be found in increased organizational effectiveness and efficiency, and in an enhanced capability to deal successfully with change.

A. Influence and Leadership

24

The Bases of Social Power

John R. P. French, Jr.,
and
Bertram Raven

In this "classic among classics," the authors start from the premise that influence stems from relationships and the effectiveness of the attempted influence depends on how the individual being influenced reacts. This, in turn, depends on the bases of power that the influencer uses.—Eds.

The processes of power are pervasive, complex, and often disguised in our society. Accordingly, one finds in political science, in sociology, and in social psychology a variety of distinctions among different types of social power or among qualitatively different processes of social influence (refs. 1, 6, 14, 20, 23, 29, 30, 38, 41). Our main purpose is to identify the major types of power and to define them systematically so we may compare them according to the changes which they produce and the other effects which accompany the use of power. The phenomena of power and influence involve a dyadic relation between two agents, which may be viewed from two points of view: (*a*) What determines the behavior of the agent who exerts power? (*b*) What determines the reactions of the recipient of this behavior? We take this second point of view and formulate our theory in terms of the life space of P, the person upon whom the power is exerted. In this way we hope to define basic concepts of power, which will be adequate to explain many of the phenomena of social influence, including some which have been described in other less genotypic terms.

Recent empirical work, especially on small groups, has demonstrated the necessity of distinguishing different types of power in order to account for the different effects found in studies of social influence. Yet there is no doubt that more empirical knowledge will be needed to make final decisions

SOURCE: John R. P. French, Jr., and Bertram Raven, "The Bases of Social Power," in *Studies in Social Power,* edited by Dorwin P. Cartwright (Ann Arbor: Institute for Social Research, The University of Michigan, 1959), pp. 150–67. Reprinted by permission of the publisher.

concerning the necessary differentiations, but this knowledge will be obtained only by research based on some preliminary theoretical distinctions. We present such preliminary concepts and some of the hypotheses they suggest.

POWER, INFLUENCE, AND CHANGE

Psychological Change

Since we shall define power in terms of influence, and influence in terms of psychological change, we begin with a discussion of change. We want to define change at a level of generality which includes changes in behavior, opinions, attitudes, goals, needs, values, and all other aspects of the person's psychological field. We shall use the word "system" to refer to any such part of the life space.[1] Following Lewin (26, p. 305) the state of a system at time 1 will be noted $s_1(a)$.

Psychological change is defined as any alteration of the state of some system a over time. The amount of change is measured by the size of the difference between the states of the system a at time 1 and at time 2:

$$ch(a) = s_2(a) - s_1(a).$$

Change in any psychological system may be conceptualized in terms of psychological forces. But it is important to note that the change must be coordinated to the resultant force of all the forces operating at the moment. Change in an opinion, for example, may be determined jointly by a driving force induced by another person, a restraining force corresponding to anchorage in a group opinion, and an own force stemming from the person's needs.

Social Influence

Our theory of social influence and power is limited to influence on the person, P, produced by a social agent, O, where O can be either another person, a role, a norm, a group, or a part of a group. We do not consider social influence exerted on a group.

The influence of O on system a in the life space of P is defined as the resultant force on system a which has its source in an act of O. This resultant force induced by O consists of two components: a force to change the system in the direction induced by O and an opposing resistance set up by the same act of O.

By this definition the influence of O does not include P's own forces nor the forces induced by other social agents. Accordingly the "influence" of O must be clearly distinguished from O's "control" of P. . . . O may be able to induce strong forces on P to carry out an activity (i.e., O exerts strong influence on P); but, if the opposing forces induced by another person or by

P's own needs are stronger, then P will locomote in an opposite direction (i.e., O does not have control over P). Thus, psychological change in P can be taken as an operational definition of the social influence of O on P only when the effects of other forces have been eliminated.

It is assumed that any system is interdependent with other parts of the life space so that a change in one may produce changes in others. However, this theory focuses on the primary changes in a system which are produced directly by social influence; it is less concerned with secondary changes which are indirectly effected in the other systems or with primary changes produced by nonsocial influences.

Commonly, social influence takes place through an intentional act on the part of O. However, we do not want to limit our definition of "act" to such conscious behavior. Indeed, influence might result from the passive presence of O, with no evidence of speech or overt movement. A policeman's standing on a corner may be considered an act of an agent for the speeding motorist. Such acts of the inducing agent will vary in strength, for O may not always utilize all of his power. The policeman, for example, may merely stand and watch or act more strongly by blowing his whistle at the motorist.

The influence exerted by an act need not be in the direction intended by O. The direction of the resultant force on P will depend on the relative magnitude of the induced force set up by the act of O and the resisting force in the opposite direction which is generated by that same act. In cases where O intends to influence P in a given direction, a resultant force in the same direction may be termed *positive influence* whereas a resultant force in the opposite direction may be termed *negative influence*.

If O produces the intended change, he has exerted positive control; but if he produces a change in the opposite direction, as for example in the negativism of young children or in the phenomena of negative reference groups, he has exerted negative control.

Social Power

The strength of power of O/P in some system a is defined as the maximum potential ability of O to influence P in a.

By this definition influence is kinetic power, just as power is potential influence. It is assumed that O is capable of various acts which, because of some more or less enduring relation to P, are able to exert influence on P[2]. O's power is measured by his maximum possible influence, though he may often choose to exert less than his full power.

An equivalent definition of power may be stated in terms of the resultant of two forces set up by the act of O: one in the direction of O's influence attempt and another resisting force in the opposite direction. Power is the maximum resultant of these two forces:

$$\text{Power of O/P}(a) = (f_{a,x} - f_{\overline{a,x}})^{\max}$$

where the source of both forces is an act of O.

Thus, the power of O with respect to system a of P is equal to the maximum resultant force of two forces set up by any possible act of O: (a) the force which O can set up on the system a to change in the direction x, (b) the resisting force,[3] in the opposite direction. Whenever the first component force is greater than the second, positive power exists; but if the second component force is greater than the first, then O has negative power over P.

It is necessary to define power with respect to a specified system, because the power of O/P may vary greatly from one system to another. O may have great power to control the behavior of P but little power to control his opinions. Of course, a high power of O/P does not imply a low power of P/O; the two variables are conceptually independent.

For certain purposes it is convenient to define the range of power as the set of all systems within which O has power of strength greater than zero. A husband may have a broad range of power over his wife, but a narrow range of power over his employer. We shall use the term *magnitude of power* to denote the summation of O's power over P in all systems of his range.

The Dependence of s(a) on O

Several investigators have been concerned with differences between superficial conformity and "deeper" changes produced by social influence (refs. 1, 5, 6, 11, 12, 20, 21, 22, 23, 26, 36, 37). The kinds of systems which are changed and the stability of these changes have been handled by distinctions, such as "public vs. private attitudes," "overt versus covert behavior," "compliance vs. internalization," and "own versus induced forces." Though stated as dichotomies, all of these distinctions suggest an underlying dimension of the degree of dependence of the state of a system on O.

We assume that any change in the state of a system is produced by a change in some factor upon which it is functionally dependent. The state of an opinion, for example, may change because of a change either in some internal factor, such as a need or in some external factor, such as the arguments of O. Likewise, the maintenance of the same state of a system is produced by the stability or lack of change in the internal and external factors. In general, then, psychological change and stability can be conceptualized in terms of dynamic dependence. Our interest is focused on the special case of dependence on an external agent, O (31).

In many cases the initial state of the system has the character of a quasi-stationary equilibrium with a central force field around $s_1(a)$ (26, p. 106). In such cases we may derive a tendency toward retrogression to the original state as soon as the force induced by O is removed.[4] Let us suppose that O exerts influence producing a new state of the system, $s_2(a)$. Is $s_2(a)$ now dependent on the continued presence of O? In principle we could answer this question by removing any traces of O from the life space of P and by observing the consequent state of the system at time 3. If $s_3(a)$ retrogresses completely back to $s_1(a)$, then we may conclude that maintenance of $s_2(a)$ was completely dependent on O; but if $s_3(a)$ equals $s_2(a)$, this lack of change shows that $s_2(a)$ has become completely independent of O. In general, the degree of dependence of $s_2(a)$ on O, following O's influence, may be defined as equal to the amount of retrogression following the removal of O from the life space of P:

$$\text{Degree of dependence of } s_2(a) \text{ on}$$
$$O = s_2(a) - s_3(a).$$

A given degree of dependence at time 2 may later change, for example, through the gradual weakening of O's influence. At this later time, the degree of dependence of $s_4(a)$ on O, would still be equal to the amount of retrogression toward the initial state of equilibrium $s_1(a)$. Operational measures of the degree of dependence on O will, of course, have to be taken under conditions where all other factors are held constant.

Consider the example of three separated employees who have been working at the same steady level of production despite normal, small fluctuations in the work environment. The supervisor orders each to increase his production, and the level of each goes up from 100 to 115 pieces per day. After a week of producing at the new rate of 115 pieces per day, the supervisor is removed for a week. The production of employee A immediately returns to 100 but B and C return to only 110 pieces per day. Other things being equal, we can infer that A's new rate was completely dependent on his supervisor whereas the new rate of B and C was dependent on the supervisor only to the extent of 5 pieces. Let us further assume that, when the supervisor returned, the production of B and of C returned to 115 without further orders from the supervisor. Now another month goes by, during which B and C maintain a steady 115 pieces per day. However, there is a difference between them: B's level of production still depends on O to the extent of 5 pieces whereas C has come to rely on his own sense of obligation to obey the order of his legitimate supervisor, rather than on the supervisor's external pressure for the maintenance of his 115 pieces per day. Accordingly, the next time the supervisor departs, B's production again drops to 110 but C's remains at 115 pieces per day. In cases like employee B, the degree of dependence is contingent on the perceived probability that O will observe the state of the system and note P's conformity (5, 6, 11, 12, 23). The level of observability will in turn depend on both the nature of the system (e.g., the difference between a covert opinion and overt behavior) and on the environmental barriers to observation (e.g., O is too far away from P). In other cases, for example that of employee C, the new behavior pattern is highly dependent on his supervisor, but the degree of dependence of the new state will be related not to the level of observability but rather to factors inside P, in this case a sense of duty to perform an act legitimately prescribed by O. The internalization of social norms is a related process of decreasing degree of dependence of behavior on an external O and increasing dependence on an internal value; it is usually assumed that internalization is accompanied by a decrease in the effects of level of observability (37).

The concepts "dependence of a system on O" and "observability as a basis for dependence" will be useful in understanding the stability of conformity. In the next section we shall discuss various types of power and the types of conformity which they are likely to produce.

THE BASES OF POWER

By the basis of power we mean the relationship between O and P, which is the source of that power. It is rare that we can say with certainty that a given empirical case of power is limited to one source. Normally, the relation between O and P will be characterized by several qualitatively different variables which are bases of power (30, Chapter 11). Although there are undoubtedly many possible bases of power which may be distinguished, we shall here define five which seem especially common and important. These five bases of O's power are: (1) reward power, based on P's perception that O has the ability to mediate rewards for him; (2) coercive power, based on P's perception that O has the ability to mediate punishments for him; (3) legitimate power, based on the perception by P that O has a legitimate right to prescribe behavior for him; (4) referent power, based on P's identification with O; (5) expert power, based on the perception that O has some special knowledge or expertness.

Our first concern is to define the bases which give rise to a given type of power. Next, we describe each type of power according to its strength, range, and the degree of dependence of the new state of the system which is most likely to occur with each type of power. We shall also examine the other effects which the exercise of a given type of power may have upon P and his relationship to O. Finally, we shall point out the interrelationships between different types of power, and the effects of use of one type of power by O upon other bases of power which he might have over P. Thus, we shall both define a set of concepts and propose a series of hypotheses. Most of these hypotheses have not been systematically tested, although there is a good deal of evidence in favor of several. No attempt will be made to summarize that evidence here.

Reward Power

Reward power is defined as power whose basis is the ability to reward. The strength of the reward power of O/P increases with the magnitude of the rewards which P perceives that O can mediate for him. Reward power depends on O's ability to administer positive valences and to remove or decrease negative valences. The strength of reward power also depends upon the probability that O can mediate the reward, as perceived by P. A common example of reward power is the addition of a piece-work rate in the factory as an incentive to increase production.

The new state of the system induced by a promise of reward (for example, the factory worker's increased level of production) will be highly dependent on O. Since O mediates the reward, he controls the probability that P will receive it. Thus P's new rate of production will be dependent on his subjective probability that O will reward him for conformity minus his subjective probability that O will reward him even if he returns to his old level. Both probabilities will be greatly affected by the level of observability of P's behavior. Incidentally, a piece rate often seems to have more effect on production than a merit rating system, because it yields a higher probability of reward for conformity and a much lower probability of reward for nonconformity.

The utilization of actual rewards (instead of promises) by O will tend over time to increase the attraction of P toward O and, therefore, the referent power of O over P. As we shall note later, such referent power will permit O to induce changes which are relatively independent. Neither rewards nor promises will arouse resistance in P, provided P considers it legitimate for O to offer rewards.

The range of reward power is specific to those regions within which O can reward P for conforming. The use of rewards to change systems within the range of reward power tends to increase reward power by increasing the probability attached to future promises. However, unsuccessful attempts to exert reward power outside the range of power would tend to decrease the power; for example if O offers to reward P for performing an impossible act, this will reduce for P the probability of receiving future rewards promised by O.

Coercive Power

Coercive power is similar to reward power in that it also involves O's ability to manipulate the attainment of valences. Coercive power of O/P stems from the expectation on the part of P that he will be punished by O if he fails to conform to the influence attempt. Thus, negative valences will exist in given regions of P's life space, corresponding to the threatened punishment by O. The strength of coercive power depends on the magnitude of the negative valence of the threatened punishment multiplied by the perceived probability that P can avoid the punishment by conformity (i.e., the probability of punishment for nonconformity minus the probability of punishment for conformity) (11). Just as an offer of a piece-rate bonus in a factory can serve as a basis for reward power, so the ability to fire a worker if he falls below a given level of production will result in coercive power.

Coercive power leads to dependent change, also; and the degree of dependence varies with the level of observability of P's conformity. An excellent illustration of coercive power leading to dependent change is provided by a clothes presser in a factory observed by Coch and French (3). As her efficiency rating climbed above average for the group, the other workers began to "scapegoat" her. That the resulting plateau in her production was not independent of the group was evident once she was removed from the presence of the other workers. Her production immediately climbed to new heights.[5]

At times, there is some difficulty in distinguishing between reward power and coercive power. Is the withholding of a reward really equivalent to a punishment? Is the withdrawal of punishment equivalent to a reward? The answer must be a psychological one—it depends upon the situation as it exists for P. But ordinarily we would answer these questions in the affirmative; for P, receiving a reward is a positive valence as is the relief of suffering. There is some evidence that conformity to group norms in order to gain acceptance (reward power) should be distinguished from conformity as a means for forestalling rejection (coercive power) (5).

The distinction between these two types of power is important because the dynamics are different. The concept of "sanctions" sometimes lumps the two together despite their opposite effects. While reward power may eventually result in an independent system, the effects of coercive power will continue to be dependent. Reward power will tend to increase the attraction of P toward O; coercive power will decrease this attraction (11, 12). The valence of the region of behavior will become more negative, acquiring some negative valence from the threatened punishment. The negative valence of punishment would also spread to other regions of the life space. Lewin (25) has pointed out this distinction between the effects of rewards and punishment. In the case of threatened punishment, there will be a resultant force on P to leave the field entirely. Thus, to achieve conformity, O must not only place a strong negative valence in certain regions through threat of punishment but O must also introduce restraining forces, or other strong valences, so as to prevent P from withdrawing completely from O's range of coercive power. Otherwise the probability of receiving the punishment, if P does not conform, will be too low to be effective.

Legitimate Power

Legitimate power is probably the most complex of those treated here, embodying notions from the structural sociologist, the group-norm and role-oriented social psychologist, and the clinical psychologist.

There has been considerable investigation and speculation about socially prescribed behavior, particularly that which is specific to a given role or position. Linton (29) distinguishes group norms according to whether they are universals for everyone in the culture, alternatives (the individual having a choice on whether to accept them), or specialties (specific to given positions). Whether we speak of internalized norms, role prescriptions and expectations (34), or internalized pressures (15), the fact remains that each individual sees certain regions toward which he should locomote, some regions toward which he should not locomote, and some regions toward which he may locomote if they are generally attractive for him. This applies to specific behaviors in which he may, should, or should not engage; it applies to certain attitudes or beliefs which he may, should, or should not hold. The feeling of "oughtness" may be an internalization from his parents, from his teachers, from his religion, or may have been logically developed from some idiosyncratic system of ethics. He will speak of such behaviors with expressions like "should," "ought to," or "has a right to." In many cases, the original source of the requirement is not recalled.

Though we have oversimplified such evaluations of behavior with a positive-neutral-negative trichotomy, the evaluation of behaviors by the person is really more one of degree. This dimension of evaluation, we shall call "legitimacy." Conceptually, we may think of legitimacy as a valence in a region which is induced by some internalized norm or value. This value has the same conceptual property as power, namely an ability to induce force fields (26, pp. 40–41). It may or may not be correct that values (or the superego) are internalized parents, but at least they can set up force fields which have a phenomenal "oughtness" similar to a parent's prescription. Like a value, a need can also induce valences (i.e., force fields) in P's psychological environment; but these valences have more the phenomenal character of noxious or attractive properties of the object or activity. When a need induces a valence in P, for example, when a need makes an object attractive to P, this attraction applies to P but not to other persons. When a value induces a valence, on the other hand, it not only sets up forces on P to engage in the activity but P may feel that all others ought to behave in the same way. Among other things, this evaluation applies to the legitimate right of some other individual or group to prescribe behavior or beliefs for a person even though the other cannot apply sanctions.

Legitimate power of O/P is here defined as that power which stems from internalized values in P which dictate that O has a legitimate right to influence P and that P has an obligation to accept this influence. We note that legitimate power is very similar to the notion of legitimacy of authority which has long been explored by sociologists, particularly by Weber (42), and more recently by Goldhammer and Shils (14). However, legitimate power is not always a role relation: P may accept an induction from O simply because he had previously promised to help O and he values his word too much to break the promise. In all cases, the notion of legitimacy involves some sort of code or standard, accepted by the individual, by virtue of which the external agent can assert his power. We shall attempt to describe a few of these values here.

Bases for Legitimate Power. Cultural values constitute one common basis for the legitimate power of one individual over another. O has characteristics which are specified by the culture as giving him the right to prescribe behavior for P, who may not have these characteristics. These bases, which Weber (42) has called the authority of the "eternal yesterday," include such things as age, intelligence, caste, and physical characteristics.

In some cultures, the aged are granted the right to prescribe behavior for others in practically all behavior areas. In most cultures, there are certain areas of behavior in which a person of one sex is granted the right to prescribe behavior for the other sex.

Acceptance of the social structure is another basis for legitimate power. If P accepts as right the social structure of his group, organization, or society, especially the social structure involving a hierarchy of authority, P will accept the legitimate authority of O who occupies a superior office in the hierarchy. Thus, legitimate power in a formal organization is largely a relationship between offices, rather than between persons. And the acceptance of an office as *right* is a basis for legitimate power—a judge has a right to levy fines, a foreman should assign work, a priest is justified in prescribing religious beliefs, and it is the management's prerogative to make certain decisions (10). However, legitimate power also involves the perceived right of the person to hold the office.

Designation by a legitimizing agent is a third basis for legitimate power. An influencer O may be seen as legitimate in prescribing behavior for P, because he has been granted such power by a legitimizing agent whom P accepts. Thus, a department head may accept the authority of his vice president in a certain area, because that authority has been specifically delegated by the president. An election is perhaps the most common example of a group's serving to legitimize the authority of one individual or office for other individuals in the group. The success of such legitimizing depends upon the acceptance of the legitimizing agent and procedure. In this case it depends ultimately on certain democratic values concerning election procedures. The election process is one of legitimizing a person's right to an office which already has a legitimate range of power associated with it.

Range of Legitimate Power of O/P. The areas in which legitimate power may be exercised are generally specified along with the designation of that power. A job description, for example, usually specifies supervisory activities and also designates the person to whom the jobholder is responsible for the duties described. Some bases for legitimate authority carry with them a very broad range. Culturally derived bases for legitimate power are often especially broad. It is not uncommon to find cultures in which a member of a given caste can legitimately prescribe behavior for all members of lower castes in practically all regions. More common, however, are instances of legitimate power where the range is specifically and narrowly prescribed. A sergeant in the army is given a specific set of regions within which he can legitimately prescribe behavior for his men.

The attempted use of legitimate power which is outside of the range of legitimate power will decrease the legitimate power of the authority figure. Such use of power which is not legitimate will also decrease the attractiveness of O (11, 12, 36).

Legitimate Power and Influence. The new state of the system which results from legitimate power usually has high dependence on O, though it may become independent. Here, however, the degree of dependence is not related to the level of observability. Since legitimate power is based on P's values, the source of the forces induced by O include both these internal values and O. O's induction serves to activate the values and to relate them to the system which is influenced, but thereafter the new state of the system may become directly dependent on the values with no mediation by O. Accordingly, this new state will be relatively stable and consistent across varying environmental situations, since P's values are more stable than his psychological environment.

We have used the term *legitimate* not only as a basis for the power of an agent but also to describe the general behaviors of a person. Thus, the individual P may also consider the legitimacy of the attempts to use other types of power by O. In certain cases, P will consider that O has a legitimate right to threaten punishment for nonconformity; in other cases, such use of coercion would not be seen as legitimate. P might change in response to coercive power of O, but it will make a considerable difference in his attitude and conformity if O is not seen as having a legitimate right to use such coercion. In such cases, the attraction of P for O will be particularly diminished, and the influence attempt will arouse more resistance (11). Similarly the utilization of reward power may vary in legitimacy; the word *bribe,* for example, denotes an illegitimate reward.

Referent Power

The referent power of O/P has its basis in the identification of P with O. By identification, we mean a feeling of oneness of P with O or a desire for such an identity. If O is a person toward whom P is highly attracted, P will have a feeling of membership or a desire to join. If P is already closely associated with O he will want to maintain this relationship (39, 41). P's identification with O can be established or maintained if P behaves, believes, and perceives as O does. Accordingly, O has the ability to influence P, even though P may be unaware of this referent power. A verbalization of such power by P might be, "I am like O, and, therefore, I shall behave or believe as O does," or "I want to be like O, and I will be more like O if I behave or believe as O does." The stronger the identification of P with O the greater the referent power of O/P.

Similar types of power have already been investigated under a number of different formulations. Festinger (7) points out that, in an ambiguous situation, the individual seeks some sort of "social reality" and may adopt the cognitive structure of the individual or group with which he identifies. In such a case, the lack of clear structure may be threatening to the individual, and the agreement of his beliefs with those of a reference group will both satisfy his need for structure and give him added security through increased identification with his group (16, 19).

We must try to distinguish between referent power and other types of power which might be operative at the same time. If a member is attracted to a group and he conforms to its norms only because he fears ridicule or expulsion from the group for nonconformity, we would call this coercive power. On the other hand, if he conforms in order to obtain praise for conformity, it is a case of reward power. The basic criterion for distinguishing referent power from both coercive and reward power is the mediation of the punishment and the reward by O: to the extent that O mediates the sanctions (i.e., has means control over P) we are dealing with coercive and reward power; but to the extent that P avoids discomfort or gains satisfaction by conformity based on identification, regardless of O's responses, we are dealing with referent power. Conformity with majority opinion is sometimes based on a respect for the collective wisdom of the group, in which case it is expert power. It is important to distinguish these phenomena, all grouped together elsewhere as "pressures toward uniformity," since the type of change which occurs will be different for different bases of power.

The concepts of "reference group" (40) and "prestige suggestion" may be treated as instances of referent power. In this case, O, the prestigeful person or group, is valued by P; because P desires to be associated or identified with O, he will assume attitudes or beliefs held by O. Similarly a negative reference group which O dislikes and evaluates negatively may exert negative influence on P as a result of negative referent power.

It has been demonstrated that the power which we designate as referent power is especially great when P is attracted to O (2, 7, 8, 9, 13, 23, 30). In our terms, this would mean that, the greater the attraction, the greater the identification, and consequently the greater the referent power. In some cases, attraction or prestige may have a specific basis, and the range of referent power will be limited accordingly: a group of campers may have great referent power over a member regarding campcraft, but considerably less effect on other regions (30). However, we hypothesize that the greater the attraction of P toward O, the broader the range of referent power of O/P.

The new state of a system produced by referent power may be dependent on or independent of O; but the degree of dependence is not affected by the level of observability to O (6, 23). In fact, P is often not consciously aware of the referent power which O exerts over him. There is probably a tendency for some of these dependent changes to become independent of O quite rapidly.

Expert Power

The strength of the expert power of O/P varies with the extent of the knowledge or perception which P attributes to O within a given area. Probably P evaluates O's expertness in relation to his own knowledge as well as against an absolute standard. In any case, expert power results in primary social influence on P's cognitive structure and probably not on other types of systems. Of course, changes in the cognitive structure can change the direction of forces and, hence, of locomotion, but such a change of behavior is secondary social influence. Expert power has been demonstrated experimentally (8, 33). Accepting an attorney's advice in legal matters is a common example of expert influence; but there are many instances based on much less knowledge, such as the acceptance by a stranger of directions given by a native villager.

Expert power, where O need not be a member of P's group, is called "informational power" by Deutsch and Gerard (4). This type of expert power must be distinguished from influence based on the content of communication as described by Hovland et al. (17, 18, 23, 24). The influence of the content of a communication upon an opinion is presumably a secondary influence produced after the *primary* influence (i.e., the acceptance of the information). Since power is here defined in terms of the primary changes, the influence of the content on a related opinion is not a case of expert power as we have defined it, but the initial acceptance of the validity of the content does seem to be based on expert power or referent power. In other cases, however, so-called facts may be accepted as self-evident because they fit into P's cognitive structure; if this impersonal acceptance of the truth of the fact is independent of the more or less enduring relationship between O and P, then P's acceptance of the fact is not an actualization of expert power. Thus, we distinguish between expert power based on the credibility of O and informational influence, which is based on characteristics of the stimulus, such as the logic of the argument or the "self-evident facts."

Wherever expert influence occurs, it seems to be necessary both for P to think that O knows and for P to trust that O is telling the truth (rather than trying to deceive him).

Expert power will produce a new cognitive structure which is initially relatively dependent on O, but informational influence will produce a more independent structure. The former is likely to become more independent with the passage of time. In both cases, the degree of dependence on O is not affected by the level of observability.

The "sleeper effect" (18, 24) is an interesting case of a change in the degree of dependence of an opinion on O. An unreliable O (who probably had negative referent power but some positive expert power) presented "facts" which were accepted by the subjects and which would normally produce secondary influence on their opinions and beliefs. However, the negative referent power aroused resistance and resulted in negative social influence on their beliefs (i.e., set up a force in the direction opposite to the influence attempt), so there was little change in the subjects' opinions. With the passage of time, however, the subjects tended to forget the identity of the negative communicator faster than they forgot the contents of his communication, so there was a weakening of the negative referent influence and a consequent delayed positive change in the subjects' beliefs in the direction of the influence attempt ("sleeper effect"). Later, when the identity of the negative communicator was experimentally reinstated, these resisting forces were reinstated, and there was another negative change in belief in a direction opposite to the influence attempt (24).

The range of expert power, we assume, is more delimited than that of referent power. Not only is it restricted to cognitive systems but the expert is seen as having superior knowledge or ability in very specific areas, and his power will be limited to these areas, though some "halo effect" might occur. Recently, some of our renowned physical scientists have found quite painfully that their expert power in physical sciences does not extend to regions involving international politics. Indeed, there is some evidence that the attempted exertion of expert power outside of the range of expert power will reduce that expert power. An undermining of confidence seems to take place.

SUMMARY

We have distinguished five types of power: referent power, expert power, reward power, coercive power, and legitimate power. These distinctions led to the following hypotheses:

1. For all five types, the stronger the basis of power the greater the power.
2. For any type of power, the size of the range may vary greatly; but, in general, referent power will have the broadest range.
3. Any attempt to utilize power outside the range of power will tend to reduce the power.
4. A new state of a system produced by reward power or coercive power will be highly dependent on O, and the more observable P's conformity the more dependent the state. For the other three types of power, the new state is usually dependent, at least in the beginning, but in any case the level of observability has no effect on the degree of dependence.
5. Coercion results in decreased attraction of P toward O and high resistance; reward power results in increased attraction and low resistance.
6. The more legitimate the coercion the less it will produce resistance and decreased attraction.

NOTES

1. The word "system" is here used to refer to a whole or to a part of the whole.
2. The concept of power has the conceptual property of *potentiality;* but it seems useful to restrict this potential influence to more or less enduring power relations between O and P by excluding from the definition of power those cases where the potential influence is so momentary or so changing that it cannot be predicted

from the existing relationship. Power is a useful concept for describing social structure only if it has a certain stability over time; it is useless if every momentary social stimulus is viewed as actualizing social power.

3. We define resistance to an attempted induction as a force in the opposite direction which is set up by the same act of O. It must be distinguished from opposition which is defined as existing opposing forces which do not have their source in the same act of O. For example, a boy might resist his mother's order to eat spinach because of the manner of the induction attempt, and at the same time he might oppose it because he didn't like spinach.

4. Miller (33) assumes that all living systems have this character. However, it may be that some systems in the life space do not have this elasticity.

5. Though the primary influence of coercive power is dependent, it often produces secondary changes which are independent. Brainwashing, for example, utilizes coercive power to produce many primary changes in the life space of the prisoner, but these dependent changes can lead to identification with the aggressor and, hence, to secondary changes in ideology which are independent.

REFERENCES

1. Asch, S. E. *Social Psychology.* New York: Prentice-Hall, 1952.
2. Back, K. W. "Influence through Social Communication." *J. Abnorm. Soc. Psychol.,* 1951, **46,** 9–23.
3. Coch, L., & French, J. R. P., Jr. "Overcoming Resistance to Change." *Hum. Relat.,* 1948, **1,** 512–32.
4. Deutsch, M., & Gerard, H. B. "A Study of Normative and Informational Influences upon Individual Judgment." *J. Abnorm. Soc. Psychol.,* 1955, **51,** 629–36.
5. Dittes, J. E., & Kelley, H. H. "Effects of Different Conditions of Acceptance upon Conformity to Group Norms." *J. Abnorm. Soc. Psychol.,* 1956, **53,** 100–07.
6. Festinger, L. "An Analysis of Compliant Behavior." In Sherif, M., & Wilson, M. O., (eds.), *Group Relations at the Crossroads.* New York: Harper & Row, 1953, 232–56.
7. Festinger, L. "Informal Social Communication." *Psychol. Rev.,* 1950, **57,** 271–82.
8. Festinger, L.; Gerard, H. B.; Hymovitch, B.; Kelley, H. H.; & Raven, B. H. "The Influence Process in the Presence of Extreme Deviates. *Hum. Relat.,* 1952, **5,** 327–46.
9. Festinger, L., Schachter, S., & Back, K. "The Operation of Group Standards." In Cartwright, D., & Zander, A. *Group Dynamics: Research and Theory.* Evanston: Row, Peterson, 1953, 204–23.
10. French, J. R. P., Jr., Israel, Joachim & Ås, Dagfinn. "Arbeidernes medvirkning i industribedriften. En eksperimentell undersøkelse." Institute for Social Research, Oslo, Norway, 1957.
11. French, J. R. P., Jr.; Levinger, G.; & Morrison, H. W. "The Legitimacy of Coercive Power." In preparation.
12. French, J. R. P., Jr., & Raven, B. H. "An Experiment in Legitimate and Coercive Power." In preparation.
13. Gerard, H. B. "The Anchorage of Opinions in Face-to-face Groups." *Hum. Relat.,* 1954, **7,** 313–25.
14. Goldhammer, H., & Shils, E. A. "Types of Power and Status." *Amer. J. Sociol.,* 1939, **45,** 171–78.

15. Herbst, P. G. "Analysis and Measurement of a Situation." *Hum. Relat.*, 1953, **2**, 113–40.
16. Hochbaum, G. M. "Self-confidence and Reactions to Group Pressures." *Amer. Soc. Rev.*, 1954, **19**, 678–87.
17. Hovland, C. I.; Lumsdaine, A. A.; & Sheffield, F. D. *Experiments on Mass Communication*. Princeton: Princeton Univer. Press, 1949.
18. Hovland, C. I., & Weiss, W. "The Influence of Source Credibility on Communication Effectiveness." *Publ. Opin. Quart.*, 1951, **15**, 635–50.
19. Jackson, J. M., & Saltzstein, H. D. "The Effect of Person-group Relationships on Conformity Processes." *J. Abnorm. Soc. Psychol.*, 1958, **57**, 17–24.
20. Jahoda, M. "Psychological Issues in Civil Liberties." *Amer. Psychologist*, 1956, **11**, 234–40.
21. Katz, D., & Schank, R. L. *Social Psychology*. New York: John Wiley & Sons, 1938.
22. Kelley, H. H., & Volkart, E. H. "The Resistance to Change of Group-anchored Attitudes." *Amer. Soc. Rev.*, 1952, **17**, 453–65.
23. Kelman, H. "Three Processes of Acceptance of Social Influence: Compliance, Identification, and Internalization." Paper read at the meetings of the American Psychological Association, August 1956.
24. Kelman, H., & Hovland, C. I. " 'Reinstatement' of the Communicator in Delayed Measurement of Opinion Change." *J. Abnorm. Soc. Psychol.*, 1953, **48**, 327–35.
25. Lewin, K. *Dynamic Theory of Personality*. New York: McGraw-Hill, 1935, 114–70.
26. Lewin, K. *Field Theory in Social Science*. New York: Harper & Row, 1951.
27. Lewin, K., Lippitt, R., & White, R. K. "Patterns of Aggressive Behavior in Experimentally Created Social Climates." *J. Soc. Psychol.*, 1939, **10**, 271–301.
28. Lasswell, H. D., & Kaplan, A. *Power and Society: A Framework for Political Inquiry*. New Haven: Yale Univer. Press, 1950.
29. Linton, R. *The Cultural Background of Personality*. New York: Appleton-Century-Crofts, 1945.
30. Lippitt, R., Polansky, N., Redl, F., & Rosen, S. "The Dynamics of Power." *Hum. Relat.*, 1952, **5**, 37–64.
31. March, J. G. "An Introduction to the Theory and Measurement of Influence." *Amer. Polit. Sci. Rev.*, 1955, **49**, 431–51.
32. Miller, J. G. "Toward a General Theory for the Behavioral Sciences." *Amer. Psychologist*, 1955, **10**, 513–31.
33. Moore, H. T. "The Comparative Influence of Majority and Expert Opinion." *Amer. J. Psychol.*, 1921, **32**, 16–20.
34. Newcomb, T. M. *Social Psychology*. New York: Dryden, 1950.
35. Raven, B. H. "The Effect of Group Pressures on Opinion, Perception, and Communication." Unpublished doctoral dissertation, University of Michigan, 1953.
36. Raven, B. H., & French, J. R. P., Jr. "Group Support, Legitimate Power, and Social Influence." *J. Person.*, 1958, **26**, 400–09.
37. Rommetveit, R. *Social Norms and Roles*. Minneapolis: Univer. Minnesota Press, 1953.
38. Russell, B. *Power: A New Social Analysis*. New York: Norton, 1938.
39. Stotland, E.; Zander, A.; Burnstein, E.; Wolfe, D.; & Natsoulas, T. "Studies on the Effects of Identification." University of Michigan, Institute for Social Research. Forthcoming.

40. Swanson, G. E.; Newcomb, T. M.; & Hartley, E. L. *Readings in Social Psychology.* New York: Henry Holt, 1952.
41. Torrance, E. P., & Mason, R. "Instructor Effort to Influence: An Experimental Evaluation of Six Approaches." Paper presented at USAF-NRC Symposium on Personnel, Training, and Human Engineering. Washington, D.C., 1956.
42. Weber, M. *The Theory of Social and Economic Organization.* Oxford: Oxford Univer. Press, 1947.

25

The Ambiguity of Leadership

Jeffrey Pfeffer

This article addresses several problems with the concept of leadership, including the ambiguity of its definition and measurement, the issue of whether leadership affects organizational performance, and the process of selecting leaders, which frequently emphasizes irrelevant criteria.—Eds.

Leadership has for some time been a major topic in social and organizational psychology. Underlying much of this research has been the assumption that leadership is causally related to organizational performance. Through an analysis of leadership styles, behaviors, or characteristics (depending on the theoretical perspective chosen), the argument has been made that more effective leaders can be selected or trained or, alternatively, the situation can be configured to provide for enhanced leader and organizational effectiveness.

Three problems with emphasis on leadership as a concept can be posed: (a) ambiguity in definition and measurement of the concept itself; (b) the question of whether leadership has discernible effects on organizational outcomes; and (c) the selection process in succession to leadership positions, which frequently uses organizationally irrelevant criteria and which has implications for normative theories of leadership. The argument here is that leadership is of interest primarily as a phenomenological construct. Leaders serve as symbols for representing personal causation of social events. How and why are such attributions of personal effects made? Instead of focusing on leadership and its effects, how do people make inferences about and react to phenomena labelled as leadership (5)?

THE AMBIGUITY OF THE CONCEPT

While there have been many studies of leadership, the dimensions and definition of the concept remain unclear. To treat leadership as a separate concept, it must be distinguished from other social influence phenomena.

SOURCE: Reprinted with permission from the publisher from "The Ambiguity of Leadership," *Academy of Management Review,* January 1977, pp. 104–12.

Hollander and Julian (24) and Bavelas (2) did not draw distinctions between leadership and other processes of social influence. A major point of the Hollander and Julian review was that leadership research might develop more rapidly if more general theories of social influence were incorporated. Calder (5) also argued that there is no unique content to the construct of leadership that is not subsumed under other, more general, models of behavior.

Kochan, Schmidt, and DeCotiis (33) attempted to distinguish leadership from related concepts of authority and social power. In leadership, influence rights are voluntarily conferred. Power does not require goal compatibility—merely dependence—but leadership implies some congruence between the objectives of the leader and the led. These distinctions depend on the ability to distinguish voluntary from involuntary compliance and to assess goal compatibility. Goal statements may be retrospective inferences from action (46, 53) and problems of distinguishing voluntary from involuntary compliance also exist (32). Apparently there are few meaningful distinctions between leadership and other concepts of social influence. Thus, an understanding of the phenomena subsumed under the rubric of leadership may not require the construct of leadership (5).

While there is some agreement that leadership is related to social influence, more disagreement concerns the basic dimensions of leader behavior. Some have argued that there are two tasks to be accomplished in groups—maintenance of the group and performance of some task or activity—and thus leader behavior might be described along these two dimensions (1, 6, 8, 25). The dimensions emerging from the Ohio State leadership studies—consideration and initiating structure—may be seen as similar to the two components of group maintenance and task accomplishment (18).

Other dimensions of leadership behavior have also been proposed (4). Day and Hamblin (10) analyzed leadership in terms of the closeness and punitiveness of the supervision. Several authors have conceptualized leadership behavior in terms of the authority and discretion subordinates are permitted (23, 36, 51). Fiedler (14) analyzed leadership in terms of the least-preferred-co-worker scale (LPC), but the meaning and behavioral attributes of this dimension of leadership behavior remain controversial.

The proliferation of dimensions is partly a function of research strategies frequently employed. Factor analysis on a large number of items describing behavior has frequently been used. This procedure tends to produce as many factors as the analyst decides to find, and permits the development of a large number of possible factor structures. The resultant factors must be named and further imprecision is introduced. Deciding on a summative concept to represent a factor is inevitably a partly subjective process.

Literature assessing the effects of leadership tends to be equivocal. Sales (45) summarized leadership literature employing the authoritarian-democratic typology and concluded that effects on performance were small and inconsistent. Reviewing the literature on consideration and initiating structure dimensions, Korman (34) reported relatively small and inconsistent results, and Kerr and Schriesheim (30) reported more consistent effects of the two dimensions. Better results apparently emerge when moderating factors are taken into account, including subordinate personalities (50), and situational characteristics (23, 51). Kerr, et al. (31) list many moderating effects grouped under the headings of subordinate considerations, supervisor considerations, and task considerations. Even if each set of considerations consisted of only one factor (which it does not), an attempt to account for the effects of leader behavior would necessitate considering four-way interactions. While social reality is complex and contingent, it seems desirable to attempt to find more parsimonious explanations for the phenomena under study.

THE EFFECTS OF LEADERS

Hall asked a basic question about leadership: Is there any evidence on the magnitude of the effects of leadership (17, p. 248)? Surprisingly, he could find little evidence. Given the resources that have been spent studying, selecting, and training leaders, one might expect that the question of whether or not leaders matter would have been addressed earlier (12).

There are at least three reasons why it might be argued that the observed effects of leaders on organizational outcomes would be small. First, those obtaining leadership positions are selected, and perhaps only certain, limited styles of behavior may be chosen. Second, once in the leadership position, the discretion and behavior of the leader are constrained. And third, leaders can typically affect only a few of the variables that may impact organizational performance.

Homogeneity of Leaders

Persons are selected to leadership positions. As a consequence of this selection process, the range of behaviors or characteristics exhibited by leaders is reduced, making it more problematic to empirically discover an effect of leadership. There are many types of constraints on the selection process. The attraction literature suggests that there is a tendency for persons to like those they perceive as similar (3). In critical decisions, such as the selections of persons for leadership positions, compatible styles of behavior probably will be chosen.

Selection of persons is also constrained by the internal system of influence in the organization. As Zald (56) noted, succession is a critical decision, affected by political influence and by environmental contingencies faced by the organization. As Thompson (49) noted, leaders may be selected for their capacity to deal with various organizational contingencies. In a study of characteristics of hospital administrators, Pfeffer and Salancik (42) found a relationship between the hospital's context and the characteristics and tenure of the administrators. To the extent that the contingencies and power distribution within the organization remain stable, the abilities and behaviors of those selected into leadership positions will also remain stable.

Finally, the selection of persons to leadership positions is affected by a self-selection process. Organizations and roles have images, providing information about their character. Persons are likely to select themselves into organizations and roles based upon their preferences for the dimensions of the organizational and role characteristics as perceived through these images. The self-selection of persons would tend to work along with organizational selection to limit the range of abilities and behaviors in a given organizational role.

Such selection processes would tend to increase homogeneity more within a single organization than across organizations. Yet many studies of leadership effect at the work group level have compared groups within a single organization. If there comes to be a widely shared, socially constructed definition of leadership behaviors or characteristics which guides the selection process, then leadership activity may come to be defined similarly in various organizations, leading to the selection of only those who match the constructed image of a leader.

Constraints on Leader Behavior

Analyses of leadership have frequently presumed that leadership style or leader behavior was an independent variable that could be selected or trained at will to conform to what research would find to be optimal. Even theorists who took a more contingent view of appropriate leadership behavior generally assumed that, with proper training, appropriate behavior could be produced (51). Fiedler (13), noting how hard it was to change behavior, suggested changing the situational characteristics, rather than the person; but this was an unusual suggestion in the context of prevailing literature, which suggested that leadership style was something to be strategically selected according to the variables of the particular leadership theory.

But the leader is embedded in a social system, which constrains behavior. The leader has a role-set (27), in which members have expectations for appropriate behavior and persons make efforts to modify the leader's behavior. Pressures to conform to the expectations of peers, subordinates, and superiors are all relevant in determining actual behavior.

Leaders, even in high-level positions, have unilateral control over fewer resources and fewer policies than might be expected. Investment decisions may require approval of others, while hiring and promotion decisions may be accomplished by committees. Leader behavior is constrained by both the demands of others in the role-set and by organizationally prescribed limitations on the sphere of activity and influence.

External Factors

Many factors that may affect organizational performance are outside a leader's control, even if he or she were to have complete discretion over major areas of organizational decisions. For example, consider the executive in a construction firm. Costs are largely determined by operation of commodities and labor markets; and demand is largely affected by interest rates, availability of mortgage money, and economic conditions, which are affected by governmental policies over which the executive has little control. School superintendents have little control over birth rates and community economic development, both of which profoundly affect school system budgets. While the leader may react to contingencies as they arise, or may be a better or worse forecaster, in accounting for variation in organizational outcomes, he or she may account for relatively little compared to external factors.

Second, the leader's success or failure may be partly due to circumstances unique to the organization but still outside his or her control. Leader positions in organizations vary in terms of the strength and position of the organization. The choice of a new executive does not fundamentally alter a market and financial position that has developed over years and affects the leader's ability to make strategic changes and the likelihood that the organization will do well or poorly. Organizations have relatively enduring strengths and weaknesses. The choice of a particular leader for a particular position has limited impact on these capabilities.

Empirical Evidence

Two studies have assessed the effects of leadership changes in major positions in organizations. Lieberson and O'Connor (35) examined 167 business firms in 13 industries over a 20-year period, allocating variance in sales, profits, and profit margins to one of four sources: year (general economic conditions), industry, company effects, and effects of changes in the top executive position. They concluded that, compared to other factors, administration had a limited effect on organizational outcomes.

Using a similar analytical procedure, Salancik and Pfeffer (44) examined the effects of mayors on city budgets for 30 U.S. cities. Data on expenditures by budget category were collected for 1951–68. Variance in amount and proportion of expenditures was apportioned to the year, the city, or the mayor. The mayoral effect was relatively small, with the city accounting for most of the variance, although the mayor effect was larger for expenditure categories that were not as directly connected to important interest groups. Salancik and Pfeffer argued that the effects of the mayor were limited both by absence of power to control many of the expenditures and tax sources and by construction of policies in response to demands from interests in the environment.

If leadership is defined as a strictly interpersonal phenomenon, the relevance of these two studies for the issue of leadership effects becomes problematic. But such a conceptualization seems unduly restrictive, and it is certainly inconsistent with Selznick's (47) conceptualization of leadership as strategic management and decision making. If one cannot observe differences when leaders change, then what does it matter who occupies the positions or how they behave?

Pfeffer and Salancik (41) investigated the extent to which behaviors selected by first-line supervisors were constrained by expectations of others in their role-set. Variance in task and social behaviors could be accounted for by role-set expectations, with adherence to various demands made by role-set participants a function of similarity and relative power. Lowin and Craig (37) experimentally demonstrated that leader behavior was determined by the subordinate's own behavior. Both studies illustrate that leader behaviors are responses to the demands of the social context.

The effect of leadership may vary depending upon level in the organizational hierarchy, while the appropriate activities and behaviors may also vary with organizational level (26, 40). For the most part, empirical studies of leadership have dealt with first-line supervisors or leaders with relatively low organizational status (17). If leadership has any impact, it should be more evident at higher organizational levels or where there is more discretion in decisions and activities.

THE PROCESS OF SELECTING LEADERS

Along with the suggestion that leadership may not account for much variance in organizational outcomes, it can be argued that merit or ability may not account for much variation in hiring and advancement of organizational personnel. These two ideas are related. If competence is hard to judge, or if leadership competence does not greatly affect organizational outcomes, then other person-dependent criteria may be sufficient. Effective leadership styles may not predict career success when other variables, such as social background, are controlled.

Belief in the importance of leadership is frequently accompanied by belief that persons occupying leadership positions are selected and trained according to how well they can enhance the organization's performance. Belief in a leadership effect leads to development of a set of activities oriented toward enhancing leadership effectiveness. Simultaneously, persons managing their own careers are likely to place emphasis on activities and developing behaviors that will enhance their own leadership skills, assuming that such a strategy will facilitate advancement.

Research on the bases for hiring and promotion has been concentrated in examination of academic positions (e.g., 7, 19, 20). This is possibly the result of availability of relatively precise and unambiguous measures of performance, such as number of publications or citations. Evidence on criteria used in selecting and advancing personnel in industry is more indirect.

Studies have attempted to predict either the compensation or the attainment of general management positions of MBA students, using personality and other background information (21, 22, 54). There is some evidence that managerial success can be predicted by indicators of ability and motivation, such as test scores and grades, but the amount of variance explained is typically quite small.

A second line of research has investigated characteristics and backgrounds of persons attaining leadership positions in major organizations in society. Domhoff (11), Mills (38), and Warner and Abbeglin (52) found a strong preponderance of persons with upper-class backgrounds occupying leadership positions. The implication of these findings is that studies of graduate success, including the success of MBAs, would explain more variance if the family background of the person were included.

A third line of inquiry uses a tracking model. The dynamic model developed is one in which access to elite universities is affected by social status (28) and, in turn, social status and attendance at elite universities affect later career outcomes (9, 43, 48, 55).

Unless one is willing to make the argument that attendance at elite universities or coming from an upper class background is perfectly correlated with merit, the evidence suggests that succession to leadership positions is not strictly based on meritocratic criteria. Such a conclusion is consistent with the inability of studies attempting to predict the success of MBA graduates to account for much variance, even when a variety of personality and ability factors are used.

Beliefs about the bases for social mobility are important for social stability. As long as persons believe that positions are allocated on meritocratic grounds, they are more likely to be satisfied with the social order and with their position in it. This satisfaction derives from the belief that occupational position results from application of fair and reasonable criteria, and that the opportunity exists for mobility if the person improves skills and performance.

If succession to leadership positions is determined by person-based criteria, such as social origins or social connections (16), then efforts to enhance managerial effectiveness with the expectation that this will lead to career success divert attention from the process of stratification actually operating within organizations. Leadership literature has been implicitly aimed at two audiences. Organizations were told how to become more effective, and persons were told what behaviors to acquire in order to become effective and, hence, advance in their careers. The possibility that neither organizational outcomes nor career success are related to leadership behaviors leaves leadership research facing issues of relevance and importance.

THE ATTRIBUTION OF LEADERSHIP

Kelley conceptualized the layman as:

an applied scientist, that is, as a person concerned about applying his knowledge of causal relationships in order to *exercise control* of his world [29, p. 2].

Reviewing a series of studies dealing with the attributional process, he concluded that persons were not only interested in understanding their world correctly, but also in controlling it.

The view here proposed is that attribution processes are to be understood not only as a means of providing the individual with a veridical view of his world, but as a means of encouraging and maintaining his effective exercise of control in that world [29, p. 22].

Controllable factors will have high salience as candidates for causal explanation, while a bias toward the more important causes may shift the attributional emphasis toward causes that are not controllable (29, p. 23). The study of attribution is a study of naive psychology—an examination of how persons make sense out of the events taking place around them.

If Kelley is correct that individuals will tend to develop attributions that give them a feeling of control, then emphasis on leadership may derive partially from a desire to believe in the effectiveness and importance of individual action, since individual action is more controllable than contextual variables. Lieberson and O'Connor (35) made essentially the same point in introducing their paper on the effects of top management changes on organizational performance. Given the desire for control and a feeling of personal effectiveness, organizational outcomes are more likely to be attributed to individual actions, regardless of their actual causes.

Leadership is attributed by observers. Social action has meaning only through a phenomenological process (46). The identification of certain organizational roles as leadership positions guides the construction of meaning in the direction of attributing effects to the actions of those positions. While Bavelas (2) argued that the functions of leadership, such as task accomplishment and group maintenance, are shared throughout the group, this fact provides no simple and potentially controllable focus for attributing causality. Rather, the identification of leadership positions provides a simpler and more readily changeable model of reality. When causality is lodged in one or a few persons, rather than being a function of a complex set of interactions among all group members, changes can be made by replacing or influencing the occupant of the leadership position. Causes of organizational actions are readily identified in this simple causal structure.

Even if, empirically, leadership has little effect, and even if succession to leadership positions is not predicated on ability or performance, the belief in leadership effects and meritocratic succession provides a simple causal framework and a justification for the structure of the social collectivity.

More importantly, the beliefs interpret social actions in terms that indicate potential for effective individual intervention or control. The personification of social causality serves too many uses to be easily overcome. Whether or not leader behavior actually influences performance or effectiveness, it is important because people believe it does.

One consequence of the attribution of causality to leaders and leadership is that leaders come to be symbols. Mintzberg (39), in his discussion of the roles of managers, wrote of the symbolic role, but more in terms of attendance at formal events and formally representing the organization. The symbolic role of leadership is more important than implied in such a description. The leader as a symbol provides a target for action when difficulties occur, serving as a scapegoat when things go wrong. Gamson and Scotch (15) noted that, in baseball, the firing of the manager served a scapegoating purpose. One cannot fire the whole team, yet, when performance is poor, something must be done. The firing of the manager conveys to the world and to the actors involved that success is the result of personal actions, and that steps can and will be taken to enhance organizational performance.

The attribution of causality to leadership may be reinforced by organizational actions, such as the inauguration process, the choice process, and providing the leader with symbols and ceremony. If leaders are chosen by using a random number table, persons are less likely to believe in their effects than if there is an elaborate search or selection process followed by an elaborate ceremony signifying the changing of control, and if the leader then has a variety of perquisites and symbols that distinguish him or her from the rest of the organization. Construction of the importance of leadership in a given social context is the outcome of various social processes, which can be empirically examined.

Since belief in the leadership effect provides a feeling of personal control, one might argue that efforts to increase the attribution of causality to leaders would occur more when it is more necessary and more problematic to attribute causality to controllable factors. Such an argument would lead to the hypothesis that, the more the *context* actually effects organizational outcomes, the more efforts will be made to ensure attribution to *leadership*. When leaders really do have effects, it is less necessary to engage in rituals indicating their effects. Such rituals are more likely when there is uncertainty and unpredictability associated with the organization's operations. This results both from the desire to feel control in uncertain situations and from the fact that, in ambiguous contexts, it is easier to attribute consequences to leadership without facing possible disconfirmation.

The leader is, in part, an actor. Through statements and actions, the leader attempts to reinforce the operation of an attribution process which tends to vest causality in that position in the social structure. Successful leaders, as perceived by members of the social system, are those who can separate themselves from organizational failures and associate themselves with organizational success. Since the meaning of action is socially constructed, this involves manipulation of symbols to reinforce the desired process of attribution. For instance, if a manager knows that business in his or her division is about to improve because of the economic cycle, the leader may, nevertheless, write recommendations and undertake actions and changes that are highly visible and that will tend to identify his or her behavior closely with the division. A manager who perceives impending failure will attempt to associate the division and its policies and decisions with others, particularly persons in higher organizational positions, and to disassociate himself or herself from the division's performance, occasionally even transferring or moving to another organization.

CONCLUSION

The theme of this article has been that analysis of leadership and leadership processes must be contingent on the intent of the researcher. If the interest is in understanding the causality of social phenomena as reliably and accurately as possible, then the concept of leadership may be a poor place to begin. The issue of the effects of leadership is open to question. But examination of situational variables that accompany more or less leadership effect is a worthwhile task.

The more phenomenological analysis of leadership directs attention to the process by which social causality is attributed, and it focuses on the distinction between causality as perceived by group members and causality as assessed by an outside observer. Leadership is associated with a set of myths reinforcing a social construction of meaning which legitimates leadership role occupants, provides belief in potential mobility for those not in leadership roles, and attributes social causality to leadership roles, thereby providing a belief in the effectiveness of individual control. In analyzing leadership, this mythology and the process by which such mythology is created and supported should be separated from analysis of leadership as a social influence process, operating within constraints.

REFERENCES

1. Bales, R. F. *Interaction Process Analysis: A Method for the Study of Small Groups.* Reading, Mass.: Addison-Wesley, 1950.
2. Bavelas, Alex. "Leadership: Man and Function." *Administrative Science Quarterly* 4 (1960), pp. 491–98.
3. Berscheid, Ellen, and Elaine Walster. *Interpersonal Attraction.* Reading, Mass.: Addison-Wesley, 1969.
4. Bowers, David G., and Stanley E. Seashore. "Predicting Organizational Effectiveness with a Four-Factor Theory of Leadership." *Administrative Science Quarterly* 11 (1966), pp. 238–63.
5. Calder, Bobby J. "An Attribution Theory of Leadership." In *New Directions in Organizational Behavior,* ed. B. Staw and G. Salancik. Chicago: St. Clair Press, 1976; in press.

6. Cartwright, Dorwin C., and Alvin Zander. *Group Dynamics: Research and Theory.* 3rd ed. Evanston, Ill.: Row, Peterson, 1960.

7. Cole, Jonathan R., and Stephen Cole. *Social Stratification in Science.* Chicago: University of Chicago Press, 1973.

8. Collins, Barry E., and Harold Guetzkow. *A Social Psychology of Group Processes for Decision-Making.* New York: John Wiley & Sons, 1964.

9. Collins, Randall. "Functional and Conflict Theories of Stratification," *American Sociological Review* 36 (1971), pp. 1002–19.

10. Day, R. C., and R. L. Hamblin. "Some Effects of Close and Punitive Styles of Supervision." *American Journal of Sociology* 69 (1964), pp. 499–510.

11. Domhoff, G. William. *Who Rules America?* Englewood Cliffs, N.J.: Prentice-Hall, 1967.

12. Dubin, Robert. "Supervision and Productivity: Empirical Findings and Theoretical Considerations." In *Leadership and Productivity* ed. R. Dubin, G. C. Homans, F. C. Mann, and D. C. Miller. San Francisco: Chandler, 1965, pp. 1–50.

13. Fiedler, Fred E. "Engineering the Job to Fit the Manager." *Harvard Business Review* 43 (1965), pp. 115–22.

14. ———. *A Theory of Leadership Effectiveness.* New York: McGraw-Hill, 1967.

15. Gamson, William A., and Norman A. Scotch. "Scapegoating in Baseball." *American Journal of Sociology* 70 (1964), pp. 69–72.

16. Granovetter, Mark. *Getting a Job.* Cambridge, Mass.: Harvard University Press, 1974.

17. Hall, Richard H. *Organizations: Structure and Process.* Englewood Cliffs, N.J.: Prentice-Hall, 1972.

18. Halpin, A. W., and J. Winer. "A Factorial Study of the Leader Behavior Description Questionnaire." In *Leader Behavior: Its Description and Measurement,* ed. R. M. Stogdill and A. E. Coons. Columbus, Ohio: Bureau of Business Research, Ohio State University, 1957, pp. 39–51.

19. Hargens, L. L. "Patterns of Mobility of New Ph.D.'s among American Academic Institutions." *Sociology of Education* 42 (1969), pp. 18–37.

20. Hargens, L. L., and W. O. Hagstrom. "Sponsored and Contest Mobility of American Academic Scientists." *Sociology of Education* 40 (1967), pp. 24–38.

21. Harrell, Thomas W. "High Earning MBA's." *Personnel Psychology* 25 (1972), pp. 523–30.

22. Harrell, Thomas W., and Margaret S. Harrell. "Predictors of Management Success." *Stanford University Graduate School of Business, Technical Report no. 3 to the Office of Naval Research.*

23. Heller, Frank, and Gary Yukl. "Participation, Managerial Decision-Making, and Situational Variables." *Organizational Behavior and Human Performance* 4 (1969), pp. 227–41.

24. Hollander, Edwin P., and James W. Julian. "Contemporary Trends in the Analysis of Leadership Processes." *Psychological Bulletin* 71 (1969), pp. 387–97.

25. House, Robert J. "A Path Goal Theory of Leader Effectiveness." *Administrative Science Quarterly* 16 (1971), pp. 321–38.

26. Hunt, J. G. "Leadership-Style Effects at Two Managerial Levels in a Simulated Organization." *Administrative Science Quarterly* 16 (1971), pp. 476–85.

27. Kahn, R. L., D. M. Wolfe, R. P. Quinn, and J. D. Snoek. *Organizational Stress: Studies in Role Conflict and Ambiguity.* New York: John Wiley & Sons, 1964.

28. Karabel, J., and A. W. Astin. "Social Class, Academic Ability, and College 'Quality'. " *Social Forces* 53 (1975), pp. 381–98.

29. Kelley, Harold H. *Attribution in Social Interaction.* Morristown, N.J.: General Learning Press, 1971.

30. Kerr, Steven, and Chester Schriesheim. "Consideration, Initiating Structure and Organizational Criteria—An Update of Korman's 1966 Review." *Personnel Psychology* 27 (1974), pp. 555–68.

31. Kerr, S., C. Schriesheim, C. J. Murphy, and R. M. Stogdill. "Toward a Contingency Theory of Leadership Based upon the Consideration and Initiating Structure Literature." *Organizational Behavior and Human Performance* 12 (1974), pp. 62–82.

32. Kiesler, C., and S. Kiesler. *Conformity.* Reading, Mass.: Addison-Wesley, 1969.

33. Kochan, T. A., S. M. Schmidt, and T. A. DeCotiis. "Superior-Subordinate Relations: Leadership and Headship." *Human Relations* 28 (1975), pp. 279–94.

34. Korman, A. K. "Consideration, Initiating Structure, and Organizational Criteria—A Review." *Personnel Psychology* 19 (1966), pp. 349–62.

35. Lieberson, Stanley, and James F. O'Connor. "Leadership and Organizational Performance: A Study of Large Corporations." *American Sociological Review* 37 (1972), pp. 117–30.

36. Lippitt, Ronald. "An Experimental Study of the Effect of Democratic and Authoritarian Group Atmospheres." *University of Iowa Studies in Child Welfare* 16 (1940), pp. 43–195.

37. Lowin, A., and J. R. Craig. "The Influence of Level of Performance on Managerial Style: An Experimental Object-Lesson in the Ambiguity of Correlational Data." *Organizational Behavior and Human Performance* 3 (1968), pp. 440–58.

38. Mills, C. Wright. "The American Business Elite: A Collective Portrait." In C. W. Mills, *Power, Politics, and People.* New York: Oxford University Press, 1963, pp. 110–39.

39. Mintzberg, Henry. *The Nature of Managerial Work.* New York: Harper & Row, 1973.

40. Nealey, Stanley M., and Milton R. Blood. "Leadership Performance of Nursing Supervisors at Two Organizational Levels." *Journal of Applied Psychology* 52 (1968), pp. 414–42.

41. Pfeffer, Jeffrey, and Gerald R. Salancik. "Determinants of Supervisory Behavior: A Role-Set Analysis." *Human Relations* 28 (1975), pp. 139–54.

42. Pfeffer, Jeffrey, and Gerald R. Salancik. "Organizational Context and the Characteristics and Tenure of Hospital Administrators." *Academy of Management Journal* 20 (1977), in press.

43. Reed, R. H., and H. P. Miller. "Some Determinants of the Variation in Earnings for College Men." *Journal of Human Resources* 5 (1970), pp. 117–90.

44. Salancik, Gerald R., and Jeffrey Pfeffer. "Constraints on Administrator Discretion: The Limited Influence of Mayors on City Budgets." *Urban Affairs Quarterly,* in press.

45. Sales, Stephen M. "Supervisory Style and Productivity: Review and Theory." *Personnel Psychology* 19 (1966), pp. 275–86.

46. Schutz, Alfred. *The Phenomenology of the Social World.* Evanston, Ill.: Northwestern University Press, 1967.

47. Selznick, P. *Leadership in Administration.* Evanston, Ill.: Row, Peterson, 1957.

48. Spaeth, J. L., and A. M. Greeley. *Recent Alumni and Higher Education.* New York: McGraw-Hill, 1970.

49. Thompson, James D. *Organizations in Action.* New York: McGraw-Hill, 1967.

50. Vroom, Victor H. "Some Personality Determinants of the Effects of Participation." *Journal of Abnormal and Social Psychology* 59 (1959), pp. 322–27.

51. Vroom, Victor H., and Phillip W. Yetton. *Leadership and Decision-Making.* Pittsburgh: University of Pittsburgh Press, 1973.
52. Warner, W. L., and J. C. Abbeglin. *Big Business Leaders in America.* New York: Harper & Row, 1955.
53. Weick, Karl E. *The Social Psychology of Organizing.* Reading, Mass.: Addison-Wesley, 1969.
54. Weinstein, Alan G., and V. Srinivasan. "Predicting Managerial Success of Master of Business Administration (MBA) Graduates." *Journal of Applied Psychology* 59 (1974), pp. 207–12.
55. Wolfle, Dael. *The Uses of Talent.* Princeton: Princeton University Press, 1971.
56. Zald, Mayer N. "Who Shall Rule? A Political Analysis of Succession in a Large Welfare Organization." *Pacific Sociological Review* 8 (1965), pp. 52–60.

26
The Contingency Model—
New Directions for
Leadership Utilization

Fred E. Fiedler

An early proponent of the contingency approach, Fiedler suggests that what constitutes effective leadership is dependent upon the situation in which the leadership attempt is made. Fiedler goes on to clearly spell out what aspects of the situation are important, namely the state of leader-member relations, task structure, and the leader's formal power. These three factors combine to determine situational favorableness, a key variable in the model. While the theory has its problems, it is a classical example of the contingency approach.—Eds.

Leadership research has come a long way from the simple concepts of earlier years, which centered on the search for the magic leadership trait. We have had to replace the old cherished notion that "leaders are born and not made." These increasingly complex formulations postulate that some types of leaders will behave and perform differently in a given situation than other types. The Contingency Model is one of the earliest and most articulated of these theories,[1] taking into account the personality of the leader as well as aspects of the situation which affect the leader's behavior and performance. This model has given rise to well over 100 empirical studies. This article briefly reviews the current status of the Contingency Model and then discusses several new developments which promise to have considerable impact on our thinking about leadership as well as on the management of executive manpower.

THE CONTINGENCY MODEL

The theory holds that the effectiveness of a task group or of an organization depends on two main factors: the personality of the leader and the

SOURCE: From the *Journal of Contemporary Business* 3, no. 4 (Autumn 1974), pp. 65–80. Reprinted by permission of the publisher.

degree to which the situation gives the leader power, control, and influence over the situation or, conversely, the degree to which the situation confronts the leader with uncertainty.[2]

Leader Personality. The first of these factors distinguishes leader personality in terms of two different motivational systems (i.e., the basic or primary goals) as well as the secondary goals which people pursue once their more pressing needs are satisfied. One type of person, whom we shall call "relationship-motivated," primarily seeks to maintain good interpersonal relationships with co-workers. These basic goals become very apparent in uncertain and anxiety provoking situations in which we try to make sure that the important needs are secured. Under these conditions the relationship-motivated individual will seek out others and solicit their support; however, under conditions in which he or she feels quite secure and relaxed—because this individual has achieved the major goals of having close relations with subordinates—he or she will seek the esteem and admiration of others. In a leadership situation where task performance results in esteem and admiration from superiors, this leader will tend to concentrate on behaving in a task-relevant manner, sometimes to the detriment of relations with immediate subordinates.

The relationship-motivated leader's counterpart has as a major goal the accomplishment of some tangible evidence of his or her worth. This person gets satisfaction from the task itself and from knowing that he or she has done well. In a leadership situation which is uncertain and anxiety provoking, this person will, therefore, put primary emphasis on completing the task. However, when this individual has considerable control and influence and knows, therefore, the task will get done, he or she will relax and be concerned with subordinates' feelings and satisfactions. In other words, business before pleasure, but business *with* pleasure whenever possible.

Of course, these two thumbnail sketches are oversimplified, but they do give a picture which tells us, first, that we are dealing with different types of people and, second, that they differ in their primary and secondary goals and, consequently, in the way they behave under various conditions. Both the relationship-motivated and the task-motivated persons may be pleasant and considerate toward their members. However, the task-motivated leader will be considerate in situations in which he or she is secure—that is, in which the individual's power and influence are high; the relationship-motivated leader will be considerate when his or her control and influence are less assured, when some uncertainty is present.

These motivational systems are measured by the Least Preferred Coworker score (LPC) which is obtained by first asking an individual to think of all people with whom he or she has ever worked, and then to describe the one person with whom this individual has been able to work least well. The description of the least preferred coworker is made on a short, bipolar eight-point scale, from 16 to 22 item-scale of the semantic differential format. The LPC score is the sum of the item scores; for example:

Friendly

: ___ : ___ : ___ : ___ : ___ : ___ : ___ : ___ :
   1   2   3   4   5   6   7   8

                                 Unfriendly

Cooperative

: ___ : ___ : ___ : ___ : ___ : ___ : ___ : ___ :
   1   2   3   4   5   6   7   8

                                Uncooperative

High-LPC persons (i.e., individuals who describe their LPC in relatively positive terms) seem primarily relationship-motivated. Low-LPC persons, those who describe their least preferred co-worker in very unfavorable terms, are basically task-motivated. Therefore, as can be seen, the LPC score is not a description of leader behavior, because the behavior of high- and low-LPC people changes with different situations.

Relationship-motivated people seem more open, more approachable, and more like McGregor's "Theory Y" managers, while the task-motivated leaders tend to be more controlled and more controlling persons, even though they may be as likeable and pleasant as their relationship-motivated colleagues.[3]

Current evidence suggests that the LPC scores and the personality attributes they reflect are almost as stable as most other personality measures. (For example, test-retest reliabilities for military leaders have been .72 over an eight-month period[4] and .67 over a two-year period for faculty members.[5]) Changes do occur, but, in the absence of major upsets in the individual's life, they tend to be gradual and relatively small.

The Leadership Situation.   The second variable, "situational favorableness,"[6] indicates the degree to which the situation gives the leader control and influence and the ability to predict the consequences of his or her behavior.[7] A situation in which the leader cannot predict the consequences of the decision tends to be stressful and anxiety arousing.

One rough but useful method for defining situational favorableness is based on three subscales. These are the degree to which (a) the leader is, or feels, accepted and supported by his or her members (leader-member relations); (b) the task is clear-cut, programmed, and structured as to goals, procedures, and measurable progress and success (task structure); and (c) the leader's position provides power to reward and punish and, thus, to obtain compliance from subordinates (position power).

Groups then can be categorized as being high or low on each of these three dimensions by dividing them at the median or, on the basis of normative scores, into those with good and poor leader-member relations, task structure, and position power. This leads to an eight-celled classification shown on the horizontal axis of Figure 1. The eight cells or "octants" are scaled from "most favorable" (octant I) to the left of the graph to "least favorable" (octant VIII) to the right. A leader obviously will have the most control and influence in groups that fall into octant I; that is, in which this leader is accepted, has high position power and a structured task. The leader will have somewhat less control and influence in octant II, where he or she is accepted and has a structured task, but little position power, and so on to groups in octant VIII where control and influence will be relatively small, because the leader is not accepted by his or her group, has a vague, unstructured task, and little position power. Situational favorableness and LPC are, of course, neither empirically nor logically related to each other.

FIGURE 1

Leader-member relations	Good	Good	Good	Good	Poor	Poor	Poor	Poor
Task structure	Structured		Unstructured		Structured		Unstructured	
Leader position power	Strong	Weak	Strong	Weak	Strong	Weak	Strong	Weak

The Personality-Situation Interaction

The basic findings of the Contingency Model are that task-motivated leaders perform generally best in very "favorable" situations; that is, either under conditions in which their power, control, and influence are very high (or, conversely, where uncertainty is very low) or where the situation is unfavorable, where they have low power, control, and influence. Relationship-motivated leaders tend to perform best in situations in which they have moderate power, control, and influence. The findings are summarized in Figure 1. The horizontal axis indicates the eight cells of the situational favorableness dimension, with the most favorable end on the left side of the graph's axis. The vertical axis indicates the *correlation coefficients* between the leader's LPC score and the group's performance. A high correlation in the positive direction, indicated by a point above the midline of the graph, shows that the relationship-motivated leaders performed better than the task-motivated leaders. A negative correlation, shown by a point which falls below the midline of the graph, indicates that the task-motivated leaders performed better than relationship-motivated leaders (i.e., the higher the LPC score, the lower the group's performance).

The solid curve connects the median correlations within each of the octants obtained in the original studies (before 1963) on which the model was based. The broken line connects the median correlations obtained in various validation studies from 1964–71.[8] As can be seen, the two curves are very similar, and the points on the curves correlate .76 (p < .01). Only in octant 2 is there a major discrepancy. However, it should be pointed out that there are very few groups in real life which have a highly structured task while the leader has low position power (e.g., in high school basketball teams and student surveying parties). Most of the validation evidence for octant II comes from laboratory studies in which this type of situation may be difficult to reproduce. However, the field study results for this octant are in the negative direction, just as the model predicts.

The most convincing validation evidence comes from a well-controlled experiment conducted by Chemers and Skrzypek at the U.S. Military Academy at West Point.[9] LPC scores as well as sociometric performance ratings to predict leader-member relations were obtained several weeks *prior* to the study, and groups then were assembled in advance, based on having the leader's LPC score and the expressed positive or negative feelings of group members about one another. The results of the Chemers and Skrzypek study are shown in the figure as a dotted line and give nearly a point-for-point replication of the original model with a correlation of .86 (p < .01). A subsequent reanalysis of the Chemers and Skrzypek data by Shiflett showed that the Contingency Model accounted for no less than 28 percent of the variance in group performance.[10] This is a very high degree of prediction, especially in a study in which variables such as the group members' intelligence, the leader's ability, the motivational factors of participants and similar effects were uncontrolled. Of course, it is inconceivable that data of this nature could be obtained by pure chance.

A different and somewhat clearer description of the Contingency Model is presented schematically in Figure 2. As before, the situational favorableness dimension is indicated on the horizontal axis, extending from the most favorable situation on the left to the relatively least favorable situation on the right. However, here the vertical axis indicates the group or organizational performance; the solid line on the graph is the schematic performance curve of relationship-motivated (high-LPC) leaders, while the dashed line indicates the performance of task-motivated (low-LPC) leaders.

These curves show, first of all, that both the relationship- and the task-motivated leaders perform well under some situations but not under others. Therefore, it is not accurate to speak of a "good" or a "poor" leader; rather, a leader may perform well in one type of situation but not in another. Outstanding directors of research teams do not necessarily make good production foremen or military leaders, and outstanding battle field command-

FIGURE 2 The Performance of Relationship- and Task-Motivated Leaders in Different Situational-Favorableness Conditions

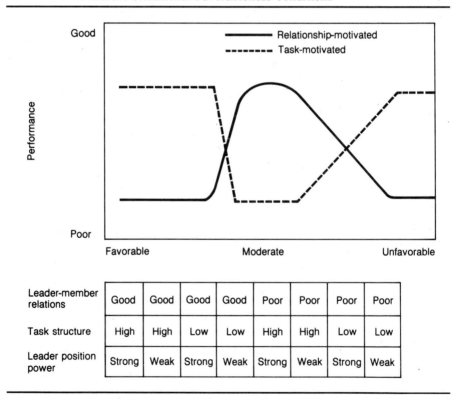

Leader-member relations	Good	Good	Good	Good	Poor	Poor	Poor	Poor
Task structure	High	High	Low	Low	High	High	Low	Low
Leader position power	Strong	Weak	Strong	Weak	Strong	Weak	Strong	Weak

ers, like General Patton, do not necessarily make good chiefs of staff or good chairmen of volunteer school picnic committees.

The second major implication of Figure 2 is that leader performance depends as much on the situation to which the organization assigns him (her) as on his or her own personality. Hence, organizational improvement can be achieved either by changing the leader's personality and motivational system—which is at best a very difficult and uncertain process—or by modifying the degree to which the situation provides the leader with power and influence. It should be obvious from the graph that certain leaders perform better with less, rather than more, power; that is, some leaders let the power "go to their heads," they become cocky and arrogant, while others need security to function well.

Extensions of the Contingency Model

Two important tests of any theory are the degree to which it allows us to understand phenomena which do not follow common-sense expectations and, second, the extent to which it predicts nonobvious findings. In both of these respects, the Contingency Model has demonstrated its usefulness. We present here several important findings from recent studies, and then discuss some implications for management.

Effects of Experience and Training.   One of the major research efforts in the area of leadership and management has been the attempt to develop training methods which will improve organizational performance. However, until now the various training programs have failed to live up to their expectations. Stogdill concluded that:

> The research on leadership training is generally inadequate in both design and execution. It has failed to address itself to the most crucial problem of leadership—. . . [the] effects of leadership on group performance and member satisfaction.[11]

The Contingency Model would predict that training should increase the performance of some leaders and also decrease the performance of others. However, it raises the question of whether any current method of training logically can result in an across-the-board increase in organizational leadership performance.[12]

As pointed out before, a group's performance depends on the leader's personality as well as the degree to which the situation provides him or her with control, power, and influence. If the leader's power and influence are increased by experience and training, the "match" between leader personality and situational favorableness would change. However, increasing the leader's power and influence is exactly the goal of most leadership training. For example, technical training increases the leader's expert power; coaching and orthodox training programs which use the case study and lecture method are designed to increase the structure of the task by providing the leader with methods for dealing with problems which, otherwise, would require him or her to think of new solutions. Human relations training is designed to develop better relations with group members, thus enabling the leader to exert more personal influence or "referent power."

For example, let us take a newly promoted supervisor of a production department in which he has not worked before. As he begins his new job, some of the tasks may seem unfamiliar and he will be unsure of his exact duties and responsibilities. He also may be uncertain of the power his position provides—how, for example, will the group react if he tries to dock an old, experienced worker who had come in late? Is this type of disciplinary measure acceptable to the group, even though it may be allowed by the union contract? He may wonder how he should handle a problem with a fellow supervisor in the plant on whom he has to depend for parts and supplies. Should he file a formal complaint or should he talk to him personally?

After several years on the job, our supervisor will have learned the ropes; he will know how far he can go in disciplining his workers, how to troubleshoot various machines, and how to deal with other managers in the organization. Thus, for the experienced supervisor, the job is structured, his position power is high, and his relations with his group are probably good. In other words, his situation is very favorable.

When he first started on the job, his leadership situation probably was only moderately favorable. If you will recall, relationship-motivated leaders tend to perform best in moderately favorable situations, while task-motivated leaders perform better in very favorable situations. Therefore, a relationship-motivated leader will perform well at first before gaining experience (e.g., by using the resources of group members and inviting their participation); a task-motivated leader will perform well after becoming experienced. In other words, the relationship-motivated leader actually should perform less well after gaining experience, while the task-motivated leader's performance should increase with greater experience.

A substantial number of studies now support this prediction.[13] A good example comes from a longitudinal study of infantry squad leaders who were assigned to newly organized units.[14] Their performance was evaluated by the same judges shortly after they joined their squads and, again, approximately five months later after their squads had passed the combat readiness test. As Figure 3 shows, the data are exactly as predicted by the Contingency Model. Similar results have been obtained in studies on the effects of training and experience of post office managers, managers of consumer cooperatives, police patrol supervisors, and leaders of various military units.

The effect of leadership training on performance also was demonstrated by a very ingenious experiment conducted at the University of Utah.[15] ROTC cadets and students were assembled *a priori* into four-man teams

FIGURE 3   Performance of High- and Low-LPC Leaders as a Function of Increased Experience and More Structured Task Assignment over Five Months

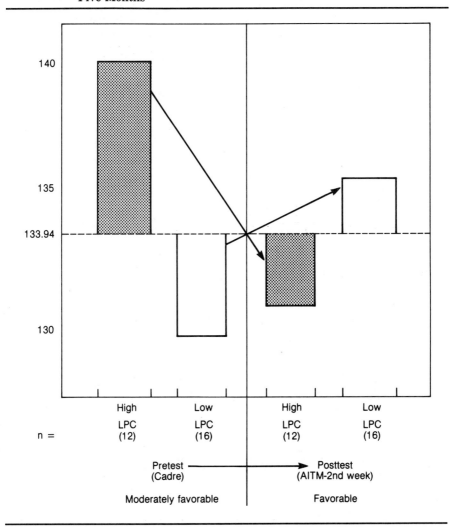

with high- and low-LPC leaders. One-half of the team leaders were given training in decoding cryptographic messages; that is, they were shown how to decode simple messages easily by first counting all the letters in the message and considering the most frequent letter an "e." A three-letter word, ending with the supposed "e" is then likely to be a "the," etc. The other half of the leaders were given no training of this type. All teams operated under a fairly high degree of tension, as indicated by subsequent ratings of the group atmosphere. Because the task is by definition unstructured, the situation was moderately favorable for the trained leaders but unfavorable for the untrained leaders. Therefore, we would expect that the relationship-motivated leaders would perform better with training, while the task-motivated leaders would perform more effectively in the unfavorable situation (i.e., without the benefit of training). As can be seen in Figure 4, the findings support the predictions of the model.

FURTHER IMPLICATIONS

Selection. It seems highly likely from these and similar findings that we need to reconsider our management selection strategies. Obviously, the old adage calling for "the right man for the right job" is not as simple as it

FIGURE 4 Interaction of Training and LPC on Group Productivity

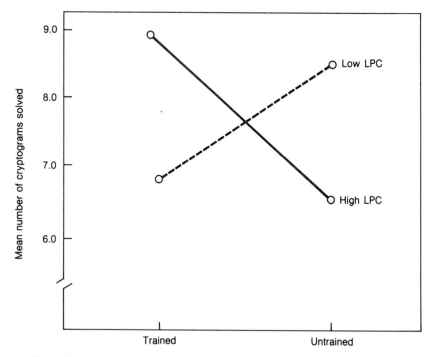

In a Harvard study, a group of underachieving 14-year-olds was given a six-week course designed to help them do better in school. Some of the boys were also given training in achievement motivation, or *n* Ach (solid lines). As the graph reveals, the only boys who continued to improve after a two-year period were the middle-class boys with the special *n* Ach training. Psychologists suspect the lower-class boys dropped back, even with *n* Ach training, because they returned to an environment in which neither parents nor friends encouraged achievement.

once appeared. The right person for a particular job today may be the wrong person in six months or in one or two years. As we have seen, the job which presents a very favorable leadership situation for the experienced leader presents a moderately favorable situation for the leader who is new and inexperienced or untrained. Hence, under these conditions a relationship-motivated leader should be chosen for the long run. The job which is moderately favorable for the experienced and trained leader is likely to represent an unfavorable leadership situation for the inexperienced leader. Hence, a task-motivated leader should be selected for the short run, and a relationship-motivated leader should be selected for the long run.

Rotation.   Figure 4 suggests that certain types of leaders will reach a "burn-out point" after they have stayed on the job for a given length of time. They will become bored, stale, disinterested, and no longer challenged. A rational rotation policy obviously must be designed to rotate these leaders at the appropriate time to new and more challenging jobs. The other types of leaders (e.g., the task-motivated leaders represented in Figure 4) should be permitted to remain on the job, so they can become maximally efficient.

Most organizations and, in particular, the military services, have a rotation system which (at least in theory) moves all officers to new jobs after a specified period of time. Such a rigid system is likely to be dysfunctional, because it does not properly allow for individual differences which determine the time required by different types of people to reach their best performance. Recent research by Bons also has shown that the behavior and performance of leaders is influenced by such other organizational changes as the transfer of a leader from one unit to a similar unit and by a reorganization which involves the reassignment of the leader's superiors.[16]

The Contingency Model clearly is a very complex formulation of the leadership problem. Whether it is more complex than is necessary, as some of its critics have claimed, or whether it is still not sufficiently complex, as others have averred, remains an open question. It is clear at this point that the theory not only predicts leadership performance in field studies and laboratory experiments but also that it serves as a very important and fruitful source of new hypotheses in the area of leadership.

NOTES AND REFERENCES

1. F. E. Fiedler, "A Contingency Model of Leadership Effectiveness," in *Advances in Experimental Social Psychology*, ed. L. Berkowitz. Academic Press, 1964. Also, *A Theory of Leadership Effectiveness* (New York: McGraw-Hill, 1967) and F. E. Fiedler and M. M. Chemers, *Leadership and Effective Management* (Glenview, Ill.: Scott, Foresman, 1974).
2. D. Nebeker, "Situational Favorability and Environmental Uncertainty: An Integrative Study," *Administrative Science Quarterly*, 1974.
3. L. K. Michaelsen, "Leader Orientation, Leader Behavior, Group Effectiveness and Situational Favorability: An Empirical Extension of the Contingency Model," *Organizational Behavior and Human Performance* 9 (1973), pp. 226–45.

4. P. M. Bons, "The Effect of Changes in Leadership Environment on the Behavior of Relationship- and Task-Motivated Leaders" (Ph.D. dissertation, University of Washington, 1974).

5. Joyce Prothero, "Personality and Situational Effects on the Job-Related Behavior of Faculty Members" (honors thesis, University of Washington, 1974).

6. F. E. Fiedler, *Leadership Effectiveness.*

7. D. Nebeker, "Situational Favorability."

8. F. E. Fiedler, "Validation and Extension of the Contingency Model of Leadership Effectiveness: A Review of Empirical Findings," *Psychological Bulletin* 76 (1971), pp. 128–48.

9. M. M. Chemers and G. J. Skrzypek, "Experimental Test of the Contingency Model of Leadership Effectiveness, *Journal of Personality and Social Psychology* 24 (1972), pp. 172–77.

10. S. C. Shiflett, "The Contingency Model of Leadership Effectiveness: Some Implications of Its Statistical and Methodological Properties," *Behavioral Science* 18 (1973), pp. 429–41.

11. R. M. Stogdill, *Handbook of Leadership: A Survey of Theory and Research* (New York: Free Press, 1974).

12. F. E. Fiedler, "The Effects of Leadership Training and Experience: A Contingency Model Interpretation," *Administrative Science Quarterly* 17 (1972), pp. 453–70.

13. Ibid.

14. F. E. Fiedler; P. M. Bons; and L. L. Hastings, "New Strategies for Leadership Utilization," in W. T. Singleton and P. Spurgeon, eds., *Defense Psychology,* NATO, Division of Scientific Affairs, 1974.

15. M. M. Chemers et al., "Leader LPC, Training and Effectiveness: An Experimental Examination," *Journal of Personality and Social Psychology,* 1974.

16. P. M. Bons, "Changes in Leadership."

B. Motivation

27

A Theory of Human Motivation

Abraham H. Maslow

A classic among classics, Maslow's article sets forth the well-known idea that all human needs may be grouped into five major categories which, in turn, are so arranged into a hierarchy of importance that the needs at one level must be minimally satisfied before higher level needs become active. This is important because, according to Maslow, only unsatisfied needs are motivators of behavior. The article includes an important discussion of the implications of the theory.—Eds.

In a previous paper (13) various propositions were presented which would have to be included in any theory of human motivation that could lay claim to being definitive. These conclusions may be briefly summarized as follows:

1. The integrated wholeness of the organism must be one of the foundation stones of motivation theory.

2. The hunger drive (or any other physiological drive) was rejected as a centering point or model for a definitive theory of motivation. Any drive that is somatically based and localizable was shown to be atypical, rather than typical, in human motivation.

3. Such a theory should stress and center itself upon ultimate or basic goals, rather than partial or superficial ones, upon ends, rather than means to these ends. Such a stress would imply a more central place for unconscious than for conscious motivations.

4. There are usually available various cultural paths to the same goal. Therefore conscious, specific, local-cultural desires are not as fundamental in motivation theory as the more basic, unconscious goals.

SOURCE: Abraham H. Maslow, "A Theory of Human Motivation," *Psychological Review* 50 (1943), pp. 370–96. Copyright 1943 by the American Psychological Association. Reprinted by permission.

5. Any motivated behavior, either preparatory or consummatory, must be understood to be a channel through which many basic needs may be simultaneously expressed or satisfied. Typically an act has *more* than one motivation.

6. Practically all organismic states are to be understood as motivated and as motivating.

7. Human needs arrange themselves in hierarchies of prepotency. That is to say, the appearance of one need usually rests on the prior satisfaction of another, more prepotent need. Man is a perpetually wanting animal. Also no need or drive can be treated as if it were isolated or discrete; every drive is related to the state of satisfaction or dissatisfaction of other drives.

8. *Lists* of drives will get us nowhere for various theoretical and practical reasons. Furthermore any classification of motivations must deal with the problem of levels of specificity or generalization of the motives to be classified.

9. Classifications of motivations must be based upon goals, rather than upon instigating drives or motivated behavior.

10. Motivation theory should be human-centered, rather than animal-centered.

11. The situation or the field in which the organism reacts must be taken into account but the field alone can rarely serve as an exclusive explanation for behavior. Furthermore, the field itself must be interpreted in terms of the organism. Field theory cannot be a substitute for motivation theory.

12. Not only the integration of the organism must be taken into account, but also the possibility of isolated, specific, partial, or segmental reactions.

It has since become necessary to add to these another affirmation.

13. Motivation theory is not synonymous with behavior theory. The motivations are only one class of determinants of behavior. While behavior is almost always motivated, it is also almost always biologically, culturally, and situationally determined as well.

The present paper is an attempt to formulate a positive theory of motivation which will satisfy these theoretical demands and at the same time conform to the known facts, clinical and observational as well as experimental. It derives most directly, however, from clinical experience. This theory is, I think, in the functionalist tradition of James and Dewey, and is fused with the holism of Wertheimer (19), Goldstein (6), and gestalt psychology, and with the dynamicism of Freud (4) and Adler (1). This fusion or synthesis may arbitrarily be called a "general-dynamic" theory.

It is far easier to perceive and to criticize the aspects in motivation theory than to remedy them. Mostly this is because of the very serious lack of sound data in this area. I conceive this lack of sound facts to be due primarily to the absence of a valid theory of motivation. The present theory then must be considered to be a suggested program or framework for future research and must stand or fall, not so much on facts available or evidence presented, as upon researches yet to be done, researches suggested perhaps by the questions raised in this paper.

THE BASIC NEEDS

The "Physiological" Needs

The needs that are usually taken as the starting point for motivation theory are the so-called physiological drives. Two recent lines of research make it necessary to revise our customary notions about these needs: first, the development of the concept of homeostasis, and second, the finding that appetites (preferential choices among foods) are a fairly efficient indication of actual needs or lacks in the body.

Homeostasis refers to the body's automatic efforts to maintain a constant, normal state of the blood stream. Cannon (2) has described this process for *(1)* the water content of the blood, *(2)* salt content, *(3)* sugar content, *(4)* protein content, *(5)* fat content, *(6)* calcium content, *(7)* oxygen content, *(8)* constant hydrogen-ion level (acid-base balance), and *(9)* constant temperature of the blood. Obviously this list can be extended to include other minerals, the hormones, vitamins, etc.

Young in a recent article (21) has summarized the work on appetite in its relation to body needs. If the body lacks some chemical, the individual will tend to develop a specific appetite or partial hunger for that food element.

Thus, it seems impossible as well as useless to make any list of fundamental physiological needs, for they can come to almost any number one might wish, depending on the degree of specificity of description. We cannot identify all physiological needs as homeostatic. That sexual desire, sleepiness, sheer activity, and maternal behavior in animals are homeostatic has not yet been demonstrated. Furthermore, this list would not include the various sensory pleasures (tastes, smells, tickling, stroking) which are probably physiological and which may become the goals of motivated behavior.

In a previous paper (13) it has been pointed out that these physiological drives or needs are to be considered unusual, rather than typical, because they are isolable, and because they are localizable somatically. That is to say, they are relatively independent of each other, of other motivations, and of the organism as a whole, and secondly, in many cases, it is possible to demonstrate a localized, underlying somatic base for the drive. This is true less generally than has been thought (exceptions are fatigue, sleepiness, maternal responses) but it is still true in the classic instances of hunger, sex, and thirst.

It should be pointed out again that any of the physiological needs and the consummatory behavior involved with them serve as channels for all sorts of other needs as well. That is to say, the person who thinks he is hungry may actually be seeking more for comfort, or dependence, than for vitamins or proteins. Conversely, it is possible to satisfy the hunger need in part by other activities, such as drinking water or smoking cigarettes. In other words, relatively isolable as these physiological needs are, they are not completely so.

Undoubtedly these physiological needs are the most prepotent of all needs. What this means specifically is that, in the human being who is missing everything in life in an extreme fashion, it is most likely that the major motivation would be the physiological needs, rather than any others. A person who is lacking food, safety, love, and esteem would most probably hunger for food more strongly than for anything else.

If all the needs are unsatisfied, and the organism is then dominated by the physiological needs, all other needs may become simply nonexistent or be pushed into the background. It is then fair to characterize the whole organism by saying simply that it is hungry, for consciousness is almost completely preempted by hunger. All capacities are put into the service of hunger-satisfaction, and the organization of these capacities is almost entirely determined by the one purpose of satisfying hunger. The receptors and effectors, the intelligence, memory, habits, all may now be defined simply as hunger-gratifying tools. Capacities that are not useful for this purpose lie dormant, or are pushed into the background. The urge to write poetry, the desire to acquire an automobile, the interest in American history, the desire for a new pair of shoes are, in the extreme case, forgotten or become of secondary importance. For the man who is extremely and dangerously hungry, no other interests exist but food. He dreams food, he remembers food, he thinks about food, he emotes only about food, he perceives only food, and he wants only food. The more subtle determinants that ordinarily fuse with the physiological drives in organizing even feeding, drinking, or sexual behavior may now be so completely overwhelmed as to allow us to speak at this time (but *only* at this time) of pure hunger drive and behavior, with the one unqualified aim of relief.

Another peculiar characteristic of the human organism when it is dominated by a certain need is that the whole philosophy of the future tends also to change. For our chronically and extremely hungry man, Utopia can be defined very simply as a place where there is plenty of food. He tends to think that, if only he is guaranteed food for the rest of his life, he will be perfectly happy and will never want anything more. Life itself tends to be defined in terms of eating. Anything else will be defined as unimportant. Freedom, love, community feeling, respect, philosophy, may all be waved aside as fripperies which are useless since they fail to fill the stomach. Such a man may fairly be said to live by bread alone.

It cannot possibly be denied that such things are true, but their *generality* can be denied. Emergency conditions are, almost by definition, rare in the normally functioning peaceful society. That this truism can be forgotten is due mainly to two reasons. First, rats have few motivations, other than physiological ones, and since so much of the research upon motivation has been made with these animals, it is easy to carry the rat picture over to the human being. Secondly, it is too often not realized that culture itself is an adaptive tool, one of whose main functions is to make the physiological emergencies come less and less often. In most of the known societies, chronic extreme hunger of the emergency type is rare, rather than common. In any case, this is still true in the United States. The average American citizen is experiencing appetite, rather than hunger, when he says "I am hungry." He is apt to experience sheer life-and-death hunger only by accident and then only a few times through his entire life.

Obviously a good way to obscure the "higher" motivations, and to get a lopsided view of human capacities and human nature, is to make the organism extremely and chronically hungry or thirsty. Anyone who attempts to make an emergency picture into a typical one, and who will measure all of man's goals and desires by his behavior during extreme physiological deprivation, is certainly being blind to many things. It is quite true that man lives by bread alone—when there is no bread. But what happens to man's desires when there *is* plenty of bread and when his belly is chronically filled?

At once other (and "higher") needs emerge and these, rather than physiological hungers, dominate the organism. And when these in turn are satisfied, again new (and still "higher") needs emerge and so on. This is what we mean by saying that the basic human needs are organized into a hierarchy of relative prepotency.

One main implication of this phrasing is that gratification becomes as important a concept as deprivation in motivation theory, for it releases the organism from the domination of a relatively more physiological need, permitting thereby the emergence of other more social goals. The physiological needs, along with their partial goals, when chronically gratified cease to exist as active determinants or organizers of behavior. They now exist only in a potential fashion in the sense that they may emerge again to dominate the organism if they are thwarted. But a want that is satisfied is no longer a want. The organism is dominated and its behavior organized only by unsatisfied needs. If hunger is satisfied, it becomes unimportant in the current dynamics of the individual.

This statement is somewhat qualified by a hypothesis to be discussed more fully later, namely that it is precisely those individuals in whom a certain need has always been satisfied who are best equipped to tolerate deprivation of that need in the future, and that, furthermore, those who have been deprived in the past will react differently to current satisfactions than the one who has never been deprived.

The Safety Needs

If the physiological needs are relatively well gratified, there then emerges a new set of needs, which we may categorize roughly as the safety needs. All that has been said of the physiological needs is equally true, although in lesser degree, of these desires. The organism may equally well be wholly dominated by them. They may serve as the almost exclusive organizers of behavior, recruiting all the capacities of the organism in their service, and we may then fairly describe the whole organism as a safety-seeking mechanism. Again we may say of the receptors, the effectors, of the intellect and the other capacities that they are primarily safety-seeking tools. Again, as in the hungry man, we find that the dominating goal is a strong determinant not only of his current world outlook and philosophy but also of his philosophy of the future. Practically everything looks less important than safety (even sometimes the physiological needs which, being satisfied, are now underestimated). A man, in this state, if it is extreme enough and chronic enough, may be characterized as living almost for safety alone.

Although in this paper we are interested primarily in the needs of the adult, we can approach an understanding of his safety needs perhaps more efficiently by observation of infants and children, in whom these needs are much more simple and obvious. One reason for the clearer appearance of the threat or danger reaction in infants is that they do not inhibit this reaction at all, whereas adults in our society have been taught to inhibit it at all costs. Thus, even when adults do feel their safety to be threatened, we may not be able to see this on the surface. Infants will react in a total fashion and as if they were endangered, if they are disturbed or dropped suddenly, startled by loud noises, flashing light, or other unusual sensory stimulation, by rough handling, by general loss of support in the mother's arms, or by inadequate support.[1]

In infants we can also see a much more direct reaction to bodily illnesses of various kinds. Sometimes these illnesses seem to be immediately and per se threatening and seem to make the child feel unsafe. For instance, vomiting, colic, or other sharp pains seem to make the child look at the whole world in a different way. At such a moment of pain, it may be postulated that, for the child, the appearance of the whole world suddenly changes from sunniness to darkness, so to speak, and becomes a place in which anything at all might happen, in which previously stable things have suddenly become unstable. Thus, a child who because of some bad food is taken ill may, for a day or two, develop fear, nightmares, and a need for protection and reassurance never seen in him before his illness.

Another indication of the child's need for safety is his preference for some kind of undisrupted routine or rhythm. He seems to want a predictable, orderly world. For instance, injustice, unfairness, or inconsistency in the parents seems to make a child feel anxious and unsafe. This attitude may be not so much because of the injustice per se or any particular pains involved, but rather because this treatment threatens to make the world look unreliable, or unsafe, or unpredictable. Young children seem to thrive better under a system which has at least a skeletal outline of rigidity, in which there is a schedule of a kind, some sort of routine, something that can be counted upon, not only for the present but also far into the future. Perhaps one could express this more accurately by saying that the child needs an organized world, rather than an unorganized or unstructured one.

The central role of the parents and the normal family setup are indisputable. Quarreling, physical assault, separation, divorce, or death within the family may be particularly terrifying. Also parental outbursts of rage or threats of punishment directed to the child, calling him names, speaking to him harshly, shaking him, handling him roughly, or actual physical punishment sometimes elicit such total panic and terror in the child that we must assume more is involved than the physical pain alone. While it is true that in some children this terror may represent also a fear of loss of parental love, it can also occur in completely rejected children, who seem to cling to the hating parents more for sheer safety and protection than because of hope of love.

Confronting the average child with new, unfamiliar, strange, unmanageable stimuli or situations will too frequently elicit the danger or terror reaction, as for example, getting lost or even being separated from the parents for a short time, being confronted with new faces, new situations or new tasks, the sight of strange, unfamiliar or uncontrollable objects, illness or death. (Particularly at such times, the child's frantic clinging to his parents is eloquent testimony to their role as protectors (quite apart from their roles as food-givers and love-givers).

From these and similar observations, we may generalize and say that the average child in our society generally prefers a safe, orderly, predictable, organized world, which he can count on, and in which unexpected, unmanageable, or other dangerous things do not happen, and in which, in any case, he has all-powerful parents who protect and shield him from harm.

That these reactions may so easily be observed in children is in a way a proof of the fact that children in our society feel too unsafe (or, in a word, are badly brought up). Children who are reared in an unthreatening, loving family do *not* ordinarily react as we have described above (17). In such children the danger reactions are apt to come mostly to objects or situations that adults, too, would consider dangerous.[2]

The healthy, normal, fortunate adult in our culture is largely satisfied in his safety needs. The peaceful, smoothly running, "good" society ordinarily makes its members feel safe enough from wild animals, extremes of temperature, criminals, assault and murder, tyranny, etc. Therefore, in a very real sense, he no longer has any safety needs as active motivators. Just as a sated man no longer feels hungry, a safe man no longer feels endangered. If we wish to see these needs directly and clearly we must turn to neurotic or near-neurotic individuals, and to the economic and social underdogs. In between these extremes, we can perceive the expressions of safety needs only in such phenomena as, for instance, the common preference for a job with tenure and protection, the desire for a savings account, and for insurance of various kinds (medical, dental, unemployment, disability, old age).

Other broader aspects of the attempt to seek safety and stability in the world are seen in the very common preference for familiar, rather than unfamiliar, things, or for the known, rather than the unknown. The tendency to have some religion or world-philosophy that organizes the universe and the men in it into some sort of satisfactorily coherent, meaningful whole is also in part motivated by safety-seeking. Here, too, we may list science and philosophy in general as partially motivated by the safety needs (we shall see later that there are also other motivations to scientific, philosophical, or religious endeavor).

Otherwise the need for safety is seen as an active and dominant mobilizer of the organism's resources only in emergencies; for example, war, disease, natural catastrophies, crime waves, societal disorganization, neurosis, brain injury, chronically bad situation.

Some neurotic adults in our society are, in many ways, like the unsafe child in their desire for safety, although in the former it takes on a somewhat special appearance. Their reaction is often to unknown, psychological dangers in a world that is perceived to be hostile, overwhelming, and threatening. Such a person behaves as if a great catastrophe were almost always impending (i.e., he is usually responding as if to an emergency). His safety needs often find specific expression in a search for a protector, or a stronger person on whom he may depend, or perhaps, a Fuehrer.

The neurotic individual may be described in a slightly different way with some usefulness as a grownup person who retains his childish attitudes toward the world. That is to say, a neurotic adult may be said to behave "as if" he were actually afraid of a spanking, or of his mother's disapproval, or of being abandoned by his parents, or having his food taken away from him. It is as if his childish attitudes of fear and threat reaction to a dangerous world had gone underground, and, untouched by the growing up and learning processes, were now ready to be called out by any stimulus that would make a child feel endangered and threatened.[3]

The neurosis in which the search for safety takes its clearest form is in the compulsive-obsessive neurosis. Compulsive-obsessives try frantically to order and stabilize the world so that no unmanageable, unexpected, or unfamiliar dangers will ever appear (14). They hedge themselves about with all sorts of ceremonials, rules, and formulas so that every possible contingency may be provided for and so that no new contingencies may appear. They are much like the brain injured cases, described by Goldstein (6), who manage to maintain their equilibrium by avoiding everything unfamiliar and strange and by ordering their restricted world in such a neat, disciplined, orderly fashion that everything in the world can be counted upon.

They try to arrange the world so that anything unexpected (dangers) cannot possibly occur. If, through no fault of their own, something unexpected does occur, they go into a panic reaction as if this unexpected occurrence constituted a grave danger. What we can see only as a none too strong preference in the healthy person (e.g., preference for the familiar) becomes a life-and-death necessity in abnormal cases.

The Love Needs

If both the physiological and the safety needs are fairly well gratified, then there will emerge the love and affection and belongingness needs, and the whole cycle already described will repeat itself with this new center. Now the person will feel keenly, as never before, the absence of friends, or a sweetheart, or a wife, or children. He will hunger for affectionate relations with people in general, namely, for a place in his group, and he will strive with great intensity to achieve this goal. He will want to attain such a place more than anything else in the world and may even forget that once, when he was hungry, he sneered at love.

In our society the thwarting of these needs is the most commonly found core in cases of maladjustment and more severe psychopathology. Love and affection, as well as their possible expression in sexuality, are generally looked upon with ambivalence and are customarily hedged about with many restrictions and inhibitions. Practically all theorists of psychopathology have stressed thwarting of the love needs as basic in the picture of maladjustment. Many clinical studies have, therefore, been made of this need and we know more about it perhaps than any of the other needs except the physiological ones (14).

One thing that must be stressed at this point is that love is not synonymous with sex. Sex may be studied as a purely physiological need. Ordinarily sexual behavior is multidetermined, that is to say, determined not only by sexual but also by other needs, chief among which are the love and affection needs. Also not to be overlooked is the fact that the love needs involve both giving *and* receiving love.[4]

The Esteem Needs

All people in our society (with a few pathological exceptions) have a need or desire for a stable, firmly based, (usually) high evaluation of themselves, for self-respect, or self-esteem, and for the esteem of others. By firmly based self-esteem, we mean that which is soundly based upon real capacity, achievement, and respect from others. These needs may be classified into two subsidiary sets. These are, first, the desire for strength, for achievement, for adequacy, for confidence in the face of the world, and for independence and freedom.[5] Secondly, we have what we may call the desire for reputation or prestige (defining it as respect or esteem from other people), recognition, attention, importance, or appreciation.[6] These needs have been relatively stressed by Alfred Adler and his followers, and have been relatively neglected by Freud and the psychoanalysts. More and more today, however, there is appearing widespread appreciation of their central importance.

Satisfaction of the self-esteem need leads to feelings of self-confidence, worth, strength, capability, and adequacy of being useful and necessary in the world. But thwarting of these needs produces feelings of inferiority, of weakness, and of helplessness. These feelings in turn give rise to either basic discouragement or else compensatory or neurotic trends. An appreciation of the necessity of basic self-confidence, and an understanding of how helpless people are without it, can be easily gained from a study of severe traumatic neurosis (8).[7]

The Need for Self-Actualization

Even if all these needs are satisfied, we may still often (if not always) expect that a new discontent and restlessness will soon develop, unless the individual is doing what he is fitted for. A musician must make music, an artist must paint, a poet must write, if he is to be ultimately happy. What a man *can* be, he *must* be. This need we may call self-actualization.

This term, first coined by Kurt Goldstein, is being used in this paper in a much more specific and limited fashion. It refers to the desire for self-fulfillment, namely, to the tendency for him (a person) to become actualized in what he is potentially. This tendency might be phrased as the desire to become more and more what one is, to become everything that one is capable of becoming.

The specific form that these needs will take will, of course, vary greatly from person to person. In one individual it may take the form of the desire to be an ideal mother, in another it may be expressed athletically, and in still another it may be expressed in painting pictures or in inventions. It is not necessarily a creative urge, although in people who have any capacities for creation it will take this form.

The clear emergence of these needs rests upon prior satisfaction of the physiological, safety, love, and esteem needs. We shall call people, who are satisfied in these needs, basically satisfied people, and it is from these that we may expect the fullest (and healthiest) creativeness.[8] Since, in our society, basically satisfied people are the exception, we do not know much about self-actualization, either experimentally or clinically. It remains a challenging problem for research.

The Preconditions for the Basic Need Satisfactions

There are certain conditions which are immediate prerequisites for the basic need satisfactions. Danger to these is reacted to almost as if it were a direct danger to the basic needs themselves. Such conditions as freedom to speak, freedom to do what one wishes so long as no harm is done to others, freedom to express one's self, freedom to investigate and seek for information, freedom to defend one's self, justice, fairness, honesty, orderliness in the group are examples of such preconditions for basic need satisfactions. Thwarting in these freedoms will be reacted to with a threat or emergency response. These conditions are not ends in themselves, but they are *almost* so since they are so closely related to the basic needs, which are apparently the only ends in themselves. These conditions are defended because without them the basic satisfactions are quite impossible, or at least, very severely endangered.

If we remember that the cognitive capacities (perceptual, intellectual, learning) are a set of adjustive tools, which have, among other functions, that of satisfaction of our basic needs, then it is clear that any danger to them, any deprivation or blocking of their free use, must also be indirectly threatening to the basic needs themselves. Such a statement is a partial solution of the general problems of curiosity, the search for knowledge, truth, and wisdom, and the ever-persistent urge to solve the cosmic mysteries.

We must, therefore, introduce another hypothesis and speak of degrees of closeness to the basic needs, for we have already pointed out that *any* conscious desires (partial goals) are more or less important as they are more or less close to the basic needs. The same statement may be made for various behavior acts. An act is psychologically important if it contributes directly to satisfaction of basic needs. The less directly it so contributes, or the weaker this contribution is, the less important this act must be conceived to be from the point of view of dynamic psychology. A similar statement may be made for the various defense or coping mechanisms. Some are very directly related to the protection or attainment of the basic needs, others are only weakly and distantly related. Indeed, if we wished, we could speak of more basic and less basic defense mechanisms, and then affirm that danger to the more basic defenses is more threatening than danger to less basic defenses (always remembering that this is so only because of their relationship to the basic needs).

The Desires to Know and to Understand

So far, we have mentioned the cognitive needs only in passing. Acquiring knowledge and systematizing the universe have been considered as, in part, techniques for the achievement of basic safety in the world, or, for the intelligent man, expressions of self-actualization. Also, freedom of inquiry and expression have been discussed as preconditions of satisfactions of the basic needs. True though these formulations may be, they do not constitute definitive answers to the question as to the motivation role of curiosity, learning, philosophizing, experimenting, etc. They are, at best, no more than partial answers.

This question is especially difficult because we know so little about the facts. Curiosity, exploration, desire for the facts, desire to know may certainly be observed easily enough. The fact that they often are pursued even at great cost to the individual's safety is an earnest of the partial character of our previous discussion. In addition, the writer must admit that, though he has sufficient clinical evidence to postulate the desire to know as a very strong drive in intelligent people, no data are available for unintelligent people. It may then be largely a function of relatively high intelligence. Rather tentatively, then, and largely in the hope of stimulating discussion and research, we shall postulate a basic desire to know, to be aware of reality, to get the facts, to satisfy curiosity, or, as Wertheimer phrases it, to see, rather than to be blind.

This postulation, however, is not enough. Even after we know, we are impelled to know more and more minutely and microscopically on the one hand, and on the other, more and more extensively in the direction of a world philosophy, religion, etc. The facts that we acquire, if they are isolated or atomistic, inevitably get theorized about, and either analyzed or organized, or both. This process has been phrased by some as the search for "meaning." We shall then postulate a desire to understand, to systematize, to organize, to analyze, to look for relations and meanings.

Once these desires are accepted for discussion, we see that they, too, form themselves into a small hierarchy in which the desire to know is prepotent over the desire to understand. All the characteristics of a hierarchy of prepotency, that we have described above, seem to hold for this one as well.

We must guard ourselves against the too easy tendency to separate these desires from the basic needs we have discussed above (i.e., to make a sharp dichotomy between "cognitive" and "conative" needs). The desires to know and to understand are themselves conative (i.e., have a striving character) and are as much personality needs as the "basic needs" we have already discussed (19).

FURTHER CHARACTERISTICS OF THE BASIC NEEDS

The Degree of Fixity of the Hierarchy of Basic Needs

We have spoken so far as if this hierarchy were a fixed order, but actually it is not nearly as rigid as we may have implied. It is true that most of the people with whom we have worked have seemed to have these basic needs in about the order that has been indicated. However, there have been a number of exceptions.

1. There are some people in whom, for instance, self-esteem seems to be more important than love. This most common reversal in the hierarchy is usually due to the development of the notion that the person who is most likely to be loved is a strong or powerful person, one

who inspires respect or fear, and who is self-confident or aggressive. Therefore, such people who lack love and seek it may try hard to put on a front of aggressive, confident behavior. But essentially they seek high self-esteem and its behavior expressions more as a means to an end than for its own sake; they seek self-assertion for the sake of love, rather than for self-esteem itself.

2. There are other, apparently innately creative people in whom the drive to creativeness seems to be more important than any other counter-determinant. Their creativeness might appear not as self-actualization released by basic satisfaction, but in spite of lack of basic satisfaction.

3. In certain people the level of aspiration may be permanently deadened or lowered. That is to say, the less prepotent goals may simply be lost, and may disappear forever, so that the person who has experienced life at a very low level (i.e., chronic unemployment) may continue to be satisfied for the rest of his life if only he can get enough food.

4. The so-called psychopathic personality is another example of permanent loss of the love needs. These are people who, according to the best data available (9), have been starved for love in the earliest months of their lives and have simply lost forever the desire and the ability to give and to receive affection (as animals lose sucking or pecking reflexes that are not exercised soon enough after birth).

5. Another cause of reversal of the hierarchy is that, when a need has been satisfied for a long time, this need may be underevaluated. People who have never experienced chronic hunger are apt to underestimate its effects and to look upon food as a rather unimportant thing. If they are dominated by a higher need, this higher need will seem to be the most important of all. It then becomes possible, and indeed does actually happen, that they may, for the sake of this higher need, put themselves into the position of being deprived in a more basic need. We may expect that after a long-time deprivation of the more basic need there will be a tendency to reevaluate both needs so that the more prepotent need will actually become consciously prepotent for the individual who may have given it up very lightly. Thus, a man who has given up his job, rather than lose his self-respect, and who then starves for six months or so, may be willing to take his job back even at the price of losing his self-respect.

6. Another partial explanation of *apparent* reversals is seen in the fact that we have been talking about the hierarchy of prepotency in terms of consciously felt wants or desires, rather than of behavior. Looking at behavior itself may give us the wrong impression. What we have claimed is that the person will *want* the more basic of two needs when deprived in both. There is no necessary implication here that he will act

upon his desires. Let us say again that there are many determinants of behavior other than the needs and desires.

7. Perhaps more important than all these exceptions are the ones that involve ideals, high social standards, high values, and the like. With such values people become martyrs; they will give up everything for the sake of a particular ideal, or value. These people may be understood, at least in part, by reference to one basic concept (or hypothesis) which may be called "increased frustration-tolerance through early gratification." People who have been satisfied in their basic needs throughout their lives, particularly in their earlier years, seem to develop exceptional power to withstand present or future thwarting of these needs simply because they have strong, healthy character structure as a result of basic satisfaction. They are the "strong" people who can easily weather disagreement or opposition, who can swim against the stream of public opinion, and who can stand up for the truth at great personal cost. It is just the ones who have loved and been well loved, and who have had many deep friendships, who can hold out against hatred, rejection, or persecution.

I say all this in spite of the fact that there is a certain amount of sheer habituation which is also involved in any full discussion of frustration tolerance. For instance, it is likely that those persons who have been accustomed to relative starvation for a long time are partially enabled thereby to withstand food deprivation. What sort of balance must be made between these two tendencies, of habituation on the one hand, and of past satisfaction breeding present frustration tolerance on the other hand, remains to be worked out by further research. Meanwhile we may assume that they are both operative, side by side, since they do not contradict each other. In respect to this phenomenon of increased frustration tolerance, it seems probable that the most important gratifications come in the first two years of life. That is to say, people who have been made secure and strong in the earliest years, tend to remain secure and strong thereafter in the face of whatever threatens.

Degrees of Relative Satisfaction

So far, our theoretical discussion may have given the impression that these five sets of needs are somehow in a stepwise, all-or-none relationship to each other. We have spoken in such terms as the following: "If one need is satisfied, then another emerges." This statement might give the false impression that a need must be satisfied 100 percent before the next need emerges. In actual fact, most members of our society who are normal are partially satisfied in all their basic needs and partially unsatisfied in all their basic needs at the same time. A more realistic description of the hierarchy would be in terms of decreasing percentages of satisfaction as we go up the hierarchy of prepotency. For instance, if I may assign arbitrary figures for the sake of illustration, it is as if the average citizen is satisfied perhaps 85 percent in his physiological needs, 70 percent in his safety needs, 50 percent in his love needs, 40 percent in his self-esteem needs, and 10 percent in his self-actualization needs.

As for the concept of emergence of a new need after satisfaction of the prepotent need, this emergence is not a sudden, saltatory phenomenon but, rather, a gradual emergence by slow degrees from nothingness. For instance, if prepotent need A is satisfied only 10 percent, then need B may not be visible at all. However, as this need A becomes satisfied 25 percent, need B may emerge 5 percent; as need A becomes satisfied 75 percent, need B may emerge 90 percent, and so on.

Unconscious Character of Needs

These needs are neither necessarily conscious nor unconscious. On the whole, however, in the average person, they are more often unconscious, rather than conscious. It is not necessary at this point to overhaul the tremendous mass of evidence which indicates the crucial importance of unconscious motivation. It would by now be expected, on a priori grounds alone, that unconscious motivations would on the whole be rather more important than the conscious motivations. What we have called the basic needs are very often largely unconscious, although they may, with suitable techniques and with sophisticated people, become conscious.

Cultural Specificity and Generality of Needs

This classification of basic needs makes some attempt to take account of the relative unity behind the superficial differences in specific desires from one culture to another. Certainly in any particular culture an individual's conscious motivational content will usually be extremely different from the conscious motivational content of an individual in another society. However, it is the common experience of anthropologists that people, even in different societies, are much more alike than we would think from our first contact with them, and that as we know them better we seem to find more and more of this commonness. We then recognize the most startling differences to be superficial, rather than basic (e.g., differences in style of hairdress, clothes, tastes in food, etc.). Our classification of basic needs is in part an attempt to account for this unity behind the apparent diversity from culture to culture. No claim is made that it is ultimate or universal for all cultures. The claim is made only that it is relatively *more* ultimate, more universal, more basic, than the superficial conscious desires from culture to culture, and makes a somewhat closer approach to common human characteristics. Basic needs are *more* common-human than superficial desires or behaviors.

Multiple Motivations of Behavior

These needs must be understood *not* to be *exclusive* or single determiners of certain kinds of behavior. An example may be found in any behavior that seems to be physiologically motivated, such as eating, or sexual play or the like. The clinical psychologists have long since found that any behavior may be a channel through which flow various determinants. Or to say it in another way, most behavior is multimotivated. Within the sphere of motivational determinants, any behavior tends to be determined by several or *all* of the basic needs simultaneously, rather than by only one of them. The latter would be more an exception than the former. Eating may be partially for the sake of filling the stomach, and partially for the sake of comfort and amelioration of other needs. One may make love not only for pure sexual release but also to convince one's self of one's masculinity, or to make a conquest, to feel powerful, or to win more basic affection. As an illustration, I may point out that it would be possible (theoretically, if not practically) to analyze a single act of an individual and see in it the expression of his physiological needs, his safety needs, his love needs, his esteem needs, and self-actualization. This contrasts sharply with the more naive brand of trait psychology in which one trait or one motive accounts for a certain kind of act (i.e., an aggressive act is traced solely to a trait of aggressiveness).

Multiple Determinants of Behavior

Not all behavior is determined by the basic needs. We might even say that not all behavior is motivated. There are many determinants of behavior, other than motives.[9] For instance, one other important class of determinants is the so-called field determinants. Theoretically, at least, behavior may be determined completely by the field, or even by specific isolated external stimuli, as in association of ideas, or certain conditioned reflexes. If in response to the stimulus word "table," I immediately perceive a memory image of a table, this response certainly has nothing to do with my basic needs.

Secondly, we may call attention again to the concept of "degree of closeness to the basic needs" or "degree of motivation." Some behavior is highly motivated, other behavior is only weakly motivated. Some is not motivated at all (but all behavior is determined).

Another important point[10] is that there is a basic difference between expressive behavior and coping behavior (functional striving, purposive goal seeking). An expressive behavior does not try to do anything; it is simply a reflection of the personality. A stupid man behaves stupidly, not because he wants to, or tries to, or is motivated to, but simply because he *is* what he is. The same is true when I speak in a bass voice, rather than tenor or soprano. The random movements of a healthy child, the smile on the face of a happy man even when he is alone, the springiness of the healthy man's walk, and the erectness of his carriage are other examples of expressive, nonfunctional behavior. Also the *style* in which a man carries out almost all his behavior, motivated as well as unmotivated, is often expressive.

We may then ask, is *all* behavior expressive or reflective of the character structure? The answer is no. Rote, habitual, automatized, or conventional behavior may or may not be expressive. The same is true for most "stimulus-bound" behaviors.

It is finally necessary to stress that expressiveness of behavior, and goal-directedness of behavior are not mutually exclusive categories. Average behavior is usually both.

Goals as Centering Principle in Motivation Theory

It will be observed that the basic principle in our classification has been neither the instigation nor the motivated behavior but, rather, the functions, effects, purposes, or goals of the behavior. It has been proven sufficiently by various people that this is the most suitable point for centering in any motivation theory.[11]

Animal- and Human-Centering

This theory starts with the human being, rather than any lower and presumably "simpler" animal. Too many of the findings that have been made in animals have been proven to be true for animals but not for the human being. There is no reason whatsoever why we should start with animals in order to study human motivation. The logic or rather illogic behind this general fallacy of "pseudosimplicity" has been exposed often enough by philosophers and logicians as well as by scientists in each of the various fields. It is no more necessary to study animals before one can study man than it is to study mathematics before one can study geology or psychology or biology.

We may also reject the old, naive behaviorism which assumed that it was somehow necessary, or at least more "scientific," to judge human beings by animal standards. One consequence of this belief was that the whole notion of purpose and goal was excluded from motivational psychology simply because one could not ask a white rat about his purposes. Tolman (18) has long since proven in animal studies themselves that this exclusion was not necessary.

Motivation and the Theory of Psychopathogenesis

The conscious motivational content of everyday life has, according to the foregoing, been conceived to be relatively important or unimportant accordingly as it is more or less closely related to the basic goals. A desire for an ice cream cone might actually be an indirect expression of a desire for love. If it is, then this desire for the ice cream cone becomes extremely important motivation. If however the ice cream is simply something to cool the mouth with, or a casual appetitive reaction, then the desire is relatively unimportant. Everyday conscious desires are to be regarded as symptoms, as surface indicators of more basic needs. If we were to take these superficial desires at their face value we would find ourselves in a state of complete confusion which could never be resolved, since we would be dealing seriously with symptoms, rather than with what lay behind the symptoms.

Thwarting of unimportant desires produces no psychopathological results; thwarting of a basically important need does produce such results. Any theory of psychopathogenesis must then be based on a sound theory of motivation. A conflict or a frustration is not necessarily pathogenic. It becomes so only when it threatens or thwarts the basic needs, or partial needs that are closely related to the basic needs (10).

The Role of Gratified Needs

It has been pointed out above several times that our needs usually emerge only when more prepotent needs have been gratified. Thus, gratification has an important role in motivation theory. Apart from this, however, needs cease to play an active determining or organizing role as soon as they are gratified.

What this means is that, for example, a basically satisfied person no longer has the needs for esteem, love, safety, etc. The only sense in which he might be said to have them is in the almost metaphysical sense that a sated man has hunger, or a filled bottle has emptiness. If we are interested in what *actually* motivates us, and not in what has, will, or might motivate us, then a satisfied need is not a motivator. It must be considered for all practical purposes simply not to exist, to have disappeared. This point should be emphasized, because it has been either overlooked or contradicted in every theory of motivation I know.[12] The perfectly healthy, normal, fortunate man has no sex needs or hunger needs, or needs for safety, or for love, or for prestige, or self-esteem, except in stray moments of quickly passing threat. If we were to say otherwise, we should also have to aver that every man had all the pathological reflexes (e.g., Babinski, etc.), because, if his nervous system were damaged, these would appear.

It is such considerations as these that suggest the bold postulation that a man who is thwarted in any of his basic needs may fairly be envisaged simply as a sick man. This is a fair parallel to our designation as "sick" of the man who lacks vitamins or minerals. Who is to say that a lack of love is less important than a lack of vitamins? Since we know the pathogenic effects of love starvation, who is to say that we are invoking value-questions in an unscientific or illegitimate way, any more than the physician does who diagnoses and treats pellagra or scurvy? If I were permitted this usage, I should then say simply that a healthy man is primarily motivated by his needs to develop and actualize his fullest potentialities and capacities. If a man has any other basic needs in any active, chronic sense, then he is simply an unhealthy man. He is as surely sick as if he had suddenly developed a strong salt hunger or calcium hunger.[13]

If this statement seems unusual or paradoxical, the reader may be assured that this is only one among many such paradoxes that will appear as we revise our ways of looking at man's deeper motivations. When we ask what man wants of life, we deal with his very essence.

SUMMARY

1. There are at least five sets of goals, which we may call basic needs. These are, briefly, physiological, safety, love, esteem, and self-actualization. In addition, we are motivated by the desire to achieve or maintain the various conditions upon which these basic satisfactions rest and by certain more intellectual desires.

2. These basic goals are related to each other, being arranged in a hierarchy of prepotency. This means that the most prepotent goal will monopolize consciousness and will tend of itself to organize the recruitment of the various capacities of the organism. The less prepotent needs are minimized, even forgotten or denied. But when a need is fairly well satisfied, the next prepotent ("higher") need emerges, in turn to dominate the conscious life and to serve as the center of organization of behavior, since gratified needs are not active motivators.

Thus, man is a perpetually wanting animal. Ordinarily, the satisfaction of these wants is not altogether mutually exclusive, but only tends to be. The average member of our society is most often partially satisfied and partially unsatisfied in all of his wants. The hierarchy principle is usually empirically observed in terms of increasing percentages of nonsatisfaction as we go up the hierarchy. Reversals of the average order of the hierarchy are sometimes observed. Also, it has been observed that an individual may permanently lose the higher wants in the hierarchy under special conditions. There are not only ordinarily multiple motivations for usual behavior, but, in addition, many determinants, other than motives.

3. Any thwarting or possibility of thwarting of these basic human goals, or danger to the defenses which protect them, or to the conditions upon which they rest, is considered to be a psychological threat. With a few exceptions, all psychopathology may be partially traced to such threats. A basically thwarted man may actually be defined as a "sick" man, if we wish.

4. It is such basic threats which bring about the general emergency reactions.

5. Certain other basic problems have not been dealt with because of limitations of space. Among these are *(a)* the problem of values in any definitive motivation theory; *(b)* the relation between appetites, desires, needs and what is "good" for the organism; *(c)* the etiology of the basic needs and their possible derivation in early childhood; *(d)* redefinition of motivational concepts (i.e., drive, desire, wish, need, goal); *(e)* implication of our theory for hedonistic theory; *(f)* the nature of the uncompleted act, of success and failure, and of aspiration level; *(g)* the role of association, habit, and conditioning; *(h)* relation to the theory of interpersonal relations; *(i)* implications for psychotherapy; *(j)* implication for theory of society; *(k)* the theory of selfishness; *(l)* the relation between needs and cultural patterns; *(m)* the relation between this theory and Allport's theory of functional autonomy. These as well as certain other less important questions must be considered, as motivation theory attempts to become definitive.

NOTES

1. As the child grows up, sheer knowledge and familiarity as well as better motor development make these "dangers" less and less dangerous and more and more manageable. Throughout life it may be said that one of the main conative functions of education is this neutralizing of apparent dangers through knowledge (e.g., I am not afraid of thunder because I know something about it).
2. A "test battery" for safety might be confronting the child with a small exploding firecracker, or with a bewhiskered face, having the mother leave the room, putting him upon a high ladder, a hypodermic injection, having a mouse crawl up to him, etc. Of course I cannot seriously recommend the deliberate use of such "tests" for they might very well harm the child being tested. But these and similar situations come up by the score in the child's ordinary day-to-day living and may be observed. There is no reason why these stimuli should not be used with, for example, young chimpanzees.
3. Not all neurotic individuals feel unsafe. Neurosis may have at its core a thwarting of the affection and esteem needs in a person who is generally safe.
4. For further details see (12) and (16, Ch. 5).
5. Whether or not this particular desire is universal we do not know. The crucial question, especially important today, is, "Will men who are enslaved and dominated inevitably feel dissatisfied and rebellious?" We may assume on the basis of commonly known clinical data that a man who has known true freedom (not paid for by giving up safety and security but, rather, built on the basis of adequate safety and security) will not willingly or easily allow his freedom to be taken away from him. But we do not know that this is true for the person born into slavery. The events of the next decade should give us our answer. See discussion of this problem in (5).
6. Perhaps the desire for prestige and respect from others is subsidiary to the desire for self-esteem or confidence in oneself. Observation of children seems to indicate that this is so, but clinical data give no clear support for such a conclusion.
7. For more extensive discussion of normal self-esteem, as well as for reports of various researches, see (11).

8. Clearly creative behavior, like painting, is like any other behavior in having multiple determinants. It may be seen in "innately creative" people whether they are satisfied or not, happy or unhappy, hungry or sated. Also, it is clear that creative activity may be compensatory, ameliorative, or purely economic. It is my impression (as yet unconfirmed) that it is possible to distinguish the artistic and intellectual products of basically satisfied people from those of basically unsatisfied people by inspection alone. In any case, here, too, we must distinguish, in a dynamic fashion, the overt behavior itself from its various motivations or purposes.

9. I am aware that many psychologists and psychoanalysts use the term *motivated* and *determined* synonymously (e.g., Freud). But I consider this an obfuscating usage. Sharp distinctions are necessary for clarity of thought, and precision in experimentation.

10. Discussed fully in a subsequent publication.

11. The interested reader is referred to the very excellent discussion of this point in Murray's *Explorations in Personality* (15).

12. Note that acceptance of this theory necessitates basic revision of the Freudian theory.

13. If we were to use the word "sick" in this way, we should then also have to face squarely the relations of man to his society. One clear implication of our definition would be that *(1)* since a man is to be called sick who is basically thwarted, and *(2)* since such basic thwarting is made possible ultimately only by forces outside the individual, then *(3)* sickness in the individual must come ultimately from a sickness in the society. The "good" or healthy society would then be defined as one that permitted man's highest purposes to emerge by satisfying all his prepotent basic needs.

REFERENCES

1. Adler, A. *Social Interest*. London: Faber & Faber, 1938.
2. Cannon, W. B. *Wisdom of the Body*. New York: W. W. Norton, 1932.
3. Freud, A. *The Ego and the Mechanisms of Defense*. London: Hogarth, 1937.
4. Freud, S. *New Introductory Lectures on Psychoanalysis* (New York: W. W. Norton, 1933).
5. Fromm, E. *Escape from Freedom*. New York: Farrar and Rinehart, 1941.
6. Goldstein, K. *The Organism*. New York: American Book, 1939.
7. Horney, K. *The Neurotic Personality of Our Time*. New York: W. W. Norton, 1937.
8. Kardiner, A. *The Traumatic Neuroses of War*. New York: Hoeber, 1941.
9. Levy, D. M. "Primary Affect Hunger." *American Journal of Psychiatry* 94 (1937), pp. 643–52.
10. Maslow, A. H. "Conflict, Frustration, and the Theory of Threat." *Journal of Abnormal (Social) Psychology* 38 (1943), pp. 81–86.
11. _____ . "Dominance, Personality and Social Behavior in Women." *Journal of Social Psychology* 10 (1939), pp. 3–39.
12. _____ . "The Dynamics of Psychological Security-Insecurity." *Character and Personality* 10 (1942), pp. 331–44.
13. _____ . "A Preface to Motivation Theory." *Psychosomatic Medicine* 5 (1943), pp. 85–92.

14. Maslow, A. H. and B. Mittelmann. *Principles of Abnormal Psychology.* New York: Harper & Row, 1941.
15. Murray, H. A. et al. *Explorations in Personality.* New York: Oxford University Press, 1938.
16. Plant, J. *Personality and the Cultural Pattern.* New York: Commonwealth Fund, 1937.
17. Shirley, M. "Children's Adjustments to a Strange Situation." *Journal of Abnormal (Social) Psychology* 37 (1942), pp. 201–17.
18. Tolman, E. C. *Purposive Behavior in Animals and Men.* New York: Century, 1932.
19. Wertheimer, M. Unpublished lectures at the New School for Social Research.
20. Young, P. T. *Motivation of Behavior.* New York: John Wiley & Sons, 1936.
21. _____ . "The Experimental Analysis of Appetite." *Psychology Bulletin* 38 (1941), pp. 129–64.

28

That Urge to Achieve

David C. McClelland

Foremost among the factors that serve to spur individuals to greater and greater efforts is thought by many to be the need to achieve. In this article, McClelland, who has devoted his professional life to understanding this need, describes what achievement motivation is, how it is measured, and, most importantly, how it can be taught. McClelland argues that the urge to achieve is an essential ingredient in business success for individuals as well as for nations.—Eds.

Most people in this world, psychologically, can be divided into two broad groups. There is that minority which is challenged by opportunity and willing to work hard to achieve something, and the majority which really does not care all that much.

For nearly 20 years now, psychologists have tried to penetrate the mystery of this curious dichotomy. Is the need to achieve (or the absence of it) an accident, is it hereditary, or is it the result of environment? Is it a single, isolatable human motive, or a combination of motives—the desire to accumulate wealth, power, fame? Most important of all, is there some technique that could give this will to achieve to people, even whole societies, who do not now have it?

While we do not yet have complete answers for any of these questions, years of work have given us partial answers to most of them and insights into all of them. There is a distinct human motive, distinguishable from others. It can be found, in fact tested for, in any group.

Let me give you one example. Several years ago, a careful study was made of 450 workers who had been thrown out of work by a plant shutdown in Erie, Pennsylvania. Most of the unemployed workers stayed home for a while and then checked back with the United States Employment Service to see if their old jobs or similar ones were available. But a small minority

SOURCE: From *THINK Magazine* 32, no. 6 (November–December 1966), pp. 19–23. Reprinted by permission from *THINK Magazine,* published by IBM, copyright 1966 by International Business Machines Corporation.

among them behaved differently; the day they were laid off, they started job-hunting.

They checked both the United States and the Pennsylvania Employment Offices; they studied the "Help Wanted" sections of the papers; they checked through their union, their church, and various fraternal organizations; they looked into training courses to learn a new skill; they even left town to look for work, while the majority when questioned said they would not under any circumstances move away from Erie to obtain a job. Obviously, the members of that active minority were differently motivated. All the men were more or less in the same situation objectively: they needed work, money, food, shelter, job security. Yet only a minority showed initiative and enterprise in finding what they needed. Why? Psychologists, after years of research, now believe they can answer that question. They have demonstrated that these men possessed in greater degree a specific type of human motivation. For the moment let us refer to this personality characteristic as "Motive A" and review some of the other characteristics of the men who have more of the motive than other men.

Suppose they are confronted by a work situation in which they can set their own goals on how difficult a task they will undertake. In the psychological laboratory, such a situation is very simply created by asking them to throw rings over a peg from any distance they may choose. Most men throw more or less randomly, standing now close, now far away; but those with Motive A seem to calculate carefully where they are most likely to get a sense of mastery. They stand nearly always at moderate distances, not so close to make the task ridiculously easy, nor so far away to make it impossible. They set moderately difficult, but potentially achievable goals for themselves, where they objectively have only about a 1-in-3 chance of succeeding. In other words, they are always setting challenges for themselves, tasks to make them stretch themselves a little.

But they behave like this only if *they* can influence the outcome by performing the work themselves. They prefer not to gamble at all. Say they are given a choice between rolling dice with one-in-three chances of winning and working on a problem with a one-in-three chance of solving in the time allotted, they choose to work on the problem even though rolling the dice is obviously less work and the odds of winning are the same. They prefer to work at a problem, rather than leave the outcome to chance or to others.

Obviously, they are concerned with personal achievement, rather than with the rewards of success *per se,* since they stand just as much chance of getting those rewards as by throwing the dice. This leads to another characteristic the Motive A men show—namely, a strong preference for work situations in which they get concrete feedback on how well they are doing, as one does, say, in playing golf, or in being a salesman, but as one does not in teaching, or in personnel counseling. A golfer always knows his score and can compare how well he is doing with par or with his own performance yesterday or last week. A teacher has no such concrete feedback on how well he is doing in "getting across" to his students.

THE *n* Ach MEN

But why do certain men behave like this? At one level the reply is simple: because they habitually spend their time thinking about doing things better. In fact, psychologists typically measure the strength of Motive A by taking samples of a man's spontaneous thoughts (such as making up a story about a picture they have been shown) and counting the frequency with which he mentions doing things better. The count is objective and can even be made these days with the help of a computer program for content analysis. It yields what is referred to technically as an individual's *n* Ach score (for "need for Achievement"). It is not difficult to understand why people who think constantly about "doing better" are more apt to do better at job hunting, to set moderate, achievable goals for themselves, to dislike gambling (because they get no achievement satisfaction from success) and to prefer work situations where they can tell easily whether they are improving or not. But why some people and not others come to think this way is another question. The evidence suggests it is not because they are born that way, but because of special training they get in the home from parents who set moderately high achievement goals but who are warm, encouraging, and nonauthoritarian in helping their children reach these goals.

Such detailed knowledge about one motive helps correct a lot of common-sense ideas about human motivation. For example, much public policy (and much business policy) is based on the simpleminded notion that people will work harder "if they have to." As a first approximation, the idea isn't totally wrong, but it is only a half-truth. The majority of unemployed workers in Erie "had to" find work as much as those with higher *n* Ach, but they certainly didn't work as hard at it. Or again, it is frequently assumed that *any* strong motive will lead to doing things better. Wouldn't it be fair to say that most of the Erie workers were just "unmotivated"? But our detailed knowledge of various human motives shows that each one leads a person to behave in *different* ways. The contrast is not between being "motivated" or "unmotivated" but between being motivated toward A or B or C, etc.

A simple experiment makes the point nicely: Subjects were told that they could choose as a working partner either a close friend or a stranger who was known to be an expert on the problem to be solved. Those with higher *n* Ach (more "need to achieve") chose the experts over their friends, whereas those with more *n* Aff (the "need to affiliate with others") chose friends over experts. The latter were not "unmotivated"; their desire to be with someone they liked was simply a stronger motive than their desire to excel at the task. Other such needs have been studied by psychologists. For instance, the need for Power is often confused with the need for Achievement, because both may lead to "outstanding" activities. There is a distinct difference. People with a strong need for Power want to command attention, get recognition, and control others. They are more active in political life and tend to busy themselves primarily with controlling the channels of communication both up to the top and down to the people so they are more "in charge." Those with high n Power are not as concerned with improving their work performance daily as those with high n Ach.

It follows, from what we have been able to learn, that not all "great achievers" score high n Ach. Many generals, outstanding politicians, great research scientists do not, for instance, because their work requires other personality characteristics, other motives. A general or a politician must be more concerned with power relationships, a research scientist must be able to go for long periods without the immediate feedback the person with high n Ach requires, etc. On the other hand, business executives, particularly if they are in positions of real responsibility or if they are salesmen, tend to score high in n Ach. This is true even in a Communist country like Poland: apparently there, as well as in a private enterprise economy, a manager succeeds if he is concerned about improving all the time, setting moderate goals, keeping track of his or the company's performance, etc.

MOTIVATION AND HALF-TRUTHS

Since careful study has shown that common sense notions about motivation are at best half-truths, it also follows that you cannot trust what people tell you about their motives. After all, they often get their own motives from common sense. Thus a general may say he is interested in achievement (because he has obviously achieved), or a businessman that he is interested only in making money (because he has made money), or one of the majority of unemployed in Erie that he desperately wants a job (because he knows he needs one); but a careful check of what each one thinks about and how he spends his time may show that each is concerned about quite different things. It requires special measurement techniques to identify the presence of n Ach and other such motives. Thus, what people say and believe is not very closely related to these "hidden" motives which seem to affect a person's "style of life" more than his political, religious or social attitudes. Thus, n Ach produces enterprising men among labor leaders or managers, Republicans or Democrats, Catholics or Protestants, capitalists or communists.

Wherever people begin to think often in n Ach terms things begin to move. Men with higher n Ach get more raises and are promoted more rapidly, because they keep actively seeking ways to do a better job. Companies with many such men grow faster. In one comparison of two firms in Mexico, it was discovered that all but one of the top executives of a fast-growing firm had higher n Ach scores than the highest-scoring executive in an equally large but slow-growing firm. Countries with many such rapidly growing firms tend to show above-average rates of economic growth. This appears to be the reason why correlations have regularly been found between the n Ach content in popular literature (such as popular songs or stories in children's textbooks) and subsequent rates of national economic growth. A nation which is thinking about doing better all the time (as shown in its popular literature) actually does do better economically speaking. Careful quantitative studies have shown this to be true in Ancient Greece, in Spain in the Middle Ages, in England from 1400–1800, as well as among contemporary nations, whether capitalist or communist, developed or underdeveloped.

Contrast these two stories for example. Which one contains more *n* Ach? Which one reflects a state of mind which ought to lead to harder striving to improve the way things are?

Excerpt from story A (4th grade reader): "Don't Ever Owe a Man—The world is an illusion. Wife, children, horses, and cows are all just ties of fate. They are ephemeral. Each after fulfilling his part in life disappears. So we should not clamour after riches which are not permanent. As long as we live it is wise not to have any attachments and just think of God. We have to spend our lives without trouble, for is it not time that there is an end to grievances? So it is better to live knowing the real state of affairs. Don't get entangled in the meshes of family life."

Excerpt from story B (4th grade reader): "How I Do Like to Learn—I was sent to an accelerated technical high school. I was so happy I cried. Learning is not very easy. In the beginning I couldn't understand what the teacher taught us. I always got a red cross mark on my papers. The boy sitting next to me was very enthusiastic and also an outstanding student. When he found I couldn't do the problems he offered to show me how he had done them. I could not copy his work. I must learn through my own reasoning. I gave his paper back and explained I had to do it myself. Sometimes I worked on a problem until midnight. If I couldn't finish, I started early in the morning. The red cross marks on my work were getting less common. I conquered my difficulties. My marks rose. I graduated and went on to college."

Most readers would agree without any special knowledge of the *n* Ach coding system, that the second story shows more concern with improvement than the first, which comes from a contemporary reader used in Indian public schools. In fact the latter has a certain Horatio Alger quality that is reminiscent of our own McGuffey readers of several generations ago. It appears today in the textbooks of Communist China. It should not, therefore, come as a surprise if a nation like Communist China, obsessed as it is with improvement, tended in the long run to outproduce a nation like India, which appears to be more fatalistic.

The *n* Ach level is obviously important for statesmen to watch and in many instances to try to do something about, particularly if a nation's economy is lagging. Take Britain, for example. A generation ago (around 1925) it ranked fifth among 25 countries where children's readers were scored for *n* Ach—and its economy was doing well. By 1950, the *n* Ach level had dropped to 27th out of 39 countries—well below the world average—and today, its leaders are feeling the severe economic effects of this loss in the spirit of enterprise.

ECONOMICS AND *n* Ach

If psychologists can detect *n* Ach levels in individuals or nations, particularly before their effects are widespread, can't the knowledge somehow be put to use to foster economic development? Obviously, detection or diagnosis is not enough. What good is it to tell Britain (or India for that matter) that it needs more *n* Ach, a greater spirit of enterprise? In most such cases, informed observers of the local scene know very well that such a need exists, though they may be slower to discover it than the psychologist hovering over *n* Ach in individuals or nations.

Since about 1960, psychologists in my research group at Harvard have been experimenting with techniques designed to accomplish this goal, chiefly among business executives whose work requires the action characteristics of people with high *n* Ach. Initially, we had real doubts about whether we could succeed, partly because like most American psychologists we had been strongly influenced by the psychoanalytic view that basic motives are laid down in childhood and cannot really be changed later, and partly because many studies of intensive psychotherapy and counseling have shown minor if any long-term personality effects. On the other hand we were encouraged by the nonprofessionals: those enthusiasts like Dale Carnegie, the communist ideologue or the church missionary, who felt they could change adults and in fact seemed to be doing so. At any rate we ran some brief (7 to 10 days) "total push" training courses for businessmen, designed to increase their *n* Ach.

FOUR MAIN GOALS

In broad outline the courses had four main goals: (1) They were designed to teach the participants how to think, talk, and act like a person with high *n* Ach, based on our knowledge of such people gained through 17 years of research. For instance, men learned how to make up stories that would code high in *n* Ach (i.e., how to think in *n* Ach terms), how to set moderate goals for themselves in the ring toss game (and in life). (2) The courses stimulated the participants to set higher but carefully planned and realistic work goals for themselves over the next two years. Then we checked back with them every six months to see how well they were doing in terms of their own objectives. (3) The courses also utilized techniques for giving the participants knowledge about themselves. For instance, in playing the ring toss game, they could observe that they behaved differently from others—perhaps in refusing to adjust a goal downward after failure. This would then become a matter for group discussion, and the man would have to explain what he had in mind in setting such unrealistic goals. Discussion could then lead on to what a man's ultimate goals in life were, how much he cared about actually improving performance versus making a good impression or having many friends. In this way the participants would be freer to realize their achievement goals without being blocked by old habits and attitudes. (4) The courses also usually created a group *esprit de corps* from learning about each other's hopes and fears, successes and failures, and from going through an emotional experience together, away from everyday life, in a retreat setting. This membership in a new group helps a man achieve his goals, partly because he knows he has their sympathy and support and partly because he knows they will be watching to see how well he does. The same effect has been noted in other therapy groups like Alcoholics Anonymous. We are not sure which of these course "inputs" is really absolutely essential—that remains a research question—but we were taking no chances at the outset in view of the general pessimism about such efforts, and we wanted to include any and all techniques that were thought to change people.

The courses have been given: to executives in a large American firm, and in several Mexican firms; to underachieving high school boys; and to businessmen in India from Bombay and from a small city—Kakinada in the state of Andhra Pradesh. In every instance save one (the Mexican case), it was possible to demonstrate statistically, some two years later, that the men who took the course had done better (made more money, got promoted faster, expanded their businesses faster) than comparable men who did not take the course or who took some other management course.

Consider the Kakinada results, for example. In the two years preceding the course 9 men, 18 percent of the 52 participants, had shown "unusual" enterprise in their businesses. In the 18 months following the course 25 of the men, in other words nearly 50 percent, were unusually active. And this was not due to a general upturn of business in India. Data from a control city, some 45 miles away, show the same base rate of "unusually active" men as in Kakinada before the course—namely, about 20 percent. Something clearly happened in Kakinada: the owner of a small radio shop started a chemical plant; a banker was so successful in making commercial loans in an enterprising way that he was promoted to a much larger branch of his bank in Calcutta; the local political leader accomplished his goal (it was set in the course) to get the federal government to deepen the harbor and make it into an all-weather port; plans are far along for establishing a steel rolling mill, etc. All this took place without any substantial capital input from outside. In fact, the only costs were for four 10-day courses plus some brief follow-up visits every six months. The men are raising their own capital and using their own resources for getting business and industry moving in a city that had been considered stagnant and unenterprising.

The promise of such a method of developing achievement motivation seems very great. It has obvious applications in helping underdeveloped countries, or "pockets of poverty" in the United States, to move faster economically. It has great potential for businesses that need to "turn around" and take a more enterprising approach toward their growth and development. It may even be helpful in developing more n Ach among low-income groups. For instance, data show that lower-class Negro Americans have a very low level of n Ach. This is not surprising. Society has systematically discouraged and blocked their achievement striving. But as the barriers to upward mobility are broken down, it will be necessary to help stimulate the motivation that will lead them to take advantage of new opportunities opening up.

EXTREME REACTIONS

But a word of caution: Whenever I speak of this research and its great potential, audience reaction tends to go to opposite extremes. Either people remain skeptical and argue that motives can't really be changed, that all we are doing is dressing Dale Carnegie up in fancy "psychologese," or they become converts and want instant course descriptions by return mail to solve their local motivational problems. Either response is unjustified. What I have described here in a few pages has taken 20 years of patient research effort, and hundreds of thousands of dollars in basic research costs. What remains to be done will involve even larger sums or more time for development to turn a promising idea into something of wide practical utility.

ENCOURAGEMENT NEEDED

To take only one example, we have not learned to develop n Ach really well among low-income groups. In our first effort—a summer course for bright underachieving 14-year-olds—we found that boys from the middle class improved steadily in grades in school over a two-year period, but boys from the lower class showed an improvement after the first year followed by a drop back in their beginning low grade average. (See the accompanying chart.) Why? We speculate that it was because they moved back into an environment in which neither parents nor friends encouraged achievement or upward mobility. In other words, it isn't enough to change a man's motivation if the environment in which he lives doesn't support at least to some degree his new efforts. Negroes striving to rise out of the ghetto frequently confront this problem: They are faced by skepticism at home and suspicion on the job, so that, even if their n Ach is raised, it can be lowered again by the heavy odds against their success. We must learn not only to raise n Ach but also to find methods of instructing people in how to manage it, to create a favorable environment in which it can flourish.

Many of these training techniques are now only in the pilot testing stage. It will take time and money to perfect them, but society should be willing to invest heavily in them in view of their tremendous potential for contributing to human betterment.

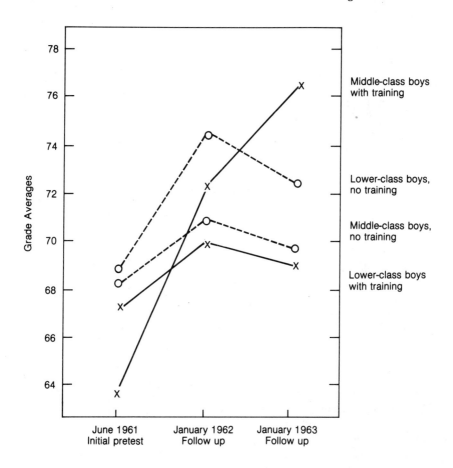

29

New Approaches in Management Organization and Job Design

Frederick Herzberg

The relationship between the nature of individuals and the satisfaction of individual's needs and the implications of this relationship on how jobs are structured is the thrust of this selection. Herzberg suggests that organizations will be most effective in situations where work is structured to maximize the opportunity for need satisfaction.—Eds.

To clarify my remarks this morning, I should like to qualify, at the beginning, many of the points that I am about to make. I must necessarily oversimplify certain positions in order to stay within allotted time limits, and also because I wish to emphasize a particular view of the problems of psychiatry in industry. Much that may appear iconoclastic is meant only for the negative aspects of the position I will be criticizing. I should like to begin by stating certain propositions regarding the goals of the American industrial enterprise.

The first two goals are traditional and provide for little or no disagreement. The third proposition will allow, I believe, for some disagreement in either its philosophy or its practicality, or both. Let me state them:

First, the function of any industrial or business enterprise is to produce goods and services required or desired by the society of which it is a part. No argument here. Second, the business should make a profit if for no other reason than to insure its survival. Again, there is no conflict. Third, the business organization, or any organization for that matter, should provide a meaningful existence for its employees during the process of producing the goods and services and maintaining its integrity. If industry is an institution to serve society, then surely its provision of the material needs of the

source: Reprinted by permission of the author from the *Journal of Industrial Medicine*, November 1962.

people should not be at the cost of denying its members the psychological income that should come from work. That it has been so is abundantly clear. That this is a tragedy is not so clear to many.

Two recent studies are relevant to this last point. In the large epidemiological survey sponsored by the Joint Commission on Mental Health and reported in *Americans View Their Mental Health,* it was discovered that tensions related to jobs are credited by the persons surveyed as the second major source for bringing them to the verge of a "nervous" breakdown. This is hardly a favorable commentary on the world of work.

In another recent study by Arthur Kornhauser of Wayne University, mental health scores of workers in the Detroit area show a strong and ominous relationship with the skill level of the jobs performed. It is the skill required by the jobs, and not other factors associated with the type of persons in the various echelons of job hierarchy, that Kornhauser claims to be the crucial factor from the analysis of his data. Only 16 percent of middle-aged workers doing repetitive semiskilled jobs showed "high" mental scores. This percentage dropped to a minuscule 7 percent for those classified in the "young" age bracket.

The student of social history and the perceptive observer of the industrial scene require little in the way of experimental proof to affirm what is so apparent—the jobs most people do are not a rich source for psychological health and, in fact, they may often best be classified as mental health hazards.

CONCEPTS OF THE WORKER

Every society develops myths to sustain its institutional forms. Paramount among these myths are those dealing with human nature. Just as each of us has beliefs about what makes people tick that satisfy our own wishes, so do institutions define the needs and nature of men to suit their own desires. Let us look at what the industrial institution has variously served up as the psychology of man.

The Economic Man

The economic man arose out of the dominant myths of the Industrial Revolution and the larger myths of the Protestant ethic. Business is religion and religion is business became the dominant theme of the rise of the modern business system. Making money was a prominent sign of religious virtue, and the motivation to succeed in making money was the true reflection of natural and supernatural man. This religious justification for the social and human evils of the revolution was buttressed by the pseudoscientism of the social Darwin doctrine, which suggested that the economically successful were the survival of the fittest in an inexorable law of competition. The worker was inferior from both a scientific evolutionary point of view as well as from an ethical religious point of view—a happy and expedient view of man to justify conditions wrought by the factory system. Humanitarian efforts, largely dictated by the fear of radicalism, were sufficient as a philosophy of employee relations, particularly when various economic incentives were added to complete the carrot and the stick by stimulating the supposed rawest motivational nerve of all—the desire for money.

The Social Man

The social man got his clearest definition and boost from the work of Elton Mayo, F. Roethlisberger et al. The interpretation of the Hawthorne studies that the overriding need of the worker was to be accepted by his fellow employee fitted in perfectly with the growth of scientific management, industrial engineering, and the consequent rationalization of jobs. Since the myth of the Horatio Alger story of the Protestant ethic no longer had pragmatic validity, and since the work required by industry became more suited for the feebleminded, what more useful concept of man than as a seeker of acceptance by people? His work contribution was relegated to an unreliable and interchangeable part of the work process, but he didn't mind as long as you paid him and offered him an opportunity to belong to informal work groups. Welfare capitalism combined with the newer science of group dynamics for a more complete view of employee relations.

The Emotional Man

While Sigmund Freud did not discover emotional man, he certainly defined him. Man is determined and is a victim of biological urges and childhood frustrations of these urges. Man is not really responsible for his irrational behavior, and, in fact, his behavior is not really irrational. Understanding and dealing with man as a victim of emotions precipitated the modern emphasis on human relations programs at all job levels and at all levels of sophistication. This concept fitted in nicely with the burgeoning bureaucracies that developed to manage the huge production plants that emerged. How to manage a rank and file of managers became a problem, particularly when the industrial engineering principles of job rationalization and restriction of individual variability and responsibility were adopted for the utilization of managerial manpower. These principles found their expression by the bureaucratic techniques of policies, rules, regulations, committees, and organizational theory. Just as the assembly line reduces the effect of the industrial worker at the production line, so do the bureaucratic techniques reduce the effect of the manager at the office. Denigrating the potentiality of the worker calls for scientific handling of the resulting partial man. Human relations becomes a means of avoiding the unpleasantness arising from the use of the adult as a child on the job. What is cause and effect here? Is the employee acting as a child because the circumstances force this kind of behavior or, as assumed by the "emotional" school, are the circumstances forced by the emotional nature of man? My thesis is the former explanation.

The economic man, the social man, and the emotional man today have been combined, with each representing one aspect of the total. This definition parallels the weird assortment of premises and practices of contemporary industrial relations. We have developed from experience and research a plethora of facts, principles, and, in many instances, workable techniques with which to deal more effectively with people on the job.

SATISFYING WORKERS' NEEDS

How to handle the economic motive has given rise to an unimaginable array of wage, salary, bonus, and benefit programs of such intricacy that an interdisciplinary team of lawyers, economists, financiers, physicians, sociologists, psychologists, and welfarists are involved in their creation, planning, and administration. Research on this aspect of man is mainly at the level of new models of economic prizes, reminiscent of the frantic efforts of the give-away shows to tantalize the audience with exotic variations of payoffs. Recently the personnel director of a local restaurant chain advertised his intention to stay awake nights to think up new variations of benefits to motivate his automaton employees.

The social needs of man have given rise to some of our most ingenious and in some cases fruitful research in industry. The problems of leadership, supervision, organizational structure, group functioning, and other social psychological issues have multiplied both our scientific and applied literature beyond anything that could be imagined a few years ago. Unfortunately, the value of this work has been tarnished by some of the evangelical zeal of its proponents; but it is of significance, because of the premise that man is essentially a social animal primarily in search of social gratification. It has already defined the form of social criticism for this era in the writings of David Reisman and his attack on the Lonely Crowd and William H. Whyte's attack on the Organization Man. Nevertheless, there is a gold mine to be worked in this research for improving personnel relations, organizational efficiency, and human happiness.

Closely allied with the work being done on the social psychology of industry has been the emphasis on understanding the role played by personal adjustment on the effectiveness of our industrial concerns. The clinical insights of psychiatry and psychology have become germane to the problems of people at work. The implementation of clinical psychiatry and psychology to industry has found expression ranging from the crude and often obnoxious misuse of personality assessment for hiring and promoting, through some of the naive psychology programs in supervisory training, to the more sophisticated managerial programs, such as the one at the Menninger Foundation and the current wave of group therapy in sensitivity

programs. Personal counseling initiated as a product of the original Hawthorne studies has never crystallized as a promised land of psychological
amelioration in our companies. It is perhaps too early to forecast the impact
that these newer uses of clinical psychiatry and psychology will have, but I
believe its effectiveness will be limited by the view of emotionally sick man
carried over from the pathological settings where the clinician is trained.
This has often led to the embarrassing necessity of labelling effective behaviors by negative terms: the well-adjusted man who earns a million dollars is overcompensating; the star football guard is a masochist relieving an
Oedipus complex.

Perhaps the greatest contribution that the behavioral sciences have
made during the last half century of research on the industrial scene has
been to broaden the concept of the needs and nature of man from a solely
determined economic organism to one that encompasses some of the more
human aspects—the emotional and social needs.

However, I do not believe that we have yet developed a complete picture.
It has been only recently that the truly human needs of man have emerged
in the research and writings of the behavioral scientists. I refer to such men
as Maslow with his emphasis on the higher actualizing needs, McGregor in
the *Human Side of Enterprise,* Argyris in the conflict of *Human Personality
and Organizations,* and, hopefully, myself in the *Motivation to Work.*

I should like now to concentrate on a view of man that I believe is
emerging and challenging our concepts of managing men. To begin, I will
briefly review certain concepts derived from research on job motivation and
reported in the book just mentioned, *The Motivation to Work,* and in other
journal publications.

FACTORS INFLUENCING JOB SATISFACTION

The implication of this research for job design and organizational structure I believe are important although difficult to conceive and implement.
But a lack of proved hardware should not lead to an alternative understanding of the problems, which may have techniques but violates reality.

Essentially, the initial study consisted of interviewing engineers and
accountants, representing a fair cross-section of Pittsburgh industry, on
events that they had experienced on jobs that resulted in either a marked
improvement in their job satisfaction or a marked reduction in their job
satisfaction.

Figure 1 shows the major findings of this study. The factors listed in this
figure are a kind of shorthand for summarizing the "objective" events that
each respondent described. The length of each box represents the frequency
with which each factor appeared in the events presented, and the width of
the box indicates the duration of time the good or bad job attitude lasted, in
terms of a classification of short duration and long duration. A short dura-

FIGURE 1   Comparison of Satisfiers and Dissatisfiers

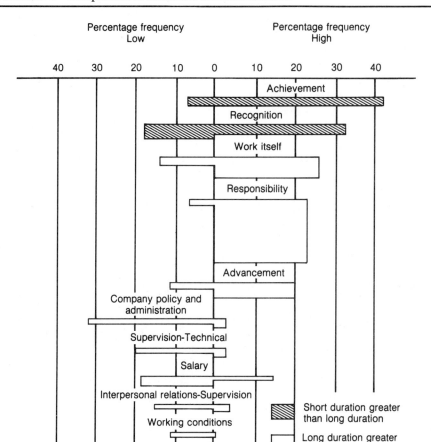

tion was usually not longer than two weeks, while a long duration attitude change may have lasted for years.

Five factors stand out as high determiners of job satisfaction: achievement, recognition, work itself, responsibility, and advancement; with the last three of greater importance for lasting change of attitudes. These five factors appeared very infrequently when the respondents described events that paralleled job dissatisfaction feelings. A further word on recognition. When it appeared in a "high" sequence of events, it referred to recognition for a task, rather than recognition as a human relations tool divorced from any accomplishment. The latter type of recognition does not serve as a "satisfier."

When we coded the factors involved in the job dissatisfaction events, an entirely different set of factors evolved. These factors were similar to the "satisfiers" in their unidimensional effect. This time, however, they served only to bring about job dissatisfaction and were rarely involved in events which led to positive job attitudes. Also contrary to the "satisfiers," the "dissatisfiers" consistently produced short-term job attitude changes.

There is a fundamental distinction between the "satisfiers" and the "dissatisfiers." The "satisfiers" all refer to the job content or job task: achievement of a task, recognition for task achievement, nature of the task, responsibility for the task, and professional growth or advancement in task capability. In contrast, the "dissatisfiers" refer to the job context or job environment: the nature of the company's policies and administrative practices under which the job is performed, the type of supervision received when doing the job, the quality of the working conditions in which the job is done, and the salary received for doing the job. Another factor that belongs on the "dissatisfiers" list and not shown in the figure, is status. Again this popular factor defines the job context.

Since the "dissatisfier" factors describe essentially the environment and serve primarily to prevent job satisfaction while having little effect on positive job attitudes, they have been named the *hygiene factors*, in analogy with the medical use of this term as preventative and environmental. The "satisfier" factors were named the *motivators,* since other findings of the study suggest that they are effective in motivating the individual to superior performance and effort.

So far, I have reported on that part of the interview that was restricted to determining the actual objective events as reported by our respondents. We also asked them to interpret the events for us; that is, to tell us why the particular event led to a change in their feelings about their jobs. The principal result of the analysis of this data was to suggest that the hygiene events led to job dissatisfaction because of a "need" to avoid unpleasantness; the motivator events led to job satisfaction because of a "need" for growth or self-actualization. At the psychological level, the two dimensions of job attitudes reflected a two dimensional "need" structure: one need system for avoidance and a parallel need system for personal growth.

In summary, there are two essential findings from this study. First, the factors which make people happy on the job are not the *same* factors that make people unhappy on the job. The distinguishing characteristic of these two sets of factors is whether they describe the job content or the job context. Second, the effects of hygiene factors on job attitudes are of a relatively short duration in contrast with the motivator factors which, three of them at least, have long lasting attitude effects.

A number of studies have subsequently been completed on a variety of different populations and with significant alterations in methods, which suggest that the motivation-hygiene concept has a considerable degree of general validity.

The two sets of factors emerge with Air Force personnel, nonsupervisory employees in the auto industry, general managers, schizophrenic patients, and physical rehabilitation patients. Age, job tenure, place of work, and other demographic variables show no substantial effect on these relationships.

EMPHASIS ON SELF-ACTUALIZATION

The importance of two distinct sets of factors to research in job satisfaction can hardly be overestimated. Traditional research in job attitudes has consistently emphasized the betterment of surrounding conditions, largely neglecting the self-actualizing factors. The self-actualizing need of man is certainly not new; Jung wrote eloquently of this need. Freud observing the Moses of Michelangelo was moved to write ". . . so that the giant frame with its tremendous physical power becomes only a concrete expression of the highest mental achievement that is possible in man, that of struggling against an inward passion for the sake of a cause to which he had devoted himself." The achievement and growth motives appear throughout our literature and experience. Why, then, has it not become a guiding principle in our employee relations philosophy? Briefly I offer these reasons.

First, it has, but mostly in a cultural noise manner. It is something to be talked about but not really implemented.

Second, it has been warped by what is now called in our national science the *new wave of conservatism.* Self-actualization and individual freedom come out as a fight against Social Security deductions to provide medical care for our aged. Hygiene is the battleground for apostles of individual integrity. They use the language of the motivators, but they do not comprehend its significance.

Third, the investment in the hardware or hygiene is too great and the number of people involved in the perpetuation too many, to relegate hygiene programs to their proper place as only maintenance needs of employees.

Fourth, and most important, we have decided that we cannot economically afford to make jobs meaningful in the sense that I have asked.

What should we do?

First, we need a new kind of therapy program. The traditional therapies are directed to the avoidance needs of man, the anxiety, the psychological pain of emotional conflict. We need, in addition, a therapy program to orient people to the satisfaction of individual accomplishment. Psychological growth does not simply unleash when we remove some discomfort.

Second, we need to reverse the philosophy of employee relations, as primarily oriented to hygiene with such motivator programs as management development merely tacked on, and put the development of man as the basic philosophy with the hygiene programs subsumed under them.

Third, we must recognize that our greatest mental health challenge is to provide jobs that have meaning. Specifically, this calls for research on job enlargement, and not the meaningless stringing of snippets of tasks that have often been defined as job enlargement. We have to go back to the traditional concepts of matching talent to the job, good old-fashioned classification of people. At the organizational level, we need to increase its variability. Line staff relations, span of control, all organizational theory has to be relooked at, not so much to increase the hygiene effectiveness of the organization but to increase individual responsibility and individual psychological income from jobs. We need a fluid structure to match achievement needs of people.

I would like to suggest the concept of the collateral organization; that is, every organization should be able to provide jobs beyond the usual organizational structure for creativity when individuals on jobs no longer are being challenged. If we sent out 100 collaterals and only one man is creative, it will pay for the other 99.

I have attempted here briefly to provide ingredients, not the recipe. Perhaps as part of this conference the recipe might be forthcoming.

C. Decision Making

30

The Myth of Management

C. West Churchman

The myth, according to the author, is of believing that the really great manager has a special ability to solve the puzzling problems found in large, complex organizations. Effective managerial decision making is seen not as a result of hidden special abilities but as a reasoned logical approach to problem analysis.—Eds.

Making decisions is, on the one hand, one of the most fascinating manifestations of biological activity and, on the other hand, a matter of terrifying implications for the whole of the human race. Although this activity is both fascinating and awesome, it is difficult to find a satisfactory name for it in any of the common languages. In English we use such terms as *manager, administrator, executive,* or simply *decision maker.* Yet each of these terms fails somehow to capture the true significance of this important activity of the human being. Because we need a label to conduct our discussion, I shall risk choosing the term *manager* and begin to say some things that will generalize on this term beyond its ordinary usage in English.

The manager is the man who decides among alternative choices. He must decide which choice he believes will lead to a certain desired objective or set of objectives. But his decision is not an abstract one, because it creates a type of reality. The manager is the man with the magic that enables him to create in the world a state of affairs that would not have occurred except for him. We say that the manager is one who has the authority to make such choices. He is also a person who has the responsibility for the choices he has made in the sense that the rest of his fellow men may judge whether he should be rewarded or punished for his choices; he is the person who justifiably is the object of praise or blame.

SOURCE: From *Challenge to Reason,* by C. West Churchman. Copyright © 1968 by McGraw-Hill, Inc. Used with permission of McGraw-Hill Book Company.

So broad a description of the manager makes managers of us all. It is a common failing of the labels that language applies to things that they may be generalized to encompass everything, as philosophers have long recognized in the case of such labels as *matter* and *mind*. It takes no great sophomoric talent to see that the world is basically matter and that everything could be reduced thereto. Nor does it take any great astuteness to see that everything a human being recognizes as natural reality is the product of some mind or collection of minds. So, too, the label *manager* may become appropriately applied to practically everything, or at least to every human, once we describe the manager as someone having the authority and responsibility for making choices. I am interested in the broad aspects of decision making, but for present purposes I want to add one more stipulation that makes the label *manager* less general. This is the stipulation that managerial activity take place within a "system": The manager must concern himself with interrelated parts of a complex organization of activities, and he is responsible for the effectiveness of the whole system. . . .

But even this further stipulation concerning the use of the label *manager* permits us to describe many activities as management. It is true that, in the history of England and the United States, the term *management* has often been narrowed to mean the managing of industrial activities, especially for the purpose of generating profit for an enterprise. In this connection management is contrasted with labor. In government activities our use of the term *manager* is often labelled *administrator,* and the term *executive* is often used to describe people who are given the legal authority to put into practice the laws of the land. All these activities, whether they be at the level of government or industry or education or health, or whatever, have a common ground which we wish to explore. The common ground is the burden of making choices about system improvement and the responsibility of responding to the choices made in a human environment in which there is bound to be opposition to what the manager has decided. Thus, the head of a labor union, the state legislator, the head of a government agency, the foreman of a shop are all managers in our sense. So is a man in his own family a manager; so is the captain of a football team. Probably all of us at some time or other in our lives become managers when, because of appointment to a committee or because of our political activities, we take on the authority and responsibility of making decisions in complex systems. Managing is an activity of which we are all aware, and its consequences concern each one of us.

I said that managers must bear the burden of the decisions they make. I could have added, in a more optimistic tone, that they enjoy the pleasures accompanying the power to make decisions. And certainly many managers in today's society do find a great deal of psychic satisfaction in the roles they play which society so clearly recognizes as important and which it credits with a great deal of prestige.

Now managing is a type of behavior, and, since it's a very important type of behavior, you might expect that we know a great deal about it. But we don't at all. We could also explore the many ways in which managers often think they know how they manage, but observers of their behavior often differ from them quite radically. The manager is frequently astonished to hear a sociologist's description of his activities, which he believes he himself knows so well, and he resents the inclination on the part of the "detached" scientist to try to describe the activity that he performs.

Imagine an observer carefully trained to study such activities as bees in a hive, or fish in a school, or birds in a flock, and suppose such a student of nature becomes curious about the behavior of judges during a trial. How might such a scientist describe what the judge actually does? He might learn a little bit from some of the reflective judges, and perhaps a little bit more from the sociologists and other scientists who have attempted to describe legal behavior, but he would find that most of the activity remains a huge mystery to the whole of humanity—a mystery that no one has ever felt inclined to investigate in detail.

The whole activity of managing, important as it is for the human race, is still largely an unknown aspect of the natural world. When man detaches himself and tries to observe what kind of living animal he is, he finds that he knows very little about the things most important to him and precious little about his role as a decision maker. Few managers are capable of describing how they reach their decisions in a way that someone else can understand; few can tell us how they feel about the decisions once they have been made. Of course, despite our ignorance about managerial phenomena, a great deal is written on the subject in popular magazines and managerial journals. It appears that the less we know about a subject, the more we are inclined to write extensively about it with great conviction. Some writings describe the various rituals followed in organizations prior and posterior to the actual managerial decision. But most of these descriptions pay little attention to the very puzzling question of *when* a decision actually occurred and *who* made it. A great deal is said about committee deliberations and other aspects of organizational rationality that go into the making of a decision, and the many checks and controls that are exerted to determine whether the decisions have been made properly. Much attention is paid to these aspects of organizational decision making, because they show up on the surface, so to speak. But the facts that a committee deliberated for three hours and then a decision emerged do not tell us *who* made the decision, *how* it was made, or *when* it was made. It might be added that the verbal assertions of the committee often do not tell us *what* decision is made.

So there is a great mystery of the natural world: the *who, when, how,* and *what* of man's decision making.

But even if we were to succeed in discovering a great deal more than we have about management, the result would be at best descriptive. It would be merely the background of the basic problem before us, namely, the question of how the manager *should* decide.

Am I right in claiming that we know so little about management? After all, most of us are quite willing, even eager, to express an opinion about managers, because we love to praise and complain. We don't hesitate to say that some men are better managers than others. We are constantly criticizing our political leaders. Biographers are accustomed to choose the most "outstanding" leaders of the age as the subject of their texts. These leaders may be great political leaders, leaders of industry, leaders of social movements, of religion, and so on. What is the quality these men of success have that their less successful colleagues lack? Since we believe we can identify "successful" leaders, surely we also believe we know a great deal about what a manager *should* decide. For example, in the case of the Presidents of the United States, we are told in our school-boy texts that we can readily recognize that some of these Presidents were "great" and some of them far from great. What is the quality of greatness that we are led to ascribe to some of these Presidents?

A ready answer is at hand—the successful and great Presidents were those who made decisions that today we clearly recognize to be correct, and those who made these decisions in the face of severe opposition. We are led to believe that the activity of great Presidents is a marvelous example of successful decision making in large complex systems.

But the skeptics among us will find this answer quite unsatisfactory as an explanation of what constitutes greatness in a President. In the first place, history has no record of what would have happened had the opposition's point of view succeeded or if serious modifications had been made in the choices of the so-called great Presidents. What if the Union had *not* been saved, or our independence declared? History seems only to have recorded the episodes that followed upon the particular decision that was made and does not provide us with an analysis of events that might have occurred if an alternative had been adopted.

More curious still is the implicit assumption that a successful President made his great decisions on the basis of his own particular abilities. Since evidence is so often lacking that great Presidents of the past had these abilities, there is a natural inclination on the part of many of us to ascribe either determinism or randomness to the activities of so-called successful managers. In the case of determinism, we might argue that the events of the world occur by the accidental conglomeration of many forces unknown to man, and that these forces produce "decisions" that man in his innocence believes that he himself makes. The decision of independence in 1776 was, according to this view, simply the outgrowth of many complex human and physical interrelationships. Those who adopt the idea of randomness simply add to the physical determinism of events a random fluctuation of the sort occurring in a roulette wheel or in the shuffling of cards. They would then be willing to admit that other decisions might have been made in 1776 or later, but that these decisions would be very much like the outcome of another spin of the roulette wheel. In either event, whether we choose to describe the world of decision making as determinism or as randomness, we conclude that ascribing greatness to the decision makers in Independence Hall would be a mistake unless one meant by greatness some recognizable features of the determined or random events occurring in the world. By analogy one might say that the man who spins the roulette wheel is its "manager" who decides nothing about the outcome of his spins; a multitude of hidden physical forces determine where the wheel will stop. Calling a President great is like calling the spinner of a roulette wheel that happens to have a satisfactory result a great spinner.

This is certainly a crass and impolite way to describe the great managerial minds of the past. Surely we can do more for their memories than to describe them as irrelevant aspects of the history of society. We might try to look into the story of their lives to find evidence that they really had superior methods of deliberation. We might try to show that they had the sort of brilliance and courage that creates an ability to handle confusing pieces of information and to reach appropriate decisions. Perhaps the great manager is an extremely adept information processor who can act so rapidly that he himself is not even aware of the comparisons and computations he has made.

Indeed, this last is more or less the popular image of the great manager. For example, many scientists who advise politicians, corporate managers, and other decision makers often state that they cannot possibly attempt to tell such men what decisions *should* be made. At best they believe they can merely tell the decision maker about certain outcomes if the decisions are adopted. Thus, the more modest among the advisers believe that they have no intent of "replacing" the managers they advise. And yet if these scientific advisers are capable of discerning at least some aspects of the managerial decision, what is it they lack? What are they incapable of doing that the politician and corporate manager are so successful in accomplishing? What is this secret ingredient of the great presidents of corporations, universities, and countries that no scientist or ordinary man could ever hope to acquire?

The answer usually given is that the President has information about many different aspects of the world and has an ability to put these aspects together in a way that no analysis could possibly do. In other words, he has a vision of the whole system and can relate the effectiveness of the parts to the effectiveness of the whole. The hidden secret of the great manager, so goes the myth, is his ability to solve the puzzling problems of whole systems that we have been discussing so far.

This answer is a myth, because it is totally unsatisfactory to the reasoning of an intellectually curious person. Are "great" managers fantastically high-speed data processors? Do great managerial minds outstrip any machinery now on the market or contemplated for decades to come? From what we know of the brain and its capabilities, the answer seems to be no.

Indeed, it is doubtful whether the great manager in reaching decisions uses very much of the information he has received from various sources. It is also doubtful whether the manager scans many of the alternatives open to him. . . . We described how the scientist, when he comes to grips with the problems of decision making, discovers that they can only be represented by fairly complicated mathematical models. Even in fairly simple decision-making situations, we have come to learn how complicated is the problem of developing a sensible way of using available information. It seems incredible that the so-called successful managers really have inbuilt models that are rich and complicated enough to include the subtleties of large-scale systems.

Suppose for the moment we descend from the lofty heights of the decision makers in Independence Hall and the White House and begin to describe a very mundane and easily recognized managerial problem concerning the number of tellers that should be available to customers in a bank. All of us have experienced the annoyance of going into a bank in a hurry and spending a leisurely but frustrating half hour behind the wrong line. How should the bank manager decide on the allocation of tellers at various times of the day?

This is a fairly simple managerial problem and its like is encountered by thousands of middle managers every day. Furthermore, this problem has been studied quite extensively in operations research, and its "solution" is often found in the elementary texts. The texts say that the scientist should try to answer the managerial question by considering both the inconvenience of the customers who wait in the lines and the possible idle time of the tellers who wait at their stations when no customers are there. Thus, the "successful" manager can be identified in an objective way, and we need not take a poll of greatness or lack thereof to ascertain whether the manager has performed well. The successful manager will be someone who has properly balanced the two costs of the operation of servicing customers in a bank: the cost of waiting customers and the cost of idle tellers. He will insist that the cost of a minute's waiting of a customer in a line must be compared to a minute's idle time of the teller. On the basis of this comparison, together with suitable evidence concerning the arrival rate of customers and the time required to service each customer, the successful manager will determine the policy concerning allocation of tellers to various stations during the day. Perhaps no one will feel inclined to write the biography of so ordinary a man as the manager of a branch of a local bank; but in any case, if this manager decides according to the rational methods just outlined, his biographer may at least be honest about his "greatness."

Nevertheless, the analysis just outlined leaves much unanswered. For example, an idle teller need not be idle while waiting at a station where there are no customers. Instead he may be occupied with other routine matters requiring attention in the administration of the bank. Consequently, if the manager can design the entire operation of his bank's many functions properly, he may be able to decrease the cost of idle time of personnel who are servicing customers. If we look on the other side of the picture, that is, the inconvenience to a customer, we may find that in fact waiting in line is not an inconvenience at all if the customer happens to meet an acquaintance there. Perhaps the manager should serve coffee and doughnuts to waiting customers. Furthermore, if the manager could somehow or other hope to control the behavior of his customers, he might be able to recognize their arrivals in such a way that inconvenience costs are vastly reduced. Add to these considerations other innovations that might be introduced: For example, in many cases banks set up express windows to handle customers who would normally have very low service times. Hence, an overall average waiting time may not make sense if there are different types of service tailored to the various needs of the customers.

But then another, broader consideration occurs to us: Handling the public's financial matters by branch banking methods may be completely wrong. Modern technology may provide ways of developing financial servicing methods far cheaper for both bank and customer. After all, handling cash and checks is an extremely awkward way for a person to acquire goods at a price. With adequately designed information centers, the retail markets need only input information about a customer purchase, and the customer's employers need only input information about his income. Thus, every purchase would become simply a matter of centralized information processing, as would a man's weekly or monthly paycheck. There would, therefore, be no real need for any of us to carry money about and no need to go to a bank and stand patiently in line. But this idea of automated purchasing and income recording is followed by another thought. We realize that any such automated financial system would probably end in eliminating a number of clerical and managerial jobs. Consequently, we must examine the social problems of displaced personnel and the need for retraining, otherwise total social costs of automated banking might be far greater than the convenience gained by introducing new technology.

Before we can decide whether the manager of the branch bank is performing "satisfactorily," we must decide a much broader issue—whether the particular system that the manager operates is an appropriate one. This question leads to deeper considerations concerning the potentials of modern technology and their implications with respect to automation, job training, and the future economics of many lives.

The simple illustration with which we started has now driven us to an almost absurd concept of the "great" manager of even so little a system as a branch bank. The really successful manager must be able to understand the optimal design of the whole bank, as well as the optimal behavior patterns of his customers, and the optimal development of the technology of automation. The great manager of a little enterprise needs to be the great manager of the great enterprise.

This is a curious concept of human behavior that we have been developing. The manager cannot manage well unless he in some sense manages all. Specifically, he must have some idea of what the whole relevant world is like to be able to justify that what he manages is managed correctly.

At the present time we understand very little about managerial behavior, because in all studies of behavior we concentrate our attention on what the observer sees the manager doing; even if we broaden our perspective of his behavior to include the manager's objectives, we usually narrow the scope of these objectives so we are capable of understanding them, that is, of representing them in some kind of analytical form. We have no apparatus in our scientific kit that enables us to observe an activity which must encompass so broad a scope as managerial activity actually implies.

In other words, when we undertake studies to assist managers, or when we try to understand how managers themselves behave, we are incapable of deciding what the behavior of the manager really means, because we are incapable of understanding or observing the manager's whole system. When a system scientist tries to solve a production problem or a government agency problem, he feels there are symptoms of trouble and he wishes to remove them. But he has no means by which he can decide whether the entire activity ought to be redesigned, thereby eliminating both the trouble and the far more serious loss entailed in a useless set of activities. This is true whether or not he claims he has used the "systems approach."

We have certainly failed to live up to the lessons that Greek philosophy tried to teach mankind, namely, that knowledge of oneself is the most important knowledge man can gain. We have undoubtedly done much in biology and psychology to study certain properties of living organisms and their minds. Our efforts in sociology have been mainly of a descriptive nature, since the sociologist typically does not try to judge that which he observes, nor even to understand what the characteristics of an excellent or healthy decision maker might be. Hence, there is a serious question whether what is observed by the "behavioral sciences" is really relevant at all with respect to the healthy life of the organization. The study of the health of organizations is thus largely neglected, even though it is the most important health problem that exists.

The heritage of Western science with its emphasis on observation and logic seems to have provided us with no tools to study managerial activity, even though this is undoubtedly the most important problem ever faced by man. We simply do not understand the part of the natural world that is of most concern to us. At best we are able to say that the good manager is one who has a faith of a proper sort in what will happen in the world, a faith that he does not attempt to examine or control. Abraham Lincoln, for example, had the faith that, by trying to preserve the Union through war, an excellent democracy would result. No matter that he failed to understand or have any evidence concerning the implications of the Civil War in the late decades of the 19th and early 20th centuries. No matter either that Lincoln's whole concept of political activity might have been wrong. No matter that today we have no adequate information about what other courses of action were available in the 1860s and what their implications might have been. We, too, have a simple faith that Lincoln was a "great" President, or else—south of the Mason-Dixon line—an equally simple faith that he was not.

If we are to be honest about our ignorance, we will have to admit that some managers become great simply because there is common agreement that they are great. The scientist, the public, and the manager all agree that the decisions made by these great managers were correct, and they agree that there were no other alternatives that would have led to far better results. They also agree that the enterprise in which the manager was engaged was a meaningful one. The scientist might contribute to this agreement by using whatever resources he has available to study the alternatives that were open to the great manager; the public can recognize the benefits they have received from the great manager's activities, because they "worked out" well, and the managers themselves through their experience can appreciate what the great manager has accomplished. The public, science, and management come to agree that certain managerial activities are beneficial to the whole system. What results is a judgment of excellence of management based upon such common agreement—not too bad a basis after all in view of the powerful role that common agreement often plays.

We must admit, though, that agreement is a dangerous basis for rational conclusions. Agreement always has its opposite side and often becomes disagreement in the next generation, especially in healthy societies where social change is bound to occur. A rational mind will want to find a far better basis for the judgment of excellence. He will want to find the rational basis in whose terms he can really prove the excellence of managerial decisions, based on an accurate account of the whole system.

Actually, we humans are quite incapable of understanding the agreements we reach. We often take common agreement as expressed in majority opinion to be the end of the matter, even though we frankly recognize that our own judgments are so often inadequate, no matter how strong the agreement behind them.

It may be that, as men become politically more astute, they will begin to develop that part of their mentality which enables them to so look at themselves that they can examine the common agreements they hold and adopt a critical attitude toward them. Instead of gaining moral support from the agreements of his fellow man, a person may instead begin to regard agreement as a kind of evidence of danger ahead. He will then be on his way toward what we may call a theory of management; that is, a knowledge about what management really is and not what it is merely perceived to be.

We have been discussing the manager as though he were an object of study of the scientist, and we have been using as an analogy the way in which the scientist observes any kind of living activity. We have seen, however, that science is incapable as yet of generating an adequate science of management simply because it has no basis or technique by which it can adequately judge the difference between good and bad, or healthy and un-healthy, types of managerial behavior. We recognize that there must be such things as a good and a bad manager, but we have no basis on which to decide whether a specific activity falls in one category or the other.

We have also been speaking as though the scientist's interest in man-agement is based mainly on the kind of intellectual curiosity that motivates him to discover the meaning of various mysteries of nature; that is, to transform myth into objectivity.

There is, however, another way in which we should look at the matter: We should realize that science itself is an organized activity—that is, a complex system—and we should examine what the management character-istics of this system are. The typical scientist regards the manager as some-one who provides resources and creates the kind of environment in which "high-level" intellectual activity can occur. The scientist has failed to see that the whole problem of management is fundamental to every aspect of his own activities. Rather, he did see this three centuries ago, but saw it in a way that for later science turned out to be unsatisfactory. Thus, the idea that management is fundamental to science disappeared in favor of other types of foundations of science. But the scientist is clearly a manager in the broad sense of the term. . . . If the concept of a great manager is a myth or a mystery, cannot the same be said of the great scientist?

31

Administrative Decision Making

Herbert A. Simon

This article surveys the broad area of managerial decisions in organizations and summarizes the current state of the art with respect to decision-making concepts and language. Of particular importance is the discussion of the role played in advancing our knowledge by (1) developments in management science, (2) the application of the experimental method to the investigation of decision making, and (3) the computer.—Eds.

There is no need, at this late date, to justify the study of organization and administration in terms of the decision-making process, for decision-making concepts and language have become highly popular in writing about administration.[1] This paper will describe some of the progress that has been made over the past quarter century, employing this approach, toward deepening our scientific knowledge—what new facts have been learned about human behavior in organizations, what new scientific procedures for ascertaining facts, what new concepts for describing them, and what new generalizations for explaining them. This progress extends both to descriptive and normative matters: to the pure science of administration, and its application to the practical business of managing.

To satisfy limits on . . . space, your patience, and my time, the account will be highly selective. Only a few notable and significant advances have been selected; others for which equally plausible claims might be made are ignored. A frequent practice in the social sciences is to bemoan our present ignorance while making optimistic predictions about future knowledge. It is a pleasure to survey an area of social science where, by contrast, we can speak without blushing about our present knowledge—indeed, where only a small sample of the gains in knowledge that have been achieved in the past quarter century can be presented.

SOURCE: Reprinted by permission of the author and the American Society for Public Administration from *Public Administration Review*, March 1965, pp. 31–37.

OPERATIONS RESEARCH AND MANAGEMENT SCIENCE

One obvious answer to the question "What's new?" is the spectacular development in the normative theory of decision making that goes under the labels of "operations research" and "management science." Through these activities, many classes of administrative decisions have been formalized, mathematics has been applied to determine the characteristics of the "best" or "good" decisions, and myriads of arithmetic calculations are carried out routinely in many business and governmental organizations to reach the actual decisions from day to day. A number of sophisticated and mathematical tools—linear programming, queuing theory, dynamic programming, combinatorial mathematics, and others—have been invented or developed to this end.

Like all scientific developments, this one has a long intellectual history and did not spring, full-grown, from the brow of Zeus. Nevertheless, the state of the art today is so remarkably advanced beyond its position before World War II that the difference of degree becomes one of kind.[2]

The quantitative decision-making tools of operations research have perhaps had more extensive application in business than in governmental organizations. It is worth recalling, however, that many of these tools underwent their early development in the American and British military services during and just after the Second World War (where the terms *operations research* and *operations analysis* were coined). Among the inventors of linear programming, for example, were Tjalling Koopmans, seeking, as statistician with the Combined Shipping Adjustment Board, a means for scheduling tanker operations efficiently; and George B. Dantzig and Marshall K. Wood, in the Office of the Air Force Controller, who used as one of their first (hypothetical) programming problems the scheduling of the Berlin Airlift.

Operations research, particularly in its governmental applications, has retained close intellectual ties with classical economic theory, and has sought to find effective ways of applying that theory to public budgeting and expenditure decisions. This has been a central preoccupation of the RAND Corporation effort, as exemplified by such works as Charles J. Hitch and Roland N. McKean, *The Economics of Defense in the Nuclear Age*.[3] In the past several years, Hitch, as Controller of the Department of Defense, and a number of his former RAND associates have played major roles in bringing the new tools to bear on Defense Department budget decisions. Thus, while the quarter century begins with V. O. Key's plaint about "The Lack of a Budgetary Theory,"[4] it ends with a distinct revitalization of the whole field of public expenditure theory, and with a burgeoning of new analytic tools to assist in allocating public resources.

OPTIMALITY AND ALL THAT

In many ways the contributions of operations research and management science to decision-making theory have been very pragmatic in flavor.

The goal, after all, is to devise tools that will help management make better decisions. One example of a pragmatic technique that has proved itself very useful and has been rapidly and widely adopted over the past five years is the scheduling procedure variously called PERT, or critical path scheduling. This technique does not use any very deep or sophisticated mathematics (which may account partly for the speed of its adoption), but is mainly an improvement of the common sense underlying the traditional Gantt Chart.

Contrasting with this pragmatic flavor, advances in operations research have been paralleled by developments in the pure theory of rational choice—a theory that has reached a very high level of mathematical and logical elegance and rigor. Among these developments perhaps the most important are: (1) rigorous, formal axiom systems for defining the concept of utility in operational terms; (2) extension of the theory of rational choice to encompass the maximization of expected utility under conditions of uncertainty; (3) extension of the theory to repeated choices over time—dynamic optimization; and (4) extension of the theory to competitive "gaming" situations. These formal advances have had an important influence, in turn, on directions of work in theoretical statistics (statistical decision theory, Bayesian statistics), and on the kinds of models that are preferred by operations researchers—or at least by the theorists among their number.[5]

An evaluation of these contributions on the pure theory of rational choice would return a mixed verdict. On the positive side, they have provided enormous conceptual clarification for discussions of "rationality." For example, it has always been unclear what rationality meant in a pure outwitting or bargaining situation, where each party is trying to outguess, and perhaps bluff, the other. If the theory of games, due to von Neumann and Morgenstern, did not solve this problem for all situations, it at least made painfully clear exactly what the problem is.

On the negative side, fascination with the pure theory of rational choice has sometimes distracted attention from the problems of decision makers who possess modest calculating powers in the face of a world of enormous complexity. (In the real world, the calculating powers of electronic computers as well as men must be described as "modest.") A normative theory, to be useful, must call only for information that can be obtained and only for calculations that can be performed. The classical theory of rational choice has generally ignored these information processing limitations. It has assumed that rationality was concerned with choice among alternatives that were already specified, and whose consequences were known or were readily calculable. It has assumed, also, comparability of consequences—that is, a practically measurable utility index.

Since these conditions, on which the classical theory rests, are so seldom satisfied in the real world, great interest attaches to procedures that make less heroic assumptions about the "givens" and the knowns; and, there is considerable progress in devising less than optimal decision procedures for situations where the optimum is unknown and practically undiscoverable. These procedures, often called *heuristic methods,* are distinguishable from optimizing techniques in three respects: they grapple, as most optimizing techniques do not, with the problems of designing and discovering alternatives, as well as with choosing among given alternatives; they frequently "satisfice," or settle for good-enough answers in despair at finding best answers; they commonly do not guarantee the qualities of the solutions they provide, and often do not even guarantee they will find a solution. The second and third of these characteristics are, of course, not virtues, but are the price that must be paid for extending our theory and tools for decision making to the wide range of real-world situations not encompassed by the classical models.

By way of illustration, a common problem of business and governmental management involves so locating a system of warehouses over a country that products can be distributed from production points to ultimate users as economically as possible. Attempts to so formulate the warehousing problem that the optimizing methods known as linear programming can be used have failed, because the computations become too lengthy. However, heuristic techniques have been applied successfully to find "good" solutions to the problem where "best" solutions are unattainable.[6]

It is traditional to observe, in any discussion of the modern decision-making tools, that knowledge of these tools runs far in advance of application, and that the domain of application has been limited largely to decisions that are well-structured or "programmed," and quantitative in character. The warehousing problem described above has both of these characteristics. Whether this limitation on applications is inherent or temporary is a more controversial question. One of the important tasks before us now is to see how far we can go in extending the applicability of the new decision-making tools to areas that are ill structured, and qualitative, calling for "judgment," "experience," and even "creativity." To do this, we shall presumably have to understand what "judgment," "experience," and "creativity" are, a topic discussed later.

EXPERIMENTS ON DECISION MAKING

A second area of significant advance has been in applying the experimental method to the investigation of decision making. This has been done both by arranging for experiments on live real-world organizations—on the model of the Hawthorne experiments—and/or by bringing organizations or organizationoid systems into the laboratory. For obvious reasons, the latter has been done more often than the former.

The first volume of the *Public Administration Review* contained a report of a large-scale field experiment on the decision-making processes of social workers,[7] but similar experiments have been exceedingly rare in the succeeding 25 years. One of the few other examples to which I can refer is the study done in the Prudential Life Insurance Company by the Survey Research Center of the University of Michigan.[8] Either researchers on organizations decided that the information attainable from field experiments was not worth the trouble and cost of carrying out such experiments, or they found it difficult to secure the cooperation of business and governmental organizations in arranging such experiments—or both. Whatever the reason, field experiments have not been an important procedure for learning about organizational decision making.

In a few cases researchers have tried to import relatively sizeable organizations into the laboratory—hence, their studies lie on the boundary line between field and laboratory experiments. The Systems Research Laboratory of the RAND Corporation, for example, studied decision making by simulating, under controlled conditions, an entire air defense control center and associated early warning stations, manned on a full-time basis over a period of several months by a staff of some 30 subjects. While the studies conducted by the Systems Research Laboratory had as their direct outgrowth a major Air Force training program, the laboratory proved less tractable as a setting for obtaining data for testing theories of the decision-making process, and there has been no subsequent rash of studies of this kind.[9]

In contrast to the dearth of field experiments and large-scale laboratory experiments, laboratory experimentation with relatively small groups has been a thriving enterprise. Several examples of methodological advances in the art of small-group experimentation can be mentioned. Fred Bales, with his interaction process analysis, developed a scheme of data processing useful for studying the interaction of task-oriented and social-system–oriented behavior in small problem-solving groups. Alex Bavelas devised a small-group task that permitted the experimenter to alter the decision-making process by opening or closing particular channels of communication between members of the group. In succeeding years, the Bales coding scheme and the Bavelas small-group task have both been used in a substantial number of studies, manipulating a great many different independent variables. Both have proved exceedingly valuable in permitting the cumulation of comparable knowledge from a whole series of experiments carried out by different investigators in different laboratories.

It is impossible to summarize here, or even to reference, the numerous contributions to the substantive knowledge of decision making that have been contributed by the small-group experiments. A single example will convey the flavor of such work. Cyert and March were able to produce bias in the estimates of members of a simulated organization by creating partial conflict of interest among them, but showed that under certain circumstances this bias did not affect organizational performance.[10]

New knowledge about organizational decision making can be obtained from appropriately planned experiments on individuals as well as from small-group experiments. Andrew Stedry, for example, has tested in this way theories about how budget controls affect behavior in organizations.[11] The series of studies of influence processes carried out at Yale by the late Carl Hovland and his associates belong in the same category.[12]

PERSUASION AND EVOCATION

Mention of the Yale research on influence processes marks a good point in our discussion to turn to several substantive developments in the theory of decision making. The notion that a decision is like a conclusion derived from a set of premises has been a useful metaphor for analyzing the decision-making process. Following the metaphor a step further, we can view each member of an organization as "inputting" certain premises, and "outputting" certain conclusions, or decisions. But each member's conclusions become, in turn, the inputs; that is to say, the premises, for other members. For one person to influence another involves inducing him to use appropriate premises in his decision making.

What happens in an organization, or in any kind of social system, when there are conflicting premises pushing a particular decision in different directions? Much of the research on influence processes has been aimed at answering this question. In much of this research, influence has been conceived as a kind of "force," so, when several influences are brought to bear simultaneously, the outcome is interpreted as a "resultant" of the impinging forces. Persuasion is then a process of exerting such a force.

An important advance in understanding decision making has been to complement the notion of persuasion with the notion of evocation. When we want someone to carry out a particular action, we may think of our task as one of inducing him to *accept* latent decision premises favorable to the action that he already possesses. Thus, writing about food will often make a reader hungry, but we would hardly say that we had "persuaded" him that he was hungry; it would be better to say that we had "reminded" him.

Processes of persuasion play their largest role in decision making in conflict situations—where the issue is already posed, and the alternatives present. This is the framework within which most of the Yale studies on attitude change were carried out. It is also the framework for the important and well-known study of *Voting* by Berelson, Lazarsfeld, and McPhee.[13]

On the other hand, in studies of decision making where the focus of attention of the participants is one of the main independent variables, the evoking processes take on larger importance. The recent study of the Trade Agreements Act renewal, by Raymond Bauer, Ithiel Pool, and Lewis Dexter indicates that these processes played a major role in deciding the issue.[14] The authors describe the setting of their study thus (p. 5): "We are interested in the sources of information for each of these populations, the bases of its attitudes on the trade issue, *and the circumstances which lead some individuals to take active roles in the making of policy.*" (Emphasis supplied.) They demonstrate convincingly that the behavior of particular Congressmen on the trade issue depended as much on the alternative claims on their time and attention as on the distribution of interests of their constituents.

To the extent that the mechanism of evocation is important for decision making, many new ways arise in which organizational arrangements may affect behavior. As example, one of the findings of the study just mentioned (p. 229) can be cited:

> In summary, we would suggest that most significant of all to an understanding of what communication went out from business on foreign trade was neither self-interest nor ideology, but the institutional structure which facilitated or blocked the production of messages. Whether a letter to a congressman would get written depended on whether organization facilitated it, whether the writer's round of daily conversations would lead up to it, whether a staff was set up to produce it, and whether the writer conceived writing this letter to be part of his job.

Evoking mechanisms take on special prominence wherever dynamic change is occurring. Studies of the diffusion of innovations show that the timing of adoption of an innovation depends critically on the means for getting people to attend to it.[15] From every point of view, the new knowledge gained about evoking and attention-directing processes is a major substantive advance in our understanding of organizational decision making.

THE STRUCTURE OF DECISIONS

A decision is not a simple, unitary event, but the product of a complex social process generally extending over a considerable period of time. As noted, decision making includes attention-directing or intelligence processes that determine the occasions of decision, processes for discovering and designing possible courses of action, and processes for evaluating alternatives and choosing among them. The complexity of decision making has posed grave difficulties in its study and description, difficulties only now being overcome by recent methodological innovations.

Traditionally, a decision-making process was captured and recorded by the common sense tools of the historian using everyday language. The notion that a decision might be viewed as a conclusion drawn from premises—a notion mentioned earlier—introduced a modicum of system into the description of decision making. According to this view, in order to record a decision-making process, it was necessary to discover the sources of the decision premises and the channels of communication they followed through the organization to the point where they became the raw materials of decision.

Studies that adopted this general approach to the description of decisions, while remaining within the traditional case study framework, became increasingly frequent during the period under discussion. One example is Herbert Kaufman's excellent study of *The Forest Ranger,* aimed at analyzing "the way their decisions and behavior are influenced within and by the Service."[16] Another is the study by the Carnegie Tech group of the influence of accounting information on operating decisions in large companies.[17]

The method of these studies is best described as "systematized common sense." The decision-premise concept provides an ordering and organizing principle; it reduces somewhat the subjectivity of the description and the dangers of observer bias; but it falls far short of allowing complete formalization of the description. And it cannot, of course, solve the problem of how to validate generalizations with data from single cases.

The invention of the modern digital computer radically changed the situation. As gradually became apparent to those who came into contact with computers, the computer is a device that is capable of making decisions. (One demonstration of this is its use to implement the analytic decision-making schemes introduced by operations research.) Hence, a language suitable for describing the processes going on in computers might well be appropriate for describing decision making in organizations. At least the notion appeared to be worth a trial: to equate "decision premise" with the concepts of data input and program of instructions in a computer, and to equate the concept of a conclusion with the concept of the output of a computer program.

An early, and rather primitive, attempt to describe an organization decision-making process in computer programming terms appeared in 1956.[18] In this study the authors recounted the steps taken by a business firm to reach a decision about the installation of an electronic computer. They then showed how this sequence of events could be explained by a program composed of an organized system of relatively simple and general information gathering, searching, problem solving, and evaluating processes. Of particular interest was the fact that the decision examined in this study was not a highly structured, quantitative one, but one that called for large amounts of professional and administrative judgment.

Encouraging results from early studies of this kind raised hopes that it might be possible to use computer programming languages formally as well as informally to construct theories of organizational decision making, and to test those theories by simulating the decision process on the computer. Computer programs seeking to explain several kinds of organizational decision-making situations have, in fact, been constructed, and have shown themselves adequate to simulate important aspects of the human behavior in these situations. The decisions that have been simulated in this way to date are still relatively simple ones, but they encompass behavior that would generally be regarded as professional, and as involving judgment. Two of the best-developed examples are a simulation of a department store buyer and a simulation of a bank trust investment officer.[19]

I am not aware that any single comparable simulation of a decision-making process in the area of public administration has yet been carried out, but it appears that several are under way in current research. Perhaps the most likely target for initial attempts is public budgeting. If we examine the strategies described in recent empirical studies, like those of Wildavsky,[20] we will see that they can be rather directly translated into components of computer programs.

Parallel with these simulations of administrative decision making there has been a considerable exploration of individual thinking and problem-solving processes, also using computer simulation as the tool of theory formulation and theory testing.[21] Today, we have a considerable specific knowledge on how human beings accomplish complex cognitive tasks. We have reasons for optimism, too, that this body of knowledge will increase rapidly, for in the digital computer language we have an analytic tool and a means for accurate expression whose powers are commensurate with the complexity of the phenomena we wish to describe and understand.

LANDMARKS AND NEW ROADS

These, then, are some of the more prominent landmarks along the road of decision-making research over the past 25 years. On the normative side, the analytic tools of modern operations research have secured an important place in the practical work of management. Their role in everyday decision making promises to be much enlarged as present techniques are supplemented by new heuristic approaches.

On the side of the pure science of administration, there have been equally fruitful developments. The experimental method, in the small-group laboratory, can now be used to study a wide range of decision-making behaviors that are relevant to organizations. We have introduced the concept of evocation into our theories of influence, and have used it to gain new understanding of the decision-making process in changing environments. Finally, the modern digital computer, a powerful new tool, has provided both a language for expressing our theories of decision making and an engine for calculating their empirical implications. Theories can now be compared with data of the real world of organizations.

The attention-directing mechanisms so important in decision making also have played their part in determining the particular developments sampled in this paper. Another scientist, with a different set of research concerns, would choose a different sample. The fact that even one such sample exists shows how far we have come during the past 25 years toward understanding human behavior in organizations.

NOTES AND REFERENCES

1. The term *decision making* occurred 3 times in the titles of articles in the first 15 volumes of the *Public Administration Review*—that is, through 1955, it occurred 10 times in the next 8 volumes, or about 6 times as often per annum as in the earlier period.

2. Some notion of the state of proto-operations-research just before World War II, as it applied to municipal administration, can be obtained from Ridley and Simon, *Measuring Municipal Activities* (Chicago: International City Managers' Association, first edition, 1938).

3. Cambridge, Mass.: Harvard University Press, 1960.

4. *American Political Science Review,* December 1940, p. 1142. Labels have an unfortunate tendency to compartmentalize knowledge. Thus, the literature of "budgeting" has been only partly informed by the literature on "decision making," and vice versa, and both of these have sometimes been isolated from the economics literature on resources allocation and public expenditure theory. Variants on the same basic sets of ideas are rediscovered each generation: "measurement of public services," "program budgeting," "performance budgeting," "engineering economy," "cost-benefit analysis," "operations analysis." What is genuinely new in this area in the past decade is the power and sophistication of the analytic and computational tools. Some impression of these tools may be gained from the Hitch and McKean book previously mentioned; from Roland N. McKean, *Efficiency in Government through Systems Analysis* (New York: John Wiley & Sons, 1958); Arthur Maass et al., *Design of Water Resource Systems* (Cambridge, Mass.: Harvard University Press, 1962); or Allen V. Kneese, *The Economics of Regional Water Quality Management* (Baltimore: Johns Hopkins University Press, 1964), and the references cited therein.

5. Since I have discoursed at length on these matters elsewhere, I shall be brief here. See "Theories of Decision Making in Economics and Behavioral Science," *American Economic Review* 49 (June 1959), pp. 253–83, and Part 4 of *Models of Man* (New York: John Wiley & Sons, 1957).

6. Alfred A. Kuehn and Michael J. Hamberger, "A Heuristic Program for Locating Warehouses," *Management Science,* July 1963.

7. Herbert A. Simon and William R. Divine, "Human Factors in an Administrative Experiment," *Public Administration Review* 1 (Autumn 1941), pp. 485–92.

8. N. C. Morse and E. Reimer, "Experimental Change of a Major Organizational Variable," *Journal of Abnormal and Social Psychology* 52 (1955), pp. 120–29.

9. Robert L. Chapman et al., "The System Research Laboratory's Air Defense Experiments," *Management Science* 5 (April 1959), pp. 250–69.

10. Richard M. Cyert and James G. March, *The Behavioral Theory of the Firm* (Englewood Cliffs, N.J.: Prentice-Hall, 1963), pp. 67–77.

11. *Budget Control and Cost Behavior* (Englewood Cliffs, N.J.: Prentice-Hall, 1960), chap. 4.

12. See the "Yale Studies in Attitude and Communication," edited by Hovland and Rosenberg, and published by the Yale University Press.

13. Chicago: University of Chicago Press, 1954.

14. *American Business and Public Policy: The Politics of Foreign Trade* (Atherton Press, 1963).

15. See J. Coleman, E. Katz, and H. Menzel, "Diffusion of an Innovation among Physicians," *Sociometry* 20 (1957), pp. 253–70; also, H. A. Simon and J. G. March, *Organizations* (New York: John Wiley & Sons, 1957), chap. 7.

16. Johns Hopkins University Press, 1960, p. 4.

17. *Centralization versus Decentralization in Organizing the Controller's Department* (New York: The Controllership Foundation, 1954). The study is summa-

rized in John M. Pfiffner and Frank P. Sherwood, *Administrative Organization* (Englewood Cliffs, N.J.: Prentice-Hall, 1960), chap. 21.

18. R. M. Cyert, H. A. Simon, and D. B. Trow, "Observation of a Business Decision," *Journal of Business* 29 (1956), pp. 237–48.

19. Descriptions of these two simulations may be found in chapters 7 and 10, respectively, of Cyert and March, *Behavioral Theory of the Firm* (see note 10).

20. Aaron Wildavsky, *The Politics of the Budgetary Process* (Boston: Little, Brown, 1964).

21. For a survey, and numerous examples, see Edward Feigenbaum and Julian Feldman, *Computers and Thought* (New York: McGraw-Hill, 1963).

32

Decision Making as a Social Process: Normative and Descriptive Models of Leader Behavior

Victor H. Vroom
and
Arthur G. Jago

This article reviews the research that has been conducted pertinent to both normative and descriptive models of decision making in organizations. It outlines a model of the decision process which, with a number of refinements that have been made, is as applicable today as when it was first developed.—Eds.

INTRODUCTION

Several scholarly disciplines share an interest in the decision-making process. On one hand, there are related fields of operations research and management science, both concerned with how to improve the decisions which are made. Their models of decision making, aimed at providing a rational basis for selecting among alternative courses of action, are termed *normative* or *prescriptive* models. On the other hand, there have been attempts by psychologists, sociologists, and political scientists to understand the decisions and choices that people do make. March and Simon [6] were among the first to suggest that an understanding of the decision-making process could be central to an understanding of the behavior of organizations—a point of view that was later amplified by Cyert and March [1] in their behavioral theory of the firm. In this tradition, the goal is understand-

SOURCE: Reprinted by permission from *Decision Sciences*, vol. 5, 1974, pp. 743-755, published by The Decision Sciences Institute, Georgia State University.

ing, rather than improvement, and the models are descriptive, rather than normative.

Whether the models are normative or descriptive, the common ingredient is a conception of decision making as an information-processing activity, frequently one which takes place within a single manager. Both sets of models focus on the set of alternative decisions or problem solutions from which the choice is, or should be, made. The normative models are based on the consequences of choices among these alternatives, the descriptive models on the determinants of these choices.

In this article, the authors take a somewhat different, although complementary, view of managerial decision making. They view decision making as a social process, with the elements of the process presented in terms of events between people, rather than events that occur within a person. When a problem or occasion for decision making occurs within an organization, there are typically several alternative social mechanisms available for determining what solution is chosen or decision reached. These alternatives vary in the person or persons participating in the problem-solving and decision-making process, and in the relative amounts of influence that each has on the final solution or decision reached.

There are both descriptive and normative questions to be answered about the social processes used for decision making in organizations. The normative questions hinge on knowledge concerning the consequences of alternatives for the effective performance of the system. The dimensions on which social processes can vary constitute the independent variables, and criteria of the effectiveness of the decisions constitute dependent variables. Ultimately, such knowledge could provide the foundation for a specification of the social and interpersonal aspects of how decisions *should be* made within organizations.

Similarly, the descriptive questions concern the circumstances under which alternative social processes for decision making *are* used in organizations. The dimensions on which social processes vary become the dependent variables, and characteristics of the manager who controls the process and the nature of the decision itself provide the basis for the specification of independent variables.

Vroom and Yetton [10] provided a start to an examination of both normative and descriptive questions through an examination of one dimension of decision making—the extent to which a leader encourages the participation of his subordinates in decision making. Participation in decision making was a logical place to start since there is substantial evidence of its importance and of the circumstances surrounding different consequences of it [3, 9, 11].

The purpose of this article is twofold: *(1)* to provide a brief summary of the objectives, methods, and results of the research pertaining to both normative and descriptive models of decision processes used in organizations (described in detail in Vroom and Yetton [10]); *(2)* to describe some recent extensions of the previous work, including an empirical investigation designed to explore facets of decision making not previously studied.

Vroom and Yetton concern themselves primarily with problems or decisions to be made by managers with a formally defined set of subordinates reporting to them. In each problem or decision, the manager must have some area of freedom or discretion in determining the solution adopted, and the solution must affect at least one of the manager's subordinates. Following Maier, Solem, and Maier [4], they further make a distinction between group problems and individual problems. If the solution adopted has potential effects on all immediate subordinates or some readily identifiable subset of them, it is classified as a group problem. If the solution affects only one of the manager's subordinates, it is called an *individual problem*. This distinction is an important one because it determines the range of decision-making processes available to the manager. Table 1 shows a taxonomy of decision processes for both types of problems. Each process is represented by a symbol (e.g., AI, CI, GII, DI), which provides a convenient method of referring to each process. The letters in the code signify the basic properties of the process (A stands for autocratic; C for consultative; G for group; and D for delegated). The roman numerals that follow the letters constitute variants on that process. Thus, AI represents the first variant on an autocratic process; AII the second variant, and so on.

The processes shown in Table 1 are arranged in columns corresponding to their presumed applicability to either group or individual problems and are arranged within columns in order of increasing opportunity for the subordinate to influence the solution to the problem.

The discrete alternative processes shown in Table 1 can be used both normatively and descriptively. In the former use, they constitute discrete alternatives available to the manager or decision maker, who presumably is motivated to choose that alternative which has the greatest likelihood of producing effective results for his organization. In the latter use, the processes constitute forms of behavior on the part of individuals which require explanation. In the balance of this paper, we will attempt to keep in mind these two uses of the taxonomy and will discuss them separately.

A NORMATIVE MODEL OF DECISION PROCESSES

What would be a rational way of deciding on the form and amount of participation in decision making to be used in different situations? Neither debates over the relative merits of Theory X and Theory Y [7], nor the apparent truism that leadership depends on the situation, are of much help here. The aim in this portion of the research is to develop a framework for matching a leader's behavior, as expressed in the alternatives presented in Table 1, to the demands of his situation. Any framework developed must be consistent with empirical evidence concerning the consequences of participation and be so operational that a trained leader could use it to determine how he should act in a given situation.

TABLE 1 Decision-Making Processes

For Individual Problems	*For Group Problems*
AI You solve the problem or make the decision yourself, using information available to you at that time.	**AI** You solve the problem or make the decision yourself, using information available to you at that time.
AII You obtain any necessary information from the subordinate, then decide on the solution to the problem yourself. You may or may not tell the subordinate what the problem is, in getting the information from him. The role played by your subordinate in making the decision is clearly one of providing specific information which you request, rather than generating or evaluating alternative solutions.	**AII** You obtain any necessary information from subordinates, then decide on the solution to the problem yourself. You may or may not tell subordinates what the problem is, in getting the information from them. The role played by your subordinates in making the decision is clearly one of providing specific information which you request, rather than generating or evaluating solutions.
CI You share the problem with the relevant subordinate, getting his ideas and suggestions. Then *you* make the decision. This decision may or may not reflect your subordinate's influence.	**CI** You share the problem with the relevant subordinates individually, getting their ideas and suggestions without bringing them together as a group. Then *you* make the decision. This decision may or may not reflect your subordinates' influence.
GI You share the problem with one of your subordinates and together you analyze the problem and arrive at a mutually satisfactory solution in an atmosphere of free and open exchange of information and ideas. You both contribute to the resolution of the problem with the relative contribution of each being dependent on knowledge, rather than formal authority.	**CII** You share the problem with your subordinates in a group meeting. In this meeting you obtain their ideas and suggestions. Then *you* make the decision which may or may not reflect your subordinates' influence.
DI You delegate the problem to one of your subordinates, providing him with any relevant information that you possess, but giving him responsibility for solving the problem by himself. Any solution which the person reaches will receive your support.	**GII** You share the problem with your subordinates as a group. Together you generate and evaluate alternatives and attempt to reach agreement (concensus) on a solution. Your role is much like that of chairman; coordinating the discussion, keeping it focused on the problem, and making sure that the critical issues are discussed. You do not try to influence the group to adopt "your" solution and are willing to accept and implement any solution which has the support of the entire group.

The normative model should provide a basis for effective problem solving and decision making by matching the desired decision process with relevant properties of particular problems or decisions to be made. Following Maier [5], the effectiveness of a decision is thought to be a function of three classes of outcomes, each of which may be expected to be affected by the decision process used. These are:

1. The quality or rationality of the decision.
2. The acceptance or commitment on the part of subordinates to execute the decision effectively.
3. The amount of time required to make the decision.

Space prevents an exposition of the empirical evidence concerning the consequences of participation, but the reader interested in these questions is referred to Vroom [9] and to Vroom and Yetton [10, pp. 20–31] for a presentation of that evidence. Since the research program began, a number of normative models for choosing among alternative decision processes have been developed. Each revision is slightly more complex than its predecessor but, in the minds of both developers and users, also is more accurate in forecasting the consequences of alternatives. Most of these models have been concerned solely with group problems (the right-hand column in Table 1). In Vroom and Yetton [10] virtually all of the discussion of normative models is oriented toward group problems; although, in their discussion of further revisions and extensions of the model, they discuss the possibility of a model for both individual and group problems and present a tentative model which governs choice of decision processes for both types.

Figure 1 shows the latest version of a model intended to deal with both types of problems. Like previous models, it is expressed in the form of a decision tree. Arranged along the top of the tree are a set of eight problem attributes, expressed here in the form of simple yes-no questions that a leader could ask himself about the decision-making situation he is presently confronting.[1] To use the model, one starts at the left-hand side of the tree and works toward the right-hand side, asking oneself the questions pertaining to any box that is encountered. When a terminal node is reached, a number will be found designating the problem type and one or more decision-making processes considered appropriate for that problem. Within each problem type there are both individual and group problems, and the feasible set of methods is different for each.

The decision processes specified for each problem type are not arbitrary. The specification of the feasible set of decision processes for each problem type is governed by a set of 10 rules that serve to protect the quality and acceptance of the decision by eliminating alternatives that risk one or the other of these decision outcomes. These rules, consistent with existing empirical evidence concerning the consequences of participation, are shown in Table 2 in both verbal and set-theoretic form. It should be noted that the

FIGURE 1   Decision-Process Flow Chart for Both Individual and Group
Problems

A.   Is there a quality requirement such that one solution is likely to be more
rational than another?
B.   Do I have sufficient info to make a high-quality decision?
C.   Is the problem structured?
D.   Is acceptance of decision by subordinates critical to effective implementation?
E.   If I were to make the decision by myself, is it reasonably certain that it
would be accepted by my subordinates?
F.   Do subordinates share the organizational goals to be attained in solving this
problem?
G.   Is conflict among subordinates likely in preferred solutions? (This question is
irrelevant to individual problems.)
H.   Do subordinates have sufficient info to make a high-quality decision?

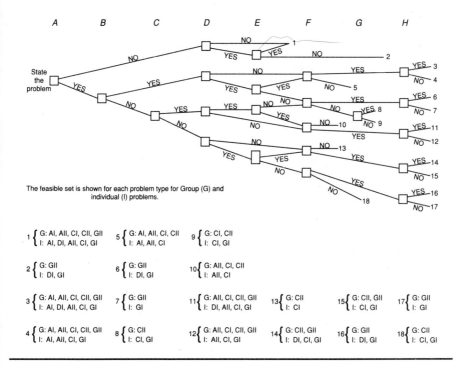

The feasible set is shown for each problem type for Group (G) and
individual (I) problems.

1 { G: AI, AII, CI, CII, GII
    I: AI, DI, AII, CI, GI

2 { G: GII
    I: DI, GI

3 { G: AI, AII, CI, CII, GII
    I: AI, DI, AII, CI, GI

4 { G: AI, AII, CI, CII, GII
    I: AI, AII, CI, GI

5 { G: AI, AII, CI, CII
    I: AI, AII, CI

6 { G: GII
    I: DI, GI

7 { G: GII
    I: GI

8 { G: CII
    I: CI, GI

9 { G: CI, CII
    I: CI, GI

10 { G: AII, CI, CII
     I: AII, CI

11 { G: AII, CI, CII, GII
     I: DI, AII, CI, GI

12 { G: AII, CI, CII, GII
     I: AII, CI, GI

13 { G: CII
     I: CI

14 { G: CII, GII
     I: DI, CI, GI

15 { G: CII, GII
     I: CI, GI

16 { G: GII
     I: DI, GI

17 { G: GII
     I: GI

18 { G: CII
     I: CI, GI

---

rules are of three distinct types. Rules 1 through 4 are designed to protect
the quality or rationality of the decision; Rules 5 through 8 are designed to
protect the acceptance of or commitment to the decision; and Rules 9
through 10 eliminate the use of group methods for individual problems and
vice versa. The decision tree is merely a convenient structure for applying
these rules, and, once the problem type has been determined, the rules have

TABLE 2 Rules Underlying the Normative Model

1. *The Leader Information Rule:* $A \cap \overline{B} \to \overline{AI}$
   If the quality of the decision is important and the leader does not possess enough information or expertise to solve the problem by himself, then AI is eliminated from the feasible set.

2. *The Subordinate Information Rule:* $A \cap \overline{H} \to \overline{DI}$
   (applicable to individual problems only)
   If the quality of the decision is important and the subordinate does not possess enough information or expertise to solve the problem himself, then DI is eliminated from the feasible set.

3a. *The Goal Congruence Rule:* $A \cap \overline{F} \to \overline{GII}, \overline{DI}$
   If the quality of the decision is important and the subordinates are not likely to pursue organization goals in their efforts to solve this problem, then GII and DI are eliminated from the feasible set.

3b. *The Augmented Goal Congruence Rule:*
   $A \cap (\overline{D} \cap E) \cap \overline{F} \to \overline{GI}$
   (applicable to individual problems only)
   Under the conditions specified in the previous rule (i.e., quality of decision is important, and the subordinate does not share the organizational goals to be attained in solving the problem) GI may also constitute a risk to the quality of the decision taken in response to an individual problem. Such a risk is a reasonable one to take only if the nature of the problem is such that the acceptance of the subordinate is critical to the effective implementation and prior probability of acceptance of an autocratic solution is low.

4a. *The Unstructured Problem Rule (Group):*
   $A \cap \overline{B} \cap \overline{C} \to \overline{AI}, \overline{AII}, \overline{CI}$
   In decisions in which the quality of the decision is important, if the leader lacks the necessary information or expertise to solve the problem by himself and if the problem is unstructured, the method of solving the problem should provide for interaction among subordinates. Accordingly, AI, AII, and CI are eliminated from the feasible set.

4b. *The Unstructured Problem Role (Individual):*
   $A \cap \overline{B} \cap \overline{C} \to \overline{AI}, \overline{AII}$
   In decisions in which the quality of the decision is important, if the leader lacks the necessary information to solve the problem by himself and if the problem is unstructured, the method of solving the problem should permit the subordinate to generate solutions to the problem. Accordingly, AI and AII are eliminated from the feasible set.

5. *The Acceptance Rule:* $D \cap \overline{E} \to \overline{AI}, \overline{AII}$
   If the acceptance of the decision by subordinates is critical to effective implementation and if it is not certain that an autocratic decision will be accepted, AI and AII are eliminated from the feasible set.

6. *The Conflict Rule:* $D \cap \overline{E} \cap G \to \overline{AI}, \overline{AII}, \overline{CI}$
   (applicable to group problems only)
   If the acceptance of the decision is critical, an autocratic decision is not certain to be accepted, and disagreement among subordinates in methods of attaining the organizational goal is likely, the methods used in solving the problem should enable those in disagreement to resolve their differences with full knowledge of the problem. Accordingly, AI, AII, and CI, which permit no interaction among subordinates, are eliminated from the feasible set.

7. *The Fairness Rule:* $\overline{A} \cap D \cap \overline{E} \to \overline{AI}, \overline{AII}, \overline{CI}, \overline{CII}$
   If the quality of the decision is unimportant, but acceptance of the decision is critical and not certain to result from an autocratic decision, the decision process used should permit the subordinates to interact with one another and negotiate over the fair method of resolving any differences with full responsibility on them for determining what is equitable. Accordingly, AI, AII, CI, and CII are eliminated from the feasible set.

8. *The Acceptance Priority Rule:*
   $D \cap \overline{E} \cap F \to \overline{AI}, \overline{AII}, \overline{CI}, \overline{CII}$
   If acceptance is critical, not certain to result from an autocratic decision and if (the) subordinate(s) is (are) motivated to pursue the organizational goals represented in the problem, then methods which provide equal partnership in the decision-making process can provide greater acceptance without risking decision quality. Accordingly, AI, AII, CI, and CII are eliminated from the feasible set.

9. *The Group Problem Rule:* Group $\to \overline{GI}, \overline{DI}$
   If a problem has approximately equal effects on each of a number of subordinates (i.e., is a group problem) the decision process used should provide them with equal opportunities to influence that decision. Use of a decision process, such as GI or DI, which provides opportunities for only one of the affected subordinates to influence that decision, may in the short run produce feelings of inequity reflected in lessened commitment to the decision on the part of those "left out" of the decision process and, in the long run, be a source of conflict and divisiveness.

10. *The Individual Problem Rule:* Individual $\to \overline{CII}, \overline{GII}$
   If a problem affects only one subordinate, decision processes which *unilaterally* introduce other (unaffected) subordinates as equal partners constitute an unnecessary use of time of the unaffected subordinates and can reduce the amount of commitment of the affected subordinate to the decision by reducing the amount of his opportunity to influence the decision. Thus, CII and GII are eliminated from the feasible set.

all been applied. It can be seen that there are some problem types for which only one method remains in the feasible set, and others for which two, three, four, or even five methods remain in the feasible set.

When more than one method remains in the feasible set, there are a number of ways in which one might choose among them. One method, called Model A and discussed at length by Vroom and Yetton, uses the number of manhours required by the process of decision making. They argue that if the alternatives within the feasible set are equal in the probability of generating a rational decision which subordinates will accept, a choice among them based on the time requirement of each will be of maximum short-run benefit to the organization.

The basis for estimating the relative requirements in manhours for the alternatives given for group problems is simple. Vroom and Yetton argue that more participative processes require more time. Therefore, the ordering of the methods shown for group problems in terms of manhours is perfectly correlated with the degree of participation they permit (AI<AII<CICII<G<II). However, the extension of the model to cover individual problems complicates this picture, since the decision process which provides greatest opportunity for subordinate influence, DI, is certainly less time consuming than GI, which requires reaching a solution that has the agreement of both superior and subordinate. While the differences in time requirements of the alternatives for individual problems is not nearly so great as the differences in the alternatives for group problems, we have assumed an ordering such that AI<DI<AII<CI<GI. The reader will note that the ordering of alternatives from left to right within the feasible sets for each problem type in Figure 1 reflects this assumption. Thus, for both group and individual problems, the minimum-manhours solution is assumed to be the alternative furthest to the left within the feasible set.

There are, however, other bases for choice within the feasible set. A manager may wish to choose the most participative alternative that can be used while still producing rational and acceptable solutions to organizational problems. Such a position could be grounded in humanistic considerations, emphasizing the intrinsic value of participation, or on pragmatic considerations, such as the utility of participation in developing informed and responsible behavior [10]. A model based on these considerations is termed *Model B*.

The reader should note that both Models A and B are consistent with the rules which generate the feasible set. They merely represent different bases for choice within it. Model A chooses the method within the feasible set, which is the most economical method in terms of manhours. Its choice is always the method furthest to the left in the set shown in Figure 1. Model B chooses the most participative method available within the feasible set, which is that method closest to the bottom of Table I. Model A seeks to minimize manhours, subject to quality and acceptance constraints, while Model B seeks to maximize participation, subject to quality and acceptance constraints. Of course, when only one process exists within the feasible set, the choices of Model A and B are identical. Perhaps the best way of illustrating the model is to show how it works in sample situations. Following are a set of actual leadership problems,[2] each based on a retrospective account by a manager who experienced the problem. The reader may wish, after reading each case, to analyze it himself using the model and then to compare his analysis with that of the authors.

Case I: You are president of a small but growing midwestern bank, with its head office in the state's capital and branches in several nearby market towns. The location and type of business are factors which contribute to the emphasis on traditional of participation in developing informed and responsible behavior [10]. A model based and conservative banking practices at all levels.

When you bought the bank five years ago, it was in poor financial shape. Under your leadership, much progress has been made. This progress has been achieved while the economy has moved into a mild recession, and, as a result, your prestige among your bank managers is very high. Your success, which you are inclined to attribute principally to good luck and to a few timely decisions on your part, has, in your judgment, one unfortunate by-product. It has caused your subordinates to look to you for leadership and guidance in decision making beyond what you consider necessary. You have no doubts about the fundamental capabilities of these men but wish that they were not quite so willing to accede to your judgment.

You have recently acquired funds to permit opening a new branch. Your problem is to decide on a suitable location. You believe that there is no "magic formula" by which it is possible to select an optimal site. The choice will be made by a combination of some simple common-sense criteria and "what feels right." You have asked your managers to keep their eyes open for commercial real estate sites that might be suitable. Their knowledge about the communities in which they operate should be extremely useful in making a wise choice.

Their support is important because the success of the new branch will be highly dependent on your managers' willingness to supply staff and technical assistance during its early days. Your bank is small enough for everyone to feel like part of a team, and you feel that this has and will be critical to the bank's prosperity.

The success of this project will benefit everybody. Directly, they will benefit from the increased base of operations, and, indirectly, they will reap the personal and business advantages of being part of a successful and expanding business.

Analysis:

A	(Quality?) = Yes	
B	(Leader's information?) = No	
C	(Structured?) = No	
D	(Acceptance?) = Yes	
E	(Prior probability of acceptance?) = Yes	
F	(Goal congruence?) = Yes	
G[3]	(Conflict?) = No	
H[3]	(Subordinate information?) = Yes	

Synthesis:

Problem type	14-Group
Feasible set	CII, GII
Model A behavior	CII
Model B behavior	GII

Case II: You are regional manager of an international management consulting company. You have a staff of six consultants reporting to you, each of whom enjoys a considerable amount of autonomy with clients in the field.

Yesterday you received a complaint from one of your major clients to the effect that the consultant whom you assigned to work on the contract with them was not doing his job effectively. They were not very explicit about the nature of the problem, but it was clear that they were dissatisfied and that something would have to be done if you were to restore the client's faith in your company.

The consultant assigned to work on that contract has been with the company for six years. He is a systems analyst and is one of the best in that profession. For the first four or five years his performance was superb, and he was a model for the other more junior consultants. However, recently he has seemed to have a "chip on his shoulder," and his previous identification with the company and its objectives has been replaced with indifference. His negative attitude has been noticed by other consultants, as well as by clients. This is not the first such complaint that you have had from a client this year about his performance. A previous client even reported to you that the consultant reported to work several times obviously suffering from a hangover and that he had been seen around town in the company of "fast" women.

It is important to get to the root of this problem quickly if that client is to be retained. The consultant obviously has the skill necessary to work with the clients effectively. If only he were willing to use it!

Analysis:

A	(Quality?) = Yes	
B	(Leader's information?) = No	
C	(Structured?) = No	
D	(Acceptance?) = Yes	
E	(Prior probability of acceptance?) = No	
F	(Goal congruence?) = No	
H^3	(Subordinate information?) = Yes	

Synthesis:

Problem type	18-Individual
Feasible set	CI, GI
Model A behavior	CI
Model B behavior	GI

Case III: You have recently been appointed manager of a new plant which is presently under construction. Your team of five department heads has been selected, and they are now working with you in selecting their own staffs, purchasing equipment, and generally anticipating the problems that are likely to arise when you move into the plant in three months.

Yesterday, you received from the architect a final set of plans for the building, and, for the first time, you examined the parking facilities that are available. There is a large lot across the road from the plant intended primarily for hourly workers and lower-level supervisory personnel. In addition, there are seven spaces immediately adjacent to the administrative offices, intended for visitor and reserved parking. Company policy requires that a minimum of three spaces be made available for visitor parking, leaving you only four spaces to allocate among yourself and your five department heads. There is no way of increasing the total number of such spaces without changing the structure of the building.

Up to now, there have been no obvious status differences among your team, who have worked together very well in the planning phase of the operation. To be sure, there are salary differences, with your administrative, manufacturing, and engineering managers receiving slightly more than the quality control and industrial relations managers. Each has recently been promoted to his new position, and expects reserved parking privileges as a consequence of his new status. From past experience, you know that people feel strongly about things which would be indicative of their status. So you and your subordinates have been working together as a team, and you are reluctant to do anything which might jeopardize the team relationship.

Analysis:		Synthesis:	
A	(Quality?) = No	Problem type	2-Group
D	(Acceptance?) = Yes	Feasible set	GII
E	(Prior probability of acceptance?) = No	Model A behavior	GII
G^3	(Conflict?) = Yes	Model B behavior	GII

Case IV: You are executive vice president for a small pharmaceutical manufacturer. You have the opportunity to bid on a contract for the Defense Department pertaining to biological warfare. The contract is outside the mainstream of your business; however, it could make economic sense since you do have unused capacity in one of your plants, and the manufacturing processes are not dissimilar.

You have written the document to accompany the bid and now have the problem of determining the dollar value of the quotation which you think will win the job for your company. If the bid is too high, you will undoubtedly lose to one of your competitors; if it is too low, you would stand to lose money on the program.

There are many factors to be considered in making this decision, including the cost of the new raw materials and the additional administrative burden of relationships with a new client, not to speak of factors which are likely to influence the bids of your competitors, such as how much they *need* this particular contract. You have been busy assembling the necessary data to make this decision but there remain several "unknowns," one of which involves the manager of the plant in which the new products will be manufactured. Of all your subordinates, only he is in the position to estimate the costs of adapting the present equipment to their new purpose, and his cooperation and support will be necessary in ensuring that the specifications of the contract will be met. However, in an initial discussion with him when you first learned of the possibility of the contract, he seemed adamantly opposed to the idea. His previous experience has not particularly equipped him with the ability to evaluate projects like this one, so you were not overly influenced by his opinions. From the nature of his arguments, you inferred that his opposition was ideological, rather than economic. You recall that he was actively involved in a local "peace organization" and, within the company, was one of the most vocal opponents to the war in Vietnam.

Analysis:		Synthesis:	
A	(Quality?) = Yes	Problem type	8 or 9 individual
B	(Leader's information?) = No	Feasible set	CI, GI
C	(Structured?) = Yes	Model A behavior	CI
D	(Acceptance?) = Yes	Model B behavior	GI
E	(Prior probability of acceptance?) = No		
F	(Goal congruence?) = No		
H[3]	(Subordinate information?) = No		

TOWARD A DESCRIPTIVE MODEL

So far, we have been concerned only with normative or prescriptive questions. But, how do managers really behave? What decision rules underlie their willingness to share their decision-making power with their subordinates? In what respects are these decision rules similar to or different from those employed in the normative model?

The manner in which these questions are posed is at variance with much of the conventional treatment of such issues. Frequently, leaders are typed as autocratic or participative or as varying on a continuum between these extremes. In effect, autocratic or participative behavior is assumed to be controlled by a personality trait, the amount of which varies from one person to another. The trait concept is a useful one for summarizing differences among people, but allows no room for the analysis of intra-individual differences in behavior. Following Lewin's [2] classic formation $B = f(P,E)$, we assumed that a leader's behavior in a given situation reflects characteristics of that leader, properties of the situation, and the interaction of the two.

Two somewhat different research methods have been used in studying the situational determinants of participative behavior. The first method [10, chapter 4] utilized what we have come to refer to as "recalled problems." Over 500 managers, all of whom were participants in management development programs, provided written descriptions of a group problem which they encountered recently. These descriptions ranged in length from one paragraph to several pages and covered virtually every facet of managerial decision making. Each manager was then asked to indicate which of the methods shown on the right-hand side of Table 1 (AI, AII, CI, CII, GII) he had used in solving the problem. Finally, each manager was asked a set of questions concerning the problem he had selected. These questions corresponded to attributes in the normative model.

Preliminary investigation revealed that managers perceived the five alternatives as varying (in the order shown in Table 1) on a scale of participation, but that the four intervals separating adjacent processes were not seen as equal. On the basis of the application of several scaling methods [10, pp. 65–71], the following values on a scale of participation were assigned to each process: AI = 0; AII = .625; CI = 5.0; CII = 8.125; GII = 10.

Using the managers' judgments of the status of the problems they described on the problem attributes as independent variables and the scale values of their behavior on the problem as a dependent variable, it is possible to use the method of multiple regression to determine the properties of situations (i.e., problems), which are associated with autocratic or participative behavior. It is also possible to insert the managers' judgments concerning their problems into the normative model and to determine the degree of correspondence between managerial and model behavior.

Several investigations have been conducted using this method—all of which have been restricted to group problems and the decision processes corresponding to them. The results are consistent with the view that there are important differences in the processes used for different kinds of problems. Specifically, managers were more likely to exhibit autocratic behavior on structured problems in which they believed that they had enough information, their subordinates lacked information, their subordinates' goals were incongruent with the organizational goals, their subordinates' acceptance of the decision was not critical to its effective implementation, and the prior probability that an autocratic decision would be accepted was high. Thus, many (but not all) of the attributes contained in the normative model had an effect on the decision processes which managers employed, and the directions of these effects are similar to those found in the model. However, it would be a mistake to conclude that the managers' behavior was always identical to that of the model. In approximately two thirds of the problems, nevertheless, the behavior which the manager reported was within the feasible set of methods prescribed for that problem, and in about 40 percent of the cases it corresponded exactly to the minimum manhours (Model A) solution.

Several observations help to account for differences between the model and the typical manager in the sample. First, as is apparent from an inspection of Figure 1, the normative model incorporates a substantial number of interactions among attributes, whereas no such interactions appeared in the results of the regression analysis. Second, the magnitude of the effects of two attributes pertaining to the acceptance or commitment of subordinates to decisions was considerably weaker in the descriptive than in the normative model, suggesting that these considerations play less of a role in determining how people behave. This inference was further supported by the fact that rules designed to protect the acceptance of the decision in the normative model were violated far more frequently than rules designed to protect decision quality.

The results of this research were supportive of the concept of intrapersonal variance in leadership style and helped to identify some of the situational factors influencing leaders' choices of decision processes. There were, however, some key methodological weaknesses to this research. Limited variance in and intercorrelations among problem attributes restricted the extent to which situational effects could be determined with precision. Furthermore, the fact that subjects selected and scored their own problems may have led to confounding of individual differences and situational effects. Finally, since only one problem was obtained from each manager, it was impossible to identify interactions between person and situational variables (i.e., idiosyncratic rules for deciding when and to what extent to encourage participation by subordinates).

The methodological problems inherent in the use of "recalled problems" dictated a search for another method with which to explore the same phenomenon. The technique selected involved the development of a standardized set of administrative problems or cases, each of which depicted a leader faced with some organizational requirement for action or decision making. Managers were asked to assume the role of leader in each situation and to indicate which decision process they would employ.

Several standardized sets of cases were developed, using rewritten accounts of actual managerial problems obtained from the previous method. These sets of cases, or problem sets, were developed in accordance with a multi-factorial experimental design, within which the problem attributes were varied orthogonally. Each case corresponded to a particular combination of problem characteristics, and the entire set of cases permitted the simultaneous variation of each problem attribute. To ensure conformity of a given case or problem with the specifications of a cell in the experimental design, an elaborate procedure for testing cases was developed [10, pp. 97–101], involving coding of problems by expert judges and practicing managers.

This method showed promise of permitting the replication of the results using recalled problems with a method that avoided spurious effects stemming from the influence of uncontrolled variables on problem selection. Since the use of a "repeated measures design" permitted a complete experiment to be performed on each subject, the main effects of each of the problem attributes on the decision processes used by the subject could be identified. By comparing the results for different subjects, the similarities and differences in these main effects and the relative importance of individual differences and of situational variables could be ascertained.

Vroom and Yetton worked exclusively with group problems and with an experimental design which called for 30 cases. The results, obtained from investigations of eight distinct populations comprising over 500 managers, strongly support the major findings from the use of recalled problems, both in terms of the amount of correspondence with the normative model and the specific attributes of situations which tended to induce autocratic and participative decision processes. Moreover, the nature of the methods used made it possible also to obtain precise estimates of the amount of variance attributable to situational factors and individual differences. Only 10 percent of the total variance could be accounted for in terms of general tendencies to be autocratic or participative (as expressed in differences among individuals in mean behavior on all 30 problems), while about 30 percent was attributable to situational effects (as expressed in differences in mean behavior among situations).

What about the remaining 60 percent of the variance? Undoubtedly, some of it can be attributed to errors of measurement, but Vroom and Yetton were able to show that a significant portion of that variance can be explained in terms of another form of individual differences (i.e., differences among managers in ways of "tailoring" their approach to the situation). Theoretically, these can be thought of as differences in decision rules that they employ concerning when to encourage participation.

NOTES

1. For a detailed definition of these attributes and of criteria to be used in making Yes-No judgments, see Vroom and Yetton [10, pp. 21–31].
2. For additional problems and their analysis, see Vroom and Yetton [10, pp. 40–44].
3. The question pertaining to this attribute is asked in the decision tree but is irrelevant to the prescribed behavior.

REFERENCES

1. Cyert, R. M., and J. G. March. *A Behavioral Theory of the Firm.* Englewood Cliffs, N.J.: Prentice-Hall, 1963.
2. Lewin, K. "Frontiers in Group Dynamics." *Field Theory in Social Science.* ed. D. Cartwright. New York: Harper & Row, 1951, pp. 188–237.
3. Lowin, A. "Participative Decision Making: A Model, Literature Critique, and Prescriptions for Research." *Organizational Behavior and Human Performance* 3(1968), pp. 68–106.
4. Maier, N. R. F.; A. R. Solem; and A. A. Maier. *Supervisory and Executive Development: A Manual for Role Playing.* New York: John Wiley & Sons, 1957.
5. Maier, N. R. F. "Problem-solving Discussions and Conferences." *Leadership Methods and Skills.* New York: McGraw-Hill, 1963.
6. March, J. G., and H. A. Simon. *Organizations.* New York: John Wiley & Sons, 1958.
7. McGregor, D., *The Human Side of Enterprise,* New York: McGraw-Hill, 1960.
8. Overall, J. E., and D. K. Spiegel. "Concerning Least Squares Analysis of Experimental Data." *Psychological Bulletin* 72 (1969), pp. 311–22.
9. Vroom, V. H. "Industrial Social Psychology." *Handbook of Social Psychology.* ed. G. Lindzey and E. Aronson. Reading, Mass.: Addison-Wesley, 1970, chap. 5, pp. 196–268.
10. Vroom, V. H., and P. W. Yetton. *Leadership and Decision-Making.* Pittsburgh: University of Pittsburgh Press, 1973.
11. Wood, M. T. "Power Relationships and Group Decision Making in Organizations." *Psychological Bulletin* 79 (1973), pp. 280–93.

D. Organizational Change and Development

33

The Coming Death of Bureaucracy

Warren G. Bennis

Warren Bennis sounds the death knell of the bureaucratically organized structure. He argues that rapid and unexpected change, growth, complexity of modern technology, and changes in managerial behavior are major threats to bureaucracies. Note Bennis's description of how future organizations will look and how inconsistent their needs will be with present-day bureaucracies.—Eds.

Not far from the new Government Center in downtown Boston, a foreign visitor walked up to a sailor and asked why American ships were built to last only a short time. According to the tourist, "The sailor answered without hesitation that the art of navigation is making such rapid progress that the finest ship would become obsolete if it lasted beyond a few years. In these words which fell accidentally from an uneducated man, I began to recognize the general and systematic idea upon which your great people direct all their concerns."

The foreign visitor was that shrewd observer of American morals and manners, Alexis de Tocqueville, and the year was 1835. He would not recognize Scollay Square today. But he had caught the central theme of our country: its preoccupation, its *obsession* with change. One thing is, however, new since de Tocqueville's time: the *acceleration* of newness, the changing scale and scope of change itself. As Dr. Robert Oppenheimer said, ". . . the world alters as we walk in it, so that the years of man's life measure not some small growth or rearrangement or moderation of what was learned in childhood, but a great upheaval."

SOURCE: Reprinted by permission from *THINK* Magazine, published by IBM, copyright 1966 by International Business Machines Corporation.

421

How will these accelerating changes in our society influence human organizations?

A short while ago, I predicted that we would, in the next 25 to 50 years, participate in the end of bureaucracy as we know it and in the rise of new social systems better suited to the 20th-century demands of industrialization. This forecast was based on the evolutionary principle that every age develops an organizational form appropriate to its genius, and that the prevailing form, known by sociologists as bureaucracy and by most businessmen as "damn bureaucracy," was out of joint with contemporary realities. I realize now that my distant prophecy is already a distinct reality so that prediction is already foreshadowed by practice.

I should like to make clear that by bureaucracy I mean a chain of command structured on the lines of a pyramid—the typical structure which coordinates the business of almost every human organization we know of: industrial, governmental, of universities and research and development laboratories, military, religious, voluntary. I do *not* have in mind those fantasies so often dreamed up to describe complex organizations. These fantasies can be summarized in two grotesque stereotypes. The first I call "Organization as Inkblot"—an actor steals around an uncharted wasteland, growing more restive and paranoid by the hour, while he awaits orders that never come. The other specter is "Organization as Big Daddy"—the actors are square people plugged into square holes by some omniscient and omnipotent genius who can cradle in his arms the entire destiny of man by way of computer and TV. Whatever the first image owes to Kafka, the second owes to George Orwell's *Nineteen Eighty-Four*.

Bureaucracy, as I refer to it here, is a useful social invention that was perfected during the Industrial Revolution to organize and direct the activities of a business firm. Most students of organizations would say that its anatomy consists of the following components:

- A well-defined chain of command.
- A system of procedures and rules for dealing with all contingencies relating to work activities.
- A division of labor based on specialization.
- Promotion and selection based on technical competence.
- Impersonality in human relations.

It is the pyramid arrangement we see on most organizational charts.

The bureaucratic "machine model" was developed as a reaction against the personal subjugation, nepotism and cruelty, and the capricious and subjective judgments which passed for managerial practices during the early days of the Industrial Revolution. Bureaucracy emerged out of the organizations' need for order and precision and the workers' demands for impartial treatment. It was an organization ideally suited to the values and demands of the Victorian era. And just as bureaucracy emerged as a creative response to a radically new age, so today new organizational shapes are surfacing before our eyes.

First I shall try to show why the conditions of our modern industrialized world will bring about the death of bureaucracy. In the second part of this article I will suggest a rough model of the organization of the future.

FOUR THREATS

There are at least four relevant threats to bureaucracy:

(1) Rapid and unexpected change.

(2) Growth in size where the volume of an organization's traditional activities is not enough to sustain growth. (A number of factors are included here, among them: bureaucratic overhead; tighter controls and impersonality due to bureaucratic sprawls; outmoded rules and organizational structures.)

(3) Complexity of modern technology where integration between activities and persons of very diverse, highly specialized competence is required.

(4) A basically psychological threat springing from a change in managerial behavior.

It might be useful to examine the extent to which these conditions exist *right now*:

1. *Rapid and unexpected change.* Bureaucracy's strength is its capacity to efficiently manage the routine and predictable in human affairs. It is almost enough to cite the knowledge and population explosion to raise doubts about its contemporary viability. More revealing, however, are the statistics which demonstrate these overworked phrases:

- Our productivity output per manhour may now be doubling almost every 20 years, rather than every 40 years, as it did before World War II.
- The federal government alone spent $16 billion in research and development activities in 1965; it will spend $35 billion by 1980.
- The time lag between a technical discovery and recognition of its commercial uses was: 30 years before World War I, 16 years between the wars, and only 9 years since World War II.
- In 1946, only 42 cities in the world had populations of more than one million. Today there are 90. In 1930, there were 40 people for each square mile of the earth's land surface. Today there are 63. By 2000, it is expected, the figure will have soared to 142.

Bureaucracy, with its nicely defined chain of command, its rules and its rigidities, is ill-adapted to the rapid change the environment now demands.

2. *Growth in size.* While, in theory, there may be no natural limit to the height of a bureaucratic pyramid, in practice the element of complexity

is almost invariably introduced with great size. International operation, to cite one significant new element, is the rule, rather than exception, for most of our biggest corporations. Firms like Standard Oil Company (New Jersey) with over 100 foreign affiliates, Mobil Oil Corporation, The National Cash Register Company, Singer Company, Burroughs Corporation, and Colgate-Palmolive Company derive more than half their income or earnings from foreign sales. Many others—such as Eastman Kodak Company, Chas. Pfizer & Company, Inc., Caterpillar Tractor Company, International Harvester Company, Corn Products Company, and Minnesota Mining & Manufacturing Company—make from 30 to 50 percent of their sales abroad. General Motors Corporation sales are not only nine times those of Volkswagen, they are also bigger than the gross national product of the Netherlands and well over the GNP of a hundred other countries. If we have seen the sun set on the British Empire we may never see it set on the empires of General Motors, ITT, Shell, and Unilever.

LABOR BOOM

3. *Increasing diversity. Today's activities require persons of very diverse, highly specialized competence.*

Numerous dramatic examples can be drawn from studies of labor markets and job mobility. At some point during the past decade, the United States became the first nation in the world ever to employ more people in service occupations than in the production of tangible goods. Examples of this trend:

- In the field of education, the *increase* in employment between 1950 and 1960 was greater than the total number of employed in the steel, copper, and aluminum industries.

- In the field of health, the *increase* in employment between 1950 and 1960 was greater than the total number employed in automobile manufacturing in either year.

- In financial firms, the *increase* in employment between 1950 and 1960 was greater than total employment in mining in 1960.

These changes, plus many more that are harder to demonstrate statistically, break down the old industrial trend toward more and more people doing either simple or undifferentiated chores.

Hurried growth, rapid change, and increase in specialization—pit these three factors against the five components of the pyramid structure described [earlier], and we should expect the pyramid of bureaucracy to begin crumbling.

4. *Change in managerial behavior.* There is, I believe, a subtle but perceptible change in the philosophy underlying management behavior. Its

magnitude, nature, and antecedents, however, are shadowy because of the difficulty of assigning numbers. (Whatever else statistics do for us, they most certainly provide a welcome illusion of certainty.) Nevertheless, real change seems under way, because of:

a. A new concept of *man*, based on increased knowledge of his complex and shifting needs, which replaces an oversimplified, innocent, push-button idea of man.

b. A new concept of *power* based on collaboration and reason, which replaces a model of power based on coercion and threat.

c. A new concept of *organizational values* based on humanistic-democratic ideals, which replaces the depersonalized mechanistic value system of bureaucracy.

The primary cause of this shift in management philosophy stems not from the bookshelf but from the manager himself. Many of the behavioral scientists, like Douglas McGregor or Rensis Likert, have clarified and articulated—even legitimized—what managers have only half registered to themselves. I am convinced, for example, that the popularity of McGregor's book, *The Human Side of Enterprise*, was based on his rare empathy for a vast audience of managers who are wistful for an alternative to the mechanistic concept of authority; that is, he outlined a vivid utopia of more authentic human relationships than most organizational practices today allow. Furthermore, I suspect that the desire for relationships in business has little to do with a profit motive per se, though it is often rationalized as doing so. The real push for these changes stems from the need not only to humanize the organization but to use it as a crucible of personal growth and the development of self-realization.[1]

The core problems confronting any organization fall, I believe, into five major categories. First, let us consider the problems, then let us see how our 20th-century conditions of constant change have made the bureaucratic approach to these problems obsolete.

1. *Integration.* The problem is how to integrate individual needs and management goals. In other words, it is the inescapable conflict between individual needs (like "spending time with the family") and organizational demands (like meeting deadlines).

Under 20th-century conditions of constant change there has been an emergence of human sciences and a deeper understanding of man's complexity. Today, integration encompasses the entire range of issues concerned with incentives, rewards, and motivations of the individual, and how the organization succeeds or fails in adjusting to these issues. In our society, where personal attachments play an important role, the individual is appreciated, and there is genuine concern for his well-being, not just in a veterinary-hygiene sense but as a moral, integrated personality.

PARADOXICAL TWINS

The problem of integration, like most human problems, has a venerable past. The modern version goes back at least 160 years and was precipitated by an historical paradox: the twin births of modern individualism and modern industrialism. The former brought about a deep concern for and a passionate interest in the individual and his personal rights. The latter brought about increased mechanization of organized activity. Competition between the two has intensified as each decade promises more freedom and hope for man and more stunning achievements for technology. I believe that our society *has* opted for more humanistic and democratic values, however unfulfilled they may be in practice. It will "buy" these values even at loss in efficiency because it feels it can now afford the loss.

2. *Social influence.* This problem is essentially one of power and how power is distributed. It is a complex issue and alive with controversy, partly because of an ethical component and partly because studies of leadership and power distribution can be interpreted in many ways, and almost always in ways which coincide with one's biases (including a cultural leaning toward democracy).

The problem of power has to be seriously reconsidered, because of dramatic situational changes which make the possibility of one-man rule not necessarily "bad" but impractical. I refer to changes in top management's role.

Peter Drucker, over 12 years ago, listed 41 major responsibilities of the chief executive and declared that "90 percent of the trouble we are having with the chief executive's job is rooted in our superstition of the one-man chief." Many factors make one-man control obsolete, among them: the broadening product base of industry; impact of new technology; the scope of international operation; the separation of management from ownership; the rise of trade unions and general education. The real power of the "chief" has been eroding in most organizations, even though both he and the organization cling to the older concept.

3. *Collaboration.* This is the problem of managing and resolving conflicts. Bureaucratically, it grows out of the very same social process of conflict and stereotyping that has divided nations and communities. As organizations become more complex, they fragment and divide, building tribal patterns and symbolic codes which often work to exclude others (secrets and jargon, for example) and on occasion to exploit differences for inward (and always fragile) harmony.

Recent research is shedding new light on the problem of conflict. Psychologist Robert R. Blake in his stunning experiments has shown how simple it is to induce conflict, how difficult to arrest it. Take two groups of people who have never before been together, and give them a task which will be judged by an impartial jury. In less than an hour, each group devolves into a tightly-knit band with all the symptoms of an "in group." They regard their product as a "masterwork" and the other group's as "commonplace" at best. "Other" becomes "enemy." "We are good, they are bad; we are right, they are wrong."

RABBIE'S REDS AND GREENS

Jaap Rabbie, conducting experiments on intergroup conflict at the University of Utrecht, has been amazed by the ease with which conflict and stereotype develop. He brings into an experimental room two groups and distributes green name tags and pens to one group, red pens and tags to the other. The two groups do not compete; they do not even interact. They are only in sight of each other while they silently complete a questionnaire. Only 10 minutes are needed to activate defensiveness and fear, reflected in the hostile and irrational perceptions of both "reds" and "greens."

4. *Adaptation.* This problem is caused by our turbulent environment. The pyramid structure of bureaucracy, where power is concentrated at the top, seems the perfect way to "run a railroad." And for the routine tasks of the 19th and early 20th centuries, bureaucracy was (in some respects it still is) a suitable social arrangement. However, rather than a placid and predictable environment, what predominates today is a dynamic and uncertain one where there is a deepening interdependence among economic, scientific, educational, social, and political factors in the society.

5. *Revitalization.* This is the problem of growth and decay. As Alfred North Whitehead has said: "The art of free society consists first in the maintenance of the symbolic code, and secondly, in the fearlessness of revision. . . . Those societies which cannot combine reverence to their symbols with freedom of revision must ultimately decay. . . .

Growth and decay emerge as the penultimate conditions of contemporary society. Organizations, as well as societies, must be concerned with those social structures that engender buoyancy, resilience, and a "fearlessness of revision."

I introduce the term *revitalization* to embrace all the social mechanisms that stagnate and regenerate, as well as the process of this cycle. The elements of revitalization are:

1. An ability to learn from experience and to codify, store, and retrieve the relevant knowledge.

2. An ability to "learn how to learn"; that is, to develop methods for improving the learning process.

3. An ability to acquire and use feedback mechanisms on performance; in short, to be self-analytical.

4. An ability to direct one's own destiny.

These qualities have a good deal in common with what John Gardner calls "self-renewal." For the organization, it means conscious attention to its own evolution. Without a planned methodology and explicit direction, the enterprise will not realize its potential.

Integration, distribution of power, collaboration, adaptation, and *revitalization*—these are the major human problems of the next 25 years. How organizations cope with and manage these tasks will undoubtedly determine the viability of the enterprise.

Against this background I should like to set forth some of the conditions that will dictate organizational life in the next two or three decades.

1. *The environment.* Rapid technological change and diversification will lead to more and more partnerships between government and business. It will be a truly mixed economy. Because of the immensity and expense of the projects, there will be fewer identical units competing in the same markets, and organizations will become more interdependent.

The four main features of this environment are:

- Interdependence, rather than competition.
- Turbulence and uncertainty, rather than readiness and certainty.
- Large-scale, rather then small-scale, enterprises.
- Complex and multinational, rather than simple national, enterprises.

"NICE"—AND NECESSARY

2. *Population characteristics.* The most distinctive characteristic of our society is education. It will become even more so. Within 15 years, two thirds of our population living in metropolitan areas will have attended college. Adult education is growing even faster, probably because of the rate of professional obsolescence. The Killian Report showed that the average engineer required further education only 10 years after getting his degree. It will be almost routine for the experienced physician, engineer, and executive to go back to school for advanced training every two or three years. All of this education is not just "nice." It is necessary.

One other characteristic of the population which will aid our understanding of organizations of the future is increasing job mobility. The ease of transportation, coupled with the needs of a dynamic environment, change drastically the idea of "owning" a job—or "having roots." Already 20 percent of our population change their mailing address at least once a year.

3. *Work values.* The increased level of education and mobility will change the values we place on work. People will be more intellectually committed to their jobs and will probably require more involvement, participation, and autonomy.

Also, people will be more "other-oriented," taking cues for their norms and values from their immediate environment, rather than tradition.

4. *Tasks and goals.* The tasks of the organization will be more technical, complicated, and unprogrammed. They will rely on intellect, instead of muscle. And they will be too complicated for one person to comprehend, to

say nothing of control. Essentially, they will call for the collaboration of specialists in a project or a team form of organization.

There will be a complication of goals. Business will increasingly concern itself with its adaptive or innovative-creative capacity. In addition, supragoals will have to be articulated, goals which shape and provide the foundation for the goal structure. For example, one might be a system for detecting new and changing goals; another could be a system for deciding priorities among goals.

Finally, there will be more conflict and contradiction among diverse standards for organizational effectiveness. This is because professionals tend to identify more with the goals of their profession than with those of their immediate employer. University professors can be used as a case in point. Their inside work may be a conflict between teaching and research, while more of their income is derived from outside sources, such as foundations and consultant work. They tend not to be good "company men," because they divide their loyalty between their professional values and organizational goals.

KEY WORD: "TEMPORARY"

5. *Organization.* The social structure of organizations of the future will have some unique characteristics. The key word will be "temporary." There will be adaptive, rapidly changing *temporary* systems. These will be task forces organized around problems-to-be-solved by groups of relative strangers with diverse professional skills. The groups will be arranged on an organic, rather than mechanical, model; they will evolve in response to a problem, rather than to programmed role expectations. The executive thus becomes a coordinator or "linking pin" between various task forces. He must be a man who can speak the polyglot jargon of research, with skills to relay information and to mediate between groups. People will be evaluated not vertically, according to rank and status, but flexibly and functionally, according to skill and professional training. Organizational charts will consist of project groups, rather than stratified functional groups. (This trend is already visible in the aerospace and construction industries, as well as in many professional and consulting firms.)

Adaptive, problem-solving, temporary systems of diverse specialists, linked together by coordinating and task-evaluating executive specialists in an organic flux—this is the organization form that will gradually replace bureaucracy as we know it. As no catchy phrase comes to mind, I call this an *organic-adaptive structure.* Organizational arrangements of this sort may not only reduce the intergroup conflicts, mentioned earlier, it may also induce honest-to-goodness creative collaboration.

6. *Motivation.* The organic-adaptive structure should increase motivation and thereby effectiveness, because it enhances satisfactions intrinsic to the task. There is harmony between the educated individual's need for tasks that are meaningful, satisfactory, and creative and a flexible organizational structure.

There will also be, however, reduced commitment to work groups, for these groups will be, as I have already mentioned, transient structures. I would predict that, in the organic-adaptive system, people will learn to develop quick and intense relationships on the job, and learn to bear the loss of more enduring work relationships. Because of the added ambiguity of roles, time will have to be spent on continual rediscovery of the appropriate organizational mix.

I think that the future I describe is not necessarily a "happy" one. Coping with rapid change, living in temporary work systems, developing meaningful relations and then breaking them—all augur social strains and psychological tensions. Teaching how to live with ambiguity, to identify with the adaptive process, to make a virtue out of contingency, and to be self-directing—these will be the tasks of education, the goals of maturity, and the achievement of the successful individual.

NO DELIGHTFUL MARRIAGES

In these new organizations of the future, participants will be called upon to use their minds more than at any other time in history. Fantasy, imagination, and creativity will be legitimate in ways that today seem strange. Social structures will no longer be instruments of psychic repression but will increasingly promote play and freedom on behalf of curiosity and thought.

One final word: While I forecast the structure and value coordinates for organizations of the future and contend that they are inevitable, this should not bar any of us from giving the inevitable a little push. The French moralist may be right in saying that there are no delightful marriages, just good ones; it is possible that, if managers and scientists continue to get their heads together in organizational revitalization, they *might* develop delightful organizations—just possibly.

I started with a quote from de Tocqueville and I think it would be fitting to end with one: "I am tempted to believe that what we call necessary institutions are often no more than institutions to which we have grown accustomed. In matters of social constitution, the field of possibilities is much more extensive than men living in their various societies are ready to imagine."

NOTE

1. Let me propose an hypothesis to explain this tendency. It rests on the assumption that man has a basic need for transcendental experiences, somewhat like the psychological rewards which William James claimed religion provided—"an assurance of safety and a temper of peace, and, in relation to others, a preponderance of loving affections." Can it be that as religion has become secularized, less transcendental, men search for substitutes, such as close interpersonal relationships, psychoanalysis—even the release provided by drugs such as LSD?

34

Criteria of Organizational Effectiveness

Stanley E. Seashore

An important objective of organization development is to improve organizational effectiveness. In this article, Seashore argues that achieving effectiveness requires taking into consideration the multiple, conflicting, and changing goals of organizations. A framework is proposed for conceptualizing organizational performance.—Eds.

MULTIPLE, CONFLICTING GOALS

The aim of the following discussion is to outline a way of viewing the relationships among the numerous criteria that might be considered in the evaluation of the performance of an organization. To understand such relationships we shall need to make some distinctions between different kinds of criterion measures. We shall need to create some encompassing conceptions that serve to aid the evaluation of performance when some desired measures are not available, or when the number of measures is inconveniently large.

The issues taken up here arise because most organizations have multiple goals, rather than a single goal, and goal achievement may not be directly measurable. The formal objectives of the organization may themselves be multiple and, in any case, there are multiple short-run goals and subgoals that need to be examined. The matter would be simple if the various goals were all of similar priority and combinable in some simple additive way; but this is not the situation. The manager making decisions that rest upon multivariate assessments of the performance of his organization has to calculate the weights and the correlation values that he will apply when estimating the net outcome of a course of action.

SOURCE: Reprinted by permission from the July 1965 issue of the *Michigan Business Review*, published by the Graduate School of Business Administration, The University of Michigan.

A typical example would be the case of a manager who wishes his firm to obtain a substantial profit, and at the same time to grow in size, to insure future profit by product improvements, to avoid financial risk, to pay a substantial annual dividend to his investors, to have satisfied employees, and to have his firm respected in the community. He cannot maximize all of these simultaneously, as increasing one (e.g., dividends or risk avoidance) may imply reduced achievement on another (e.g., growth, product research). He must consider their trade-off value, their contingencies, and the presence of negative correlations among them. To estimate an optimum course of action he has to evaluate the dependability and relevance of the various measures and then estimate the way in which they combine to provide an overall evaluation of performance or a prediction of future change in performance. This task will be easier when we have for his use a theory to describe the performance of organizations. The following suggestions are a step in that direction.

CRITERIA AND THEIR USES

To begin, we need to make some distinctions among different kinds of criteria and their uses.

1. *Ends vs. means.* Some criteria are close to the formal objectives of the organization in the sense that they represent ends or goals that are valued in themselves; others have value mainly or only because they are thought to be necessary means or conditions for achieving the main goals of the organization. Substantial profit, for example, may be a goal sought by a business organization, while employee satisfaction may be valued because it is thought to be an aid in reaching the goal of substantial profit.

2. *Time reference.* Some criterion measures refer to a past time period (profit for the past year), others to current states (net worth), and still others to anticipated future periods (projected growth). Whatever their time reference, all may be used for drawing inferences about past or future conditions or changes.

3. *Long vs. short run.* Some criterion measures refer to a relatively short time, others to a longer period; they may refer to performances that are relatively stable (do not change much in the short run) or relatively unstable (erratic or highly variable in the short run). The usefulness of a criterion measure is limited if the period covered is not appropriate to the usual or potential rate of change in the variable.[1]

4. *"Hard" vs. "soft."* Some criteria are measured by the characteristics of, or number or frequency of, physical objects and events, while others are measured by qualitative observation of behavior or by evaluative questions put to people. Dollar measures, for example, or tons of

scrap, or number of grievances, are "hard" measures; while employee satisfaction, motivation to work, cooperation, product quality, customer loyalty, and many others are usually "soft." *The distinction is useful, but it contains a trap,* for we commonly think of the hard variables as being in some way inherently more valid, more reliable, and more relevant to the performance evaluation problem, when this is not necessarily true. Profit rate, for example—a popular hard variable—is a rather vague concept to begin with (accountants dispute about definition and about conventions for measurement) and it is often in the short run unreliable as a performance indicator and thus quite irrelevant to the evaluation problem, even for an organization whose long-run goals include making a profit. Similarly, a soft variable, such as one representing the intentions of key executives to stay with the organization, may be measured with high reliability in some circumstances and may be vital in the assessment of the organization's performance.

5. *Values.* Some variables appear to have a linear value scale (more is always better than less), while others have a curvilinear scale (some optimum is desired; more and less are both to be avoided). The shape of the curves determines in part the trade-off relationship among assessment variables under conditions where simultaneous optimization is not possible. Examples: profit rate is usually linear in value, in the sense that more is better than less; maintenance costs, by contrast, are usually curvilinear in value, in the sense that either excessively high or low costs may be judged to diminish overall firm performance.

THE HIERARCHY OF CRITERIA

A full accounting for the performance of an organization requires consideration for (1) achievement of the organization's main goals over a long span of time; (2) performance over shorter periods on each of those criteria that represent ends valued in themselves, and which, jointly, as a set, determine the net ultimate performance; and (3) performance on each of a number of subsidiary criteria that provide an immediate or current indication of the progress toward, or probability of achieving, success on end-result variables. The network of criteria of performance can be viewed as a pyramid-shaped hierarchy:

1. *At the top* is the "ultimate criterion"—some conception of the net performance of the organization over a long span of time in achieving its formal objectives, whatever they may be, with optimum use of the organization's environmental resources and opportunities. The ultimate criterion is never measured (except possibly by historians); yet some concept of this kind is the basis for evaluation of lesser criteria of performance.

2. *In the middle* are the penultimate criteria. These are shorter-run performance factors or dimensions comprised by the ultimate cri-

terion. They are "output" or "results" criteria: things sought for their own value and having trade-off value[2] in relation to each other. Their sum, in some weighted mixture, determines the ultimate criterion. Typical variables of this class for business organizations are: sales volume, productive efficiency, growth rate, profit rate, and the like. There may be included some "soft" (usually behavioral) variables, such as employee satisfaction or customer satisfaction. In the case of some non-business organizations these penultimate criteria might be predominantly of the behavioral kind, as in the case of a school whose output is judged in terms of learning rates, proportion of students reaching some standard of personal growth or development, etc.

3. *At the bottom* of the hierarchy of assessment criteria are measures of the current organizational functioning, according to some theory or some empirical system concerning the conditions associated with high achievement on each of the penultimate criteria.[3] These variables include those descriptive of the organization as a system and also those representing subgoals or means associated with penultimate criteria. The number of criteria in this class is very large (over 200 have been used in some studies without sensing that the limits were being approached), and they are interrelated in a complex network that includes causal, interactional, and modifier types of relationships. Included are some criteria that are not valued at all except for their power to reduce the amount of uncontrolled variance in the network. Among the "hard" criteria at this level, for a business organization, might be such as: scrappage, short-run profit, productivity against standards, meeting of production schedules, machine downtime, ratio of overtime to regular time, product return rate, rate of technological innovation, and the like. Among the "soft" criteria at this level may be such as these: employee morale, credit rating, communication effectiveness, absenteeism, turnover, group cohesiveness, customer loyalty, pride in firm, level of performance motivation, and others.

CHARACTERISTICS OF BEHAVIORAL CRITERIA

Such a model locates the behavioral criteria—those descriptive of the members (in this context, customers and clients are also "members") of the organization and of their values, attitudes, relationships, and activities—mainly in the lower regions of the network of assessment criteria, distant and perhaps only indirectly related to the ultimate goals by which the organization is eventually judged.

If behavioral criteria appear near the top of the network, it is because they are valued in themselves and have trade-off value in relation to other priority goals of the organization. In general, however, the hard—nonbehavioral—criteria are the preferred ones for most business organizations for the good reason that they are more relevant to the formal objectives of the organization.

The behavioral measures are presumed to have some stable relationships to the various nonbehavioral measures; these relationships may be causal, interactional, or merely one of covariance. It is further presumed that the criteria and their relationships are not entirely unique to each organization, nor transient, but are to some degree stable and to some extent common to all or many organizations. These presumptions appear to have some partial confirmation from analyses performed so far.[4]

We come now to the question of the role of behavioral criteria in the light of this broader conception of the evaluation of organizational performance. It appears that behavioral criteria are not likely, for most business organizations, to have a prominent place in the roster of penultimate criteria although they may and do appear there. Their chief role will arise from their power to improve the prediction of future changes in the preferred "hard" criteria; that is, their power to give advance signals of impending problems or opportunities.

A second use that they may commonly have is to complement the available hard criteria in such a way as to give the manager a more balanced and more inclusive informational basis for his decisions in the case where the hard variable measures are incomplete or not reliable for short-run evaluation.[5]

In some rare instances, the behavioral criteria have to be used exclusively instead of the preferred hard criteria of organizational performance for the reason that measurements of hard criteria are not available at all or not at reasonable cost.

There are three basic strategies that may be applied in formulating a unique version of this general scheme that may be appropriate for a particular organization.

1. There exist several partially developed general theories concerning the survival requirements of organizations. These assumed requirements may be defined in performance terms and posited as the roster of penultimate criteria or organizational goals. From this starting point, a set of subsidiary goals and performance criteria may be constructed on empirical grounds, on theoretical grounds, or on some combination of the two.

2. The existing personal values of the owners of a firm, or of the managers as representatives, may be pooled to form an agreed-upon roster of penultimate criteria together with their corresponding performance indicators, and from this starting point the set of subsidiary goals and performance criteria can be constructed.

3. Comparative empirical study can be made of the performance characteristics of a set of organizations assumed to share the same ultimate criterion but clearly differing in their overall success as judged

by competent observers (e.g., such a study might be made of a set of insurance sales agencies, some clearly prospering and others clearly headed for business failure). Using factorial analysis methods and actual performance data to identify the sets of lower-order performance criteria, and using trend and correlational analyses to detect the relationships among these sets of criteria over time, one can, in principle, draw conclusions about the penultimate components of performance that bear upon organizational survival or failure in that particular line of business.

ALTERNATIVE THEORETICAL APPROACHES

These three approaches can and do produce strikingly different systems for describing the network of criteria to be used in evaluating organizational performance. One of the general theories, for example, proposes that there are nine basic requirements to be met, or problems to be continuously solved, for an organization to achieve its long-run goals; these include such requirements as adequate input of resources, adequate normative integration, adequate means of moderation of organizational strain, adequate coordination among parts of the organization, etc. Theories of this kind are produced mainly by general organizational sociologists and stem from the view that an organization is a living system with intrinsic goals and requirements that may be unlike those of individual members. By contrast, the second mentioned approach stems from the personal values of managers. The resulting networks of criteria are different.[6]

A start has been made at the Institute for Social Research in exploring such alternative strategies. With respect to the first approach, two theoretical models have been tested against empirical data from a set of organizations in a service industry, using executive judgments of unit overall effectiveness as the ultimate criterion. Both models proved to be about equally valid, but of limited utility in explaining variance on the ultimate criterion: each "accounted for" about half of the ultimate criterion variance, with the unexplained portion arising from measurement errors or faulty theory, or both. An attempt to apply the wholly empirical approach to the same set of data proved to be a failure in the sense that it was no more powerful in explaining variance on the ultimate criterion than were the simpler, theory-based models; and, furthermore, the resulting roster of performance dimensions was not very satisfactory in common-sense terms.

A third effort is now in progress, using objective data about the performance of a set of insurance sales agencies over a span of 12 years; the early results look very promising on first examination. It appears that there will be identified a roster of about 10 penultimate criteria of agency performance, each independent of the others and of varying weight in relation to ultimate performance, and each associated with a roster of subsidiary criteria of kinds that lend themselves to ready measurement and statistical combination. It remains to be seen whether these criteria are unique to this particular line of business, or have some applicability to other kinds of organizations.

NOTES AND REFERENCES

1. May firms' current operating and financial statistics, although appropriate for control and accounting purposes, prove to be of little value for performance evaluation for the reason that they are short-period measures of unstable performances? Monthly plant maintenance costs, for example, may be extremely variable (perhaps seasonal) and may be useful as a performance criterion measure only when applied to longer periods of time. In the short run, apart from other considerations, low maintenance costs may or may not be a favorable indicator.
2. By trade-off value we mean only that an amount of one kind of performance may be substituted for an amount of another; for example, an increase in sales volume may be judged to offset a decline in profit rate per sales unit.
3. One large U.S. firm has published what appears to be a carefully considered formulation of its own roster of assessment criteria at this penultimate level. It includes one behavioral category, "employee attitudes," which is further defined in operational terms in a manner compatible with the system outlined here.
4. See "Applying Modern Management Principles to Sales Organizations," Foundation for Research on Human Behavior seminar report, 1963, for an illustration of the similarity across three sales organizations in the relevance of behavioral measures to hard penultimate criteria of organizational performance. Also, "Models of Organization Performance," an unpublished manuscript by Basil Georgopoulos, Stanley Seashore, and Bernard Indik; and "Relationships among Criteria of Job Performance," by Stanley Seashore, Bernard Indik, and Basil Georgopoulos, *Journal of Applied Psychology* 44 (1960), pp. 195–202.
5. As an example, a decision to raise prices is likely to rest not only upon estimates of hard performances, past and future, but also upon estimates of political and economic climate, of customer loyalty, of the feasibility of alternatives, such as employee collaboration in cost reduction, etc.
6. To illustrate, take the criterion of profit: in one case, profit is likely to be treated as one of a few penultimate criteria (ends valued in their own right), while in the other case profit is relegated to a subsidiary role as one of several alternative means for insuring adequate input of resources. If this seems implausible, note that some organizations—government, educational, and religious organizations, for example—have survived and prospered without profit from their own activities.

35

How to Prevent
Organizational Dry Rot

John W. Gardner

Organizational renewal is the concern of this essay. The author proposes nine rules to follow to achieve positive renewal or development. Do not be misled by the lighter tone of this article; what it has to say is important food for thought.—Eds.

Like people and plants, organizations have a life cycle. They have a green and supple youth, a time of flourishing strength, and a gnarled old age. We have all seen organizations that are still going through the diseases of childhood, and others so far gone in the rigidities of age that they ought to be pensioned off and sent to Florida to live out their days.

But organizations differ from people and plants in that their cycle isn't even approximately predictable. An organization may go from youth to old age in two or three decades, or it may last for centuries. More important, it may go through a period of stagnation and then revive. In short, decline is not inevitable. Organizations need not stagnate. They often do, to be sure, but that is because the arts of organizational renewal are not yet widely understood. Organizations can renew themselves continuously. That fact has far-reaching implications for our future.

We know at least some of the rules for organizational renewal. And those rules are relevant for all kinds of organizations—U.S. Steel, Yale University, the U.S. Navy, a government agency, or your local bank.

The first rule is that the organization must have an effective program for the recruitment and development of talent. People are the ultimate source of renewal. The shortage of able, highly trained, highly motivated men will be a permanent feature of our kind of society; and every organization that wants its share of the short supply is going to have to get out and fight for it. The organization must have the kind of recruitment policy that

---

SOURCE: Copyright © 1965 by *Harper's Magazine*.

will bring in a steady flow of able and highly motivated individuals. And it cannot afford to let those men go to seed, or get sidetracked or boxed in. There must be positive, constructive programs of career development. In this respect, local, state, and federal government agencies are particularly deficient and have been so for many years. Their provisions for the recruitment and development of talent are seriously behind the times.

The second rule for the organization capable of continuous renewal is that it must be a hospitable environment for the individual. Organizations that have killed the spark of individuality in their members will have greatly diminished their capacity for change. Individuals who have been made to feel like cogs in the machine will behave like cogs in the machine. They will not produce ideas for change. On the contrary, they will resist such ideas when produced by others.

The third rule is that the organization must have built-in provisions for self-criticism. It must have an atmosphere in which uncomfortable questions can be asked. I would lay it down as a basic principle of human organization that the individuals who hold the reins of power in any enterprise cannot trust themselves to be adequately self-critical. For those in power the danger of self-deception is very great, the danger of failing to see the problems or refusing to see them is ever-present. And the only protection is to create an atmosphere in which anyone can speak up. The most enlightened top executives are well aware of this. Of course, I don't need to tell those readers who are below the loftiest level of management that even with enlightened executives a certain amount of prudence is useful. The Turks have a proverb that says, "The man who tells the truth should have one foot in the stirrup."

But it depends on the individual executive. Some welcome criticism, others don't. Louis Armstrong once said, "There are some people that if they don't know, you can't tell 'em."

The fourth requirement for the organization that seeks continuous renewal is fluidity of internal structure. Obviously, no complex modern organization can exist without the structural arrangements of divisions, branches, departments, and so forth. I'm not one of those who imagine that the modern world can get away from specialization. Specialization and division of labor are at the heart of modern organization. In this connection I always recall a Marx Brothers movie in which Groucho played a shyster lawyer. When a client commented on the dozens of flies buzzing around his broken-down office, Groucho said, "We have a working agreement with them. They don't practice law and we don't climb the walls."

But jurisdictional boundaries tend to get set in concrete. Pretty soon, no solution to a problem is seriously considered if there is any danger that it will threaten jurisdictional lines. But those lines aren't sacred. They were established in some past time to achieve certain objectives. Perhaps the objectives are still valid, perhaps not. *Most organizations have a structure that was designed to solve problems that no longer exist.*

The fifth rule is that the organization must have an adequate system of internal communication. If I may make a rather reckless generalization, I'd say that renewal is a little like creativity in this respect—that it depends on the existence of a large number of diverse elements in a situation that permits an infinite variety of combinations and recombinations. The enormous potentialities of the human brain are in part explainable in terms of such possibilities for combination and recombination. And such recombination is facilitated by easy communication, impeded by poor communication.

The sixth rule: The organization must have some means of combating the process by which men become prisoners of their procedures. The rule book grows fatter as the ideas grow fewer. Thus, almost every well-established organization is a coral reef of procedures that were laid down to achieve some long-forgotten objective.

It is in our nature to develop an affection for customary ways of doing things. Some years ago a wholesale firm noted that some of its small shopkeeper customers were losing money because of antiquated merchandising methods. The firm decided that it would be good business to assist the shopkeepers in bringing their methods up to date, but soon discovered that many had no desire to modernize. They loved the old, money-losing ways.

Sometimes the organization procedures men devise to advance their purposes serve in the long run to block those purposes. This was apparent in an experience a friend of mine had in Germany in the last days of World War II. He was in Aachen, which had only recently been occupied by the American forces, when he received a message instructing him to proceed to London immediately. He went directly to U.S. Army headquarters, and showed the message to a sergeant in the adjutant's office.

The sergeant said that the only plane for London within the next few days was leaving from the nearest airfield in 30 minutes. He added that the airfield was 25 minutes away.

It was discouraging news. My friend knew that he could not proceed to London without written orders, and that was a process that took from an hour to a couple of days in a well-established and smoothly functioning headquarters. The present headquarters had been opened the day before, and was in a totally unorganized state.

My friend explained his dilemma to the sergeant and handed over his papers. The sergeant scratched his head and left the room. Four minutes later he returned and said, "Here are your orders, sir."

My friend said he had never been in such an efficient headquarters. The sergeant looked at him with a twinkle in his eye and said, "Sir, it's just lucky for you we weren't organized!"

The seventh rule: The organization capable of continuous renewal will have found some means of combating the vested interests that grow up in every human institution. We commonly associate the term *vested interests* with people of wealth and power, but in an organization vested interests exist at every level. The lowest employees have their vested interests, every foreman has his, and every department head has his. Every change threatens someone's privileges, someone's authority, someone's status. What wise managers try to do, of course, is to sell the idea that in the long run everyone's overriding vested interest is in the continuing vitality of the organization itself. If that fails, everyone loses. But it's a hard message to get across.

Nowhere can the operation of vested interests be more clearly seen than in the functioning of university departments. There are exceptions, of course: some departments rise above their vested interests. But the average department holds like grim death to its piece of intellectual terrain. It teaches its neophytes a jealous devotion to the boundaries of the field. It assesses the significance of intellectual questions by the extent to which they can be answered without going outside the sacred territory. Such vested interests effectively block most efforts to reform undergraduate instruction.

The eighth rule is that the organization capable of continuous renewal is interested in what it is going to become and not what it has been. When I moved to New London, Connecticut, in 1938, I was astonished at the attitude of New Londoners toward their city's future. Having grown up in California, I was accustomed to cities and towns that looked ahead habitually (often with an almost absurd optimism). I was not prepared for a city that, so far as I could discover, had no view of its future, though it had a clear view of its past.

The need to look to the future is the reason so many corporations today have research-and-development programs. But an organization cannot guarantee its future by ritualistic spending on research. Its research-and-development program must be an outgrowth of a philosophy of innovation that guides the company in everything it does. The research program, which is a way of looking forward, cannot thrive if the rest of the organization has the habit of looking backward.

The ninth rule is obvious but difficult. An organization runs on motivation, on conviction, on morale. Men have to believe that it really makes a difference whether they do well or badly. They have to care. They have to believe that their efforts as individuals will mean something for the whole organization and will be recognized by the whole organization.

Change is always risky, usually uncomfortable, often painful. It isn't accomplished by apathetic men and women. It requires high motivation to break through the rigidities of the aging organization.

So much for the rules.

One of the ominous facts about growth and decay is that the present success of an organization does not necessarily constitute grounds for optimism. In 1909 it would have been unwise to judge the future of the Central Leather Company by the fact that it ranked seventh in the nation in total assets. It would have been a disastrous long-term investment. A better bet would have been the relatively small Ford Motor Company, which had been founded only six years earlier and was about to launch its Model T. As a company it wasn't huge or powerful; but, to borrow a phrase from C. P. Snow, it had the future in its bones. (Not many of 1909's top 20 companies did—only 4 of them are in the top 20 today.)

Businessmen are fond of saying that, unlike other executives, they have a clear measure of present performance—the profit-and-loss statement. But the profits of today *may* be traceable to wise decisions made a good many years earlier. And current company officers may be making bad decisions that will spell disaster 10 years from now.

I have collected many examples of organizations that experienced crises as a result of their failure to renew themselves. In the great majority, certainly 9 out of 10, the trouble was not difficult to diagnose and there was ample warning of the coming catastrophe. In the case of a manufacturing concern that narrowly averted bankruptcy recently, the conditions that led to trouble were diagnosed by an outside consultant two years before the crisis came. In the case of another well-known organization, a published article outlined every essential difficulty that later led to disaster.

But if warning signals are plentiful, why doesn't the ailing organization take heed? The answer is clear: most ailing organizations have developed a functional blindness to their own defects. They are not suffering because they can't *solve* their problems but because they won't see their problems. They can look straight at their faults and rationalize them as virtues or necessities.

I was discussing these matters with a corporation president recently, and he said, "How do I know that *I* am not one of the blind ones? What do I do to find out? And if I am, what do I do about it?"

There are several ways to proceed. One way is to bring in an outside consultant who is not subject to the conditions that create functional blindness inside the organization.

A more direct approach, but one that is surrounded by subtle difficulties, is for the organization to encourage its internal critics. Every organization, no matter how far deteriorated, has a few stubbornly honest individuals who are not blinded by their own self-interest and have never quite accepted the rationalization and self-deceptions shared by others in the organization. If they are encouraged to speak up they probably will. The head of a government agency said to me recently, "The shrewdest critics of this organization are right under this roof. But it would take a major change of atmosphere to get them to talk."

A somewhat more complicated solution is to bring new blood into at least a few of the key positions in the organization. If the top level of the organization is salted with vigorous individuals too new to be familiar with all the established ways of doing and thinking, they can be a source of fresh insights for the whole organization.

Still another means of getting fresh insights is rotation of personnel between parts of the organization. Not only is the individual broadened by the experience but he brings a fresh point of view to his new post. After a few years of working together, men are likely to get so used to one another that the stimulus of intellectual conflict drops almost to zero. A fresh combination of individuals enlivens the atmosphere.

In the last analysis, however, everything depends on the wisdom of those who shape the organization's policy. Most policy makers today understand that they must sponsor creative research. But not many of them understand that the spirit of creativity and innovation so necessary in the research program is just as essential to the rest of the organization.

The future of this nation depends on its capacity for self-renewal. And that in turn depends on the vitality of the organizations and individuals that make it up. Americans have always been exceptionally gifted at organizational innovation. In fact, some observers say that this is the true American inventiveness. Thanks to that inventiveness we now stand on the threshold of new solutions to some of the problems that have destroyed the vitality of human institutions since the beginning of time. We have already made progress in discovering how we may keep our institutions vital and creative. We could do even better if we put our minds to it.

Index to Readings

How to stay
out of
Court

Settling
Dispute
New Emot